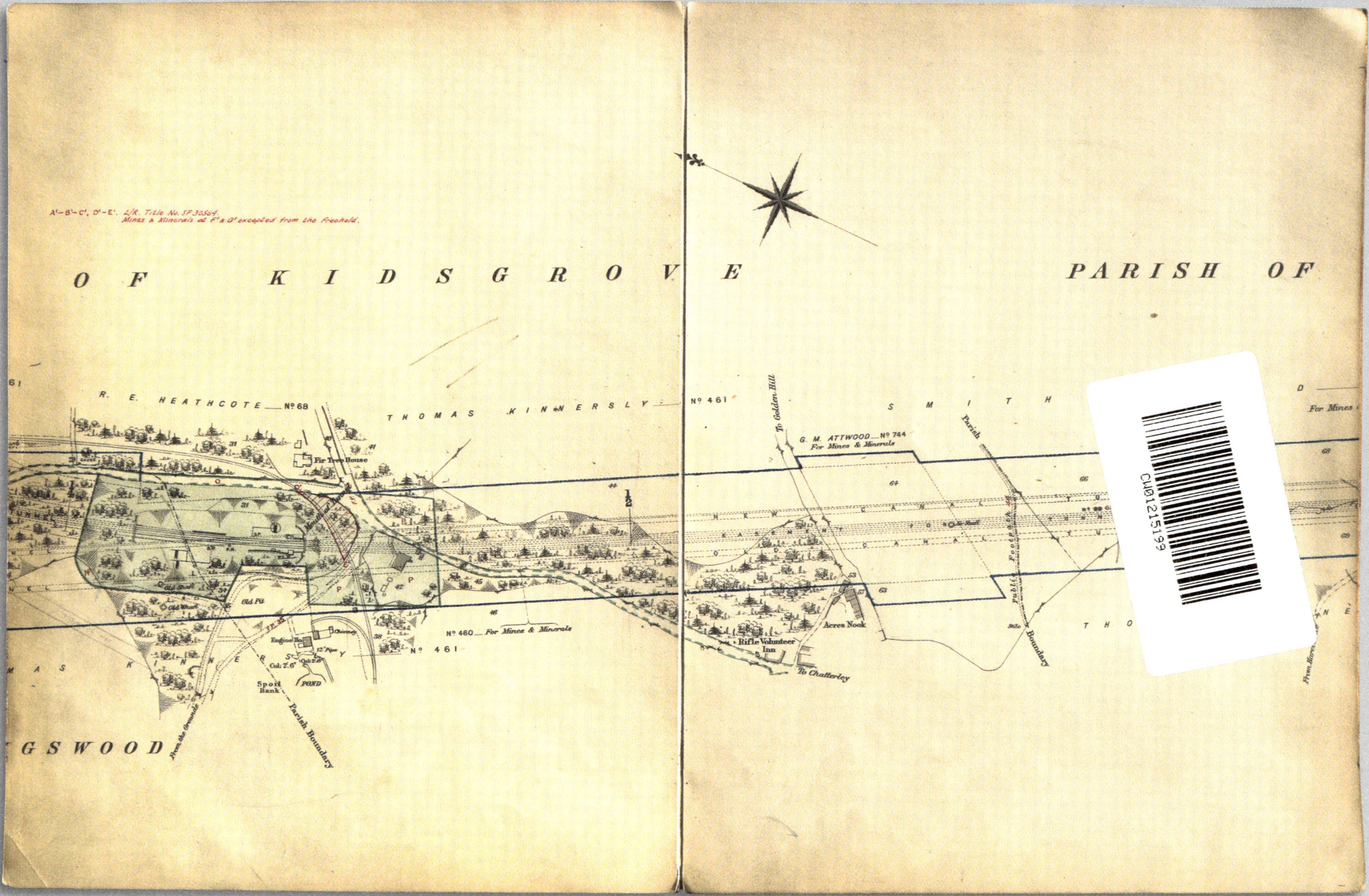

A'-B'-C', D'-E'. L/R. Title No. SF 30564.
Mines & Minerals at F' & G' excepted from the Freehold.
OF KIDSGROVE
PARISH OF
R. E. HEATHCOTE — Nº 68
THOMAS KINNERSLY — Nº 461
Fir Tree House
G. M. ATTWOOD — Nº 744
For Mines & Minerals
To Golden Hill
Parish
Public Footpath
Boundary
Nº 460 — For Mines & Minerals
Nº 461
Acres Nook
Rifle Volunteer Inn
To Chatterley
Old Pit
Spoil Bank
POND
Parish Boundary
From the Grounds
GSWOOD

HARECASTLE'S
CANAL AND RAILWAY
TUNNELS

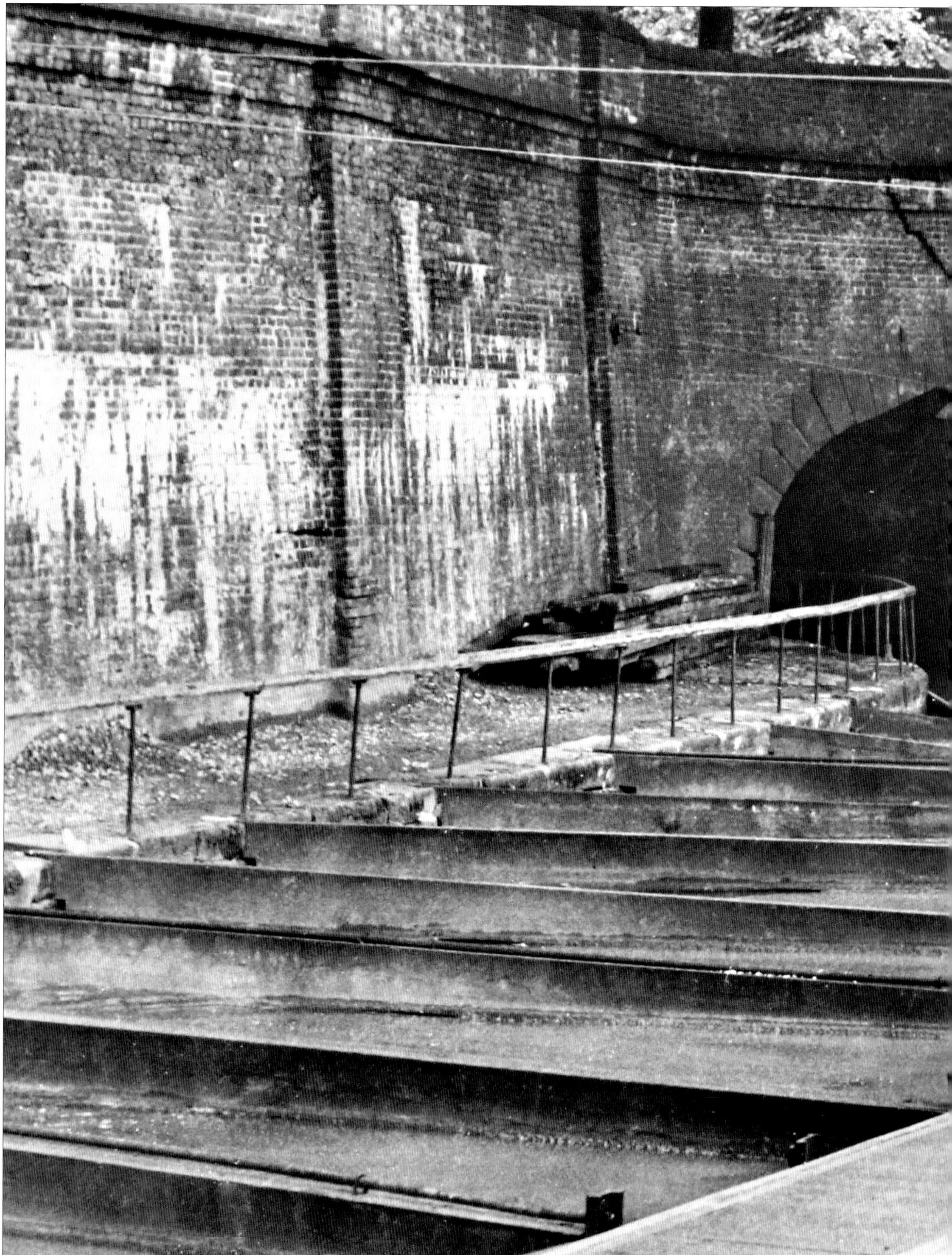

HARECASTLE'S CANAL AND RAILWAY TUNNELS

ALLAN C. BAKER AND MIKE G. FELL OBE

Lightmoor Press

COVER IMAGES
The front cover features a narrow boat about to enter the northern end of Brindley's tunnel (top left) and a Stanier Class '4' 2-6-4 tank engine on a parcels train emerging from the northern portal of the middle railway tunnel (top right). The bottom of the front cover features an elevation of Telford's tunnel mouth, while the book's title is wrapped around a general arrangement drawing of one of the electric tugs. The rear cover is illustrated with two North Staffordshire Railway advertisements highlighting both the railway and the Trent & Mersey Canal. Also shown is a goods train leaving the southern end of the south railway tunnel behind a Fowler Class '4F' 0-6-0 tender engine and a modern day cruising narrow boat and work boat moored at the northern end of the canal tunnels. All these illustrations appear again within the book with expanded captions and accreditations.

TITLE SPREAD
A tug with trolley pole extended at the north end of Telford's tunnel; the abandoned Brindley tunnel is to the right. The structure on the left jutting out into the canal must have assisted the passage of boats being towed into the tunnel. Note the permanently moored barge which supports a walkway blocking the way to Brindley's tunnel.
Cyril Arapoff/National Waterways Museum

END PAPERS
The end papers portray sections of a North Staffordshire Railway line survey plan undertaken in 1922 featuring both the railway and the Trent & Mersey Canal. They show in great detail the area surrounding the northern entrance to the canal tunnels at Harecastle, together with the old north railway tunnel and the northern mouth of the middle railway tunnel. Also included are sections showing the industrial railway that ran over the extreme northern end of the south railway tunnel and the village of Line Houses, both of which are mentioned in the text. The extracts are concluded with the section showing the area surrounding the south end of the tunnels at Chatterley.

© Lightmoor Press, Allan C. Baker, Mike G. Fell OBE, 2019.
Designed by Stephen Phillips.

British Library Cataloguing-in-Publication Data.
A catalogue record for this book is available from the British Library.
ISBN 978-1-911038-62-7

All rights reserved. No part of this publication may be reproduced, stored in a retrieval system or transmitted in any form or by any means, electronic, mechanical, photocopying, recording or otherwise, without the written permission of the publisher.

LIGHTMOOR PRESS
Unit 144B, Lydney Trading Estate, Harbour Road, Lydney, Gloucestershire GL15 5EJ
www.lightmoor.co.uk

Lightmoor Press is an imprint of Black Dwarf Lightmoor Publications Ltd.
Printed in Poland www.lfbookservices.co.uk

The famous potter Josiah Wedgwood (1730-1795) was instrumental in the promotion of the Grand Trunk Canal and became well acquainted with canal pioneer James Brindley who masterminded the first Harecastle canal tunnel. Wedgwood relocated his pottery from Burslem to a position alongside the canal at Etruria and established his family home at Etruria Hall which was built between 1768 and 1771. The hall and the canal are depicted on this serving plate which is part of the Frog Service produced by Wedgwood for Empress Catherine the Great of Russia, which comprised no less than 944 pieces. The dinner and dessert service was completed in 1774. The majority of the pieces are now in the Hermitage Museum in St Petersburg.

Turnhurst Hall was located near to Newchapel in North Staffordshire and its most famous resident was James Brindley. The hall was built around 1700 and demolished in 1929. This view dates from c.1847, long after Brindley's death. On 26th September 1772, Josiah Wedgwood wrote to his friend and partner Thomas Bentley (1731-1780): *I have been at Turnhurst almost every day this week and can give you but a melancholy account from thence. Poor Mr. Brindley has nearly finished his course in this world. He says he must leave us and indeed I do not expect to find him alive in the morning.* Brindley died at Turnhurst Hall the following day.

An enlarged Etruria Hall as depicted on one of a pair of Queen's Ware plates produced at Wedgwood's Barlaston factory in 1980 to commemorate the 250th anniversary of the birth of Josiah Wedgwood. It was a limited edition of 3,000 pairs in the famous cream ware similar to that used for the service completed for Catherine the Great. The hall survives and is now a Grade II listed building.

Dedication

The authors are dedicating this book to the memories of their fathers:
STEPHEN ALLAN BAKER and ARTHUR JAMES FELL.
How they would have enjoyed it and how proud they would have been.

CONTENTS

Abbreviations		8
Authors' notes		8
Preface		10
Introduction		11
Chapter 1	BRINDLEY'S TUNNEL	13
Chapter 2	TRENT & MERSEY CANAL	23
Chapter 3	TELFORD'S TUNNEL	29
Chapter 4	NORTH STAFFORDSHIRE RAILWAY	61
Chapter 5	AN AVOIDING ROUTE	69
Chapter 6	ELECTRIC TUGS	81
Chapter 7	BRITISH WATERWAYS BOARD	101
Chapter 8	THE RAILWAY TUNNELS	111
Chapter 9	THE HARECASTLE DIVERSION	145
Chapter 10	COAL AND IRONSTONE MINING	161
Acknowledgements		189
Appendix 1	Estimate of a Line of Locks to pass the Summit of the Grand Trunk Canal in place of a new Tunnel through Harecastle Hill – 1820	190
Appendix 2	Inspection of Brindley's Tunnel – 1979	191
Bibliography		203
Index		204

Abbreviations

B&DJR	Birmingham & Derby Junction Railway
BR	British Railways
BRB(R)	BRB (Residuary) Ltd
BTC	British Transport Commission
BWB	British Waterways Board
CRO	County Record Office, Stafford – now known as Staffordshire & Stoke-on-Trent Archive Service, Staffordshire Record Office, Stafford
GJR	Grand Junction Railway
HLRO	House of Lords Record Office
ICE	Institution of Civil Engineers
LM&SR	London Midland & Scottish Railway
L&NWR	London & North Western Railway
NA	National Archives
NSR	North Staffordshire Railway
T&FC	NSR Traffic & Finance Committee

Authors' notes

Currency

In the text, amounts of money are quoted in pre-decimal currency of pounds, shillings and pence (£sd). Rather than interpret this every time as pounds and new pence (£p), a brief conversion table is given here. In pre-decimal money: £1 = 20 shillings; 1 shilling (s) = 12 pence (d). Decimal conversions: 1 shilling = 5 new pence (p); 10 shillings = 50p; 6d = 2.5p. In 1775, 1827 and 1848 – the dates which mark the completion of Brindley's and Telford's canal tunnels and the NSR railway tunnels – one pound, taking into account inflation has the respective equivalent values today: £151.00, £90.90, £95.70.

Stoke-upon-Trent/Stoke-on-Trent

The six pottery towns of Tunstall, Burslem, Hanley, Stoke-upon-Trent, Fenton and Longton combined to form a single County Borough of Stoke-on-Trent on 31st March 1910, which later acquired city status on 5th June 1925.

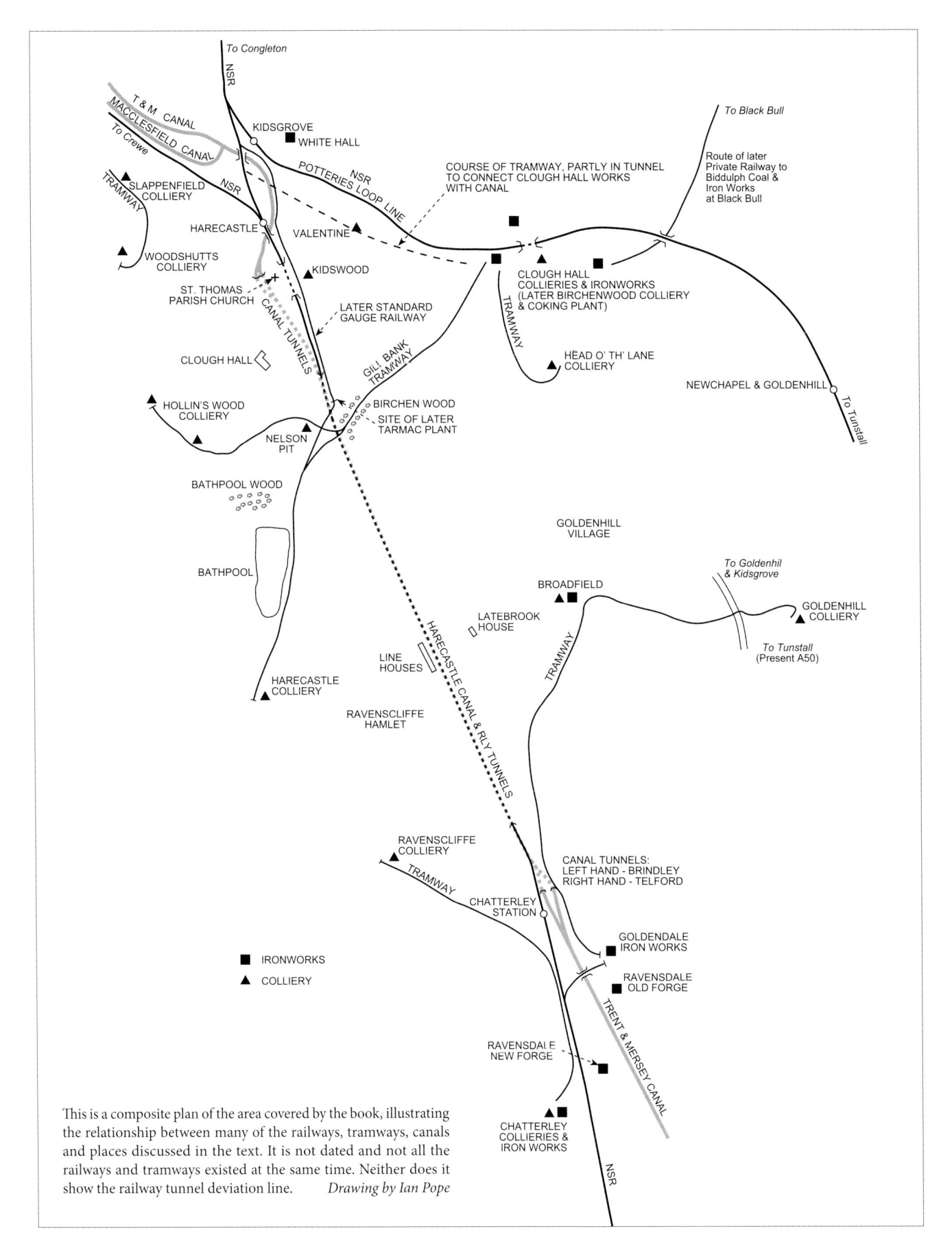

This is a composite plan of the area covered by the book, illustrating the relationship between many of the railways, tramways, canals and places discussed in the text. It is not dated and not all the railways and tramways existed at the same time. Neither does it show the railway tunnel deviation line. *Drawing by Ian Pope*

PREFACE

This work was originally intended to appear in the twice-yearly *North Staffordshire Railway Study Group Journal*. However, once we began to put pen to paper we realised that the results of our researches were rapidly exceeding the size acceptable for a *Journal* article. One thing that has surprised us is the extent of the mining that once took place whereby coal and other minerals extracted from within Harecastle Hill was removed by canal boats, so much so that we have devoted the last chapter solely to coal and ironstone mining even though this duplicates some of the information included in earlier chapters. We suspect that the mining was far more extensive than once thought and was akin to the better known but larger operations at the Duke of Bridgewater's Worsley mines in Lancashire. We were also surprised to discover that the diaries of James Caldwell (1759-1838) had survived with transcriptions readily available via the Internet. Caldwell was onetime Chairman of the Select Committee that managed the Trent & Mersey Canal (originally known as the Grand Trunk Canal) and was instrumental in influencing the decision to construct the second canal tunnel. Moreover, access to original documents about the second canal tunnel in the archives of the Institution of Civil Engineers has revealed a lot of hitherto unpublished information. These findings, plus the need to cover the electric tugs that once traversed the second canal tunnel, the Harecastle Diversion that put paid to the original railway tunnels and the mining that went on in the vicinity of all the tunnels, have resulted in this much longer work than we originally anticipated and we are delighted that Lightmoor Press have agreed to publish it as a book.

We both hail from North Staffordshire and have known each other for well over half a century. While we both now live away from the Potteries our writings are very much motivated by what we remember of the railway and canal in the Chatterley Valley and through the Harecastle tunnels. One of us, for the last four years or so of the original railway route through the tunnels, travelled that way, twice a day for five days a week, to and from his work at Crewe. The Deviation route was brought into use over the weekend of 25th-26th June 1966, during a total engineering occupation, trains being diverted via the Potteries Loop Line, including the Pinnox branch, sometimes referred to as the Spur Line. On the Friday evening prior to closure, he travelled on one of the last trains through the tunnels, while on the following Monday morning he travelled on only the third Down train to use the new line. About fifteen years later, along with a group of friends, he was able to walk through the old middle and south tunnels, from north to south, finding it even then, very wet in many places. Kidsgrove and its surrounding area are extremely rich in industrial history with the operations at Clough Hall, touched on within these pages, among the earliest in North Staffordshire of what could be called integrated coal and ironstone mining, along with the production of finished iron. The area has long fascinated the authors, such that putting this book together, growing as it has with more information coming to light as we delved deeper and deeper into various archive depositories, has been most rewarding.

A great number of people, several friends of long standing, along with staff from various organisations have helped us in our endeavours and we sincerely hope that we have not inadvertently missed anybody in the Acknowledgements. However, we would like to single out one or two who we feel are deserved of special praise. Lloyd Boardman, a friend of one of us for well over fifty years, latterly Chief Geologist for the National Coal Board Western Area, has been extremely helpful on issues connected with mining where his professional guidance and advice has been invaluable, not least in poring over various documents and drafts on our behalf. Richard Dean from Biddulph has placed at our disposal, completely unfettered, maps and plans from his extensive collection built up over many years. Peter Trewin, a former British Railway's colleague of one of the authors, has been able to unlock information on the railway tunnels that had formerly been under his control. Last, but by no means least, thanks to our dear wives, Angela and Darral, for their continued support in our activities, embracing many hours locked away in studies, or far away depositories. In concluding these few Preferential remarks, we hope it goes without saying, that despite all the help that has been freely given, we bear total responsibility for the interpretation of our source material, along with any errors or omissions readers might detect. If any reader can help in any way in enhancing our knowledge, or correcting any errors, then we will be more than pleased to hear from them via the publisher.

ALLAN C. BAKER, High Halden, Kent
MIKE G. FELL OBE, Elloughton, East Yorkshire

INTRODUCTION

The book traces the history of the two canal and four railway tunnels that have been driven through Harecastle Hill in North Staffordshire, from first aspirations, inception and building, along with the vicissitudes of fortune to the present day. Once a vital transport artery, only one of the two canal tunnels remains in use today – Telford's canal tunnel opened in 1827. James Brindley's earlier pioneering tunnel which became navigable in 1775, two years ahead of the completion of the Grand Trunk Canal as it was then called, but more familiarly known as the Trent & Mersey Canal, was closed in 1918. In its day, as far as is known, this was the longest tunnel of its kind anywhere in the world. Of the railway tunnels, two of those built for the North Staffordshire Railway (NSR) on its 1848 mainline from Stoke-upon-Trent to Macclesfield, known by the designations south and middle, were taken out of use in June 1966. The original route, from Chatterley at the south end to Kidsgove at the north end, was replaced by a deviation line as part of the 1960s British Railways London Midland Region electrification scheme. This scheme embraced the routes from London Euston to Manchester and Liverpool, along with the line via Birmingham and Wolverhampton. As the shortest distance between London and Manchester was via the former NSR line, the scheme included the railway through North Staffordshire from Colwich and Norton Bridge via Stoke to Macclesfield and onwards via the former London & North Western Railway line to Stockport and Manchester. The two tunnels that were redundant remain in situ and have only comparatively recently, had some quite extensive work undertaken on them, largely because of flooding. The third tunnel, a short one, known as the north tunnel, which in any event only had a very shallow top cover, was opened out to form a cutting. The deviation line has a short tunnel at its northern end, roughly parallel with the older middle tunnel, albeit to its west and at a higher elevation. This is on a steeply graded section of the new line as it descends to re-join the original formation where the former north tunnel has been opened out.

The two canal tunnels run parallel with each other with the long south railway tunnel in between them but at a higher level. As the railway runs from the west of the canal at the southern end of the tunnels and to the east at the opposite, northern end, in order for the long south tunnel to run in a straight line parallel to and between the canal tunnels for its entire length, the route of the railway crosses over both canal tunnels. Brindley's tunnel is crossed at its south, Chatterley end and Telford's tunnel in the cutting between the south and middle railway tunnels at the northern end. Just to make matters even more complicated, at various periods a number of industrial railways and tramways ran over parts of the railway tunnels and these too, are explored in this work.

All the tunnels through the hill were once owned by the NSR which acquired the canal as part of its original statutory powers obtained in 1846. Within the hill at Harecastle, which is part of a range of high ground which divides the extreme northern part of Staffordshire from the Pottery towns of the City of Stoke-on-Trent, all the coal and ironstone seams of the North Staffordshire Coalfield are to be found. The mineral resources of this coalfield are completely separate from other coalfields in the southern part of the county. Although limited coal and ironstone mining in the Harecastle area predates building of the original canal tunnel, it was the construction of the Trent & Mersey Canal that provided the important link of efficient and economic transport. Extensive development of the mineral resources, both coal and ironstone, came hard on the heels of the canal opening, not least by Brindley and his business associates as the extent of the resources became more and more apparent as the canal tunnel was being driven.

Using as a model what the Duke of Bridgewater had achieved on his Worsley Estate near Manchester, side tunnels were driven from the main canal tunnel, some of them probably concurrent with driving the main bore, to tap the various seams. One of these side tunnels was over 600 yards long and built to the same dimensions and standards as the main construction. Because of this strong connection between the canal tunnels and extracting the minerals, a chapter of this book has been devoted to exploring mining in the Harecastle area and while this is by no means definitive, hopefully it will enable readers to better appreciate the environment into which the owners of the Trent & Mersey Canal and no less the later NSR, found themselves.

The issue of the side tunnels has long fascinated the authors, along with many others interested in the industrial archaeology of the district. As a result, probably for the first time, it has been possible to place on record the results of detailed investigations into the issue of the underground side tunnels and associated mining. That part of the mineral estate developed by the Gilbert and later Kinnersly families at the northern, Kidsgrove end of the tunnels, is also explored within these pages and again, while not exhaustive, sufficient detail has we feel, been given to once again enable readers to appreciate its inseparable connection from both the canal and later railway, in passing through Harecastle Hill.

In closing these introductory remarks, one of the authors in his schoolboy days, while cycling along the canal towpath to explore past industrial history, often wondered as he approached the southern end of the tunnel, why the canal water took on an orangey brown colour. It was, as he later found out, due to the ironstone that abounds in the area.

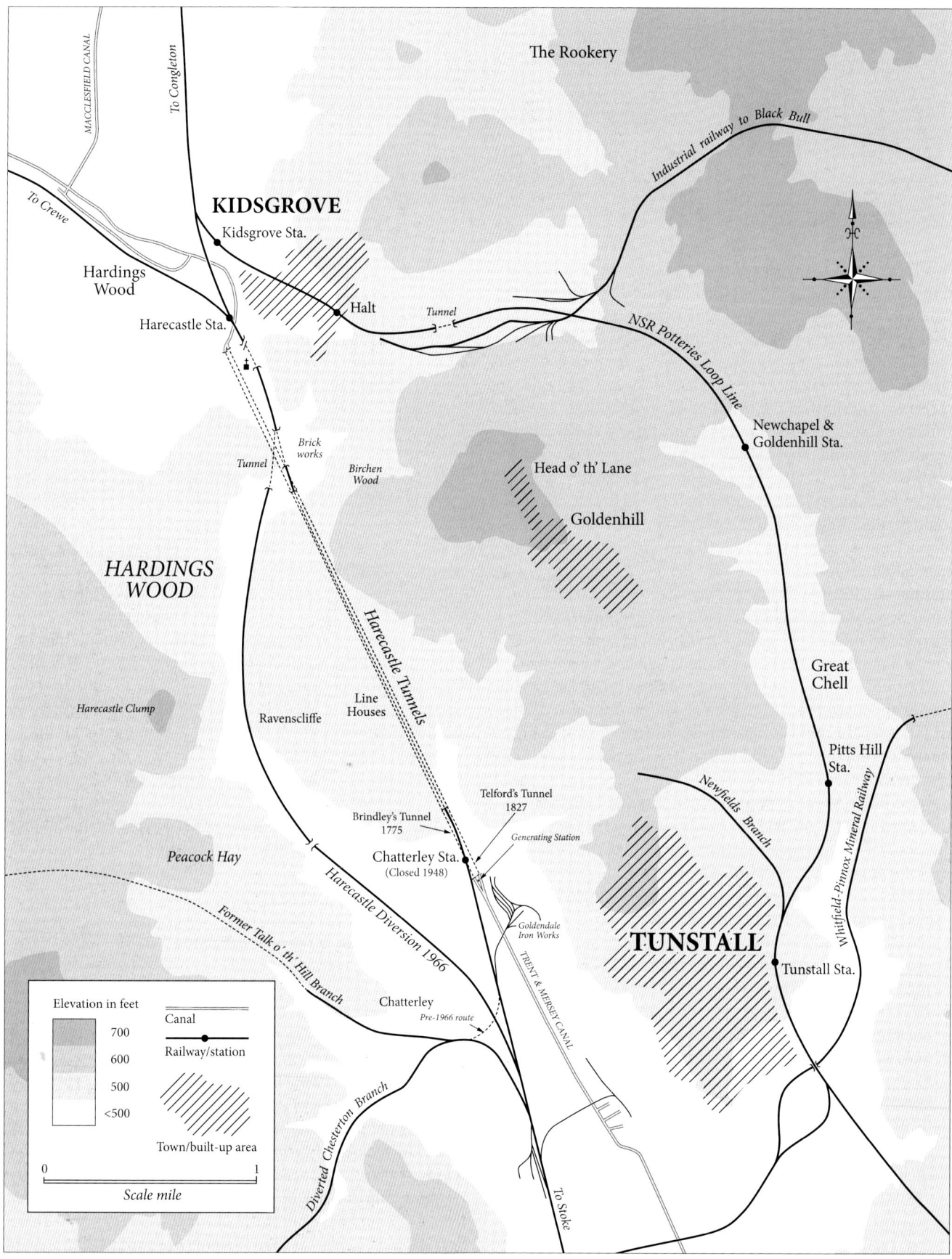

This contour map well illustrates the topography through which the Harecastle tunnels were bored and the surrounding area. *Drawing by Stephen Phillips*

1

BRINDLEY'S TUNNEL

The Trent and Mersey Canal, originally known as the Grand Trunk Canal, was authorised by an Act of Parliament which received the Royal Assent on 14 May 1766 during the reign of George III.[1] It ran from a junction with the Duke of Bridgewater's Canal at Preston Brook in Cheshire for a distance of ninety-three miles and three furlongs to a junction with the River Trent at Derwent Mouth in Derbyshire, where the River Derwent joins the Trent. The first sod was cut by the famous potter Josiah Wedgwood (1730-1795) at Brownhills on 26th July 1766. Wedgwood was instrumental in the promotion of the canal and moved his factory from Burslem to Etruria in 1769 so that it could be alongside the new transport artery. He received much support for the canal from Dr Erasmus Darwin FRS (1731-1802), grandfather of the famous naturalist Charles Darwin (1809-1882). Erasmus and Josiah were founder members of the very influential Lunar Society established to draw together innovating men of science and industry.[2] During the digging of Brindley's tunnel several fossil bones were discovered which were sent by Josiah to Erasmus for identification. Erasmus could not identify the species and joked that they might have been from a *Patagonian ox*! However, the finds stimulated the famous doctor to conceive the first comprehensive Evolutionary Theory of the Universe.[3] Erasmus Darwin's son, Robert Waring Darwin (1766-1848), married Josiah Wedgwood's daughter Susannah (1775-1817) on 18th April 1796.[4] They had six children, the fifth of whom was Charles Darwin.

Not everyone was in favour of the canal as a whole. For example, the Weaver Navigation Trustees fearing loss of trade wanted the northern end of the canal to terminate at Northwich, not Preston Brook. On 17th April 1766, just one month ahead of the inaugural Act receiving the Royal Assent, a pamphlet headed *OBJECTIONS to Part of the Proposed Canal from Wilden Ferry to the Mersey* was published by the *true Friends of the Scheme for opening a Communication between Hull and Liverpool*.[5] The *Friends*, who do not seem to have identified themselves, believed that the canal ought to have been first cut between Burton and Northwich. With regard to Harecastle they pronounced as follows: *It is suspected, that the Projectors do not entertain the chimerical Idea of cutting thro' Hare Castle. It is rather believed, that they are desirous of cutting their Canal at both Ends; and of leaving the Middle for the Project of a future Day. Are these Projectors jealous of their Honour? Let them adopt a Clause (which Reason and Justice strongly enforce) to restrain them from meddling with either End, till they have finished the great [sic] Trunk? This, and this alone will shield them from Suspicion.* There was nothing chimerical about Brindley's Harecastle Tunnel, it just took time for the vision to come about.

A portrait of James Brindley (1716-1772) by Francis Parsons. Parsons was active as an artist by 1763 and died in 1804. Notice that, to the bottom right of his painting, he has featured the famous Barton Aqueduct crossing the River Irwell on the Duke of Bridgewater's Canal. *National Portrait Gallery*

---

1 6 Geo III ch. xciv.
2 The Lunar Society was so called because it met once a month on the afternoon of the Monday nearest the time of a full moon. Informal contacts between members were of equal importance.
3 *Erasmus Darwin – A life of Unequalled Achievement* by Desmond King-Hele, Giles de la Mare 1999, ISBN 9781900357081 and *'Evolution' Evolving – Part 1: Dr Erasmus Darwin* by Jonathan Powers, iOpening Books 2014, ISBN 9780954577971.
4 Susannah Wedgwood was known as *Sukey*.
5 NA RAIL 878.

A miniature watercolour on ivory of Thomas Gilbert (1720-1798) by an unknown artist. Thomas and his brother John (1724-1795) were land agents to both the Marquess of Stafford and the Duke of Bridgewater. They were responsible for introducing Brindley to the Duke.
National Portrait Gallery

A miniature portrait on ceramic of the famous potter Josiah Wedgwood (1730-1795) by George Stubbs (1724-1806). Wedgwood was instrumental in the promotion of the Trent & Mersey Canal.
Phil Sayer/UK Art Fund

Once opened, the canal provided a waterway connection between the Humber Estuary to the River Mersey via the River Trent. James Brindley (1716-1772) along with Thomas Gilbert (1720-1798) had successfully surveyed and engineered the Bridgewater Canal and so it was not surprising that the *Company of Proprietors of the Navigation from the Trent to the Mersey* should appoint Brindley to their Committee of Management as Surveyor-General at a salary of £200 per annum. Brindley's brother-in-law Hugh Henshall (1734-1816), a former pupil/assistant, became Clerk of Works at a salary of £150 for himself and his clerk. Brindley had married Henshall's sister Anne (1747-1826) on 8th December 1765 when she was aged but 18; Brindley was thirty-one years her senior. They became good friends with the Wedgwoods and met often.

Harecastle tunnel was a truly pioneering work, especially when the concept of such a long tunnel for transport purposes had never before been attempted.[6] It was Brindley's surveying that established the summit level of the canal at Harecastle. On its south side it fell 316ft by means of forty locks to Derwent Mouth; to the north it fell by 326ft to Preston Brook via thirty-five locks.[7] It is interesting to note that Telford – and later the NSR – also chose to tunnel through Harecastle Hill rather than go around it. Brindley's tunnel was 2,880 yards in length, had a minimum width at water level of 8ft 6in and a minimum height above water level of only 5ft 10in. The highest point of Harecastle Hill was 191ft above the water level with approximately 1,500 yards of the tunnel being at around this depth, the rest having a much shallower cover. Construction commenced on 27th July 1766 when the excavation of fifteen vertical shafts spaced along the line of the tunnel was started at the same time, together with excavations at each end. Once the vertical shafts reached the required depth, the horizontal headings were driven simultaneously from a total of thirty-two faces. Fires were lit below the shafts to improve the ventilation by drawing air through the workings. The strata through which the tunnel passed included millstone grit, coal measures, ironstone and running sand. The tunnel was not bricked throughout its length, a stretch of about 100 yards towards the northern end through the harder rock was left unlined – see Appendix 2. Large quantities of water were encountered, cleared by wind pumps erected above the shafts and Newcomen stationary atmospheric steam engines. The excavated material was also drawn to the surface through the vertical shafts by means of horse-operated gins. The abundance of water was later used to feed the canal. At a general meeting of the proprietors held on 1st October 1768 it was reported that only 409 yards of tunnel had been completed but, of course, a vast amount of the work undertaken at that stage had been occupied in sinking the fifteen shafts.

The *Derby Mercury* published on 26th November 1773 quoted an extract from a letter posted in Burslem on 1st November.

---

6 The Malpas Tunnel on the Canal du Midi in France was excavated in 1679 but while of greater proportions, only has a short length of 180 yards.

7 Under an Act of 1809 (49 Geo III ch. lxxiii) a staircase of three locks at Lawton was reconstructed as four separate locks, so increasing the number of locks from Harecastle to Preston Brook to thirty-six.

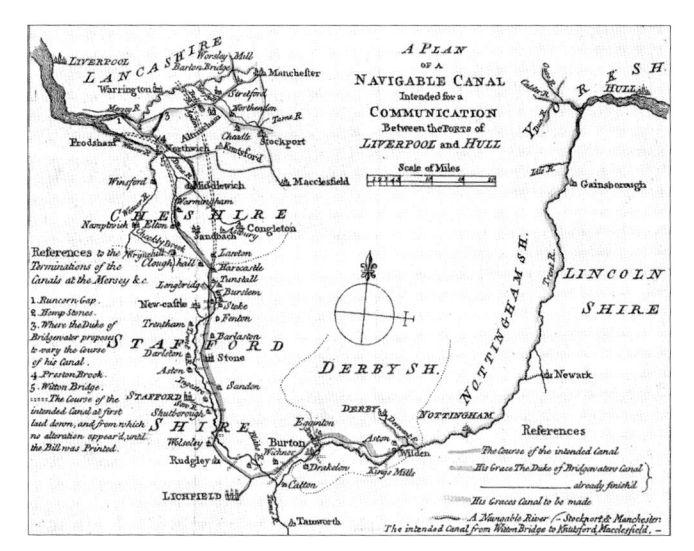

CHAPTER 1 – BRINDLEY'S TUNNEL

A contemporary plan showing the raison d'être for the Trent & Mersey Canal – to link the Port of Liverpool with the Port of Hull.

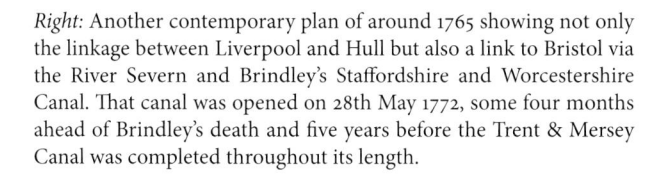

Right: Another contemporary plan of around 1765 showing not only the linkage between Liverpool and Hull but also a link to Bristol via the River Severn and Brindley's Staffordshire and Worcestershire Canal. That canal was opened on 28th May 1772, some four months ahead of Brindley's death and five years before the Trent & Mersey Canal was completed throughout its length.

The extract reads as follows: *On Wednesday last the Duke of Bridgewater, Earl Gower, the Hon. Keith Stewart, with several Gentlemen of Distinction, attended by the Agents to the Company of Proprietors of the Navigation from the Trent to the Mersey, sailed up the subterraneous tunnel at Harecastle, near a measured mile, where they were highly entertained, and expressed great satisfaction at that wonderful work of art; at night they returned in the Company's boat to Trentham, the seat of Earl Gower. This canal is now opened from the River Trent in Derbyshire to Harecastle, which is upwards of sixty-one miles, by which means goods may be conveyed to any part of the globe by water; the earth that is got by making the tunnel is now brought out in boats, and we are well informed that Harecastle Tunnel will be quite complete in another year, the length of which is near 3,000 yards, and that the whole canal is expected to be complete and join the Duke of Bridgewater's in about two years.* The trip into the tunnel took place on 27th October 1773 and clearly shows that the tunnel had been driven almost a mile into the hill from the south end. However, the estimates given for completion of the tunnel and canal were optimistic. The tunnel was completed by April 1775 when the canal was opened through the tunnel to Sandbach, but it took until May 1777 for it to be opened throughout. Contrary to popular belief, it was not the completion of the tunnel that delayed the final opening but the cutting of the canal between Middlewich and Acton where the original line ran very close to the banks of the River Weaver. This was overcome by Hugh Henshall, who had taken over as engineer after Brindley's death on 27th December 1772; he re-routed the intended line of the canal through new tunnels at Saltersford and Barnton. This northern section of the canal was, therefore, surveyed and engineered entirely by Henshall, completely independently of Brindley. Henshall would have taken this in his stride. He had been tutored by Brindley and no doubt had hands-on experience in the construction of Harecastle tunnel, taking full responsibility when Brindley was away pursuing his many other schemes. It seems that Henshall was assisted by Josiah Clowes (1735-1794) who had considerable mining experience.[8] The first Harecastle Tunnel took nine years to build; how sad that Brindley never saw its completion.

The *Derby Mercury* newspaper report referred to above clearly indicates that by 1773 the majority of spoil from the excavation

---

8 His brother, William Clowes (1728-1782), married Jane Henshall of Newchapel on 1st January 1750. She was the older sister of Anne Henshall who had married James Brindley.

This Trent & Mersey Navigation notice dated 1st June 1802 predates the construction of Telford's Tunnel. It describes the regulations, bye-laws and rules then applicable to the masters and owners of vessels employed on the navigation and to wagons and carriages used on the primitive railways or plateways that connected with the canal system. The RULES for PASSING THROUGH the TUNNEL at HARECASTLE are particularly interesting as they describe how Brindley's Tunnel was operated at that time. Boats travelling north were only allowed to enter the south end of the tunnel between 4am and 5am, between noon and 1pm and between 8pm and 9pm. Entry at the north end for boats heading south was permitted between 8am and 9am and between 4pm and 5pm. So there were three time slots for northbound traffic but only two for boats travelling in the opposite direction. Boats were expected to navigate the tunnel within three hours and the boat-masters or other persons in charge of the boats were expected to stay on board during the passage to ensure safe navigation.

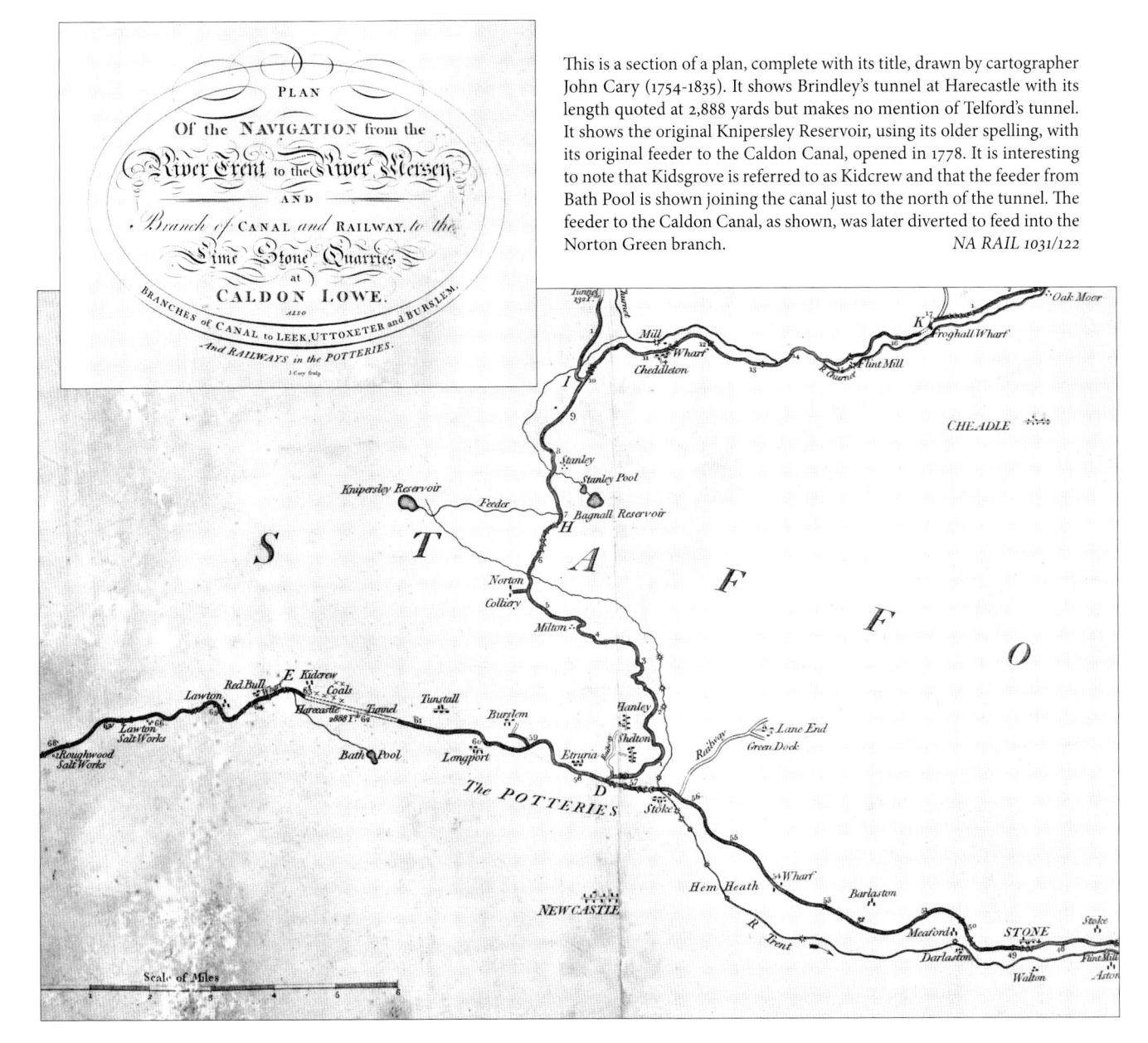

This is a section of a plan, complete with its title, drawn by cartographer John Cary (1754-1835). It shows Brindley's tunnel at Harecastle with its length quoted at 2,888 yards but makes no mention of Telford's tunnel. It shows the original Knipersley Reservoir, using its older spelling, with its original feeder to the Caldon Canal, opened in 1778. It is interesting to note that Kidsgrove is referred to as Kidcrew and that the feeder from Bath Pool is shown joining the canal just to the north of the tunnel. The feeder to the Caldon Canal, as shown, was later diverted to feed into the Norton Green branch.

NA RAIL 1031/122

of the tunnel was being brought out by boats implying that the vertical shafts at the southern end of the tunnel had been abandoned or only remained for ventilation purposes. The report covers another very interesting aspect of the workings, viz: *Harecastle tunnel cuts across 40 different mines of coal, besides mines of cannel, iron, stone, etc. In one of the principal mines of coals and cannel, the owners have made a collateral tunnel out of the grand tunnel, navigable for boats, where coals are loaded into them out of the mine, at 3s 6d per ton, and will supply most of the towns and villages bordering upon the canal, as well as supplying great parts of the Pottery. Cannel [9] will be sent as far as London by way of Hull. The owners of the said mines, are now making a passage for the men to go from the surface to work in the said mines, where they may walk by easy descent,* *till they meet the boats in the tunnel, which is upwards of sixty yards perpendicular from the surface; this is the only work of its kind in this Kingdom, or perhaps in the Universe.* Brindley was the part owner of Golden Hill Colliery which was located on the Turnhurst estate acquired by him in March 1760 with the following partners: John Brindley (1719-1807) – his brother; Hugh Henshall; Thomas Gilbert and John Gilbert (1724-1795). The Gilbert brothers were land agents to the both the Marquess of Stafford[10] and the Duke of Bridgewater. Indeed it was they who introduced Brindley to the Duke of Bridgewater. The co-operation of the two landed gentlemen, who owned large tracts of the land over which the Trent & Mersey passed, plus the drive of Josiah Wedgwood and other pottery manufacturers, was fundamental in securing the statutory powers to build the canal.

---

9   Cannel is more akin to oil shale than coal.

10 Granville Leveson-Gower (1721-1803), 1st Marquess of Stafford also known as Earl Gower from 1754 to 1786.

The north end of Brindley's tunnel in NSR days with boats about to be legged through the tunnel. Note the NSR Engineer's Department narrow boat on the left and the onlookers above the tunnel mouth at the start of Boat Horse Road. This road went over the hill to connect Kidsgrove with Chatterley.

Right: This view at the north end of Harecastle tunnels dates from c.1900 and shows a NSR Engineering Department narrow boat moored between Telford's tunnel on the left and Brindley's tunnel on the right. The narrow boat *Westwood* entering Brindley's tunnel is owned by pottery manufacturers, J. & G. Meakin of Hanley. *Basil Jeuda Collection*

Another view in NSR days in an almost identical position. The mouth of Telford's tunnel can just be seen on the left. The narrow boat *Westwood* will shortly be legged through Brindley's tunnel and the horse walked over the top of the hill along Boat Horse Road to Chatterley. The narrow boat is owned by pottery manufacturers, J. & G. Meakin of Hanley, a business founded in 1851. The firm's famous Eagle Pottery alongside the Caldon Canal was opened in 1859 and was taken over by the Wedgwood Group in 1970. It was demolished in 2005. The other identifiable narrow boat is NSR Engineer's Department number 44 displaying its Staffordshire knot; such craft seemed to have a permanent mooring here, no doubt readily available for any tunnel maintenance issues. The photograph was produced by E. Harrison & Son of Newcastle-under-Lyme. Edwin John Harrison (1836- 1903) had a studio at 77 Liverpool Road where his son Alfred William Harrison (1865-1947) assisted him. We wonder whether the young man on the right could be Alfred. *Keele University Special Collections & Archives, William Jack Collection*

CHAPTER 1 – BRINDLEY'S TUNNEL

A close-up of the north entrance to Brindley's tunnel taken on 3rd March 1958 with the tunnel keeper's cottage above.

Brindley had previously experienced the removal of coal by boat from the Worsley mines on the Duke of Bridgwater's estate and the prospect of repeating the practice at Harecastle may have been a factor in his decision to tunnel through the hill rather than finding a route around it. After completion, distance markers were placed on the east wall of the tunnel at 100 yard intervals starting with number 1, exactly 100 yards from the tunnel mouth at the Kidsgrove end. These enabled those legging the boats through the tunnel to measure their progress – see Appendix 2. A distance table published in 1795 by Newcastle-under-Lyme printer James Smith, shows two places within Harecastle where coal could be loaded underground.[11] Progressing from south to north, they were known as *Turnrail Coal* which was half a mile from the south entrance and *Birchenwood Coal* which was half a mile from the north entrance. Mining in the vicinity of Harecastle is covered in detail in Chapter 10.

In 1823, the year in which statutory powers were acquired for the second tunnel, Telford described Brindley's tunnel as follows: *This tunnel, where largest, is but 12ft high and 9ft wide, so that a 7ft wide boat, with a moderate loading, can scarcely pass through. The operation of thrusting a boat through this tunnel is by a class of men called leggers, who lie on their backs on the top of the loading, and push against the roof and sides with their feet. This tunnel, from commencement to completion, took no less than 11 years,* [authors – it actually took nine years] *so inexpert*

This is the tunnel keeper's cottage above the north end of Brindley's tunnel, a photograph taken *c*.1925.

Kidsgrove Library Local History Collection

11 NA RAIL 878/117.

This is the horse drawn narrow boat *Percy* owned by canal carrier Henry Rathbone. It is probably loaded with china clay and appears to be waiting to enter the north end of Brindley's tunnel. Above the carrier's name is the legend *Registered 187 Manchester*. The narrow boat was previously registered as number 232 with the Leigh Urban Registration Authority on 23rd October 1883 when it was recorded as recently repaired and painted and paired with another horse drawn narrow boat named *Gilbert*, number 233. They were then working on the Bridgewater and Leeds & Liverpool Canals. The master, James Lawson of Runcorn and his wife were on *Percy* with the mate on *Gilbert*. We just wonder whether the tiller is surrounded by Mrs Lawson and her six children.

Basil Jeuda Collection, Staffordshire Museums Service

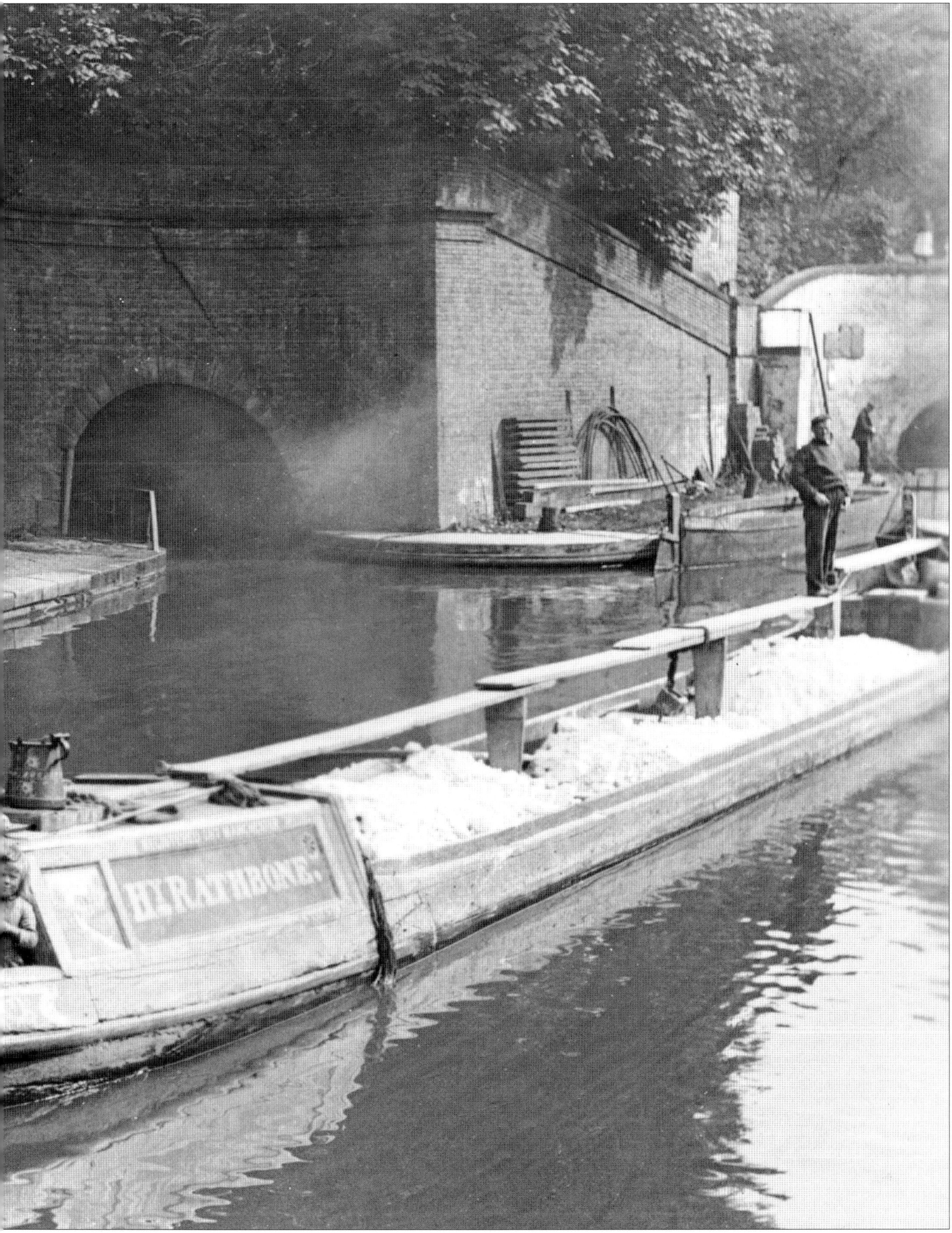
RATHBONE

were the workmen of that day, although under the direction of an able master. The inadequate dimensions of this tunnel were, no doubt, advisable in an untried project, and for several years after the navigation was opened, the imperfect and tedious passage was probably found sufficient; but, as trade increased, the delay and inconvenience became grievous. The time allotted for passing each way was two hours and before the expiration of that time a great number of boats was usually collected.[12] These same words were used by Telford in his *Atlas to the Life of Thomas Telford* published in London in 1838 by Payne & Foss (see Chapter 3).

In an endeavour to reduce the congestion at either end of Brindley's tunnel, the Select Committee which managed the canal company's affairs, at its meeting on 28th December 1824, approved a reduction in the time for passing alternately from north to south from six hours to two hours. This meant that the tunnel was open for north-bound traffic for two hours after which priority was given to south-bound traffic for the following two hours and so on throughout each day.[13]

---

12 Transcript by L. Allsop, National Waterways Museum, Ellesmere Port, ref BW 135.00 of the Minutes of the Select Committee of the Trent and Mersey Canal Company 7th September 1824 to 21st January 1828, ref BW 110/1/19.
13 *Ibid.*

This image taken on 15th February 2018 shows the barred southern entrance to Brindley's tunnel at Chatterley. The portal became a Grade II listed structure in 1989 and is now a lasting memorial to the great engineer.
Barry Knapper

Left: Brindley's gravestone at St James Church, Newchapel, Stoke-on-Trent – *The Church on the Hill*. Latterly he lived at nearby Turnhurst Hall and the stone is quite remarkable in that it featured an early use of the title *ENGINEER* to describe his profession.

2

THE TRENT AND MERSEY CANAL

The Trent and Mersey Canal was indeed immediately successful so much so that Brindley's once innovative and much praised tunnel quickly became a bottleneck, exactly as Telford had described. There was no room for boats to pass within the tunnel which led to congestion as boats queued to get through at either end and there was no towpath, necessitating the practice of *legging* referred to by Telford.

I must see the greater Part of the Men that pass along the Line, inasmuch as there is a Tunnel called the Harecastle Tunnel, and the Boats pass through that Tunnel. One Part of them are propelled by a Body of Men who are called Leggers, and there is a Way for the Horses returning back again, and Part of the Families always pass along by my Parsonage Door over the Tunnel. The Reverend Frederick Tobias Wade [14] made that statement on 13th May 1841 before a Government Select Committee on Sunday Trading. It is particularly interesting as it makes absolutely clear that it was not always the boatmen who legged the boats through Brindley's tunnel, rather a separate body of men who lived locally. They would charge for their services while one of the boatmen led his horse over Harecastle Hill along Boat Horse Road, which is still so named today. Two leggers were required for each boat; they lay on their sides on two wooden boards that were put out at the front of the boat and secured. The leggers then used their feet to propel the boat forward by pushing against the tunnel walls.[15] This is somewhat contrary to Telford's description that they also pushed against the roof but is probably more accurate, especially for an empty or lightly-laden boat when there would be very little space between the roof and men pushing against it. In 1853, Reverend Wade was still concerning himself with the leggers. On 3rd May that year at a meeting of the NSR Canal Traffic Committee held at Stoke Station, a letter from him was read out recommending that the company should provide porters at the Harecastle tunnels to supersede the leggers, whose habits and practices he considered to be highly prejudicial to the neighbourhood they lived in.[16] Nothing was done. Legging remained the only means of propelling boats through Brindley's tunnel throughout its entire existence. An analysis of the 1901 census return for Church Lawton which was just to the north of the tunnels revealed ten Boatman's Leggers living in huts near the canal or on boats moored alongside. Their ages ranged from 40 to 74; six were single, three were married and there was one widower.[17]

---

14 Frederick Tobias Wade was born in Mealiffe, Tipperary, Ireland in 1809 and was the vicar at St. Thomas' Church, Kidsgrove from 1837 to 1880. He died on 15th March 1884 at Tatenhill Rectory, Staffordshire.

15 *The Best of Kidsgrove Times Vol. V – The Leggers of Kidsgrove* by Philip R. Leese, published by the author at Kidsgrove, 2004.

16 NA RAIL 878/1.

17 Information provided to Philip R. Leese by R. Burndred.

Boat Horse Road, Kidsgrove

A mid-1950s postcard view of Boat Horse Road which was taken at Kidsgrove just after the road leaves The Avenue, running roughly parallel to the railway between the old middle and south railway tunnels and immediately prior to the road crossing over the northern end of the south tunnel. The trees are part of Kidswood with Clough Hall Park to the right and the old gas lamp once illuminated the way for the boat horses. The view was, of course, taken before the disruption caused by the diversion of the railway.

Kidsgrove Library Local History Collection

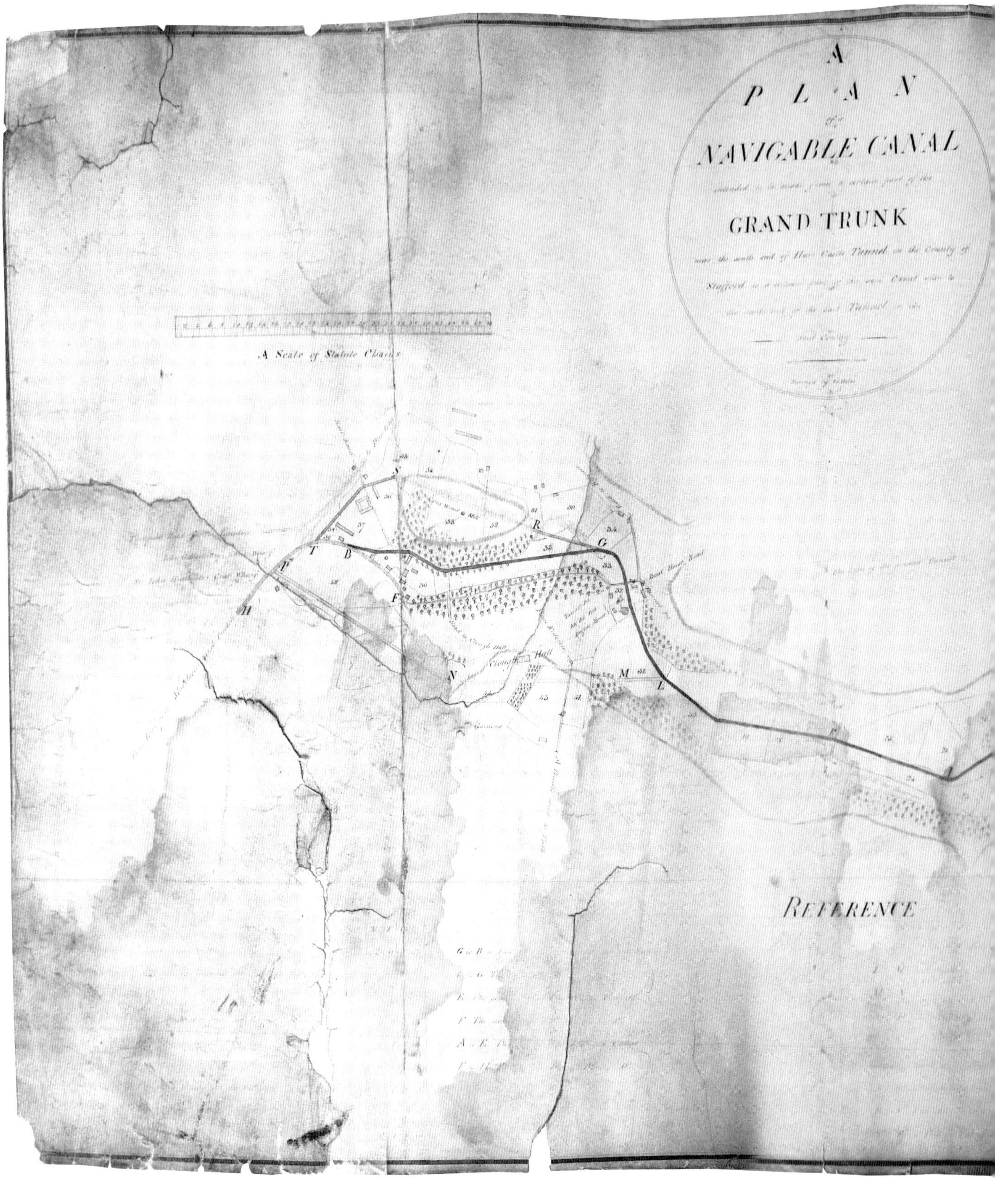
A
PLAN
NAVIGABLE CANAL
GRAND TRUNK
A Scale of Statute Chains
Clough Hall
REFERENCE

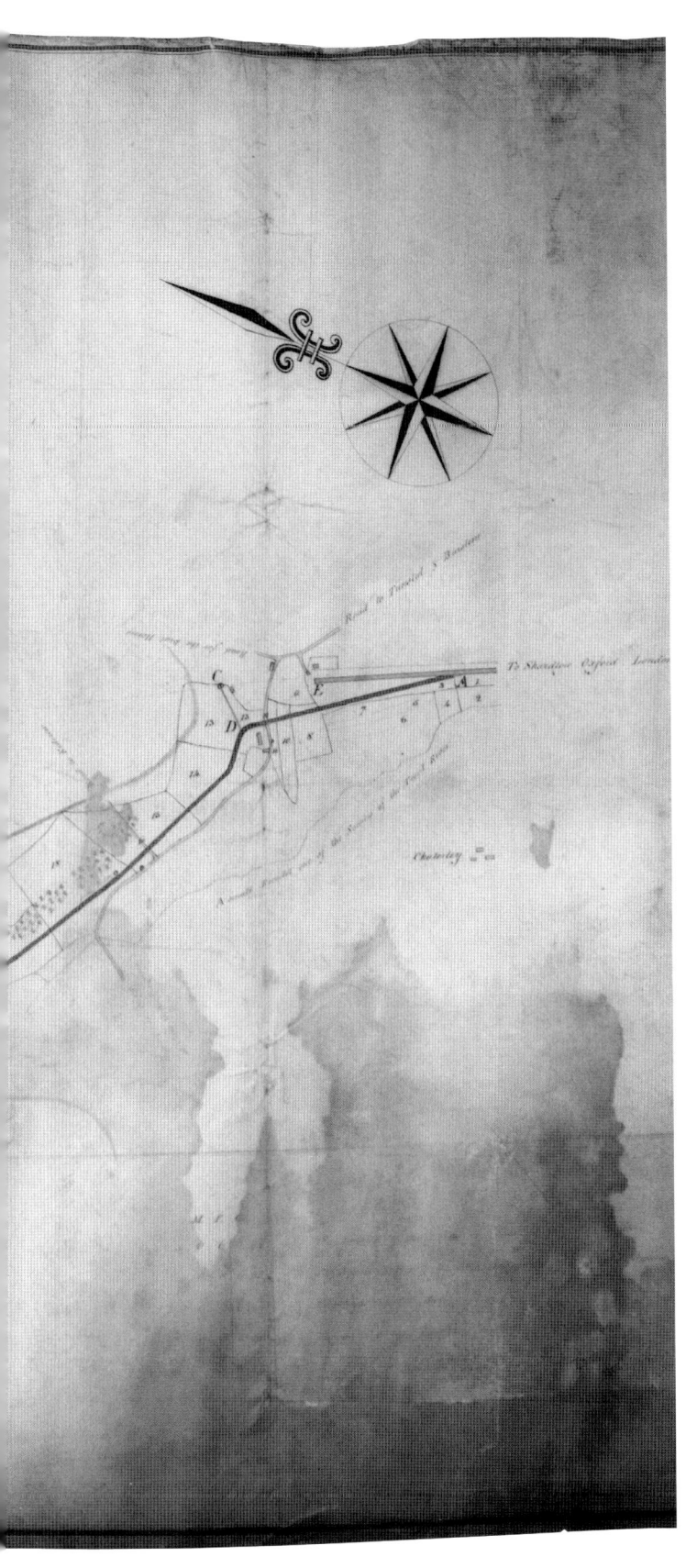

The congestion problem at the tunnel had been recognised at an early date as in the 1807-1808 Parliamentary Session an application was made by the Company of Proprietors *to vary the line of their Canal at or through Harecastle Hill*. A plan of a survey for a route to the west of the hill by Ralph Hales was deposited on 24th September 1807 and a Book of Reference on 28th September, but the proposal was later withdrawn.[18] A year earlier on 30th September 1806 a plan had also been deposited in the previous Parliamentary Session for a proposed horse-drawn railway *from or near Hardings Wood* near the north end of Brindley's tunnel *in the County of Stafford to the Trent & Mersey Canal at Treble Locks in the County of Chester*. It ran from *Mr. Kinnersley's* [sic] *Coal Works*, gave off a short branch to *Mr. Gilbert's stables*, and passed by a lime kiln near to the *Red Bull* before passing Lawton Mill and reaching its destination at *Treble Locks*.[19] That proposal also came to nothing.

---

18 CRO Q/Rum/42.
19 CRO Q/Rum/41.

Left: This is the plan by Ralph Hales referred to above. Although the original is, as can be seen, in very poor condition, the staff at the Staffordshire & Stoke-on-Trent Archives have made as good a job as possible to secure its conservation. It is particularly interesting for our purpose, as it shows a number of proposals for a canal to bypass Brindley's tunnel, prior to the construction of Telford's tunnel. The plan was deposited on 30th September 1807 and the *Book of Reference* outlining ownership of the land over which the alternative routes would pass, is dated 28th September 1807.

On the plan Harecastle is to the left and Chatterley to the right. The canal as built runs from *H* on the left to *A* on the right, via the existing tunnel, which is shown dotted from *F* to *E*. The heavy line between *A* and *L* is the principal part of the proposed new canal, but there are two alternatives for part of it at the Harecastle end, the part between *L*, via *G* to *B*. They are referred to in the *Book of Reference* as the Eastern and Western alternatives. Both involved tunnels, albeit much shorter than the existing one, along with flights of locks. The Eastern route, which is shown from *T* to *G*, has a tunnel 506 yards long from *S* to *R*, with a fall via lockage of 60ft from *S* to *T*. The Western route tunnel, from *N* to *M*, would have been approximately 630 yards long, with a similar flight of locks from *P* to *N*, also falling 60 ft. The section *B* to *G* would have been 970 yards long, obviating the need for the tunnels, but also requiring a fall by lockage of 60ft, along with a very deep cutting in which most of the locks would have had to be located. Assuming locks with a rise of, say, eight feet, around eight locks would have been required in each case. The rest of the line of the canal, from *L* to *A*, would have followed, more or less, the route later selected for the railway tunnel deviation scheme.

Notice that line of the canal would have passed through the Bathpool, using the pool as part of its passage. The supply of water would have been a crucial issue in this scheme as relying on the Bathpool and its catchment area, would not have been sufficient. This was of course, why Brindley elected to tunnel through the hill at a much lower level. It would have been necessary to install steam engines to pump water to the higher level, making the whole scheme a very expensive one. Little wonder that nothing came of it.

CRO QRum/42

An early miniature portrait of James Caldwell (1759-1838). He was a Trent & Mersey Canal Proprietor and for many years Chairman of the Select Committee that controlled the company's affairs.
Heath-Caldwell Family Archive

James Caldwell in later life, c.1830. Heath-Caldwell Family Archive

At this point it is appropriate to introduce James Caldwell (1759-1838). He was one of the canal proprietors and for many years chairman of the Select Committee referred to earlier. L.T.C. Rolt in his celebrated book *Thomas Telford*, first published by Longmans in 1958, is rather dismissive of Caldwell but he cannot have had the benefit of seeing his diaries covering the years 1770 to 1838, all of which have been preserved, with transcriptions available via the internet.[20] Caldwell was a lawyer, estate owner and a very shrewd businessman with interests in pottery and brewing. He was born on 21st January 1759 in Nantwich, Cheshire and became a protégé of Josiah Wedgwood[21] who, having been impressed with Caldwell's numeracy and literacy employed him at a very early age. On 20th February 1777, Caldwell began employment as a clerk for lawyer John Sparrow (1736-1821) of Newcastle-under-Lyme. Caldwell's father paid Sparrow a sum of £315 so that over a period of five years his son could be trained in the profession of an attorney and solicitor. Sparrow, together with Wedgwood, had been prime movers in promoting the Trent & Mersey Canal.

On 8th June 1784 in Derby, Caldwell married Elizabeth Stamford (1754-1831) whose father Thomas Stamford (1712-1787) was a close friend of Josiah Wedgwood. They had seven children, six girls and one boy, called James Stamford Caldwell (1786-1858) who was educated at Cambridge and is referred to in the diaries as Stamford. Initially the family lived in Newcastle-under-Lyme and Elizabeth's unmarried sister, Hannah Stamford (1753-1832), lived with them. Throughout the diaries Caldwell refers to his wife as Eliza and to Hannah as Miss Stamford. In 1789 Caldwell purchased the Linley Wood estate at Talke, a small mining village to the north of Newcastle, but the family did not move into the house there until 1794, as substantial alterations were required.

Caldwell had qualified as an attorney on 22nd April 1782 and in the following year became a partner in the law firm of Sparrow and Caldwell. This lasted for only a few years as, from 1788 to 1795, he was in partnership with John Martin, Attorney at Law. In 1797 he became a Deputy Lieutenant for Staffordshire. Insofar as his other commercial business interests were concerned he was in partnership with potter Enoch Wood (1759-1840) from 1791 to 1818. The firm traded as Wood & Caldwell and produced a wide range of pottery products, including dinner services, jugs and figurines to a high standard. In the late 1790s he went into the brewery business in partnership with William Bent (1764-1820) which lasted more than twenty years. The partnership had breweries at Newcastle-under-Lyme, Shrewsbury, Macclesfield and Liverpool.[22]

The first mention of his involvement with the Trent and Mersey Canal appears in 1799, but it was not until 1806 that he was invited to take office on the Select Committee. Thereafter his entries are peppered with navigation business, involving regular meetings at Stone, where the canal company had its headquarters, or occasionally elsewhere, thus demonstrating his close, almost passionate, involvement with the canal. On 29th June 1815 while inspecting the canal from Wolseley Bridge near Colwich to Fradley Junction, where the Trent & Mersey joined the Coventry Canal, he proposed that the company's new boat being used for the inspection should be named *Waterloo* as a compliment to the Duke of Wellington. The suggestion was immediately and unanimously adopted by all those taking part in the inspection. At a meeting of the Select Committee held on 3rd November 1818, the Clerk, William Vaughan (1770-1834), reported that 240 boats had recently passed the summit pound in one day.

In 1820 the celebrated engineer John Rennie the Elder (1761-1821) was engaged to inspect Brindley's tunnel and put forward

---

20 http://www.jjhc.info/caldwellnotes.htm
21 Caldwell became an executor for Josiah Wedgwood's will, a responsibility he shared with Josiah's eldest son, John Wedgwood (1766-1844).

22 The firm of Bent's continued to have a long history as brewers and in 1902 purchased the brewery in Stone, Staffordshire from Liverpudlian, Thomas Montgomery (1855-1911). The brewery was built in 1889.

proposals to relieve what had become a very serious bottleneck. Caldwell's diary entry for 16th August 1820 reads as follows: *Mr. Rennie and his two daughters having arrived at the Red Bull this morning, I immediately went down with Mr. Potter, who had come to Linley Wood to inform me of his arrival. Long conversations with Mr. Rennie relative to the objects of his survey and report, and afterwards walked with him to the entrance of the tunnel, where I left him and Mr. Potter.* The *Red Bull* was undoubtedly the coaching inn at Lawton which survived until the 1960s. Mr. Potter was the canal's engineer, James Potter (1801-1857), who became the resident engineer for the second Harecastle tunnel.

Rennie stayed for three further days. On 17th August Caldwell joined him and Potter visiting Etruria Locks and Leek from where they took pack horses to inspect parts of the River Churnet. They then proceeded to inspect the dam across the reservoir at Rudyard, returning to the locks at Hazlehurst on the Caldon Canal,[23] before proceeding to Knypersley to consider the construction of another reservoir at that location. The provision of additional water supplies for the canal was obviously also receiving serious consideration. Rennie stayed at the Red Bull throughout his visit but dined at Linley Wood during the evening of 18th August. The following day Rennie read over to Caldwell the rough draft of his intended report on Harecastle tunnel before departing for Scotland.

Rennie's final report was completed in Edinburgh and is dated 11th September 1820 and a copy survives in the archives of the Institution of Civil Engineers. Another copy is deposited with the Twemlow papers at the Staffordshire & Stoke-on-Trent Archives, at the Record Office in Stafford. Francis Twemlow (1783-1865) of Betley Court was a proprietor of the Trent & Mersey Navigation. The report graphically describes the condition of Brindley's tunnel after being in service for some forty-five years and explains the reasoning that led to the construction of a second tunnel. It is of great significance and is reproduced in its entirety below.

Edinburgh, September 11th 1820

To the General Meeting of Proprietors
of the Grand Trunk Canal

Gentlemen,

According to your request signified to me in Mr. Potter's letter of March last, I took a view of the tunnel at Harecastle on the 16th which on the whole I found to be in better condition than I expected, but far from being in such a condition as a canal so important to the country as the Grand Trunk requires.

It is not possible by word to describe minutely the various parts in which the work is deficient in size and in quality – suffice it to say that in many places the roof is not more than six feet above the ordinary level of the water – in others it is 6½, 7, 7½ and 8 feet, in some places it is too narrow, in others crooked – and generally speaking the brickwork which forms the bottom, sides and top of the tunnel is not more than 9 inches thick; it has throughout been made with bad mortar so that in all the brickwork under water and wherever there is springs or moisture that keeps it damp, the mortar is as soft as clay, the bricks in many places can therefore be pulled out with little labour and in the low parts of the roof and in some of the projecting parts of the sides, the brickwork is worn away by the rubbing of the boats and their cargoes to nearly half its thickness. The tunnel on the sides that are made to communicate with the various coalworks are generally in bad condition, their arches at the junction being torn to pieces by the barges turning into and out of them and little care is taken in cleaning them out. Mud and rubbish therefore slides down into the canal tunnel and greatly obstructs the Navigation. The colliers break into it in various places where they require a communication with the canal without even as I am informed giving notice to the company's agents and therefore in such places it can scarcely be called safe – considerable repairs were made last winter but much is still to do and it will require a good deal of time to complete these repairs which may be reckoned as temporary, but were a thorough repair to be given to the whole it would occupy several months, and if the low parts of the arch were to be taken out and raised to one general level or height with the higher parts it would require at least a year to complete the work. To say that there is any immediate danger of any considerable part of the tunnel giving way would certainly be saying too much. On the contrary I am of opinion that in all probability by strict attention and partial repairs the tunnel may be preserved in its present imperfect state for years to come; but when the whole state of it is considered, my opinion is, that the company should not risk the whole of their trade unless it is under the contemplation of giving it a thorough repair at no very distant period and as the time that this will occupy will of course be considerable, and it is a subject which in my humble estimation claims imperiously their serious attention – the inconvenience the trade of the country will sustain while such repairs are in hand and the loss the company is likely to sustain during that period – If this on the whole view of the case shall appear to them as it does to me, it may be worthy of consideration whether it would not be better to provide in the interim some means by which the trade may be carried on while these repairs are in hand; for this purpose various modes present themselves – a railway might be laid across the hill and the cargoes of the boats might be unloaded at each end of the tunnel and transported across the hill – a new tunnel might be made through the hill nearby parallel to the present, or a chain of locks with an open cutting might be made through the Bath Pool Valley.

The first plan would no doubt be soonest executed and at the least expense, and by means of two inclined planes and two steam engines would be rendered as convenient as such a plan could be, the loading and discharging the cargoes of the boats however at each end of the railway or those inclined planes would occasion much detention, damage and loss of property – as well as a heavy expense in loading and discharging of the cargoes, in working of the steam engines and haling of the wagons, without giving that facility and dispatch which the trade requires, and when the repairs of the tunnel were completed the bulk of the expense incurred in the formation of the railway and inclined planes would in a great measure be lost.

The second plan, namely a new tunnel would cost about £58,000 but when done its benefits would be great and permanent. It would afford ample time to repair the present tunnel and when completed it would give great dispatch to the trade, as all the boats passing one way might go by one tunnel, while those passing the other way might go by the

---

23 The Caldon Canal, opened *c*.1779, is a branch of the Trent & Mersey running from its summit level at Etruria to Froghall, 17½ miles away in the Churnet Valley. The canal reservoir at Rudyard (now known as Rudyard Lake) was opened in 1797; its feeder runs into the Leek Branch of the Caldon Canal which joins the Caldon at Hazlehurst Junction. Springs initially supplied the water for the reservoir at Rudyard but these proved insufficient and a feeder via a weir from the River Dane was built in 1809 to supplement supplies.

other tunnel, and thus the stoppage occasioned by the present tunnel of three hours for the alternate passage of boats would be avoided.

The third plan would in like manner be a permanent improvement, but would be attended with much more expense to the company as well as detention to the trade than a tunnel. It appears from my calculation that the expense of an open cut with 16 locks thro' Bath Pool Valley including steam engines, shafts, etc would amount to about £88,000 [24] and that the expense of working these steam engines annually including fuel, engine men, repairs, etc would be about £3,066 and when done would not be so complete or expeditious as a second tunnel. I presume that the time consumed in passing the present tunnel cannot averagely exceed two hours and if there were a second tunnel there would be no interruption which would of course lesson [sic] this time. I should think in this case an hour and a half quite sufficient. Now a boat will pass a six foot lock in about 4 minutes and as there would in the case in question be 16 locks, 64 minutes would be consumed in passing the locks and the length of the Navigation would occupy about 68 minutes more thus making two hours and nearly a quarter, but as frequent interruption would be occasioned by boats taking their turns at the respective locks the time could not be reckoned less on the average than two hours and a half perhaps even more, thus there would be a clear saving in time of at least an hour and from what I have stated a saving in money of at least £30,000. I think no doubt is left as to the choice between a tunnel and a new cutting through Bath Pool Valley.

If the company shall adopt the plan of a second tunnel, they will no doubt in addition to the arguments already used keep in view the perfect state to which their canal would be brought, the great additional facility that would be given to the trade and the removal of the temptation to the making of other lines of canal in opposition to the Grand Trunk. Schemes of this sort have already been before the public and others are now in embryo which may at no distant period be brought forward. The Proprietors of the Grand Trunk Canal will therefore best promote the interests of the concern by making the Navigation as complete as the nature of the case will admit. Much has already been done in the bringing of additional supplies of water and in removing many of the chains and locks and if they persevere in getting more water, in cutting off the remaining chain of locks at Etruria, in making an additional tunnel and in cleaning the canal from mud, the Navigation will be as complete as the nature of the case will admit, and in this state although I will not say that they may defy all rival schemes, yet I must say that they will in great measure remove the temptation to rival adventures.

I am Gentlemen, your most humble servant,

John Rennie

Rennie confirmed the overall integrity of Brindley's tunnel which was in a better state than he anticipated even though there were obvious signs of subsidence, but he was critical of the mortar used and highly critical of the connections made within the tunnel linking the canal with underground mining operations. It is clear from the report that there were several such connections, some of which were unauthorised! Repairs to the damaged brickwork were urgently required and the canal through the tunnel needed dredging to clear accumulated mud and rubbish. He estimated that proper remedial action could involve a stoppage of up to a year which was obviously unacceptable. His three solutions to the problem are summarised below:

1. Carry out the complete repairs required to Brindley's tunnel but construct a temporary railway with two inclined planes over Harecastle Hill to transport the traffic while the repairs were undertaken.

2. Drive a second tunnel.

3. Build a by-pass canal to the west of the hill through Bath Pool Valley which would require a deep cutting, the construction of 16 locks and two steam engines to pump water for the summit level.

Of the three options, Rennie preferred a new tunnel. His estimated cost for a tunnel 3,000 yards long with a width of 10ft 6in and a height of 14 feet with a deep cutting at each end was £57,561, broken down as follows:

	£	s	d
To 176 running yards of cutting at north end, 15ft deep	1,320	0	0
To 3,000 running yards of tunnel	49,500	0	0
To 230 running yards of cutting south end, 25ft deep	3,248	14	0
To 460 running yards of cutting south end, 15ft deep	1,863	0	0
To 8 acres of land	800	0	0
To damage	500	0	0
To 866 running yards of towing path	129	6	0
To 2 stop gates	200	0	0
TOTAL COST	**57,561**	**0**	**0**

Clearly Rennie did not recommend a towpath through the new tunnel and it seems odd that his estimates did not include expenditure for the sinking of vertical shafts to the tunnel level. His costing for the by-pass canal through the Bath Pool Valley can be seen in Appendix 1. On 15th September 1821, a year after Rennie had submitted his report, a notice appeared in *The Staffordshire Advertiser* ascribed to the Navigation Office, Stone stating that the Company of Proprietors of the Navigation from the Trent to the Mersey intended to make an application to Parliament in the next session for leave to bring a Bill to enable the company to make a navigable tunnel through Harecastle Hill and an additional reservoir at Knypersley, on which Rennie had actually reported unfavourably. Unfortunately, there was to be a delay brought about by Rennie's untimely death on 4th October 1821. At the General Assembly of the Proprietors held at the Crown Inn, Stone on 10th December 1821, the consequences of Rennie's death were discussed.[25] Having been deprived of his services and losing the benefit of him giving evidence before Parliament, the Assembly approved the Select Committee's recommendation to postpone the proposed Bill to another year.

---

24 The two surviving hand written reports have a figure of £57,000 which is clearly an error so this has been corrected here to £80,000 to make sense. There is no point in perpetuating an obvious error. The precise figure in Rennie's estimate (see transcript in Appendix 1) quotes £88,061, i.e. about £30,000 more than the cost of a second tunnel.

25 CRO – Twemlow papers. Ref. D3098/8/11.

3

TELFORD'S TUNNEL

On 4th March 1822, on returning from a meeting of the Select Committee at Stone, Caldwell met Thomas Telford (1757-1834)[26] at the *Roebuck* at Newcastle-under-Lyme.[27] Earlier that day Telford had been to Harecastle Hill to meet Messrs Heath and Johnson who were conversant with the mines and minerals and general stratification of the hill and its vicinity.[28] They accompanied him over the ground upon and adjacent to Brindley's tunnel and *afforded very full and satisfactory information*. The following morning Telford and James Potter breakfasted at Linley Wood with Caldwell to discuss the proposed tunnel and other works. They then went to see Brindley's tunnel which Telford examined, accompanied by Potter. In the evening all three dined at the *Red Bull* at Lawton and during the conversation Telford discussed his findings. His report was written on his return to London. A copy dated 25th March 1822 has survived and the following are quotations from it.[29]

I passed through and examined the state of the tunnel and found it tolerably good. I observed no symptoms of immediate danger or failure and none but what occasional repairs may remedy. In some instances, more especially near each extremity, the crown of the arch has an imperfect shape and from being too low has been worn away for about half its thickness, these parts require attention; much has already been done towards repairing and securing the lower parts, which is very important. The tunnel as regards general intercourse is, in several parts too narrow and low and has certainly from long experience been found quite inadequate for the business transacted. The only effectual remedy, simple and practically useful, is another tunnel. This would perfectly accommodate the intercourse of the country and save much time, trouble and expense.

A second tunnel being therefore absolutely necessary, the question is resolved into the most advisable line of direction. Upon duly weighing up all the circumstances connected with the nature of the mines and attending the construction of a tunnel, I do not hesitate to recommend fixing the line on the eastern side of the present tunnel and as near to it as prudences will admit. I conceive 25 yards between them to be quite sufficient and preferable to a greater distance. I have from the information furnished me, reason to think that in this situation, the new tunnel would be in original undisturbed ground, which has been drained by the present tunnel. It would be clear of the coal workings and would securely extend the prohibition to which the [mine] owners are already subjected. Upon the whole by keeping the new tunnel near to the present tunnel the interests of the coal masters and canal proprietors would be mutually promoted.

With regard to the expense; in works of this nature an accurate estimate is what no Engineer can be expected to give but comparing it with other works of a similar nature which have come under my inspection, I am disposed to state it at about £60,000.

Caldwell recorded that he was at home on 4th June 1822 closely engaged all morning in redrawing the Bill for the new tunnel and the additional reservoir at Knypersley which Telford supported.

In the House of Lords Record Office[30] there is a plan with the title 'PLAN of the proposed NEW TUNNEL through HARECASTLE HILL'. It is signed by James Potter of Lichfield and is dated September 1822. The plan shows the route of the proposed new tunnel alongside the old one, a section through the hill and an elevation of the proposed tunnel mouth. It also shows the landowners under whose land the tunnel would pass. Accompanying this plan is a breakdown of the estimated cost by James Potter with an indication that the work may be completed in seven years.[31] The document bears Potter's signature but is not dated. It is counter-signed by William Vaughan who certifies that the Company of Proprietors of the Navigation will defray the estimated costs which totalled £48,547 17s 4d – some £10,000 less than Rennie's estimate. This is Potter's breakdown:

	£	s	d
44,000 yards cube digging, open cutting, carrying away spoil @ 1/3 per cube	2,750	0	0
12,000 yards open cutting and carrying away shale rock @ 3/6 per cube	2,100	0	0
82,401 yards tunnelling in coal shale and clay and winding it to the bank @ 3/- per cube	12,360	0	0
2,955 yards tunnelling in hard rock and winding it to the bank @ 15/- per cube	2,216	5	0
44,497 yards super 1½ brick, sides, top and bottom arches @ 1/4 per cube	2,966	9	4
1,834 cube masonry tunnel mouths, buntings inside, etc @ 10/- per cube	917	0	0
49,509 feet cube stone @ 8d per cube	1,650	6	0
6,624,000 bricks @ 23/- per thousand	7,617	12	0

---

26 Telford had been appointed as the first President of the Institution of Civil Engineers in 1820.

27 The *Roebuck* was a coaching inn handling some forty coaches a day. It was subsequently converted into shops but demolished in 1936 to be replaced by the present Lancaster Buildings at the top of the Ironmarket.

28 Heath was undoubtedly Robert Heath (1779-1849) who managed Thomas Kinnersly's Clough Hall Estate.

29 ICE Archive T/TR. 12.

30 HLRO – HL/PO/PB/3 plan 33 1823.

31 HLRO – HL/PO/PB/3 1823. The reference to Barrow lime refers to limestone sourced from Barrow-on-Soar, Leicestershire.

	£	s	d
2,208 tons Barrow lime @ 34/- per ton	3,753	12	0
4,500 tons of sand @ 3/- per ton	675	0	0
Sinking 14 shafts, say, 315 yards run @ 15/- per yard	236	5	0
Carriage of bricks, loading and unloading and letting them down the shafts 6,624,000 @ 9/- per thousand	2,980	16	0
Making and shifting centres, timber for shoring, pumping the water from the shafts and contingencies, say, 20% of all above costs	8,044	12	0
Damage and trespass of 20 acres of land for seven years at £2 per acre	280	0	0
TOTAL COST	**£48,547**	**17s**	**4d**

The Act for the second tunnel entitled: *An Act to enable the Company of Proprietors of the Navigation from the Trent to the Mersey, to make an additional Tunnel through Harecastle Hill, in the county of Stafford, and an additional Reservoir in Knypersley Valley*, inter alia, received the Royal Assent on 17th June 1823.[32] As previously mentioned, there was already a reservoir at Knypersley which had been completed by 1787, but the additional water capacity was required to cope with the expected increase in traffic following the opening of the second tunnel. The contractors for the reservoir were Dutton & Buckley who also played a small part at Harecastle in constructing the southern approach cutting for the tunnel. The combined capacity of the old reservoir, known as the Serpentine Pool and the new, known as Knypersley Pool, is 41 million cubic feet. The feeder from Knypersley connects with the Caldon Canal via the Norton Green Branch which opened in 1778.

The main tunnel works were put out to tender in 1824 and the successful contractor was the firm of Pritchard & Hoof of Kings Norton who were experienced in driving canal tunnels. Daniel Pritchard (1777-1843) and his son-in-law William Hoof (1788-1855) were the contractors for the Strood Tunnel on the Thames & Medway Canal; Telford was the engineer. Work on that tunnel which was 3,946 yards long had commenced in 1819 and was completed on 6th May 1824. Pritchard had written to Telford a few days later on 13th May saying that he had seen newspaper reports about the proposed new tunnel at Harecastle. He asked Telford whether the main contract had been let and, if not, could he provide the name of the engineer as he was keen to play a part.[33] Obviously his enquiry proved fruitful as before the end of the month Telford had been appointed! Pritchard & Hoof's estimate for the work dated 12th January 1825 was as follows.[34]

	£	s	d
Sinking 16 shafts amounting to 538 yards at 55/- per yard	1,479	10	0
Supposing to drive 16 cross headings to the old tunnel 30 yards each amounting to 480 yards at 30/- per yard	720	0	0
Heading in the line of tunnel for the purpose of relieving water, communicating one shaft to the other to get rid of foul air, and also to keep the range and levels – 2,900 yards at 57/- per yard	8,265	0	0
Furnishing 10 shafts with gins, ropes, skips, interest upon iron rail stays, tools, trucks, etc	1,750	0	0
Supposing the tunnel to require 2,400 bricks in a yard run. Loading and wheeling the bricks to the shafts, loading them into the skips, lowering them down the shafts and conveying them underground to such places as they may be wanted at 8/6 per yard for 2,900 yards	1,232	10	0
2,900 yards of brick work in the tunnel at 30/- per yard	4,350	0	0
Excavating the main tunnel, timbering etc ready for the brick work at £14 per yard	40,600	0	0
Five foremen constantly employed upon the tunnel for conducting and looking after the same, 3 in the day with 2 in the night at £10 per week in total for 2 years	1,040	0	0
Carpenter work, blacksmiths' work keeping materials in repair, contingencies and other unforeseen accidents	1,560	0	0
TOTAL COST	**£60,997**	**0s**	**0d**

The total cost was therefore some £12,500 higher than Potter's 1822 estimate and more in line with Rennie's 1821 estimate of £58,000. However, the canal company had the responsibility of finding bricks, lime, sand, coals, timber, centres and laggings and conveying them to the pit banks and for keeping the tunnel clear from water and there is a separate costing for this dated 16th November 1824.[35] This adds another £21,473 15s 0d to the cost, explained as follows.

	£	s	d
Brick work to 2,900 yards, lime, sand etc at £5 per yard	14,500	0	0
425 thousand bricks for the purpose of sinking 17 shafts 600 yards deep, including the carting of the bricks at 27/- per thousand	573	15	0
Pumping water, sinking engine wells at 10/- per yard	1,450	0	0
Timber at 20/- per yard	2,900	0	0
Conveying 7 millions of bricks to various parts of the tunnel at 4/- per thousand	1,400	0	0

---

32 4 Geo IV ch. lxxxvii.
33 ICE Archive T/TR. 16.
34 ICE Archive T/TR. 36.
35 ICE Archive T/TR. 30.

120 curbs for the purpose of sinking the above 17 shafts at 25/- per curb, including the carting to each shaft	150	0	0
Loss on iron rail way	500	0	0
TOTAL EXTRA COST	**£21,473**	**15s**	**0d**

The total estimated cost was, therefore £82,470 15s 0d.

From these estimates we can learn some interesting aspects of the proposed construction methodology. Of the intended sixteen vertical shafts it was originally anticipated that only ten would be fitted with gins and ropes for removing spoil, lowering bricks and conveying the manpower and tools required for the excavation. The other shafts would be for ventilation as would the sixteen cross headings to the old tunnel, although the latter could possibly also have been used to convey men and bricks and remove some of the spoil by boat. It was estimated to cost £175 to furnish each of the ten working shafts with the materials required which included the cost of three horses to work each gin, so that work could be carried out during the day and night as indeed it was throughout the entire construction period. It appears from the reference to interest charges that some of the railway equipment could have been hired. In practice fifteen working shafts were sunk, six to the north of the summit and nine to the south.[36]

Caldwell's diary records that on 30th March 1824 he met Potter at the south end of the tunnel about half past eleven o'clock and *dug up myself the first clod of the open cutting for the intended new tunnel.* On 17th April Caldwell and Potter went to the site to review progress and they both rode over the hill on horseback viewing the line of the additional tunnel which had been marked out. The digging of the open cutting at the south end of the tunnel by contractors Dutton & Buckley was undertaken independently of the main tunnel contract. It was not until 25th May 1824, at the Select Committee meeting at Stone, that the engagement of Telford was formally agreed. He was in attendance and afterwards went with Potter to view the progress of works in the open cutting, with which he was well satisfied. Telford recommended that Potter be appointed as resident engineer for the tunnel works and that was agreed by the Select Committee.

Telford was again on site on 3rd July 1824, dining the following day at Linley Wood with Caldwell and Potter. On 5 July he was at Longport and wrote on one piece of paper a series of key tasks for himself, Potter and the contractors to perform. The document headed *Memorandums* has survived and in parts is difficult to decipher but it does convey the urgency with which he set about directing the work. The key tasks agreed that day were noted as follows:[37]

- North End – open cutting, engine to remove ground to be purchased and put up and the cutting be let to Mr. Pritchard in order to get a beginning made at that end.
- To negotiate with Mr Kinnersly about the rail road and trees to be cut down in the line of the tunnel
- An inclined plane to be made from summit to the railway
- Proper and substantial stages to be made to set out the line from
- Railways to be constructed from the brick yards and workshops along the whole of the line
- Shafts – beginning at south end – No. 1 at 10 chains from proposed entrance now begun
- Next shaft to be put down about 11 chains from proposed entrance at north end of tunnel
- Postpone fixing any more shafts until it has been ascertained what measures these two pass through
- Say at what rate it is wished that the tunnel should be carried on – perhaps to be completed in two years
- Headings to be driven from old tunnel to new shafts
- Mr James Potter to get some bricks made from well ground clay from several of the adjacent yards and ascertain at what rate per thousand a certain quantity can be delivered in a certain time
- Enquire of Mr Potter what mode he has thought of grinding clay
- Mortar to be made from Barrow lime from stone to be burnt on the spot
- The contractor to find gins or engines to raise the earth – also skips, candles, powder, etc.
- Make arrangements as to payments
- Query if the tunnel to have towing path

Telford strongly recommended that the new tunnel should have a towpath for horses. This was subject to a separate report which was presented on that day to a meeting of the Select Committee held at Stone. Telford recommended a towpath of about 4 feet 6 inches wide which would require the whole width of the tunnel to be increased to 14 feet. There was a slight delay but his proposal was approved at a further meeting held at Stone on 8th July.[38] Another recommendation to widen Brindley's tunnel with a towpath after the new tunnel had been completed was not pursued.

It is now time to learn more about James Potter who was born at Lichfield, Staffordshire on 10th March 1801. His father was Joseph Potter (1755-1842), architect of the City of Lichfield and also onetime engineer to the Trent & Mersey Canal Company. James quit school at the age of sixteen and spent several years in his father's office before being articled to William Brunton (1777-1857) of the Eagle Foundry in Birmingham. After that he rejoined his father's service and acted as resident engineer for several bridges for which his father was responsible, including the Chetwynd Bridge, an iron bridge of three arches over the River Tame at Alrewas which has survived to carry today's A513 trunk road. Shortly afterwards Potter was employed by the canal company. On 1st June 1824 he was recommended to become a Corresponding Member of the Institution of Civil Engineers. His principal sponsor was Thomas Telford, seconded by Bryan Donkin (1768-1855) and Joshua Field (1786-1863). He was elected a Member of the Institution on 25th June 1824 at the exceedingly young age of twenty-three. Telford was instrumental if fixing Potter's salary at £500 per annum which was twice his

---

36 *Atlas to the Life of Thomas Telford*, published by Payne & Foss, 1838.
37 ICE Archive T/TR. 23.

38 James Caldwell Diary for 1821-1825.

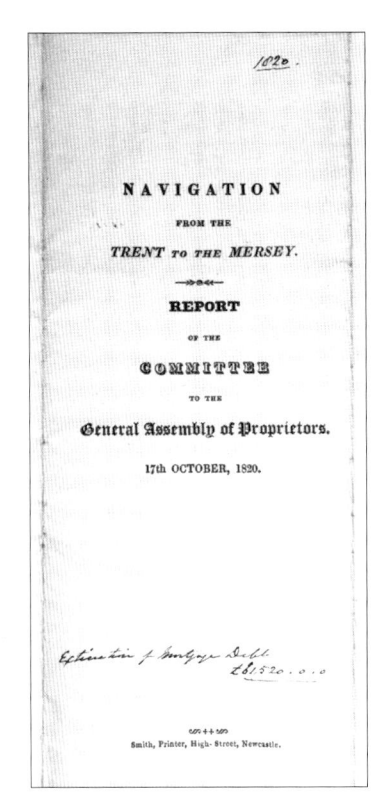

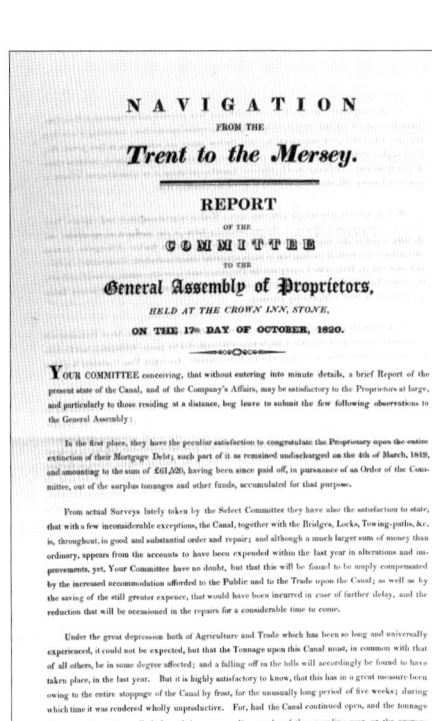

Report of the Committee of the Proprietors of the Trent & Mersey Canal, to be presented to the Proprietors on 17th October 1820. This discusses, inter alia, the issue of an additional tunnel through Harecastle Hill, along with the need for an increased supply of water for the summit level of the canal.
CRO D3098/8/11

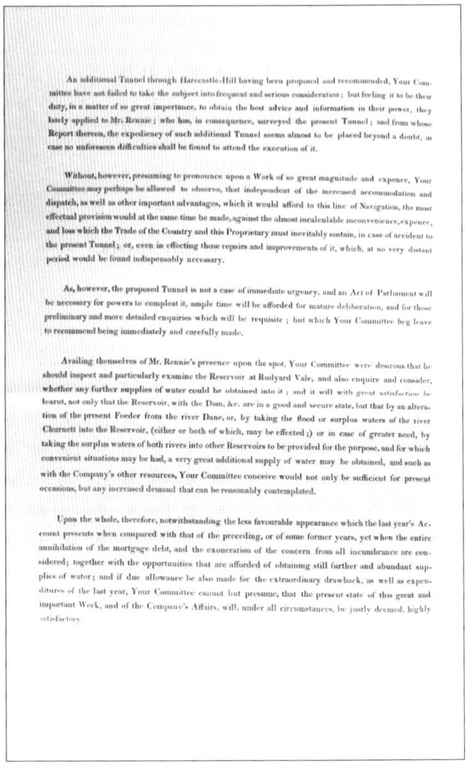

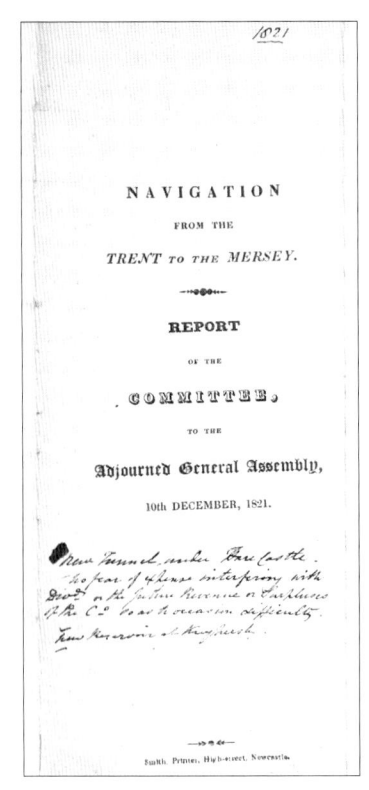

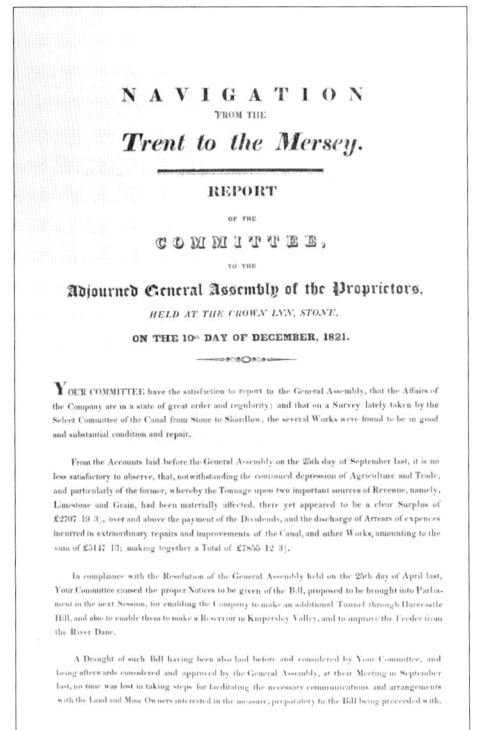

Report of the Committee of the Proprietors of the Trent & Mersey Canal dated 8th December 1821, to be presented to the Proprietors on 10th December, outlining progress being made in regard to the additional tunnel and water supply.
CRO D3098/8/11

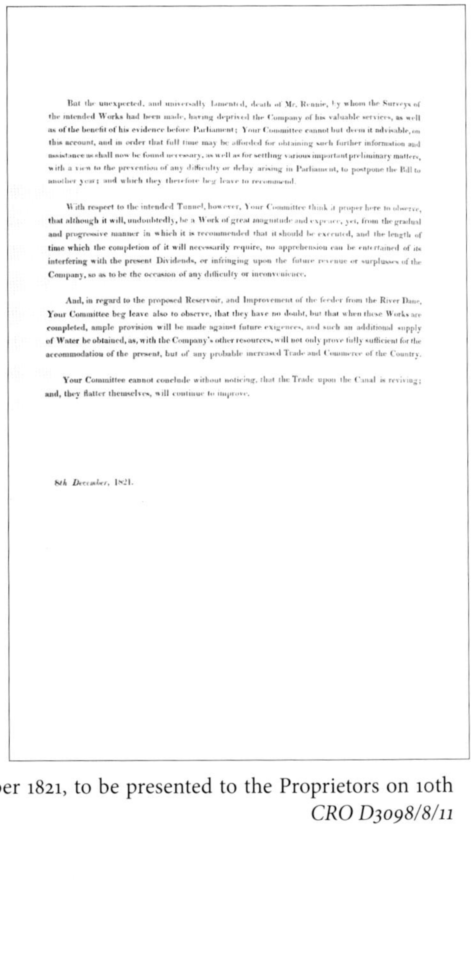

CHAPTER 3 – TELFORD'S TUNNEL

This collection of toll tickets and waybills all relate to traffic that passed through the Harecastle tunnels in the early 1830s. There are three southbound passages – two from Preston Brook to Fradley with sundry goods and one from Middlewich to Shelton with cheese. Going northbound, there are two examples – one from Wolverhampton to Middlewich with a variety iron goods and the other also to Middlewich with coal beans from Etruria, earthenware from Longport and coals from Harecastle. The southbound traffic would have been legged through Brindley's tunnel, the northbound traffic being horse drawn through Telford's, utilising the towpath. The partnership of Robins, Mills & Co, canal carriers and wharfingers, was dissolved on 15th March 1838. The partnership of Thomas Bache & Co., canal carriers based at Coventry, was dissolved on 26th November 1839. Thomas Bache died on 30th August 1843. Crowley, Hicklin, Batty & Co was based at the Union Wharf on the Birmingham Canal Navigations in Wolverhampton; the key founders of the business died in the early 1840s, Benjamin Hicklin on 19th December 1841 and John Crowley on 7th April 1843 and William Batty during the first quarter of 1844.

David Kitching Collection

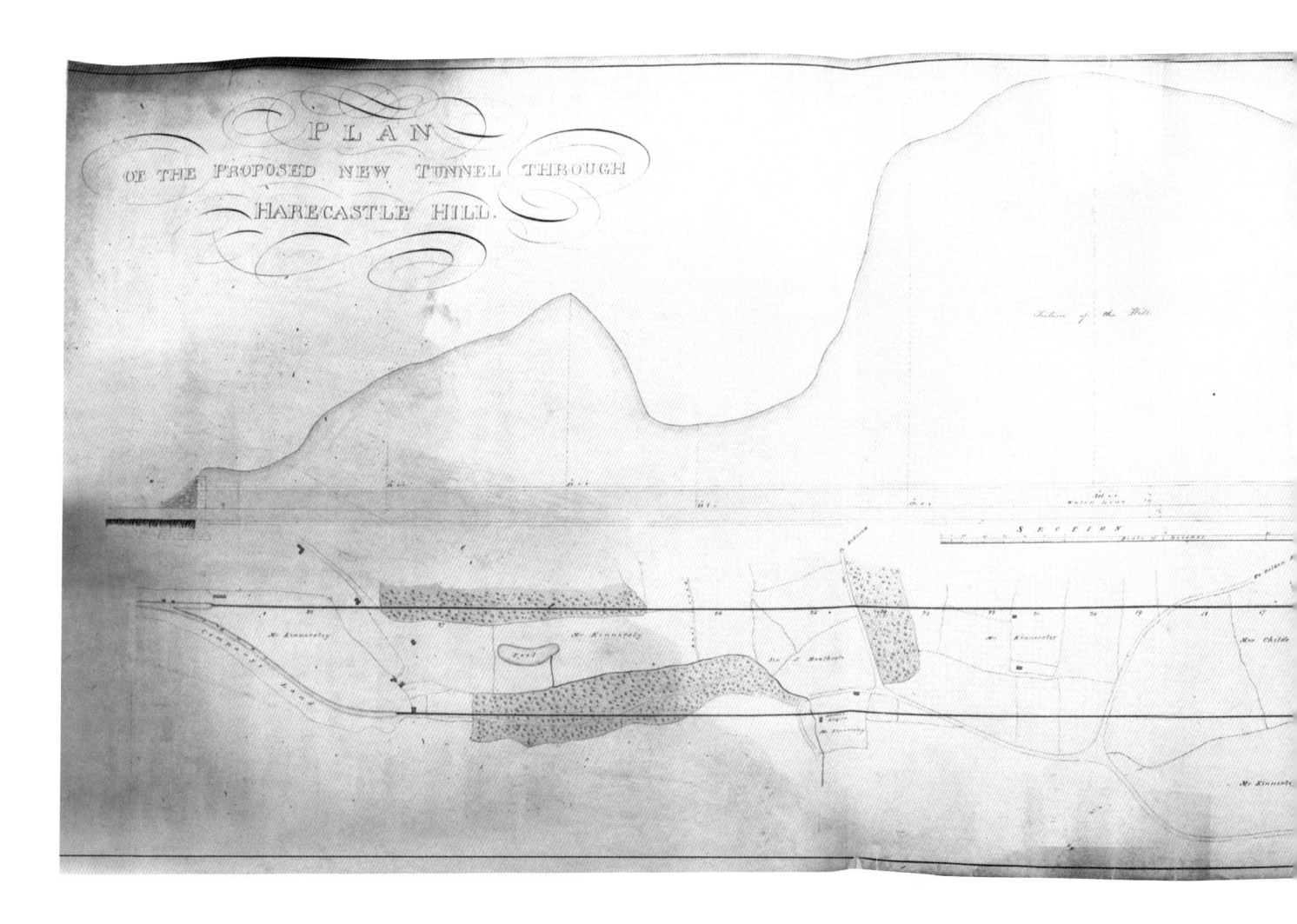

This is a plan and section of an early proposal for the second tunnel. It has the date 28th September 1821 and was signed by Joseph Potter in Lichfield. Notice in the case of this scheme the new tunnel would have been further east, with therefore, a greater distance between the two tunnels than eventually proved to be the case. Harecastle is to the left and Chatterley to the right, with the proposed tunnel at the top. Notice also the reference to the Nelson Engine at the Harecastle end and a forge towards the Chatterley end, adjacent to the line of the proposed tunnel, both of which are discussed in Chapter 10. The plan also includes an elevation of the projected portals. The various individuals' names indicate areas of land ownership.

CRO QRum 50-51a

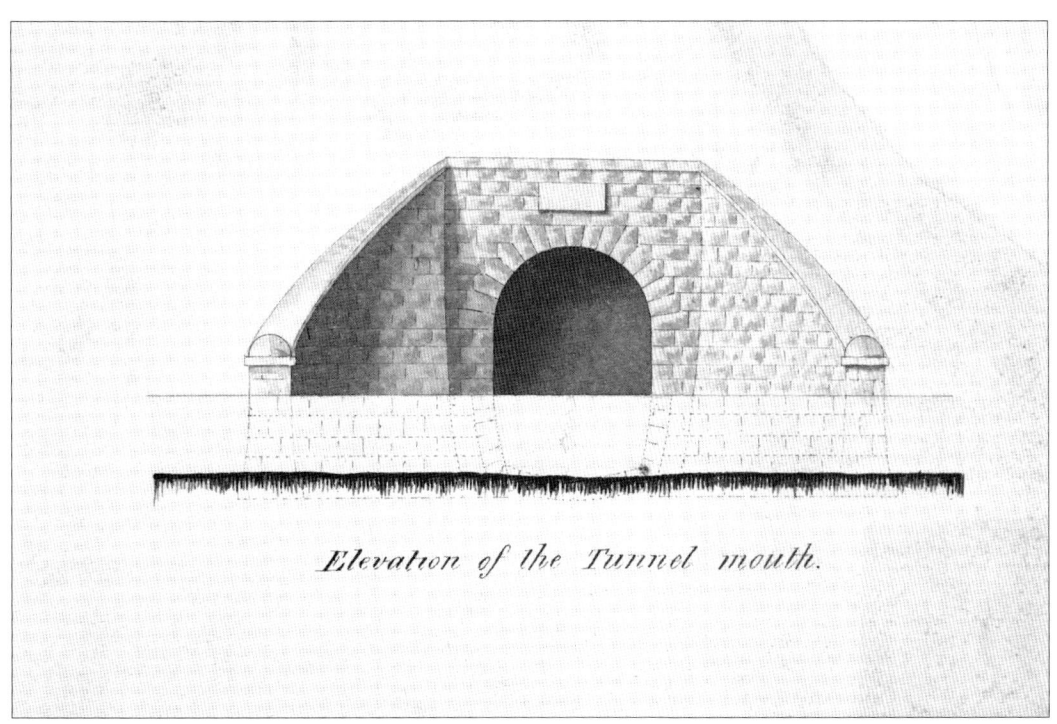

Elevation of the Tunnel mouth.

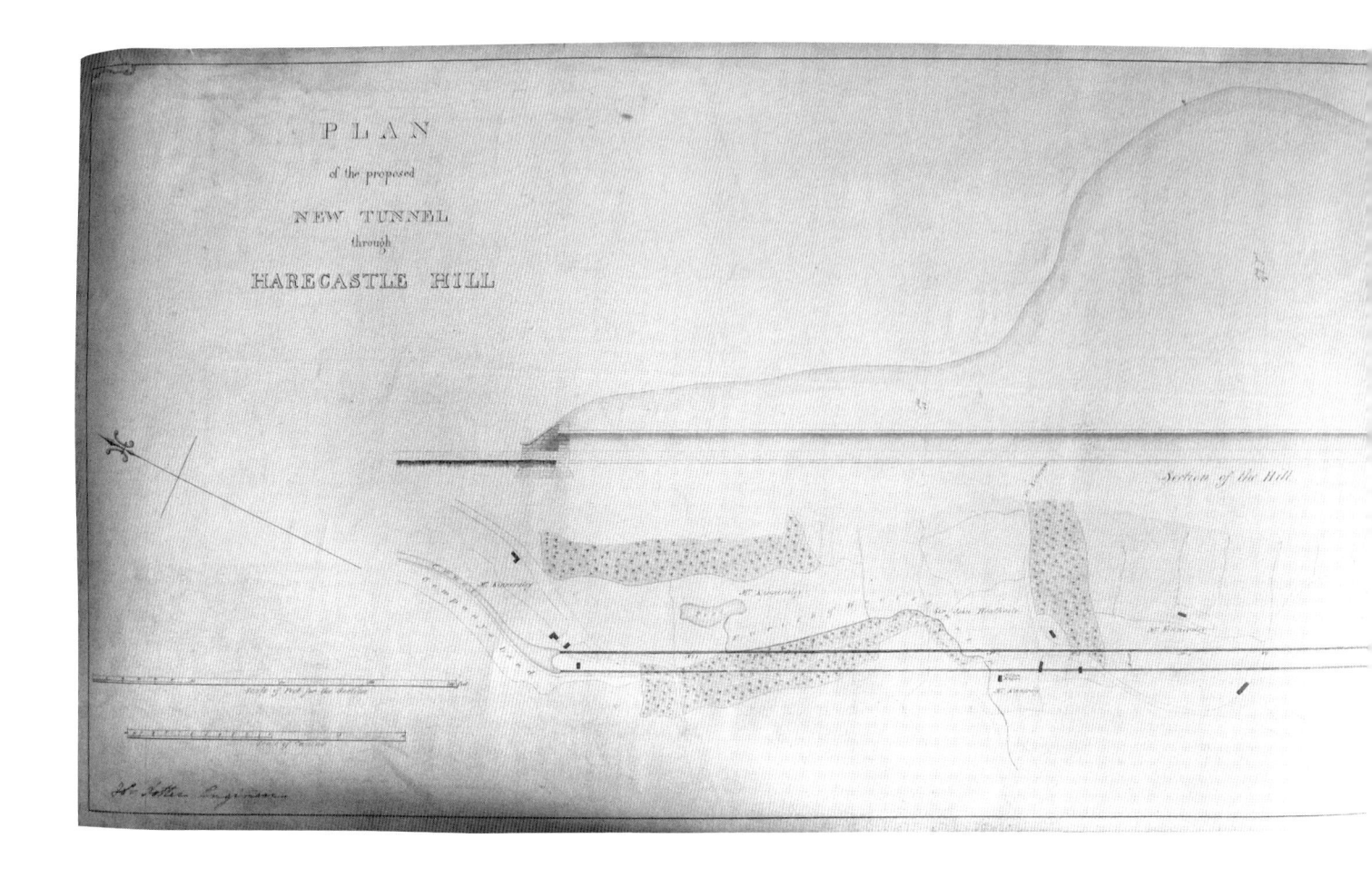

Here is a plan and section of the second tunnel as it was eventually built. It has a date of September 1822 and was also signed by James Potter in Lichfield. He was the site engineer for the tunnel's construction. The plan also includes an elevation of the tunnel mouth complete with the invert, as shown on the front cover of the book. The Nelson Engine and Forge, the latter now designated as an Iron Furnace, are also shown. *HLRO HL/PO/PB/3/plan 33 1823*

CHAPTER 3 – TELFORD'S TUNNEL

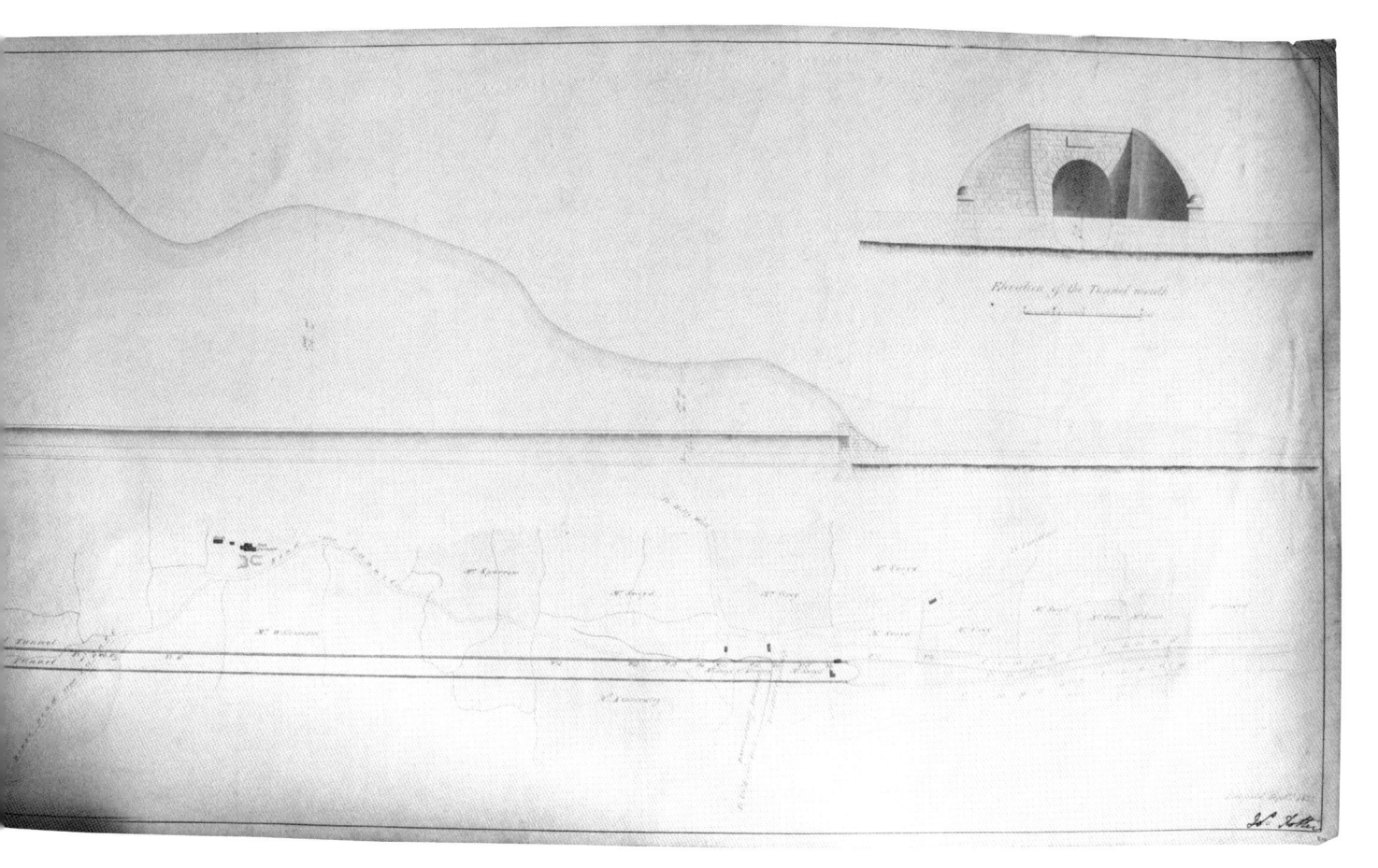

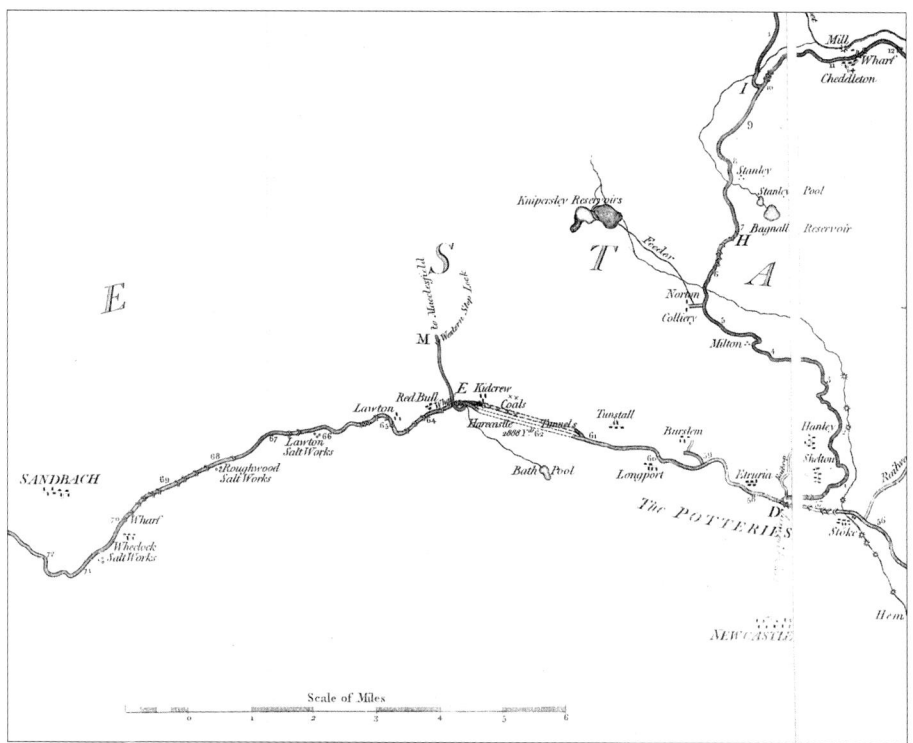

This is an updated version of the plan that appears on page 17 in Chapter 1. It now shows Telford's tunnel alongside Brindley's and the extended reservoir at Knypersley (still spelt Knipersley). Note also that the feeder from the reservoir has been diverted to feed into the Norton Green Branch Canal.

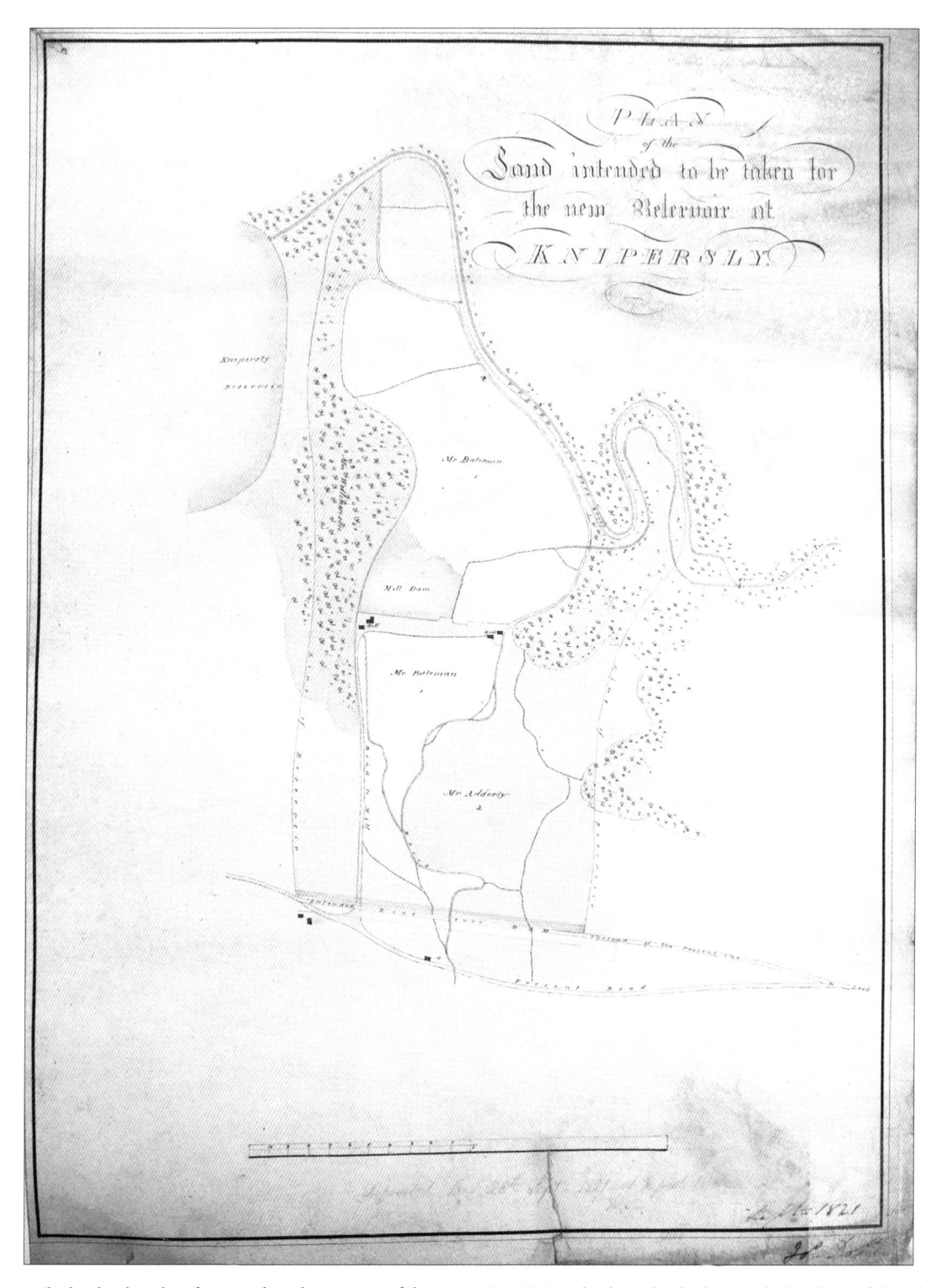

Plan showing the land to be taken for extending the capacity of the reservoir at Knipersly, the individual names being those of the relevant land owners. It is dated 28th September 1821 and once again signed by James Potter in Lichfield. Notice the earlier spelling of Knypersley. The original reservoir, part of which is shown to the left, dates from shortly after the opening of the Caldon branch canal in 1779. This canal ran from the main line of the Trent & Mersey at Etruria, a little over seventeen miles due east into the Staffordshire Moorlands at Froghall. There connection was made with the limestone quarries at Caldon Low by an early form of railway. The reservoir was certainly in existence by 1782. The water originally entered the canal at Stockton Brook via a specially constructed feeder and it is interesting to note that while the reservoir is only about three and a half miles due east from Harecastle, the distance from the reservoir to the tunnel is some fourteen miles! The feeder was later altered to flow into the Norton Green branch of the canal, which reduced the distance to Harecastle by about a mile. For much of its length the feeder follows the course of the infant River Trent, which rises on Biddulph Moor, about a mile east of the town of Biddulph.

CRO Q/Rum 50-51a

ANNO PRIMO

GULIELMI IV. REGIS.

****

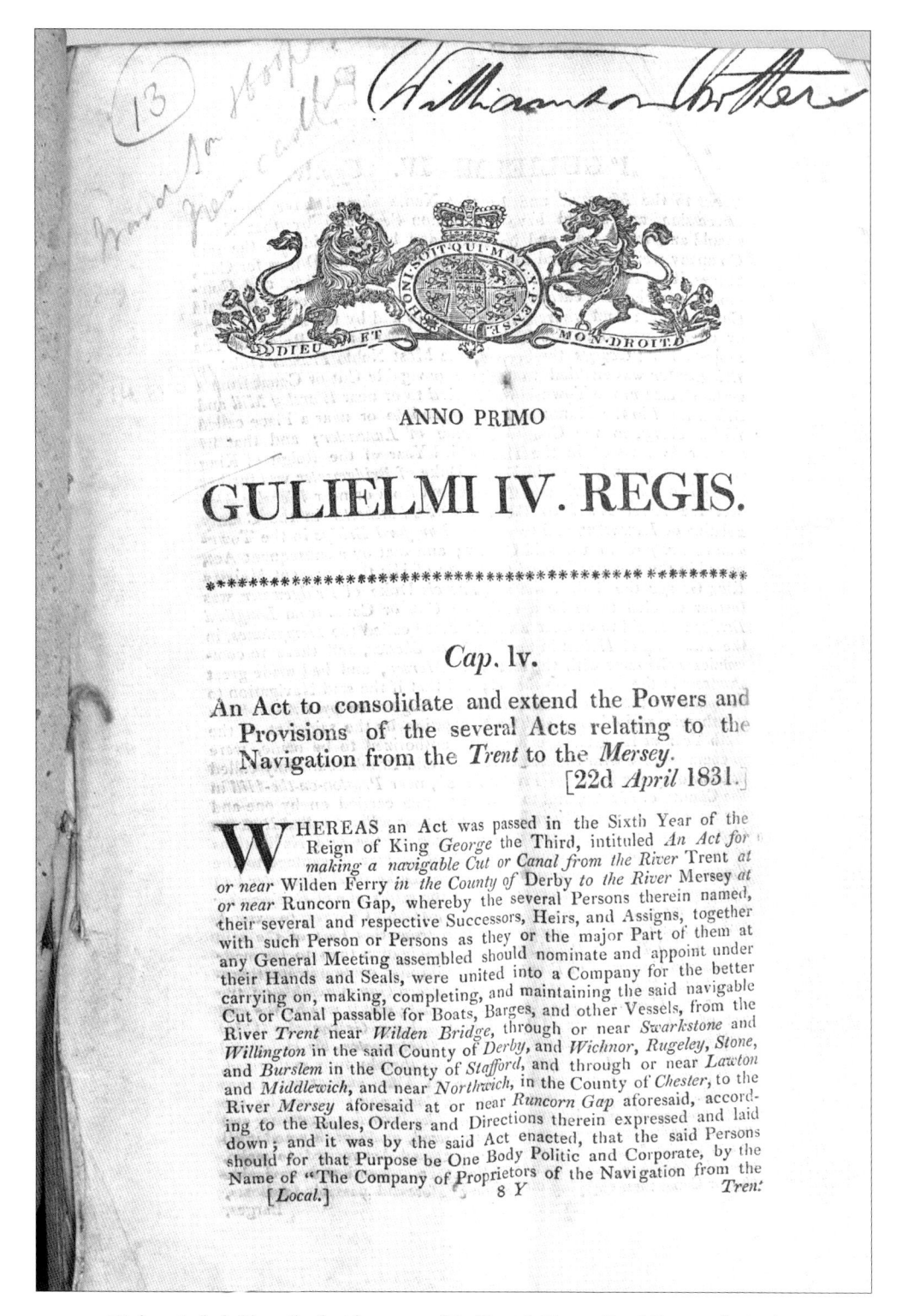

Cap. lv.

An Act to consolidate and extend the Powers and Provisions of the several Acts relating to the Navigation from the *Trent* to the *Mersey*.

[22d *April* 1831.]

WHEREAS an Act was passed in the Sixth Year of the Reign of King *George* the Third, intituled *An Act for making a navigable Cut or Canal from the River* Trent *at or near* Wilden Ferry *in the County of* Derby *to the River* Mersey *at or near* Runcorn Gap, whereby the several Persons therein named, their several and respective Successors, Heirs, and Assigns, together with such Person or Persons as they or the major Part of them at any General Meeting assembled should nominate and appoint under their Hands and Seals, were united into a Company for the better carrying on, making, completing, and maintaining the said navigable Cut or Canal passable for Boats, Barges, and other Vessels, from the River *Trent* near *Wilden Bridge*, through or near *Swarkstone* and *Willington* in the said County of *Derby*, and *Wichnor, Rugeley, Stone,* and *Burslem* in the County of *Stafford*, and through or near *Lawton* and *Middlewich*, and near *Northwich*, in the County of *Chester*, to the River *Mersey* aforesaid at or near *Runcorn Gap* aforesaid, according to the Rules, Orders and Directions therein expressed and laid down; and it was by the said Act enacted, that the said Persons should for that Purpose be One Body Politic and Corporate, by the Name of "The Company of Proprietors of the Navigation from the

[*Local.*]   8 Y   *Tren:*

We have included here the first few pages of the Trent & Mersey Canal Company's 1831 Act of Parliament, 1-2 Will IV ch lv, which received the Royal Assent on 22nd April 1831. It is particularly interesting and useful for our purpose as in its Preamble, it reviews the original Act for the canal and a number of later ones of significance to subsequent improvements and other developments. They include the Caldon and Leek Branch Canals, the second Harecastle Tunnel and the reservoir extension at Knypersley.

730 **1° GULIELMI IV. *Cap.*lv.**

Trent to the *Mersey*," and by that Name should have perpetual Succession, and should have a Common Seal, and by that Name should and might sue and be sued; and by the said Act the said Company were authorized to take certain Rates and Duties for Coal, Stones, Timber, and other Goods, Wares, Merchandise, and Commodities navigated, carried, or conveyed upon or through the said Cut or Canal: And whereas it is recited in and by the said Act, that, by an Act passed in the Thirty-second Year of the Reign of His Majesty King *George* the Second, the Most Noble *Francis* Duke of *Bridgewater* was enabled to make a navigable Cut or Canal from a certain Place in the Township of *Salford* to or near *Worsley Mill* and *Middlewood* in the Manor of *Worsley*, and to or near a Place called *Hollin Ferry*, in the County Palatine of *Lancaster*; and that by another Act, passed in the Thirty-third Year of the Reign of King *George* the Second, the said *Francis* Duke of *Bridgewater* was further enabled to make a navigable Cut or Canal from or near *Worsley Mill* over the River *Irwel* to the Town of *Manchester* in the County Palatine of *Lancaster*, and to or near *Longford Bridge* in the Township of *Stretford* in the said County; and that by a subsequent Act, passed in the Second Year of the Reign of His then present Majesty King *George* the Third, the said *Francis* Duke of *Bridgewater* was further enabled to make a navigable Cut or Canal from *Longford Bridge* aforesaid to or near a certain Place called the *Hempstones*, in the Township of *Halton* in the County of *Chester*, and there to communicate the same with the said River *Mersey*, and had made great Progress in the Execution thereof; and that if the said Navigation to be made by the said *Francis* Duke of *Bridgewater* by virtue of the last therein recited Act, and the Navigation by the said Act of the Sixth Year of King *George* the Third authorized to be made, were to communicate with each other at a certain Brook commonly called or known by the Name of *Preston Brook*, near *Preston-on-the-Hill* in the County of *Chester*, and to be from thence carried on by one and the same Canal to the River *Mersey* at or near a Place called *Runcorn Gap*, such Communication would render both the said Navigations more convenient and complete, and be of greater Advantage to the Public than if the Navigation of the said Duke of *Bridgewater* had terminated at the *Hempstones*; and that the said Duke of *Bridgewater* was willing and desirous, at his own Costs and Charges, to extend, carry on, and maintain such Navigation from that Part of the said Brook called *Preston Brook*, where the Navigation then to be made by the said Company of Proprietors should first communicate therewith, to the River *Mersey* at or near *Runcorn Gap* aforesaid, on the Terms and Considerations therein mentioned; and it was by the said Act of the Sixth Year of the Reign of King *George* the Third enacted, that the said *Francis* Duke of *Bridgewater*, his Heirs and Assigns, should be and he and they were thereby fully authorized, empowered, and required, from Time to Time and at all Times thereafter, at his and their own proper Costs and Charges, by the Ways and Means, and by and under the like Provisions, Powers, and Authorities in all respects as were authorized, made, or directed in all or any of the Acts in the said last-mentioned Act recited, to make, extend, complete, and maintain the therein-mentioned navigable Cut or Canal then carrying on by him as aforesaid, passable for Boats, Barges,

1° GULIELMI IV. *Cap.*lv. 731

Barges, and other Vessels, to that Part of the said Brook called *Preston Brook* where the said Navigation by the said Act passed in the Sixth Year of the Reign of King *George* the Third authorized to be made should first communicate therewith, and from thence into the said River *Mersey* at or near *Runcorn Gap* aforesaid, as fully, completely, and effectually, to all Intents and Purposes, as if the Course of the said Navigation had been described and the said Termination thereof fixed by the said Act passed in the Second Year of the Reign of King *George* the Third, and the same to be and remain for ever a free Navigation on Payment of the Tolls in and by the said Act of the Sixth Year of the Reign of King *George* the Third mentioned, and to be supplied with Water from both the said Canals when so united as aforesaid; and it was further enacted by the said Act of the Sixth Year of the Reign of King *George* the Third, that if the said Duke of *Bridgewater*, his Heirs or Assigns, should fail to make, carry on, and complete the said Cut or Canal from such Part as aforesaid of the said Brook called *Preston Brook* to the River *Mersey* at or near *Runcorn Gap* aforesaid within the Space of Four Years from the passing of the last-mentioned Act, or should not for ever thereafter repair, support, and maintain the said Cut or Canal with the other Works authorized and directed to be made, then and in every such Case it should and might be lawful to and for the said Company of Proprietors, their Successors and Assigns, to make, carry on, and complete the said Cut or Canal from such Part as aforesaid of the said Brook called *Preston Brook* to the River *Mersey* at or near *Runcorn Gap* aforesaid, and to repair, support, and maintain the same from Time to Time as Occasion should require; and all the Costs and Charges thereof, to be settled and allowed by the Commissioners appointed by the last-mentioned Act, or any Seven or more of them, should be repaid to the said Company of Proprietors, their Successors and Assigns, within the Space of Two Calendar Months after the same should have been settled and allowed, and an Account and Demand thereof should have been delivered and made to the said Duke of *Bridgewater*, his Heirs or Assigns, or his known Agent; and in default of Payment of the said Costs and Charges within the Time aforesaid, the said Commissioners, or any Seven or more of them, should and they were thereby empowered and required, by Warrant under their Hands and Seals, or the Hands and Seals of any Seven or more of them, to levy the said Costs and Charges by Distress and Sale of the Goods and Chattels of the said Duke of *Bridgewater*, his Heirs and Assigns, in or upon the said Cut or Canal, or the Wharfs, Quays, and Warehouses adjoining or near to the same, to and for the Use of the said Company of Proprietors, their Successors and Assigns; and that such Commissioners might moreover, in manner aforesaid, appoint One or more Person or Persons to receive the Tolls, Rates, and Duties in and by the said Act of the Sixth Year of the Reign of King *George* the Third granted to the said Duke, and thereout, in the first place, pay all such Costs and Charges, rendering to the said Duke of *Bridgewater*, his Heirs and Assigns, his or their Agents or Overseers of the said Cut or Canal, the Overplus, if any such there were, after the Deduction of the reasonable Charge of making such Distress and Sale, to be settled by the Commissioners or any Seven or more of them; and after such Costs and Charges should be so paid

732 **1° GULIELMI IV. *Cap.*lv.**

paid and satisfied, the Power of the said Receivers to be appointed by the said Commissioners should cease and determine; or otherwise the said Company of Proprietors, their Successors and Assigns, upon the Failure or Neglect of the said Duke of *Bridgewater*, his Heirs or Assigns, doing the same, or paying the Costs and Charges as aforesaid, should and might have such and the like Remedy against the said Duke of *Bridgewater*, his Heirs or Assigns, for the Recovery of such Costs and Charges, by Action at Law, to be commenced and prosecuted in such Manner as in other Cases was in and by the therein recited Acts or any of them mentioned and directed: And whereas the said Cut or Canal from such Part as aforesaid of the said Brook called *Preston Brook*, to the River *Mersey* at or near *Runcorn Gap* aforesaid, and other the Works authorized by the Act passed in the Sixth Year of King *George* the Third, were made and completed by the said Duke of *Bridgewater*, who has since departed this Life: And whereas another Act was passed in the Tenth Year of the Reign

10G. 3 c. 102. of King *George* the Third, intituled *An Act to amend an Act made in the Sixth Year of the Reign of His present Majesty, for making a navigable Cut or Canal from the River* Trent, *at or near* Wilden Ferry *in the County of* Derby, *to the River* Mersey *at or near* Runcorn Gap; *and for granting further Powers for that Purpose*: And whereas another Act was passed in the Fifteenth Year of the Reign of King

15 G. 3. c. 20. *George* the Third, intituled *An Act to amend and render more effectual Two Acts passed in the Sixth and Tenth Years of the Reign of His present Majesty, for making a navigable Cut or Canal from the River* Trent *at or near* Wilden Ferry *in the County of* Derby *to the River* Mersey *at or near* Runcorn Gap: And whereas another Act was passed in the Sixteenth Year of the Reign of King *George*

16 G. 3. c. 32. the Third, intituled *An Act to enable the Company of Proprietors of the Navigation from the* Trent *to the* Mersey *to make a navigable Canal from the said Navigation on the South Side of* Harecastle *in the County of* Stafford *to* Froghall, *and a Railway from thence to or near* Caldon *in the said County, and to make other Railways*, whereby the said Company, their Successors and Assigns, were fully authorized and empowered to make, complete, and maintain a navigable Cut or Canal, passable for Boats, Barges, and other Vessels, from the said Canal so made and completed on the South Side of *Harecastle* in the County of *Stafford*, by *Hanley*, *Norton*, and *Chedleton*, to *Froghall*, and from thence to make, complete, and maintain a Railway for the Conveyance of Coal, Stone, and other Goods to or near several Lime Works and Limestone Quarries at or near *Caldon* in the County of *Stafford*, and also to make, complete, and maintain other Railways from the said proposed Canal and Railway to the several Coal Mines and Limestone Quarries lying near the Course of the said Canal and Railway first mentioned, or the Termination thereof, from Time to Time, as they should think proper, so that no such other or collateral Railway should exceed the Length of One thousand Yards: And whereas another Act was passed in the Twenty-third Year of the

23 G. 3. c. 33. Reign of King *George* the Third, intituled *An Act to amend and render more effectual several Acts passed in the Sixth, Tenth, Fifteenth, and Sixteenth Years of the Reign of His present Majesty, for making a navigable Canal from the* Trent *to the* Mersey, *and a Branch from the said Canal to* Froghall, *and a Railway from thence to or near* Caldon in

1° GULIELMI IV. *Cap.*lv.

in the County of Stafford, whereby the said Company, their Successors and Assigns, were authorized and empowered to extend the said Canal at *Froghall* aforesaid about the Distance of Five hundred and thirty Yards on a Level, and to make, complete, and maintain a Railway from thence to the said Lime Works and Limestone Quarries at or near *Caldon* aforesaid, and to make a Reservoir at some convenient Place, within the Distance of Three thousand Yards of the South Side of the Summit of the said Canal at *Stanley Moss*, for the better supplying the said Canal with Water, and, for the better making such new Railway as aforesaid, to remove the Materials which formed the then existing Railway, or any Part thereof: And whereas another Act was passed in the Thirty-seventh Year of the Reign of

King *George* the Third, intituled *An Act to enable the Company of* 37 G. 3. c. [illegible]
Proprietors of the Navigation from the Trent *to the* Mersey *to make a navigable Canal from and out of a certain Branch of their said Navigation called the* Caldon Canal, *at or near* Hendon, *to or near the Town of* Leek *in the County of* Stafford, *and also a Reservoir for supplying the several Canals of the said Company with Water*, whereby the said Company of Proprietors, their Successors and Assigns, were authorized and empowered to make and complete, and at all Times thereafter to support and maintain, a Cut or Canal, navigable and passable for Boats, Barges, and other Vessels, from and out of the said Canal called the *Caldon Canal*, at or near *Hendon* aforesaid, to or near the Town of *Leek* aforesaid, and to supply the said Canal, whilst the same should be making and when made, with Water from such Springs as should be found in making the same; and also to make and at all Times maintain a Reservoir in the said Vale lying between *Horton* and *Rudyerd*, called *Rudyerd Vale*, in the said County of *Stafford*, and also a Trench or Feeder from the said Reservoir for conveying Water to the said Canal for the Purpose of supplying the same and also the said other Canals belonging to the said Company with Water; and also to form a Communication between the said proposed Canal and such Part of the said *Caldon* Canal as lies between *Hazlehurst Wood* near *Hendon* and *Froghall* aforesaid; and to do and perform all such Matters and Things as might be necessary for making, effecting, using, and maintaining the said Canal, and the said Reservoir, Trench or Feeder, and other Works: And whereas another Act was passed in the same Thirty-seventh Year of the Reign of

King *George* the Third, intituled *An Act to enable the Company of* 37 G. 3. c. [illegible]
Proprietors of the Navigation from the Trent *to the* Mersey *to extend several Branches of Canal from and out of their said Navigation*, whereby the said Company, their Successors and Assigns, were authorized and empowered to make and complete, and at all Times thereafter to support and maintain, a Cut or Canal, navigable and passable for Boats, Barges, and other Vessels, from and out of the said Canal called the *Caldon Canal*, at *Froghall*, to or near to the Town of *Uttoxeter* in the County of *Stafford*; and also another navigable Cut or Canal from and out of the said *Caldon* Canal at *Shelton* to or near *Cobridge* in the County of *Stafford*; and also another navigable Cut or Canal from and out of the said *Trent* and *Mersey* Canal at *Longport* to a Place called *Dale Hall*, in *Burslem* aforesaid, together with necessary Towing Paths, Wharfs, and other Conveniences for the said Cuts or Canals respectively; and to do and perform all such Matters and

[*Local.*] 8 Z

734 1° GULIELMI IV. *Cap.*lv.

and Things as might be necessary for making, effecting, using, and maintaining the said proposed Cuts or Canals and other Works: And whereas another Act was passed in the Forty-second Year of the
42 G. 3. c. 25. Reign of King *George* the Third, intituled *An Act to enable the Company of Proprietors of the Navigation from the* Trent *to the* Mersey *to make Railways, to alter the Course of the Railway from* Froghall *to* Caldon, *and Part of the Course of the Canal from* Froghall *to* Uttoxeter, *and to amend the* Trent *and* Mersey *Canal Acts,* whereby the said Company, their Successors and Assigns, were fully authorized and empowered to make and complete, and at all Times thereafter to support and maintain, a Railway from the said Canal from the *Trent* to the *Mersey* at *Stoke-upon-Trent* to *Lane End*, and another Railway from the said Canal at *Etruria* to *Hanley*, and also another Railway from the said Canal at or near *Dale Hall* to *Burslem* in the said County of *Stafford*, for the Passage of Waggons and Carriages of Forms and Constructions and with Burthens suitable to such Railways, to be approved of by the said Company; and also to alter and vary the Course of the said Railway from *Froghall* to *Caldon*, and a Part of the said proposed Canal from *Froghall* to *Uttoxeter*, near *Alveton Mill* in the Parish of *Alveton* in the said County of *Stafford*; and to do and perform all such Matters and Things as might be necessary for making, effecting, using, and maintaining the said proposed Railways, Alterations, and other Works: And whereas another Act was passed in the Forty-ninth Year of the Reign of King *George* the
49 G. 3. c. 73. Third, intituled *An Act to amend and enlarge the Powers of the several Acts passed for making a navigable Canal from the* Trent *to the* Mersey, *and other Canals connected there with,* whereby the said Company were (amongst other Things) authorized and empowered to make and maintain a Trench or Gutter from the said Reservoir in *Rudyerd Vale* to the said River *Dane*, between a Bridge called *Dane Bridge*, and the Paper Mill standing on the said River a short Distance below the said Bridge, and there to erect a Weir in manner therein mentioned: And whereas another Act was passed in the Fourth Year of the Reign of His said late Majesty King *George* the Fourth, intituled
4 G. 4. c. 87. *An Act to enable the Company of Proprietors of the Navigation from the* Trent *to the* Mersey *to make an additional Tunnel through* Harecastle Hill *in the County of* Stafford, *and an additional Reservoir in* Knypersley Valley *in the said County, and to amend and enlarge the Powers of the several Acts for making and maintaining the said Navigation, and the several Canals connected therewith,* whereby the said Company of Proprietors, their Successors and Assigns, were authorized and empowered (amongst other Things) to make and complete, and at all Times thereafter to continue, support, and maintain, an additional Tunnel or Cut or Canal, navigable for Boats, Barges, and other Vessels, from and out of their said Canal on the South Side of the said Tunnel called *Harecastle Tunnel*, unto and into their said Canal on the North Side of the said Tunnel, in a parallel Course or Direction thereto, and on the Eastern Side thereof, together with necessary Towing Paths, Wharfs, and other Conveniences for the said additional Tunnel or Cut or Canal; and to make, form, and complete an additional Reservoir at *Knypersley Valley*, for the Purpose of supplying the several Canals of the said Company of Proprietors with Water, with a Dam thereto not exceeding Forty-five Feet in Height; and also

1° GULIELMI IV. *Cap.*lv. 735

also to deepen, alter, and extend the said Trench or Gutter by the said last-recited Act authorized to be made, so as not to prejudice or affect the necessary Supplies of Water to the River *Dane*, or to the adjacent Farms and Lands; and to do and perform all such Matters and Things as might be necessary for making, effecting, using, and maintaining the said additional Tunnel or Cut or Canal, and the said additional Reservoir and other Works: And whereas the Powers of the Commissioners appointed by the said recited Acts, some or one of them, are repealed by the last-recited Act of the Fourth Year of the Reign of His said late Majesty: And whereas an Act was passed in the Seventh Year of the Reign of His
late Majesty King *George* the Fourth, intituled *An Act for making* 7 G. 4. c. 30
and maintaining a navigable Canal from the Peak Forest *Canal in the Township of* Marple *in the County Palatine of* Chester, *to join the Canal Navigation from the* Trent *to the* Mersey *at or near* Hardings-wood *Lock in the Township or Hamlet of* Talk *or* Talk-on-the-Hill *in the County of* Stafford, whereby certain Persons were declared to be a Body Politic and Corporate by the Name of the Company of Proprietors of the *Macclesfield* Canal, and were authorized and empowered to make, complete, and maintain a Canal or Navigation, navigable and passable for Barges, Boats, and other Vessels, from and out of and into the Canal belonging to the Company of Proprietors of the *Peak Forest* Canal, to and to join and communicate with the Canal belonging to the Company of Proprietors of the Navigation from the *Trent* to the *Mersey* at or near a certain Lock upon such Canal called *Hardingswood Lock* in the said Township or Hamlet of *Talk* or *Talk-on-the-Hill* in the Parish of *Audley* and County of *Stafford*, and near to the northernly End of the *Harecastle* Tunnel: And whereas an Act was passed in the Seventh and Eighth Years of
the Reign of His said late Majesty, intituled *An Act for enabling the* 7 & 8 G. c. 81.
Company of Proprietors of the Navigation from the Trent *to the* Mersey *to make Two Branches or Cuts from and out of the same Navigation, and for further amending the Acts of the said Company,* whereby the said Company of Proprietors of the Navigation from the *Trent* to the *Mersey* were authorized and empowered to make, complete, and maintain so much and such Part of the said Canal authorized by the said recited Act of the Seventh Year of the Reign of His said late Majesty to be made and constructed as extended from the Western Extremity of the Western Regulating Pound or Stop Lock directed by the said last-mentioned Act to be erected and made in a certain Field in the Township of *Oddrode*, numbered Three hundred and thirty-two on the Plan of the said then intended Canal lodged with the Clerk of the Peace for the said County of *Chester* (then in the Possession of *Matthew Owen*), and near a certain Place called *Hall Green*, in the said County of *Chester*, to join the said Navigation from the *Trent* to the *Mersey* at or near *Hardingswood* Lock in the Township or Hamlet of *Talk* or *Talk-on-the-Hill* in the Parish of *Audley* in the County of *Stafford*, and to construct, erect, make, and do all Aqueducts, Bridges, Towing Paths, Culverts, Wharfs, Quays, Landing Places, Cranes, Weighbeams, Warehouses, and all other Works, Matters, and Things auxiliary to or for the Purpose of making, completing, maintaining, supplying, and rendering fit for Use and using such Part of the said Canal or Navigation and Works aforesaid,

736 1° GULIELMI IV. *Cap.*lv.

aforesaid, or in any other Manner whatsoever in respect thereof, which the said Company of Proprietors of the *Macclesfield* Canal were by the said last-mentioned Act authorized to construct, erect, make, and do in that Behalf, under and subject nevertheless to all such Rules, Regulations, Conditions, Directions, and Provisions as the said last-mentioned Company were by the said last-mentioned Act made subject to in that Behalf, except as the same were in and by the said Act passed in the Seventh and Eighth Year of the Reign of His said late Majesty altered, varied, or repealed: And whereas by the said Act of the Seventh and Eighth Year of the Reign of His said late Majesty the said Company of Proprietors of the Navigation from the *Trent* to the *Mersey* were also authorized and empowered to make, complete, and maintain a navigable Cut or Canal, passable for Boats, Barges, and other Vessels, from and out of the said Navigation from the *Trent* to the *Mersey*, on the East Side of a certain Bridge called the *Brickkiln Field Bridge* or *Brook's Lane Bridge* in the Township of *Newton* in the Parish of *Middlewich* in the County of *Chester*, to the Extent of One hundred Yards from the said Navigation from the *Trent* to the *Mersey*, to and to communicate with a certain Branch Cut or Canal then intended to be made and which is now in progress of making by the united Company of Proprietors of the *Ellesmere and Chester* Canal; and the said Company of Proprietors of the Navigation from the *Trent* to the *Mersey* were also thereby authorized and empowered to make, construct, erect, sink, and drive such and so many Reservoirs, Aqueducts, Feeders, Tunnels, Perforations, Weirs, Shafts, Wheels, Engines, and other Machinery, for the Purpose of filling and supplying the said Cut or Canal authorized to be made by them as last aforesaid, or any Part or Parts thereof, and such Reservoirs, with Water, and for conveying Water to and from the same for the Purposes of Navigation, and for the Purpose of better making and maintaining of such Cut or Canal, as the said Company of Proprietors of the Navigation from the *Trent* to the *Mersey* should from Time to Time think necessary or expedient; and also to supply such Cut or Canal and Reservoirs with Water from all such Brooks, Springs, Streams, Watercourses, Mines, Hollows, Caverns, and other Sources or Repositories of Water as should be found in making such Cut or Canal and Reservoir or Reservoirs; and to enlarge, widen, deepen, divert, alter, or vary such Roads or Ways and also the Courses of such Brooks, Streams, or Watercourses, as might be situated within the Line of such Cut or Canal, or which might prevent or otherwise impede or obstruct the making of the same: And whereas the several Cuts or Canals, Branches, Extensions, Railways, Tunnels, Reservoirs, and Works authorized by the said several Acts passed in the Sixth, Tenth, Fifteenth, Sixteenth, Twenty-third, Thirty-seventh, Forty-second, and Forty-ninth Years of the Reign of King *George* the Third, and by the said Two several Acts passed in the Fourth Year and in the Seventh and Eighth Year of the Reign of His said late Majesty, to be made by the said Company of Proprietors of the Navigation from the *Trent* to the *Mersey*, have been duly made and completed by them, except a Part of the Railway from *Stoke-upon-Trent* to *Lane End*, authorized to be made by the said Act passed in the Forty-second Year of the Reign of King *George* the Third, extending from the Western End of the Lower

1° GULIELMI IV. *Cap.*lv. 737

Lower Market Place in *Lane End* into the Lands of the Most Noble *George Granville* Marquis of the County of *Stafford*, at a Place called *Mill Field Lane*, computed to be about One thousand Yards in Length: And whereas the said Company of Proprietors of the Navigation from the *Trent* to the *Mersey* were authorized to take certain Tolls on all Goods, Wares, and Merchandise passing along such Cuts or Canals, Branches, Extensions, and Railways so authorized to be made and completed by them: And whereas a large Sum of Money has been expended by the said Company of Proprietors of the Navigation from the *Trent* to the *Mersey* in making and completing the said several Canals and other Works so authorized to be made by the said Company as aforesaid, and considerable Sums of Money have been borrowed, and are now owing, under the Authority and on the Credit of the said recited Acts, or some or one of them: And whereas it is expedient that so much of the said recited Act of the Sixth Year of the Reign of King *George* the Third as relates to such Part of the said Navigation from the *Trent* to the *Mersey* as was thereby authorized to be made by the said Company of Proprietors of the Navigation from the *Trent* to the *Mersey*, and which extends from the River *Trent*, at or near *Wilden Ferry* in the County of *Derby*, to the Junction of the same with the said Duke of *Bridgewater's* Canal at *Preston Brook* in the County of *Chester*, and also the said several Acts of the Tenth, Fifteenth, Sixteenth, Twenty-third, Thirty-seventh, Forty-second, and Forty-ninth Years of the Reign of King *George* the Third, and the said Two several Acts of the Fourth and of the Seventh and Eighth Year of the Reign of His said late Majesty King *George* the Fourth, should be repealed, and new Powers and Provisions granted and made instead thereof, for the Maintenance and Management of the said Part of the said Navigation from the *Trent* to the *Mersey* so made by the said Company of Proprietors of such last-mentioned Navigation, and the said several other Cuts or Canals, Branches, Extensions, Railways, Reservoirs, Feeders, and other Works so authorized to be made and completed by them, and for the other Purposes herein-after mentioned: May it therefore please Your Majesty that it may be enacted; and be it enacted by the King's most Excellent Majesty, by and with the Advice and Consent of the Lords Spiritual and Temporal, and Commons, in this present Parliament assembled, and by the Authority
of the same, That from and immediately after the passing of this Acts repealed.
Act so much of the said Act of the Sixth Year of the Reign of King *George* the Third, and the Powers, Authorities, Provisoes, Clauses, Matters, and Things therein contained, as relate to such Part of the said navigable Cut or Canal from the *Trent* to the *Mersey* as was thereby authorized to be made by the said Company of Proprietors incorporated by the same Act, and which Part of the said navigable Cut or Canal extends from the River *Trent* at or near *Wilden Ferry* in the County of *Derby* to the Junction of the same navigable Cut or Canal with the said late Duke of *Bridgewater's* Canal at *Preston Brook* in the County of *Chester*, and also the said several herein-before recited Acts of the Tenth, Fifteenth, Sixteenth, Twenty-third, Thirty-seventh, Forty-second, and Forty-ninth Years of the Reign of King *George* the Third, and the said Two several recited Acts of the Fourth Year and of the Seventh and Eighth Year of the Reign

[*Local.*] 9 *A* of

father's salary as County Surveyor! The Select Committee was somewhat reluctant to pay this amount but Telford was insistent. On hearing that after a year and a quarter Potter had not received any adequate remuneration he wrote to the company on 6th May 1825 as follows:[39]

I have in a former letter which, I understand has been communicated to you, stated that the proper management of the tunnel works, joined with those of the Knypersley reservoir, including the expenses to which any person having this charge, is unavoidably subjected, is a service deserving a salary of £500 a year and this is what would have been required by any other duly qualified person I could have provided and this more especially when there is such an unusually great demand for persons of this description.

Although it has so happened that Mr James Potter, a very young man, has been appointed to this charge and that this salary may appear large for his first essay, yet, as by the due exertion of talents and unwearied assiduity aided by the experience and judgement of his father, the whole of the complicated and in many instances dangerous operations, have been arranged and in every respect carried on in a well regulated and successful manner under the management of persons in whom the company have cause to place confidence, I do not see any reason why less remuneration is due, than what a stranger would have required. Praise indeed!

It is now time to study how Potter commenced his task. Bricks were obtained from Haywoods' brickyard and those of Greys & Bancks and Peake & Shufflebotham, all located near to the tunnel. A four horse power steam engine was erected for grinding clay at Haywoods' brickyard, a six horse power engine was put up for Peake & Shufflebotham and the canal company's steam engine located at Lawton locks was repaired and used to grind clay for Greys & Bancks and also mortar for the tunnel. In addition an apparatus for grinding mortar *similar to that employed at Liverpool Docks* was procured.[40] On 5th September 1824 Potter sent two sketches to Telford, one illustrated a *Clay Mule* and the other showed a section of the strata passed through in sinking the second shaft at the south end of the tunnel.[41] Both sketches are reproduced here. The *Clay Mule* was described as a machine for mixing and crushing clay for making bricks. Potter pointed out that the sketch showed it as geared to be worked by a horse but added that four or five such machines might easily be worked by a six horse power engine all driven by one shaft with bevil [sic] wheels. He was clearly impressed with the machine. With regard to the second shaft at the south end of the tunnel Potter reported that it had been sunk to its proper depth and that headings were being driven northwards and southwards but the hardness of the rock was hampering progress. Pritchard also commented on the hardness of the rock saying that he found it *much harder than ever any tunnel has been driven in before – excepting the one that is executed by the side of it*.[42] Potter commented that rapid progress was being made in sinking shafts to the north and south of the hard rock and work had also commenced on sinking the third shaft from the south end of the tunnel. He reported that the *heading at Shaft 1 south end is also driven to a considerable distance and the cross heading is opened into the old tunnel.* At the Select Committee meeting held on 7th September 1824 Potter reported that work on the tunnel *was going on well and with all due dispatch*.[43]

Telford reported on the state of the works as at 20th February 1825 noting that at the north end of the tunnel a steam engine had been erected on the west bank of the canal to drain that end of the tunnel and raise the excavated earth. A length of brickwork had been completed at the north end with dimensions 14 feet wide and 15 feet high. He commented that the materials and workmanship were excellent and that the general shape was very perfect. Twelve shafts had been sunk to the bottom level of the tunnel and work on some of the headings had commenced with about 1,000 yards already driven. Work on sinking the remaining shafts was proceeding. Judging from the comments in his report, he clearly approved of the arrangements Potter had made for brick making and estimated that about seven million bricks would be required in total with from four to five million needed during 1825. He said that the railway should be extended to all the brickyards. The railway had been laid right across the hill enabling materials to be conveyed to the shafts and an inclined plane was about to be constructed *down the valley to the Nelson Engine*. The *Nelson Engine* is discussed in Chapter 10. A quantity of sound Norwegian and Swedish timber poles and Swedish baulks was to be obtained from Hull for use in the construction works.[44] In the event the timber was purchased from Liverpool.

On 5th April 1825 Caldwell inspected the works with Potter at the north end noting that only 10 yards was complete and fearing that costs would be *much more than was estimated expense*. Perhaps he had not fully appreciated the magnitude of the work and the extent of the work already undertaken within the hill. On 9th April Potter wrote to Telford saying that the brickwork for Shafts Nos 2 and 3 at the south end and No. 2 at the north end had commenced as had tunnelling in Shaft No. 4 at the south end and Shaft Nos 2 and 3 at the north end. This enabled tunnelling to be carried on at seven different places, including the north entrance. The running sand at the north end was causing difficulties but Potter assured Telford that it was under control as indeed it was. On 31st May, Potter reported that the heading to drain the sand at the north end of the tunnel had been thurled, an expression he used a lot to indicate when one shaft was connected to another or when the shafts at the extreme north and south ends were connected with the tunnel entrances. At this stage 81 yards of the tunnel had been bricked.[45]

---

39 ICE Archive T/TR. 48.
40 ICE Archive T/TR. 118.
41 ICE Archive T/TR. 120.
42 ICE Archive T/TR. 29.
43 Transcript by L. Allsop, op.cit.
44 ICE Archive T/TR. 39 and T/TR. 40.
45 ICE Archive T/TR. 43 and T/TR. 45.

This and the following sketch by Potter, sent to Telford on 5th September 1824, illustrate the Clay Mule, a machine for mixing and crushing clay for making bricks.
ICE Archive T/TR/120

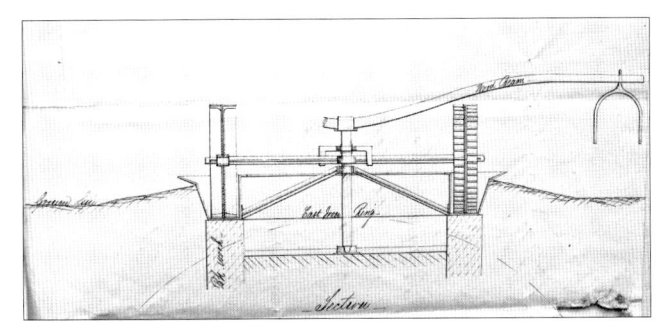

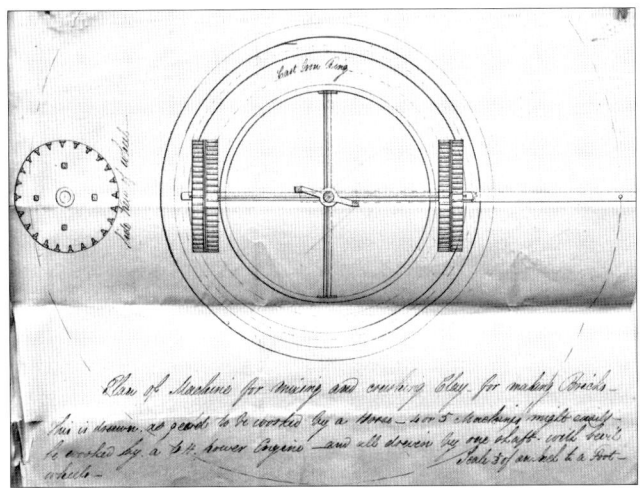

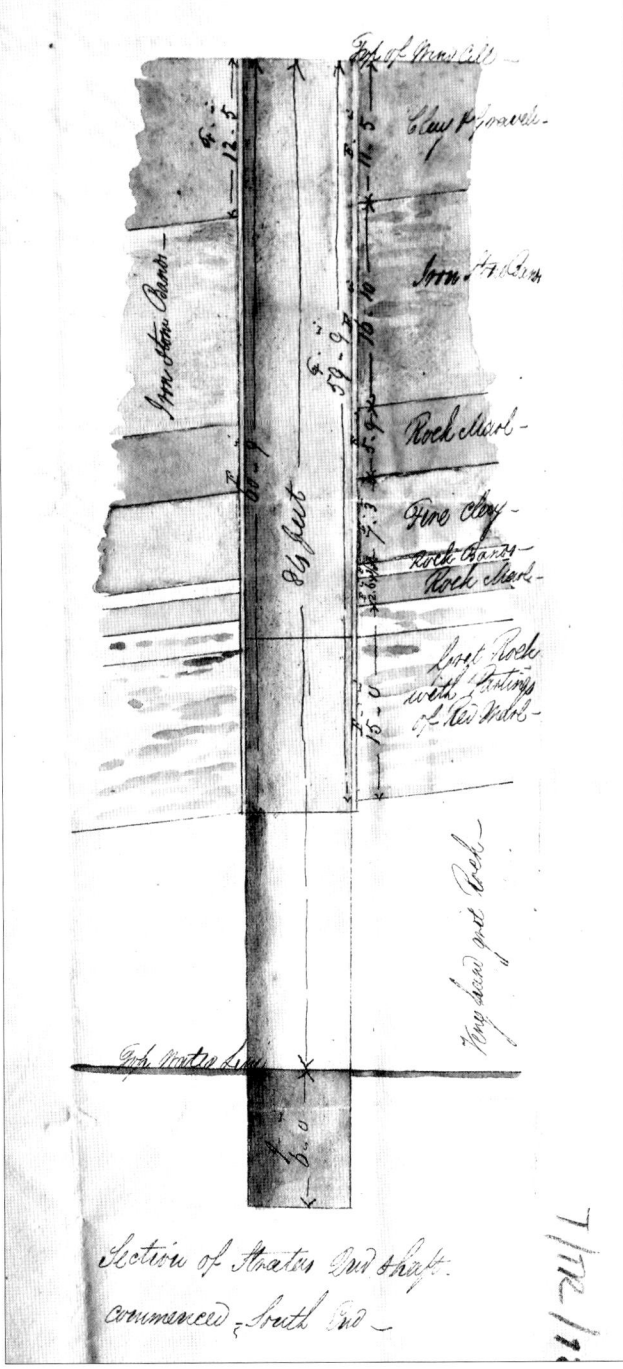

This sketch by James Potter (1801-1857) shows the strata passed through in sinking the second shaft at the south end of Telford's tunnel. The shaft is 84ft from the surface to the top of the normal water level in the canal. The strata encountered from top to bottom includes clay and gravel, ironstone bands, red marl, fire clay, rock bands, rock marl, rock with partings of red marl and very hard grit rock.
ICE Archive T/TR/120

Left: Thomas Telford (1757-1834) was the engineer responsible for the second Harecastle tunnel which opened in 1827. This engraving is by William Holl, the elder (1771-1838), after a portrait by Samuel Lane (1780-1859). It dates from around 1810. In 1820 Telford became the first President of the Institution of Civil Engineers.

The Select Committee at its meeting on 5th July 1825 deferred an application made by coalmine owner Hugh Henshall Williamson (1785-1867) for turn-outs in the new tunnel until Telford had undertaken a survey.[46] Telford was present at the tunnel on 4th August when he was able to give a most satisfactory account of the progress to Caldwell. His written report, completed two days later, stated that the machinery and arrangements for grinding the clay and mortar had been completed in a very workmanlike manner and that the materials were provided in sufficient quantities to ensure the uninterrupted progress of the work. The bricks were excellent and the mortar had hardened completely on the second day after its use in the tunnel. The railway from the brick and mortar yards to the several shafts and the inclined plane at the north end of the tunnel were all completed and an adequate supply of wagons was in use. A steam engine, similar to the one provided at the north end of the tunnel, had been provided at the south end to pump water and remove spoil. Some small dwelling houses, stables and workshops had been constructed on the summit of the tunnel to accommodate workmen and horses so that they could be accommodated as close to their work as possible and avoid unnecessary exposure to bad weather. Telford expressed himself as well pleased with Potter. All fifteen of the shafts (one less than anticipated) had been sunk to the requisite depth and it was expected that the heading all through the hill would be completed by the end of October. It was a difficult operation due to the varied strata encountered. The excavation and brickwork of the tunnel was being carried on at nineteen different places and 250 yards had already been completed in a very perfect manner. Considering what had been accomplished to date, Telford anticipated that the tunnel might be ready for opening towards the latter end of 1827. With regard to coal workings being connected to the new tunnel Telford said he had directed Potter to provide him with a plan of the ground where the coal workings were at present and where they were likely to take place in the future with observations on the nature of the measures and the effects which using the drifts as navigations would have on the integrity of the tunnel. Once he had the data, Telford said he would let the Select Committee have his opinion.[47] Telford's full written report was tabled at the meeting of the Select Committee held at Stone on 30th August. The committee found the report to be highly satisfactory and it was at this meeting that Potter's salary of £500 was finally confirmed.[48]

On 3rd September 1825 *The Staffordshire Advertiser* carried the following advertisement:

WANTED IMMEDIATELY, From twenty to thirty **BRICKLAYERS**; those who have been accustomed to underground work would be preferred; good steady workmen will meet with immediate employment by applying to Mr. DANIEL PRITCHARD, the Contractor, at Harecastle Tunnel, near Newcastle-under Lyme.

Work was clearly gathering pace. On 19th September Potter wrote to Telford reporting on the state of work. A total of 421 yards of the tunnel had been bricked and it was anticipated that the tunnel from the south entrance as far as No. 5 Shaft at the south end would be thurled and completed by Christmas, excepting the towpath. He expected a complete opening through the hill would be made by early November. His next report dated 17th October showed that 577⅔ yards of tunnel had been bricked with almost 157 yards being achieved in a single month. The heading between Nos. 5 and 6 Shafts at the north end had been thurled and Potter commented that the whole of the headings would have been thurled had the workmen not met with strong ground and been troubled with foul air. Part of the stone work for the towpath had been put in place. His report dated 14th November showed that 717⅔ yards of brickwork had been completed but foul air was still proving to be a problem and there had been an ingress of water. His last report in 1825 dated 10th December indicated that progress with the tunnel brickwork had slowed slightly with a total now completed of 846 yards but brickwork for the open cutting at the south end of the tunnel had commenced.[49]

News of the new tunnel was of international interest and so it is an appropriate time to pause from our account of the tunnel's construction and use one of the overseas accounts to summarise the project. The following is a report given in 1825 by architect and engineer, William Strickland (1787-1854) to the newly formed Pennsylvania Society for the Promotion of Internal Improvement.

The old tunnel, on the Grand Trunk Canal, at Harecastle, in Staffordshire, was executed by the celebrated Brindley; and is built with a semi-circular brick arch, springing from the water line of the canal: it is but ten feet in diameter, and consequently without a towing path. The increase of the trade on this canal, together with the delay occasioned from the want of a towing path, has made it expedient to form a new tunnel, alongside of the present one; and this is now rapidly progressing, under the superintendence of Mr. Telford. His plan is to arch the whole, from end to end, with an elliptic brick arch, eighteen inches in thickness, resting on a flat reversed arch, forming the bottom of the tunnel. The breath of the opening is fourteen feet; and the height, from the bottom to the crown of the arch, is fifteen feet in the clear; having a towpath of four feet in width, supported upon piers and arches. The whole length of the tunnel will be one mile and three quarters, formed principally through sand, rock, marl, and coal, at a depth of sixty-five yards below the top surface. There are to be fifteen working shafts, eight feet in diameter; and twelve or fourteen air wells. The loose nature of the different strata of soil through which the tunnel is to be made, renders every precaution necessary: and this has led to the determination of arching every portion of it. The accompanying cross section of the tunnel, also showing the centering, formed part of Strickland's report.[50]

---

46 Transcript by L. Allsop, *op. cit.*
47 ICE Archive T/TR. 49.
48 Transcript by L. Allsop, *op. cit.*
49 ICE Archive T/TR. 51-54.
50 Reports on Canals, Railways, Roads and other subjects, made to The Pennsylvania Society for the Promotion of Internal Improvement by William Strickland, H.C. Carey & I. Lea, Philadelphia, 1826.

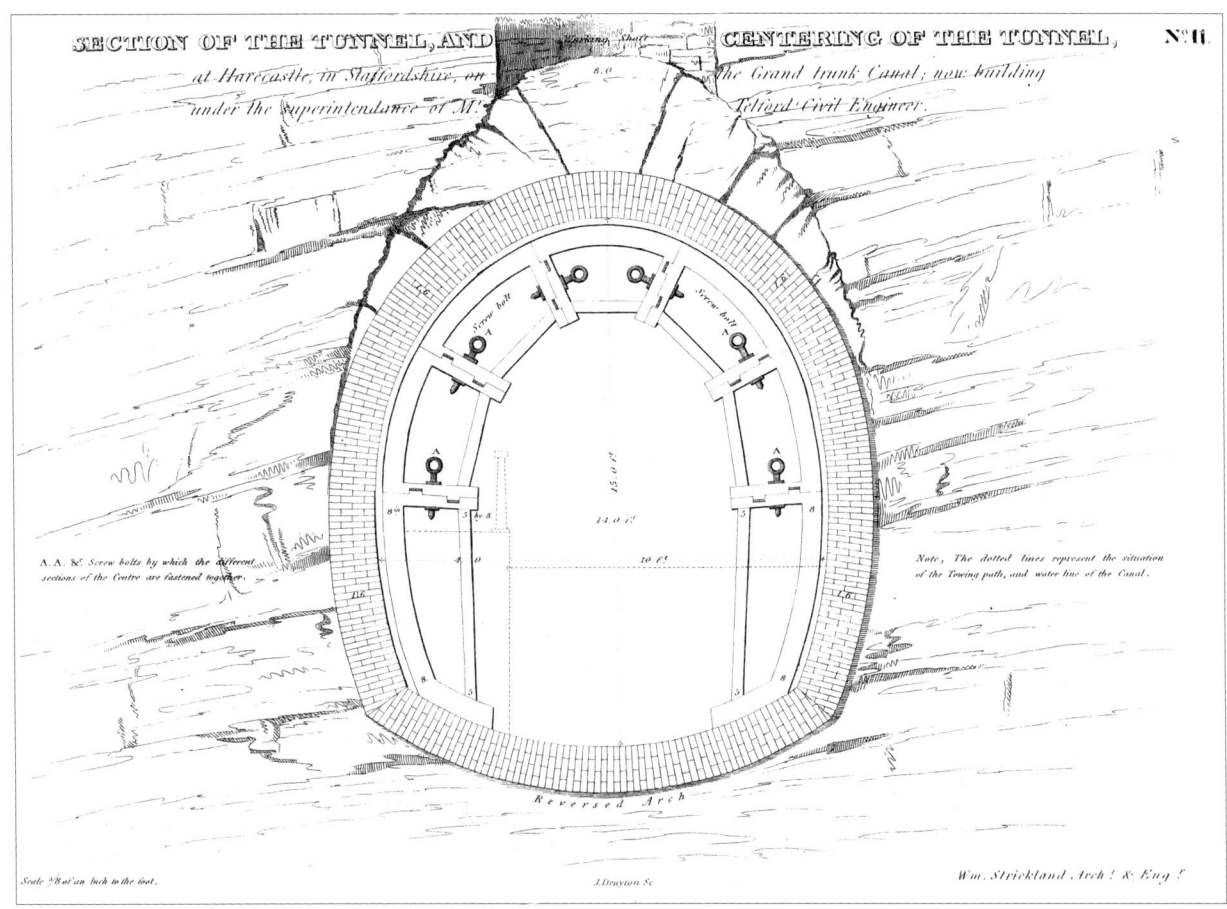

This is the extract from the report by William Strickland (1787-1854) referred to in the text. *Courtesy Richard Dean*

Potter's report dated 13th March 1826 showed that 1,297⅔ yards of the tunnel had been bricked with 1,323 yards excavated. He was becoming increasingly concerned about the lack of a decision concerning the connection of the various coal mine drifts which crossed the tunnel. He had earlier explained to Telford that a particular drift was driven through strata comprising coal, ironstone and metals or argillaceous rock. He explained that the obstruction caused by the boats bringing out the coal was not trifling. Six or seven or more of them were used at any one time which took up a lot of time in getting them in and out. He believed that they should be obliged to go through the new tunnel and return down the old tunnel to the mouth of the drift unless the drifts where connected to the new tunnel were made very wide.[51] Telford did not reply to Potter until 7th July when he had this to say: *Having examined the parts of the old tunnel and new tunnels where the coal mine drifts enter and had plans made showing the direction and dimensions of the said drifts and having duly considered the nature of the grounds, the trouble and risk of constructing such entrances as would admit ingress and egress, also the interruption to the general intercourse of trade, I consider it would be very inadvisable for the canal company to agree to their being constructed and used and am therefore of opinion that, in the new arrangement, any communication by this means, should be discontinued.*[52] At the Select Committee meeting held on 31st July 1826 the chairman tabled a report from Telford in which he voiced his strong objection to the coal mine drifts being linked to the new tunnel on the grounds that the proposed turn-outs would involve considerable expense as well as obstructing the general intercourse of trade.[53] This sound advice was later ignored.

At the previous meeting of the Select Committee held at Stone on 5th July 1826, the present state of the company's finances were considered as it appeared that *a considerable Sum of Money will still be wanting* to complete the new tunnel and the additional reservoir at Knypersley. It was resolved to borrow the sum of £20,000 under the powers of the 1823 Act and the company's clerk was instructed to send a copy of the resolution to some of the principal proprietors.[54] After an overnight stay at the Crown Inn, Caldwell and other members of the committee left Stone by boat early the following day for Harecastle. They noted that the new tunnel works were proceeding in a most satisfactory manner and anticipated that the tunnel would be open for the passage of boats the following spring, which proved to be an accurate forecast. They went over the hill on the Rail

---

51 ICE Archive T/TR. 55-56.
52 ICE Archive T/TR. 61.
53 Transcript by L. Allsop, *op. cit.*
54 Transcript by L. Allsop, *op. cit.*

Road which Caldwell found very shaking and uncomfortable. They then proceeded to Middlewich where the party arrived between eight and nine o'clock in the evening after, according to Caldwell's description, a good voyage.

Potter's report dated 12th June 1826 stated that 2,080 yards of tunnel had been completed with 829 yards remaining which he anticipated would be done by Christmas, adding that by September only three shafts would remain working. The whole quantity of bricks required would be made by the end of June; work had commenced on the towpath and he anticipated that the whole job would be completed before 1st June 1827. On 2nd August 1826, with Cladwell in the chair, the General Committee of the Proprietors, held at the Crown Inn, Stone, passed the following resolution: *That this Meeting has heard with great satisfaction the Report of the Select Committee, that the important works of the new Tunnel through Harecastle Hill and the additional Reservoir in Knypersley Valley have been so nearly executed from the resources of the Company, unaided by any Loan, that not more than about £45,000, will be required to complete the same.*[55]

Potter's report dated 5th September advised that 2,688⅓ yards had been completed and that the tunnel was thurled from the south entrance to the drift to Golden Hill mines which was nine yards from No. 7 Shaft. The report does not clarify whether or not the drift was to be connected or blocked off. The towpath was complete throughout except the railing from the south entrance to the No. 6 Shaft at the south end – a distance of 766 yards. He enquired of Telford whether or not the towpath should be paved with pebbles and added that the masonry for the south entrance would be completed the following week.[56]

On 3rd October 1826 Potter reported that 2,796⅓ yards of the tunnel had been completed and on the 17th of that month Caldwell recorded a proposal to light the new tunnel with gas but it came to nothing.[57] On 13th November Pritchard and Hoof wrote to Telford from Market Drayton to say that the excavation of the Harecastle Tunnel had been completed during the morning of Saturday, 11th November. The letter said they *have the satisfaction of saying it is a straight line from end to end, so that we can stand at one end and see the other. We flatter ourselves that the workmanship thereof will give you the utmost satisfaction.*[58] The Institution of Civil Engineers archive does not include monthly status reports from Potter after October 1826. Maybe this is because they are missing or were no longer required by Telford who obviously had absolute faith in the resident engineer. However, on 1st March 1827 Potter wrote to Telford announcing that the new tunnel would be completed and ready for his inspection by the end of that month.[59] He also said that: *the general stoppage for repairing the canal will take place on the 8th of April during which we shall take out the dams at each end of the tunnel and open it to trade on the 16th.*

Telford described the making of the tunnel in his *Atlas to the Life of Thomas Telford* published in London by Payne & Foss in 1838. This is what he said about it.

Upon the Trent and Mersey Canal a work of considerable magnitude was entrusted to my direction. On the summit of the canal it is well known that the celebrated James Brindley, in forming the Trent and Mersey Canal, found it expedient to construct a tunnel through Harecastle Hill for a distance of 2,888 yards, at 197 feet perpendicular, under the highest surface of the hill. This tunnel, where largest, is but 12 feet high and 9 feet wide, so that a seven-foot wide boat, with a moderate lading [sic], can scarcely pass through. The operation of thrusting a boat through this tunnel is by a class of men called *Leggers*, who lie on their backs on the top of the loading, and push against the roof and sides with their feet. This tunnel, from commencement to completion, cost no less then eleven [sic] years, so inexpert were the workmen of that day, although under the direction of an able master.

The inadequate dimensions of this tunnel were, no doubt, advisable in an untried project, and for several years after the navigation was opened, the imperfect and tedious passage was probably found sufficient; but, as trade increased, the delay and inconvenience became grievous. The time allotted for passing each way was two hours, and before the expiration of that time a great number of boats waiting for passage was usually collected, and, not withstanding strict regulations, much contention and confusion took place. This continued to increase with the increase of trade, and loud complaints were made, which the proprietors (although profiting by very large dividends) for many years disregarded; and it was not till after the threatened establishment of railroads, and the formation of rival canals, that they were forced into an expensive improvement.

Early in the year 1822, the Canal Company applied to me to examine Harecastle Hill, and report upon the practicability of making a second tunnel. I proceeded accordingly, and in the ensuing month of March reported it practicable and advisable; and after a pause of two years, in July 1824, I was authorised to recommend Mr. James Potter, an active, intelligent young man, as resident engineer, and Daniel Pritchard, a person of much experience in tunnels, as contractor. I also settled the terms of contract, and made arrangements for machinery and materials. The line of the tunnel contained 15 pit-shafts; the deepest pit being 179 feet. This great number of pits was for the sake of expedition. During the year 1824 some of the pits were sunk, and part of the heading accurately driven. On the 21st of February 1825, the first brick of the tunnel was laid, and with such energy and success were the various operations prosecuted, that the last brick was laid on the 25th November 1826, after which the towing-path was completed, and the passage opened to the public on the 30th April 1827, not quite three years from the commencement of operations.

The length of the tunnel (which is parallel with the former tunnel, at a distance of 26 yards) is 2,926 yards; it is 16 feet in height, and 14 feet in breadth, of which 4ft 9in is covered by the haling-path[60], leaving 9ft 3in for the passage of the boat; and as the path is supported by small pillars, the refluent water readily passes under it. The tunnel is so accurately strait [sic] that its whole length can be seen through at one view, and the workmanship is so perfect that the joinings of the separate portions in which the brickwork was built are seldom discernible, although, by means of 15 pits, it was carried out in several places at the same time, through ground of very different qualities.

---

55 CRO – Twemlow papers. Ref. D3098/8/11.
56 ICE Archive T/TR. 59 and T/TR. 63.
57 ICE Archive T/TR. 65, Transcript by L. Allsop, *op. cit.* and the Caldwell diaries.
58 ICE Archive – document unreferenced.
59 ICE Archive T/TR. 66.

60 Another term for a towpath or towing path.

CHAPTER 3 – TELFORD'S TUNNEL

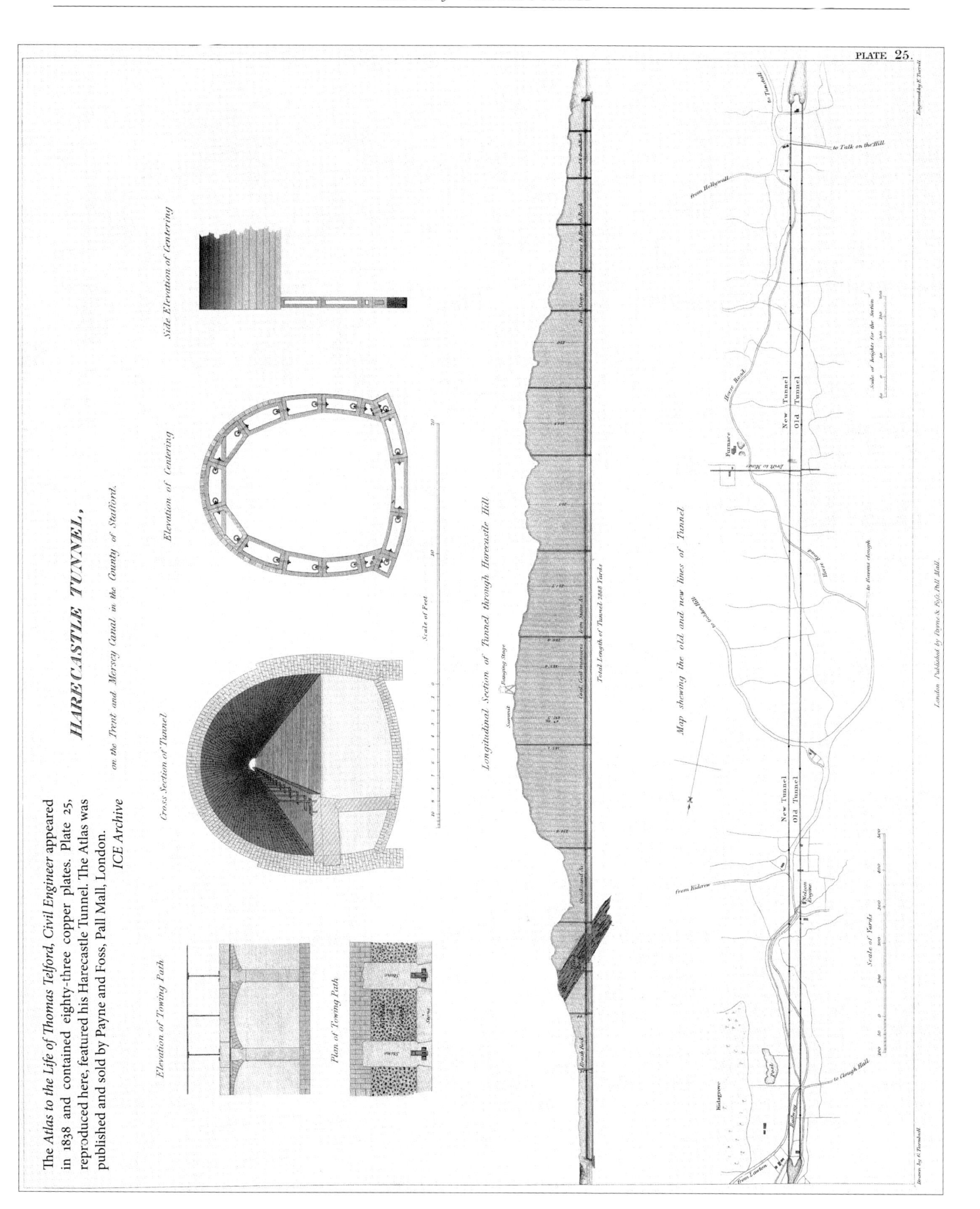

PLATE 25.

The Atlas to the Life of Thomas Telford, Civil Engineer appeared in 1838 and contained eighty-three copper plates. Plate 25, reproduced here, featured his Harecastle Tunnel. The Atlas was published and sold by Payne and Foss, Pall Mall, London.

ICE Archive

HARECASTLE TUNNEL,

on the Trent and Mersey Canal in the County of Stafford.

Side Elevation of Centering

Elevation of Centering

Cross Section of Tunnel

Elevation of Towing Path

Plan of Towing Path

Longitudinal Section of Tunnel through Harecastle Hill

Total Length of Tunnel 2888 Yards

Map shewing the old and new lines of Tunnel

Scale of Yards

Scale of heights for the Section

London Published by Payne & Foss, Pall Mall.

47

The bricks being made of clay peculiarly good in quality, and triturated by machinery, and being carefully molded [sic] and burnt, are in fact the best *Newcastle blue brick*,[61] the hardest and most durable of any made in England. They are laid in mortar made of Barrow lias limestone, ground in a mill, which, in setting, becomes impervious to water, so that, on a careful inspection on the 21st March 1829, the following Report was made by me to the Committee:-

I walked along the towing-path, and by means of a lanthorn [sic] and candle examined the whole very minutely, and found that the tunnel, after being worked for two years, remained in every part quite perfect, so that in all the 2,926 yards I did not observe one crack or fissure, or even one decayed brick, which, in a work of such magnitude and difficulty, performed in the short period of three years, is, I venture to believe, without parallel. Although the materials are thus excellent, and every facility was afforded, I consider it just to state the merit which is due to the resident engineer, Mr James Potter, for the accuracy with which he set out the line, and his unceasing attention and perseverance in providing materials and conducting the works. David Pritchard fully justified his character as a contractor, in which he was ably assisted by his son-in-law, Mr Hoof.

The above description accompanied Plate 25 of the Atlas which is reproduced herewith. Telford clearly relied very heavily upon Potter to carry out his instructions and oversee the construction of the tunnel. Much responsibility was delegated to Potter for the procurement of materials and machinery. For example, on 10th July 1824 he travelled to Birmingham to order a steam engine for work at the north end of the tunnel and he went again on 5th October that year to order *high pressure steam engines*,[62] *pumps and pumping gear* to draw water from the tunnel workings. During 1825 he travelled to Liverpool on five separate occasions to take particulars of the mortar mills used in the building of the dock and purchase timber. He went to Liverpool on two further occasions in 1826 to purchase more timber and also went to Runcorn on 19th August that year to examine the quarries there to check whether stone from that source could be used for the towpath. Earlier that year on 20th March he travelled to London to present Pritchard and Hoof's accounts for approval so Telford clearly relied on Potter to ensure their accuracy.[63] All Potter's journeys would, of course, have been made on horseback or by horse-drawn stage coaches.

Telford in his Atlas made reference to the last brick being laid on 25th November 1826. This task was undertaken by James Caldwell. His diary entry makes for some distorted reading as some of the words are indistinct but the gist is clear. *Saturday 25. Snow. I this morning accompanied by Stamford, went to Harecastle Tunnel and laid the Lock or central Key Brick of this great work, a little before 12 o'clock, attended by the two Mr. Pritchards, Mr. Hough the Head Bricklayer and Mr. James Potter, having on the 30th March 1824 first broke the ground for it, & nearly at the same time of day. The Brick was put in upright into the top of the Arch & not long.....A number of the Workmen also attended "Success to the new Tunnel & the.....of Miss Pritchard & Mr. James Potter. Prosperity to the Company of Proprietors of the Navigation".* This must have been a toast, he then goes on to record that: *The two other Members of the Select Committee, Sir George Chetwynd & Thomas Lister Esq, Mr Vaughan & the Agents & Servants of the Company, were severely drunk with whom came three cheers with great admiration from the Men. The Tunnel to the Midway when the Break was part filled with water & part laid with a Platform of Planks and a small stage created on which I stood when I laid the brick & to which I ascended by a Ladder. A Bottle of Wine was then broke against the Brick that I had laid & we returned to the Entrance amidst repeated Hugging. When having told the Men that I had directed a dinner to be given to all the workmen at the Company's expense, I made then a personal present of 5 Guineas to which Stamford added too.* Maybe Caldwell had partaken of a little too much wine when he made this particular entry in his diary, although the reference to other attendees being *severely drunk* surely meant that several toasts were made rather than them all being intoxicated! Select Committee members Sir George Chetwynd, 2nd Bart (1783-1850) of Brocton Hall and Thomas Lister (1772-1828) feature frequently in Caldwell's diaries.

With regard to the opening of the new tunnel for traffic, the diary has the following entry: *Monday 30th April 1827. Went with Mr. Vaughan to the South end of the additional Tunnel through Harecastle Hill when the Company's Boat met us in order that I might be the first to pass through it. We entered the tunnel at 4 minutes (by my watch) before 12 & arrived at the other end at 27 minutes past 12 making the passage in about 31 or 32 minutes. Mr. Hill of Stallington who had come purposely, having been informed by Mr. Vaughan, accompanied us through, the only other persons on board being Mr. Vaughan, James Potter and myself. At the North end we were met by Eliza & Miss Stamford who returned with us through the Tunnel & we went on to Etruria Locks being desirous to show Mr. Hill as much as possible of the Canal.* Mr. Hill was Reginald Clarke Hill (1782-1852) of Stallington Hall. James Potter attended the Select Committee meeting at Stone on 26th June 1827 and reported that the additional tunnel at Harecastle had been completed and was in full operation and that the new reservoir at Knypersley was in a state to contain 5,000 or 6,000 locks of water *in case sufficient rain were to fall and that it will be entirely completed by the end of September next.* At the same meeting it requested that an inventory and valuation be made of the *Engines, Rail Road, Houses and other Articles used in making the additional Tunnel at Harecastle and which may now be disposed of.* Caldwell, Sir George and Lister passed through the new tunnel on 1st August 1827 on a tour of inspection, acknowledging that it appeared to have been executed in a complete and satisfactory manner. They then

---

61 Here we think Telford must have been referring to nearby Newcastle-under-Lyme and traditional Staffordshire blue engineering bricks for which an abundance of Etruria marl was readily to hand. Etruria marl is red clay which when fired at a high temperature in a low-oxygen reducing atmosphere takes on a deep blue colour and attains a very hard, impervious surface with high crushing strength and low water absorption. Such bricks were ideal for canal tunnels.
62 This would be a reference to Boulton & Watt's improved design obviating the separate condenser without any assistance from atmospheric pressure.
63 ICE Archive T/TR. 64.

went on to Knypersley to survey the reservoir works, Potter assuring them that the whole would be complete by the end of September next.[64]

On 3rd November 1827 Potter wrote to Telford concerning the cost of the various additional works at the tunnel not taken into consideration in Telford's original estimate. It seems clear that the Select Committee was expressing some concern at the extra cost. Potter's letter, posted from Lawton, is quoted in full below.[65]

Dear Sir,

Underneath I send you an account of the amounts of various works at Harecastle new tunnel and which works were not taken into consideration in your Report presented to the Committee previous to the commencement of the work:

	£ s d
Towing Path. Materials and labour	9,600 0 0
Extra expense in providing engines and machinery necessary for grinding marl and clay for making bricks also the expense of extra labour and the extra expense of making bricks in shales during the winter months	4,300 0 0
Expense of making railway and providing railway wagons	7,000 0 0
Supposed extra expense in making tunnel of sufficient dimensions to allow putting in the towing path	12,000 0 0
TOTAL COST	**£32,900 0s 0d**

The nature of the ground must be taken into consideration, it proving much stronger and more difficult to pass through than was expected, particularly the quick sand at the north end of the tunnel which caused considerable extra expense in drainage and timbering. Also owing to expedition being so great an object, we sunk double the number of shafts that would have been requisite if the same space of time had been allowed as works of the same description and magnitude have taken to execute.

As regards the railway, without it we could not have had the quantity of materials used delivered in the time required as carting them would have been utterly impossible or if possible equally, if not more expensive, as roads must have been made, the making of which and keeping them in repair owing to the surface of the ground would have been an enormous expense, but I do not consider it would have been practicable, that is as regards dispatch. But if 8 or 9 years had been allowed to execute the work in, then we could have boated all our bricks and other materials into the tunnel and also have boated part of the spoil out, which would have made a considerable saving.

With regard to the machinery used for grinding the clay for the bricks, setting aside the great improvement in the quality, it would have been perfectly necessary as without them the quality of bricks could not have possibly been obtained in the neighbourhood in the time employed in the execution of the work.

I remain, Dear Sir, Yours most respectfully

James Potter

The extensive use of primitive railways and the number of stationary steam engines employed were significant features of the construction. In response to Potter's letter, Telford produced a report for the Select Committee dated 10th November. He said he had passed through and examined the new tunnel with Potter and *found the whole quite perfect*. He then validated the extra expense incurred using all the points made by Potter and concluded his report as follows: *These circumstances it is hoped will satisfactorily account for the expense which has been increased and this improved and very rapid mode of proceeding was certainly preferable to the cheaper but slow progress of 9 or 10 years which must otherwise have been occupied. Upon the whole, I have to congratulate the Company in having a tunnel more perfect than any other that has hitherto been constructed.* A classic example of short shrift!

On 14th November 1827 an auction of surplus equipment was held at the south end of the tunnel.[66] The items included:

TWO STEAM ENGINES, viz. one 14 horse power, made by Boulton and Watt, and one 6 horse power, upon a very portable construction, and nearly new, made by Francis Smith and Brunton, of Birmingham, two mills for grinding mortar, also rollers and machinery for crushing marl and tempering clay for making bricks, &c. about 100 railway wagons, 150 tons of cast iron, three feet railway plates, several cast iron turn tables for railways, and cast-iron and wood hand pumps, three very good gins and pit frames, a variety of cast-iron spur and bevil [sic] wheels, shafts, and plummer blocks or chains, a quantity of old timber, tiles, and other building materials, also a considerable quantity of old wrought iron screw pins, large and small.

On 20th November, Potter reported to the Select Committee that the public auction has raised a total sum of £2,500 but many items remained unsold.[67]

During the following year on 1st April, Caldwell records that Brunel called to see him at Linley Wood. This must have been Marc Isambard Brunel (1769-1849) as his son, Isambard Kingdom Brunel (1806-1859), was at that time still recovering from his injuries following the collapse on 12th January 1828 of his father's Thames tunnel during its construction from Rotherhithe to Wapping. The collapse became a topic of conversation over dinner that evening. During the afternoon they went to see the new Harecastle tunnel and Brunel expressed the *highest admiration and approbation and pronounced it to be the best and finest work of its kind*. In the evening they were joined by Pritchard and James Potter. The following day Caldwell asked Brunel for his opinion on the seeping of water from the roof of the new canal tunnel. Brunel explained that it was impossible to avoid this spring water entirely as it made its way through the bricks and mortar, but held the view that it was not of the smallest consequence and would in time probably *reach up*. Brunel commented that the spring water might be drained and carried off backwards but considered it not worth the expense. Caldwell was obviously still concerned about the overall costs for the new tunnel as he raised the matter with

---

64 Transcript by L. Allsop, *op cit*.
65 ICE Archive T/TR. 69.

66 *The Staffordshire Advertiser*, 27th October 1827.
67 Transcript by L. Allsop, *op cit*.

NAVIGATION
From the Trent to the Mersey.

THE ELLESMERE and CHESTER Canal Company, having given notice of their intention to apply to Parliament, in the present Session, for powers to enable them to make a Canal from the Ellesmere and Chester Canal, in the Township of WARDLE, in the County of Chester, to communicate with, and to be *cut into* this NAVIGATION, in the Township of MIDDLEWICH, in the same County, although expressly restrained by Act of Parliament, (17 Geo. 3, Cap. 67, Sect. 20, a copy of which is annexed) *from making, carrying on, or extending the same nearer in any part to the navigable Canal from the Trent to the Mersey than One hundred Yards;*

And it being apprehended that such Communication will be very prejudicial to this Company of Proprietors, as well as a direct violation of that Parliamentary protection, upon the confidence of which, not only a vast Capital has long since been expended in rendering this important public Work beneficial and convenient to the Trade and Commerce of the Kingdom, and in particular to that of Liverpool, Manchester, Birmingham, and London, for which it is amply sufficient; but with a view to affording still greater accommodation and dispatch, THIS PROPRIETARY are now actually expending, under the sanction of an Act passed only in the Session of 1823, and without requiring the smallest increase of Tonnage or other remuneration, the further sum of £130,000 and upwards, in making an additional Tunnel of nearly two miles in length, and an additional Reservoir for Water; and for the more speedy and effective execution of which great Works, now nearly completed, they have already been compelled to borrow the sum of £50,000 at interest, on Mortgage of their Tolls:

It is therefore hoped that the Proprietors will exert their immediate and strenuous endeavours in resisting a Bill, not only so injurious to their rights and interests, and so violent in its nature, as that now projected, but uncalled for by any adequate public necessity; and which, if passed into a law, would afford a precedent, that would shake the credit and security of all property embarked in the public Works of the Kingdom, or otherwise dependent upon the good faith and the obligation of Acts of Parliament.

Signed by desire of the SELECT COMMITTEE,

STONE, *November 21st*, 1826.

JAMES CALDWELL,

CHAIRMAN.

This document dated 21st November 1826 and signed by James Caldwell, Chairman of the Trent and Mersey Navigation's Select Committee, exhorts the Proprietors to resist a Bill being promoted by the Ellesmere and Chester Canal Company to link that canal to the Trent and Mersey at Middlewich. Clearly Caldwell saw the Ellesmere and Chester Company as a rival and did not want the capital expended on the new tunnel and reservoir to be of benefit to a competitor. The plea to the Proprietors did not succeed as the branch to Middlewich was authorised but it was not opened until 1833. *William Salt Library, M743*

Brunel who said that in a work of this kind, where the ground was so difficult, it was impossible to estimate the actual expense.

We only have access to a transcript of the Select Committee minutes from 7th September 1824 to 21st January 1828. The other minutes are missing[68] but reading between the lines, which is the only course open to us, it seems that Caldwell was coming under increasing pressure from other members of the committee to justify all the extra costs. On 4th April 1829 he wrote to Telford from 8 Palace Yard in the following terms.[69]

As you have so lately inspected the additional tunnel through Harecastle Hill your report upon which has afforded one great satisfaction, may I request the favour of you to inform me at your leisure whether in the course of your examination of it you observed any instance of wasteful or unnecessary expense – whether it would have been prudent to have executed a work of such a nature in a less perfect and durable manner – and whether the expense amounting in the whole to about £118,000 is more than it would reasonably and properly have been executed for.

I think you mentioned to me a short time ago in reply to my enquiries relative to the expense of the Knypersley Reservoir that the prices charged were very moderate – that taking the whole amount independent of the reparations now making at about £27,000, it was by no means unreasonable but less in proportion, than the expense of another reservoir which you had recently completed and that no such saving as £15,100 could, as has been said, have been made.

Pray excuse the trouble I am now giving you.

I am, Dear Sir, very truly yours
James Caldwell

A copy of Telford's reply dated 7th April has survived but it is damaged and in parts difficult to read. However, it is very clear that he did not budge on either count. Insofar as the new tunnel was concerned he expressed the opinion that all materials and labour employed were necessary to render it substantial. He confirmed that the sum of £118,000 had been laudably expended in accomplishing so useful a work in so short a time and added that any attempt at saving expense would not only have occasioned delay but would have increased the risk of serious accidents, which the extensive tunnel had fortunately been free from, an instance he expected was unexampled in such an undertaking. In spite of Telford's comments there were accidents and some workmen were killed. This is evidenced by the minutes of the meeting of the Select Committee held on 18th July 1827 which refers to the *allowances proposed to be made on account of the Persons killed or hurt in the making of Harecastle additional Tunnel*.[70] We have been unable to identify the individuals concerned or the circumstances in which they lost their lives or were injured.

---

68 A note at the CRO Stafford, in the Twemlow family papers, records that when the Trent & Mersey Canal was sold to the NSR, the minute books were deposited with bankers Stevenson, Salt & Company of Stafford. That business, founded in 1737, was sold to Lloyds Bank in 1866 but unfortunately Lloyd's archives do not include the missing minutes.
69 ICE Archive T/TR. 112.
70 Transcript by L. Allsop, *op cit.*

In 1829, schoolmaster Simeon Ackroyd Shaw (1785-1859) published his book *History of the Staffordshire Potteries* which recorded his visit to the new tunnel in the following terms: *Urged by curiosity, the author presumed to visit this monument of industrious perseverance. The strata cannot easily be ascertained from the interior, because of the brick work; but fossils of various kinds have been found in the substances excavated. After being wholly excluded from the light of day, and introduced into these dreary regions, suddenly is presented to view, glimmering in the distance, the lights of an extensive coal mine, where are busily employed the murky-visaged colliers; and small boats are seen approaching the tunnel by means of a small subterraneous canal. Passing forward, at a considerable distance, the first appearance of light adds a pleasing object to the vision, cheering the adventurer, like as the pole star cheers the returning mariner who has unfortunately lost his compass; – the beams of light increase to the view, the land in the distance is faintly presented; and at length the bark emerges from the cavity, the visitor looks with eagerness for objects known or recognizable, and almost conjectures he has passed thro' the chambers of Hades, and entered upon the scenery of another world.* The extract clearly indicates the author's wonderment at passing through the new tunnel but, more importantly, gives clear evidence that mining within Harecastle Hill was continuing apace and that Telford's advice on this matter had clearly been ignored.

The new tunnel was an immediate success. It took the northbound traffic with the old tunnel taking the southbound. Making use of the towpath, horse drawn boats could navigate the new tunnel in less than an hour and a half. On 25th February 1833, James Potter, then based at Brinklow, presented a detailed statement of the expense incurred in the construction of the new tunnel:

	£
Fifteen shafts 9ft diameter	1,610
Driving heading through hill	7,057
Driving cross headings to carry off water	470
Driving heading in coal measures to drain the sand at north end of tunnel	540
Excavating the body of the tunnel and turning brickwork including timber - length 2,926½ yards	43,435
Expense of towing path	9,600
Length of railway - 6½ miles	7,000
Length providing bricks and mortar and centering	22,750
Labour on mortar and centering	1,537
Carriage of materials	4,060
Expense of open cutting, entrances and turnover bridges at each end of the tunnel, erecting workshops, mortar mills, clay mills, engine houses pumping water, damages to land, fence, agencies, etc	14,622
TOTAL COST	**£112,681**

This appears to be the final cost of the work. Potter recorded that a total of 8,814,681 bricks were used on the project.[71] He

---

71 The statement was reproduced in a British Waterways Board booklet *Harecastle Tunnel*, published by BWB in April 1977.

left the service of the Trent & Mersey Canal and from 1830 to 1834 was employed on the improvement works on the northern section of the Oxford Canal. He married Sarah Brown Power at Monks Kirby, Warwickshire on 5th August 1830 and continued to pursue his engineering career. His final appointment was Engineer to the Manchester, Sheffield & Lincolnshire Railway. He died in Kensington, Middlesex on 23rd August 1857 and was buried in his home town of Lichfield on 31st August.[72]

---
72 Potter's last address was 9 Eldon Road, Kensington.

His involvement in the construction of the second Harecastle tunnel and the reservoir at Knypersley was paramount but his talents, although fully recognised by Telford, do not seem to have been fully appreciated by certain members of the Trent & Mersey Select Committee who at times treated him rather badly. He was particularly annoyed when in November 1828 two local men were engaged to express a view on the new reservoir after some settlement had occurred. These were George Ernest Hamilton (1799-1872) and James Trubshaw (1777-1853), both architects and civil engineers. In referring to the matter, Potter

An early engraving illustrating the canal to the south of Longport. The church is St. Paul's at Dale Hall, between Burslem and Tunstall, which was completed at the close of 1830, surviving until its most unfortunate demolition in 1974. The Pottery town of Burslem and its pottery manufactories, locally known as potbanks with their distinctive bottle ovens, is on the horizon to the right.

This view in NSR days looks north towards Kidsgrove from the northern portals of the tunnels. The first bridge is turnover bridge No. 132; the second carries the NSR main Pottery Line over the canal. A barge from the NSR Engineer's Department occupies the right foreground adorned with its emblematic Staffordshire knot.
National Waterways Museum

CHAPTER 3 – TELFORD'S TUNNEL

A view in the opposite direction taken on 3rd March 1958, showing the northern tunnel portals. Telford's on the left and Brindley's on the right.

The same view at a later date. The walkway over the permanently moored barge seen in earlier views has been removed and the tunnel keeper's cottage has, unfortunately, been demolished.

wrote to Telford 24th November 1828 stating that: *This is, of course, not only an insult to me but also to you*. It seems that without the backing of Telford, Potter was no longer treated with the respect he deserved.

Caldwell continued to serve as chairman on the Select Committee until 1836 when he retired from that position. As a proprietor he continued to attend meetings of the general committee and the general assembly but not for long as he died on 16th January 1838 at Linley Wood. William Vaughan died on 5th December 1834. John Ward's *The Borough of Stoke-upon-Trent* [73] contains an extremely useful table showing a breakdown by commodity of the tonnage carried on the canal to and from Stoke for one year ending 30th June 1836 – Caldwell's last year as chairman. The table reproduced herewith shows a total traffic of 328,110 tons of which 143,610 tons was imported and 184,500 exported. Of this tonnage 92% (132,300 tons) of the imports came through the tunnels and 66% (121,500 tons) of the exports. Taking an average of, say, twenty tons per boat this equates to 12,705 fully-laden boats passing through the tunnels annually plus, no doubt, a large number of empty ones being repositioned. All this goes to show how much the industry of the Potteries and its wealth relied upon the canal before the coming of the railway.

---

[73] Published by W. Lewis and Son, London in 1843 and reprinted by Webberley Ltd of Hanley in 1984.

Right: Table showing tonnage carried on the Trent & Mersey Canal for the year ending 30th June 1836. (John Ward's *The Borough of Stoke-upon-Trent* published by W. Lewis and Son, London 1843).

A TABLE, *shewing the amount of conveyance of Goods and Merchandize to and from the Borough of Stoke-upon-Trent, by the navigation from the Trent to the Mersey, for One Year ending 30th June, 1836.*

INWARD TRADE.—*From Liverpool.*

	Tons.	Aggregate Tonnage
Clay and Stone from Devonshire, Dorset, and Cornwall	70,000	
Flint-stone from Gravesend and Newhaven	30,000	
Borax, Boracic Acid, Tincal, Cobalt, Colours, Bones, Ashes, and other Materials used in the manufacture of China and Earthenware	4,000	
Timber	9,000	
Corn, Grain, and Flour	7,000	
Groceries and Colonial Produce	6,500	
Butter, Bacon, and other Provisions	1,500	
Wine, Spirits, Ale, and Porter	800	
Miscellaneous Goods	1,000	129,800

From South Staffordshire.

Iron	7,000	
Copper and Steel	60	
Stourbridge Bricks	1,200	8,260

From London, &c.

Mercery, Haberdashery, &c. from London and the West	500	
Groceries, &c. from London	1,500	
Copper	50	
Miscellaneous Goods and Articles	1,000	3,050

From Manchester.

Cotton, Silk, and Woollen Goods	1,200	
Window Glass and Lead	300	
Malt, &c.	500	
Miscellaneous Goods from the North	500	2,500

| Total Imports | | 143,610 |

OUTWARD TRADE.—*To Liverpool.*

Earthenware and China, for shipment to America and other Foreign Countries, and to Ireland, Scotland, &c.	51,000	
Bricks and Tiles	10,000	61,000

To Manchester.

Earthenware and China	3,500	
Bricks and Tiles	30,000	
Coals (Manchester and Stockport)	25,000	
Miscellaneous Goods	1,000	59,500

To South Staffordshire.

Ironstone		15,000

To Birmingham and the West of England.

Earthenware and China		6,000

To London and the South.

Earthenware and China	12,000	
Coals, Cannel, and Slack	30,000	42,000

To Chester and North Wales.

Earthenware and China		1,000

| Total Exports | | 184,500 |

This illustration from the *Illustrated London News* features the unveiling, on 24th February 1863, of the statue of Josiah Wedgwood in Winton Square, which is opposite Stoke-on-Trent railway station. It seems entirely appropriate that the Directors of the NSR and owners of the canal which Wedgwood promoted should agree to his statue having such a prominent position on land owned by the railway company. The bronze statue, mounted on a sandstone pedestal, was sculpted by Edward Davies (1813-1878) and remains in situ today.

This 1898 view well illustrates the importance of the Trent & Mersey Canal to Josiah Wedgwood – it ran right alongside his Etruria factory in the village he built to house his employees! The factory opened for business on 13th June 1769. *www.thepotteries.org*

This much later view of the Wedgwood factory from almost the same position graphically illustrates the problems caused by mining subsidence. The factory as portrayed here was some 10 feet below the level of the canal. The factory was vacated by the Wedgwood Company in 1940, when production was transferred to a new purpose built factory south of the pottery towns at Barlaston. Most unfortunately, the original factory, which was of such enormous historical significance, was demolished in the 1960s and the round building to the left centre, is all that remains. It is however, a listed structure. The industrial complex in the distance to the right is part of the iron and steel works of the Shelton Iron, Steel & Coal Company Limited. Colloquially known to the local populace from an earlier title as Shelton Bar, it too, has now been erased. The blast furnace and steel making plant closed in 1978 and the rolling mill and remaining parts in 2000.

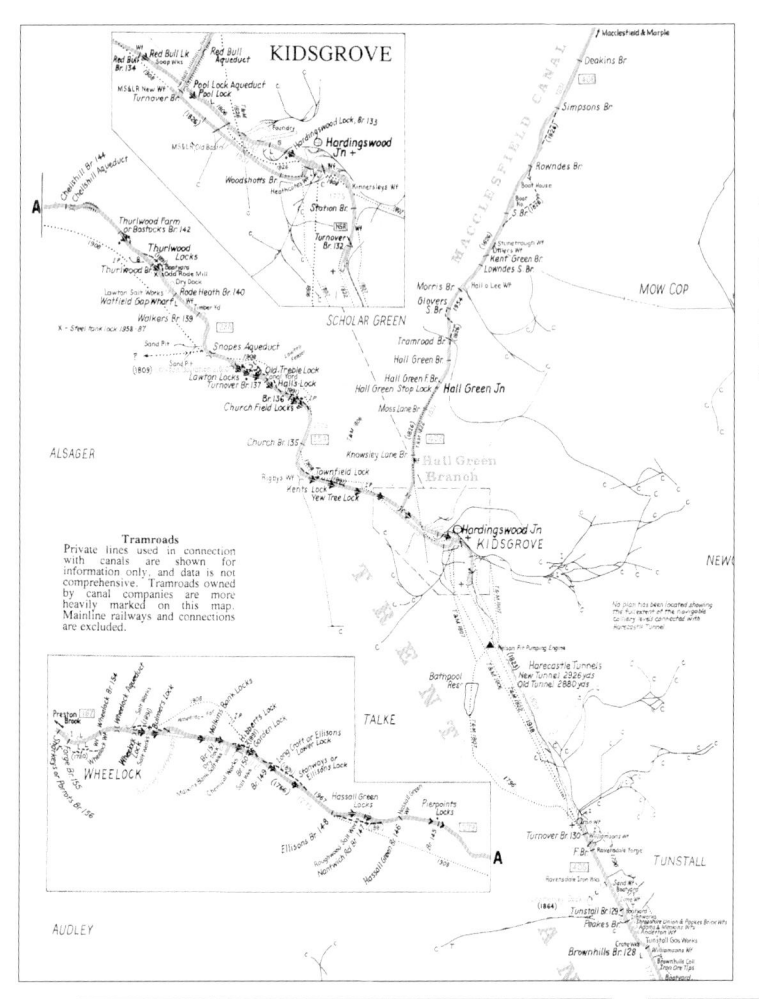

This extract is from a map entitled *Canals of North Staffordshire* by Richard Dean, published in 1997 in association with M. & M. Baldwin. The extract shows the Trent & Mersey Canal both to the south and north of the Harecastle tunnels and its junction with the Macclesfield Canal at Kidsgrove. Also shown are tramroads used in connection with the canals but not mainline railways.

Richard Dean and M. & M. Baldwin,
24 High Street, Cleobury Mortimer, Kidderminster,
Worcestershire, DY14 8BY. ISBN 0-947712-32-1

Key:
B - Brick Works
C - Colliery
I - Iron Works/Iron Mine
L - Lime Kiln/Lime Works
T - Tile Works

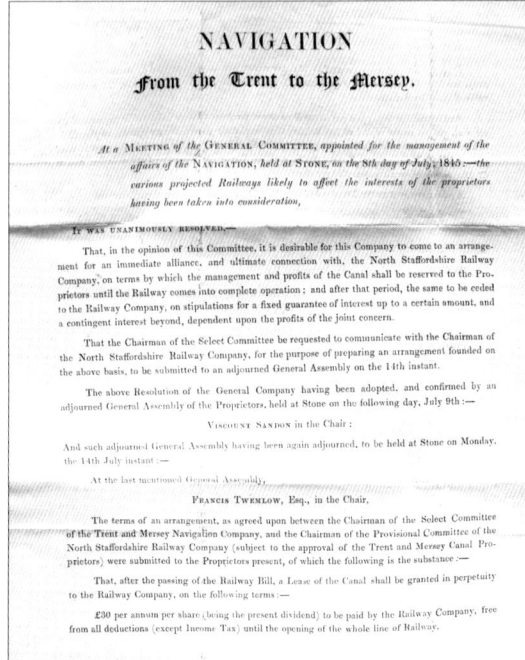

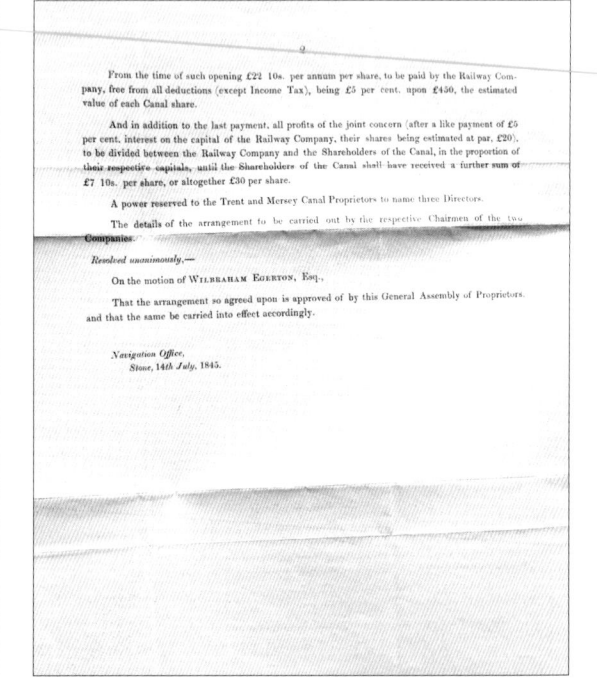

This Notice issued from the Trent and Mersey Navigation Office at Stone on 14th July 1845 neatly summarises the Navigation's attitude towards the new North Staffordshire Railway Company and the financial arrangement to be agreed between the two organisations.

William Salt Library, M743

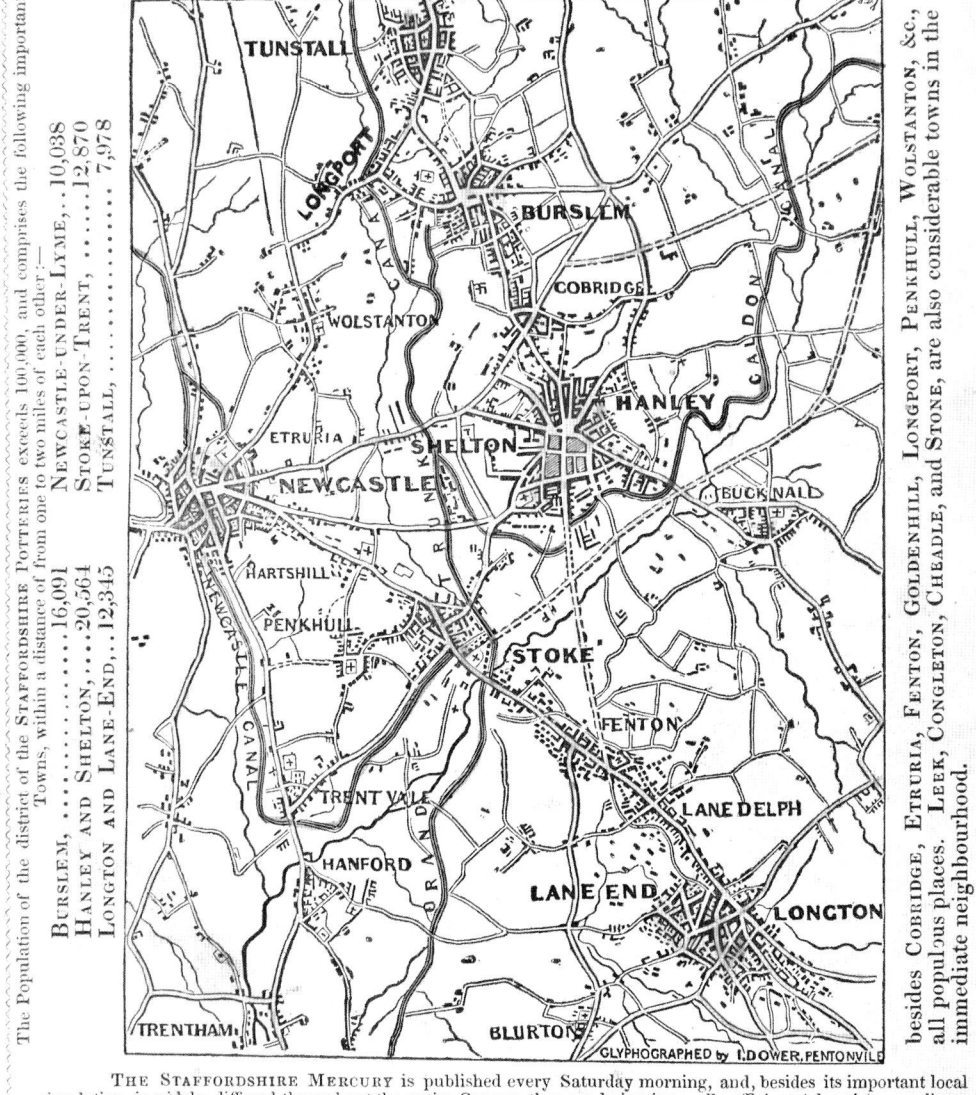

This map extracted from *The Staffordshire Mercury and Potteries Gazette* shows how the canal system served the Potteries and Newcastle-under-Lyme in 1845, just before the coming of the railways. The Grand Trunk Canal (the Trent & Mersey) runs from top to bottom, north to south. Stemming from it to the right is the Caldon Canal and by Stoke to the left is the Newcastle-under-Lyme Canal which connected to the main canal through a short tunnel; in 1864 it was leased in perpetuity to the NSR. The canals towards the top left of the map also served Newcastle-under-Lyme but were never connected to the main canal system. They were the Gresley Canal from the coal mines and ironworks at Apedale with its short branch known as the Newcastle-under-Lyme Junction Canal.

CRO D1453/1

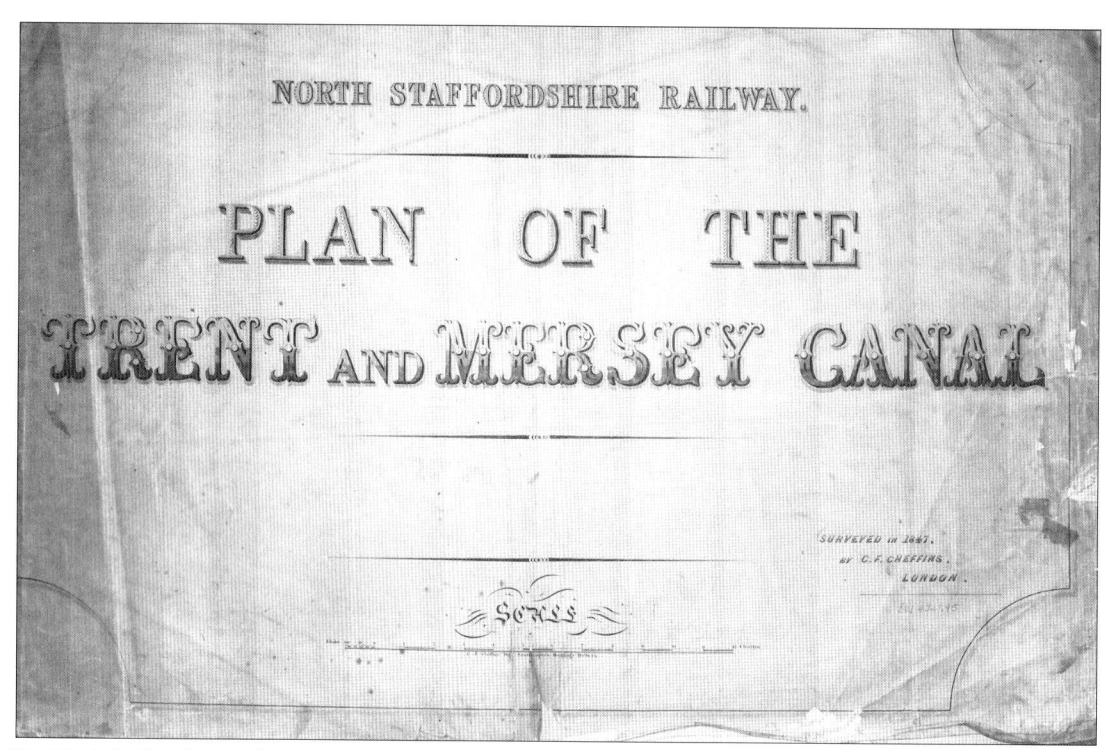

The North Staffordshire Railway commissioned a survey of the Trent & Mersey Canal in 1847. The survey was carried out by Charles Frederick Cheffins (1807-1860) of Holborn, London and runs from Chatterley to Harecastle. The five images that follow show both canal tunnels and the route of the projected railway. The images are taken from the copy of the survey deposited in the Canal & River Trust archive at the National Waterways Museum, Ellesmere Port; reference 86/74.

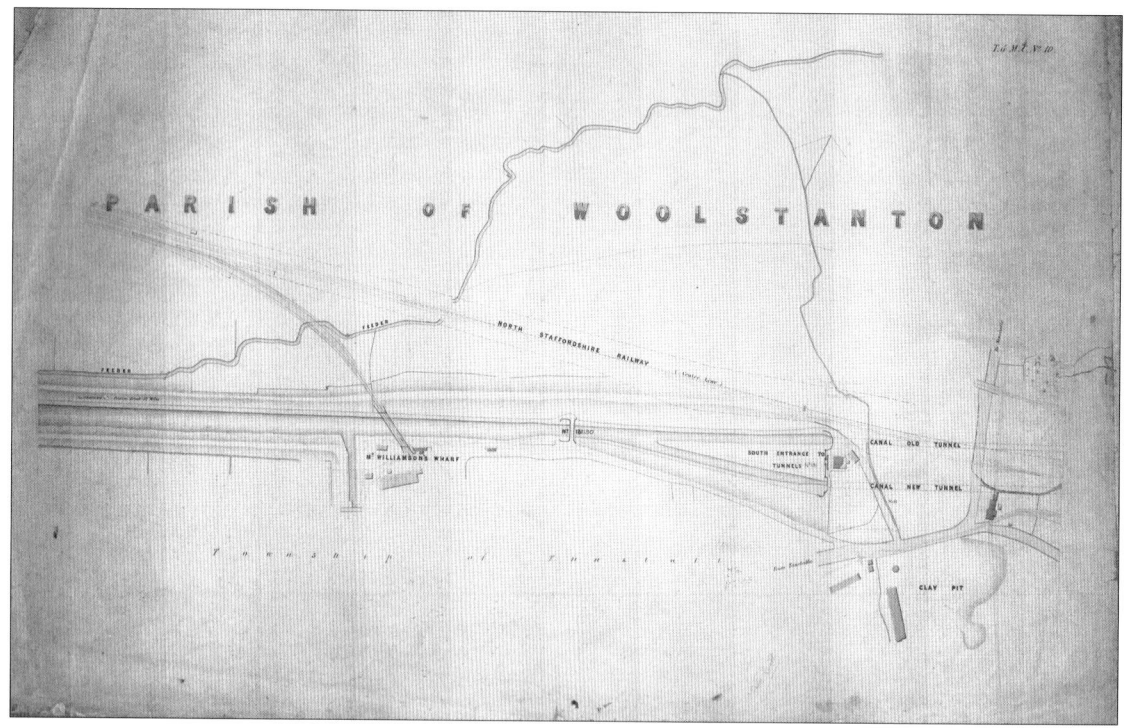

This section shows the two southern canal tunnel entrances at Chatterley and the centre line of the proposed NSR Pottery Line crossing over Brindley's tunnel in order to gain its central position above and in between the two canal tunnels. The tunnel keeper's cottage is shown above the tunnel entrances and to the left, or to the south of that, is the turnover bridge and then a bridge showing a rail link and short branch canal to the wharf and ironworks owned by Hugh Henshall Williamson (1785-1867). The ironworks began operating in 1841 and became known as the Goldendale Ironworks. Note that at this period the whole area of the canal tunnels was in the parish of Wolstanton.

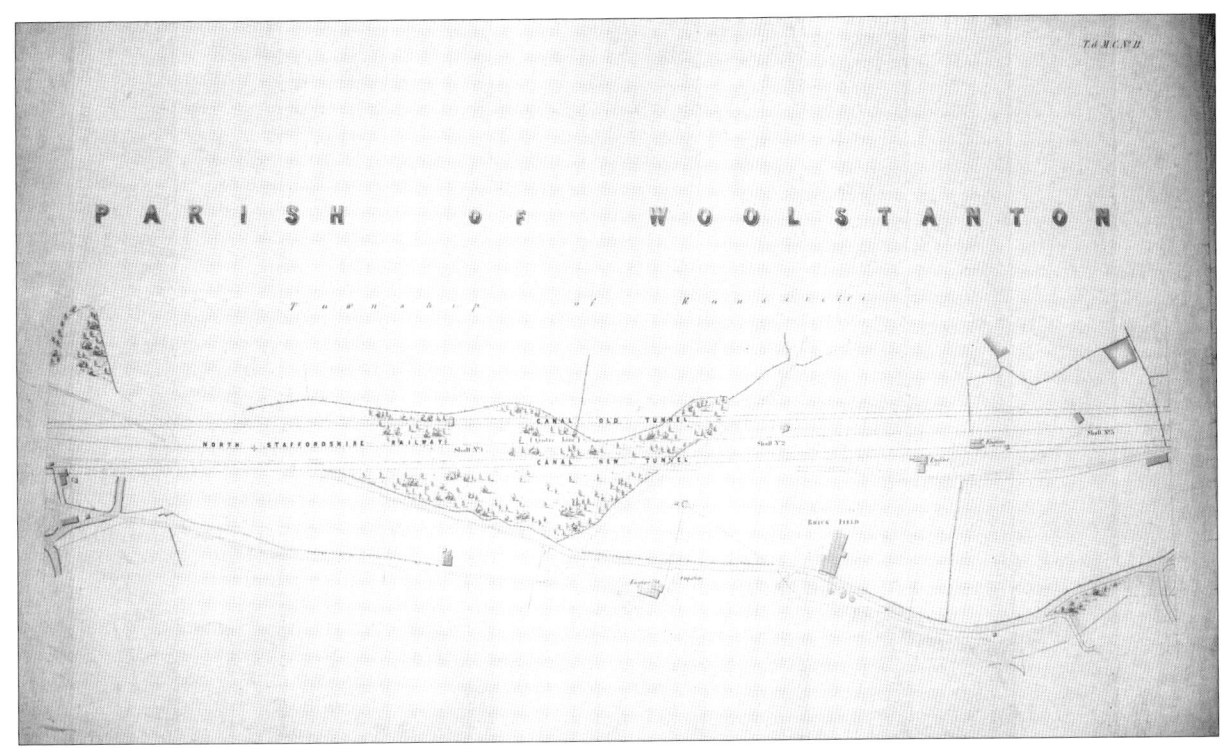

The centre line of the proposed railway can clearly be seen between the old and new tunnels and the position of Nos. 1, 2 and 3 construction shafts is marked, together with a brick field, the position of three stationary engines and a capstan. The brick field would cover an area of clay suitable for making bricks for lining the railway tunnel. The engines and the capstan were probably employed in hauling materials over the contractor's temporary tramways which are also shown.

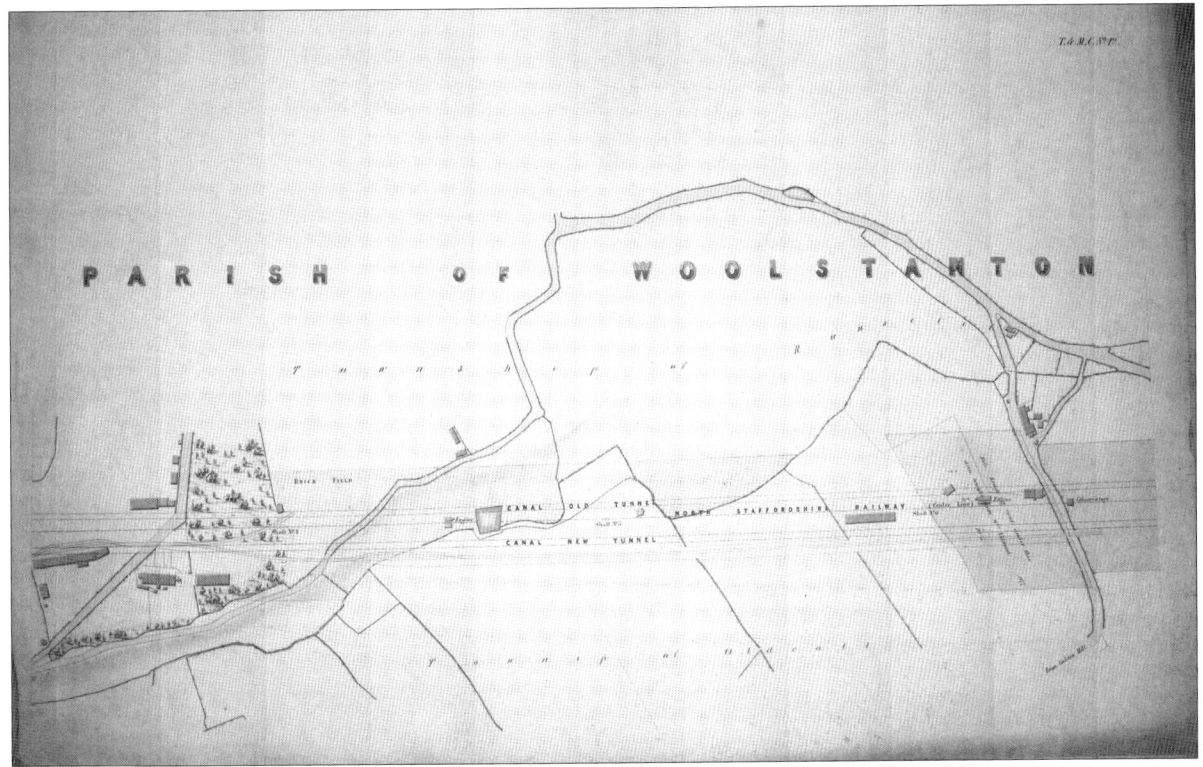

This section from left to right shows the position of shafts Nos 4, 5 and 6. It also shows another brick field and the position of another two stationary engines. The oblong highlighted to the left of shaft No. 6 represents the hamlet of Line Houses. The note written across the tunnels at an obtuse angle to the right says: *Note: Rough coal under this area bought from Miss Attwood*. Georgina Mary Attwood (1821-1885) was a niece of the Kinnerslys and at the time, owner of the Clough Hall Collieries and Ironworks which, however still traded as Kinnersly & Company.

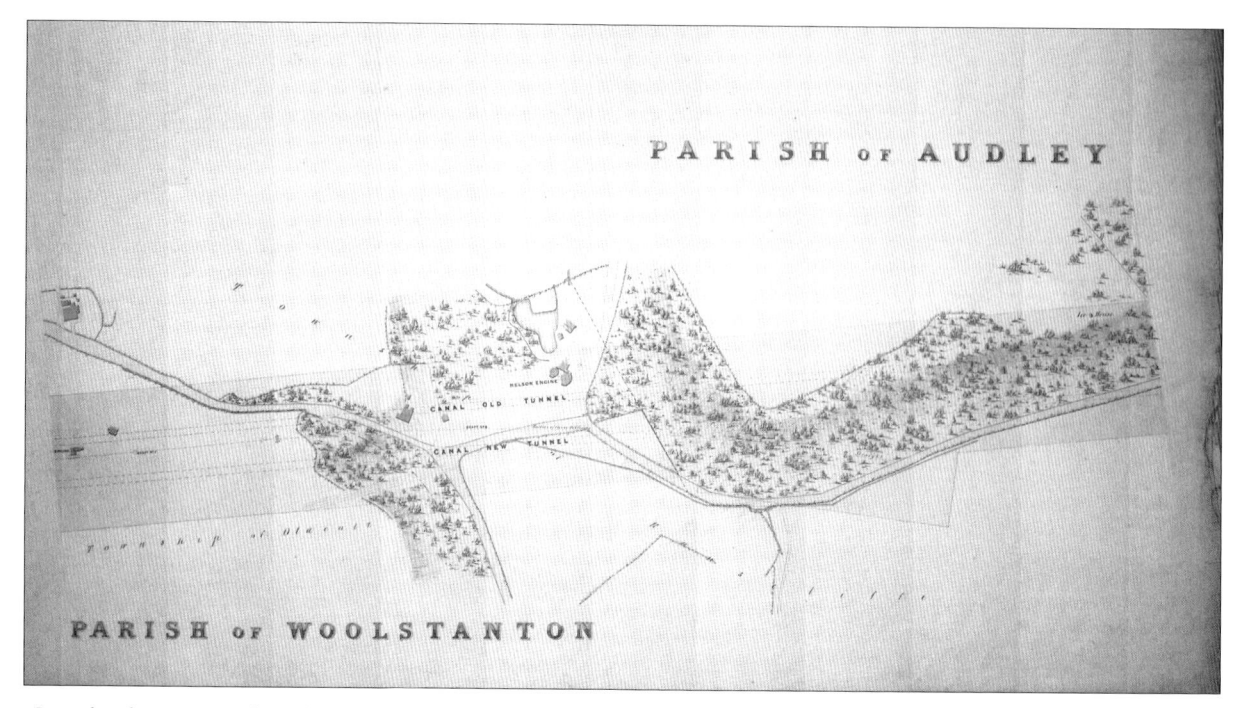

Central to this section is the *Nelson Engine* and its condensing pool. The engine, named after Admiral Viscount Lord Nelson, was part of the Clough Hall Collieries and Ironworks estate. As well as being used to pump water from nearby coal workings, the shaft was connected underground to Brindley's canal tunnel. The name was bestowed on the engine by the first John Gilbert who, along with his son, was a great admirer of the famous Admiral. Shafts Nos. 7, 8 and 9 are marked and between the latter two shafts the proposed railway leaves its central position over the two canal tunnels to cross over Telford's tunnel with a curve of 80 chains radius. Another stationary engine is shown to the far left. The wooded area above the tunnels at this point, is part of Birchen Wood.

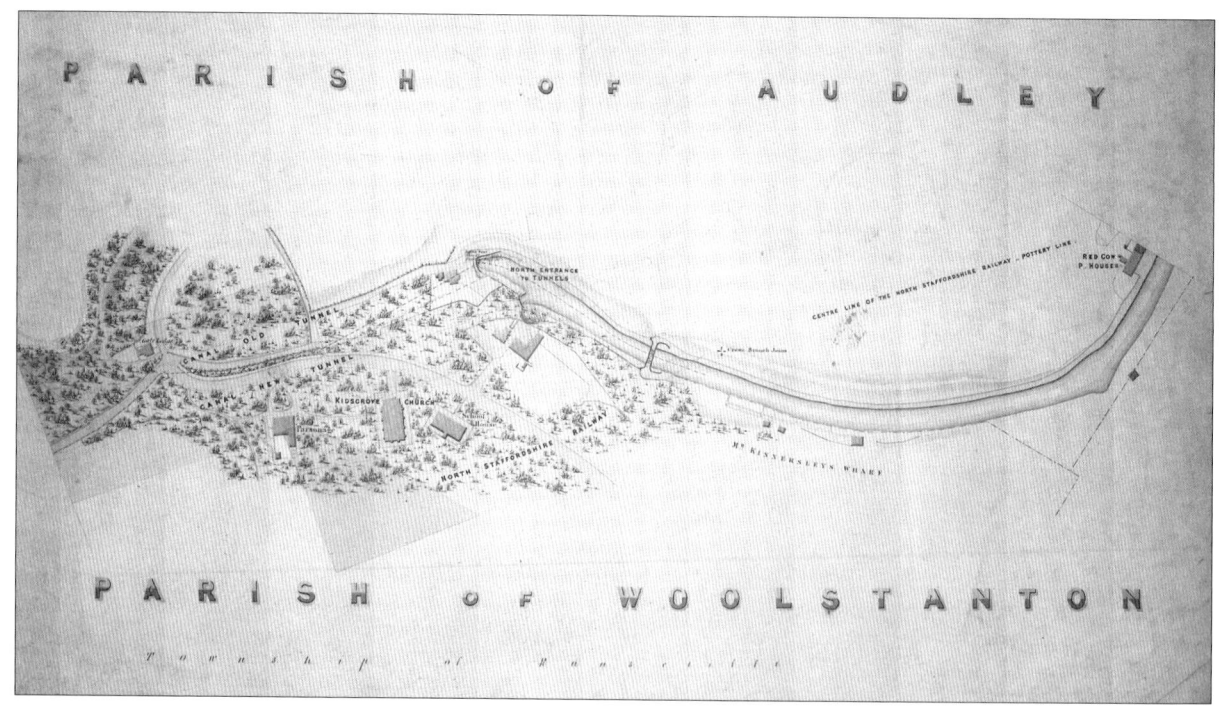

Here we have the northern entrance to the two canal tunnels with the turnover bridge to the right of them. The centre line of the proposed railway is now well clear of the canal and the site of the future Harecastle station is marked by a cross with the legend *Crewe Branch Joins*. St. Thomas' church in The Avenue is shown as is its parsonage and the Church School; all three were gifts to the town by the second Thomas Kinnersly. The incumbent of the parish at the time was the Reverend Tobias Wade (1809-1884) who is mentioned in Chapter 2. Thomas Kinnersly's wharf is shown but the family name is spelt incorrectly. Note too, the Gate Lodge for Clough Hall.

4

NORTH STAFFORDSHIRE RAILWAY

The North Staffordshire Railway (NSR) was incorporated as a statutory body in 1846, following the granting of the Royal Assent to no less than three Acts of Parliament on 26th June that year.[74] All three Acts included a provision for the railway company to acquire the shares held by the Proprietors of the Trent and Mersey Navigation either by a share swap, exchanging canal shares for railway shares or, for those shareholders not wanting to swap, by an outright purchase. There was much duplication in the three Acts and the powers were consolidated in the following year.[75] In consolidating the three Acts several concessions were made including two additional railways and the diversion of others. This followed a House of Lords Select Committee's consideration of several objections and observations from landowners and local industrialists concerning the original proposals. The shareholders of the canal company made an extremely hard and lucrative bargain for themselves in selling their undertaking to the NSR. Each canal share was exchanged for 22½ preference shares in the railway company which valued each share at £450. The holders could either take the railway shares or accept £450 in cash per share held.

Canal shareholders opting to take railway preference shares were guaranteed a twice-yearly payment of £1 6s 8d per share and 13s 4d per half share. These payments were payable from the date Royal Assent was granted until such time as all the railway lines authorised were built, or after the passage of five years, whichever was the shorter. If necessary, these sums were payable out of the NSR's capital account prior to the opening of the railway and, if required, additional capital could be created for the purpose. Once the railway lines were completed, or after five years, if that was the shorter period, the preference shareholders were entitled each half year (prior to any dividend being paid to the ordinary shareholders) to £1 per share and 10s 0d per half share. Moreover, if a dividend equal to £5 per share had been declared, the sum of £1 6s 8d per share and 13s 4d per half share was payable in addition to the sums mentioned above before any payment was made to ordinary shareholders. Once the lines were complete or the five years had elapsed, each preference share was valued at £20 and each half share at £10 for the purpose of any dividends made by the company.

As a result of this arrangement, the NSR had to make a minimum annual payment to the preference shareholders of £58,000 in perpetuity, irrespective of whether any dividend was declared and even if the company made a loss. The canal company was dissolved on 15th January 1847, no doubt leaving its former shareholders very happy with the deal. Three NSR directors represented the interests of the former canal shareholders who took preference shares in the railway company. Those directors had to hold at least 100 preference shares as a pre-qualification. The canal company chose to extract a very high price from the railway company by way of settlement rather than pursue litigation for compensation once the lines were authorised.

At their meeting held on 19th February 1847, the NSR directors considered the possibility of upgrading the canal from Preston Brook to Stoke, including an estimate of £78,000 for enlarging Brindley's tunnel but that particular proposal came to nothing. At their meeting held on 16th April 1847 the NSR's engineer, George Parker Bidder (1806-1878), reported that he had examined Telford's tunnel and found that *it had not been properly constructed and was now much out of repair*. The issue cannot have been of great magnitude as on 17th May, the following month, it was reported that repairs had been carried out with the exception of some further repairs to the towpath which would require the canal to be *stopped-up* for a week.

On 7th August 1848 the NSR completed a deed of indemnity whereby in return for a payment of £10,000 the Trent & Mersey Navigation was indemnified by the railway company against any claims arising from owners and workers of mines in the vicinity of Harecastle Hill.[76] John Henshall Williamson (1797-1867) and his brother Robert Williamson (1780-1869)[77] were specifically mentioned in the deed. Under the canal legislation owners and workers of such mines could not work within 40 yards of Harecastle tunnels without the consent of the Navigation, but they could seek compensation for ungotten coal and minerals.

On 17th June 1860 there was a problem in Telford's tunnel when a portion of the towpath fell in. It was repaired the

---

74 9-10 Vic ch. lxxxiv – The North Staffordshire Railway (Harecastle & Sandbach Line) Act; 9-10 Vic ch. lxxxv – The North Staffordshire Railway (Pottery Line) Act; 9-10 Vic ch. lxxxvi – The North Staffordshire Railway (Churnet Valley Line) Act.

75 10-11 Vic ch. cviii – The North Staffordshire Railway (Alterations & Branches) Act, Royal Assent 2nd July 1847. For a detailed explanation see *The Statutory Origins of the North Staffordshire Railway* by Allan C. Baker, *Back Track*, Vol. 27, No. 2, February 2013 and the *North Staffordshire Railway Study Group Journal* No. 32, April 2013.

76 NA RAIL 532/4. NSR Directors' meeting, 23rd May 1848, Minute 299, also NA RAIL 532/122.

77 Their father was Robert Williamson (1743-1799) who married James Brindley's widow Anne, née Henshall (1747-1826), on 30th December 1775.

This photograph dating from 1900 shows the canal adjacent to Harecastle station goods yard. The view looks south towards the northern portals of the tunnels. The main NSR Pottery Line can be seen crossing the canal and Harecastle Junction signal box is to the right behind the crane. This was used for transferring traffic from rail to canal and vice versa. The narrow boats moored alongside the towpath appear to be fully laden and their attendant horses are alongside. A private-owner Settle Speakman wagon is one of those in the goods yard. This company owned a number of local collieries, also acting as coal factors and export agents. The company was formed in 1911 by Joel Settle and Philip Speakman; in an earlier part of his life, Joel Settle had been the manager at the Birchenwood Colliery. On the opposite bank of the canal is the industrial railway which ran parallel to but above the mainline railway and then crossed over it (and consequently the canal tunnels) close to the north end of Harecastle South railway tunnel. The line served the Kidswood and Nelson Pits and ran onwards to serve another old pit and brickworks beyond Bathpool. The locomotive blowing off steam is *Alexander*, which was an outside cylinder 0-4-0 tank engine with very distinctive front tanks built by W.G. Bagnall Ltd of Stafford in 1892 (Maker's No. 1402). The locomotive was owned by the Birchenwood Colliery Company Limited. The firm's locomotives had running powers over the NSR in order to gain access to the Bathpool line which it owned.

Kidsgrove Library Local History Collection

A broadside view of the locomotive *Alexander*, which had been ordered by an agent, John Needham of Manchester, for the Birchenwood Colliery Company and delivered in March 1892. It had 12in × 18in outside cylinders, 3ft 0in diameter wheels and a wheelbase of 5ft 6in. The marbling pattern on the paintwork was achieved by dextrously rubbing tallow with a cotton rag. John Needham was a business associate of Alexander Dickinson, Managing Director of the colliery company at the time, hence the locomotive's name. Only a few years after it had been delivered the colliery company was acquired by Robert Heath & Sons, although the locomotive retained its name. When it was replaced in 1922 by a new one from the same builder, the nameplates were transferred. The line which both locomotives worked, to the Nelson and Bathpool areas, was colloquially known as Old Alex's Line; a tradition which continued, even when worked by the new locomotive!

CHAPTER 4 – NORTH STAFFORDSHIRE RAILWAY

ADDITIONAL BYE-LAWS & REGULATIONS

MADE BY
THE NORTH STAFFORDSHIRE RAILWAY COMPANY
AS OWNERS OF THE
NAVIGATION from the TRENT to the MERSEY,
On the 7th day of February, 1905.

4785

(a) Any boatman or person having the care or command of any boat or vessel who shall loiter in either of the Harecastle Tunnels, or continue any unnecessary time therein, shall forfeit and pay for every such offence a sum not exceeding Five Pounds.

(b) All pleasure boats used on the Navigation shall have affixed to them in some conspicuous place a plate bearing a distinctive number, which, subject to compliance with the provisions relating to Pleasure Boats in their several Acts of Parliament, will be supplied by the Company on application to their Canal Engineer, and any person using pleasure boats not bearing a plate in accordance with this Rule shall forfeit and pay a sum not exceeding Ten Shillings in respect of each day upon which the said boat shall be used upon the said Navigation.

(c) That no boat shall pass through any lock or shall travel along any part of the said Navigation stern first unless it be necessary to do so for the purpose of reaching a turning place, but every boat shall turn at the nearest place used for that purpose. Any person contravening this Bye-Law shall forfeit and pay for every such offence a sum not exceeding Twenty Shillings.

(d) Any boatman or other person going down the said Navigation, on coming to a lock, shall if there be another lock which is empty within 200 yards, fill the empty lock before drawing off the water from the upper lock, unless there be a boat approaching the empty lock in the opposite direction within 300 yards, in which case the said boat approaching up-hill shall go through the lock first. Every person contravening this Bye-Law shall forfeit and pay for every such offence a sum not exceeding Twenty Shillings.

(e) The Company may, if it be found necessary at any time through scarcity of water, upon giving notice thereof arrange the working of boats by turns through any of the locks on the said Navigation, and when such turns are in force no boatman or other person shall fill or cause to be filled any lock with water, if there be no boat to pass up such lock with such water, or shall empty any lock or cause to be emptied any lock on the said Navigation if there be no boat to pass down such lock with such water, but all boats shall pass up and down by turns so that one lock of water may serve for two boats.

Every person contravening this Bye-Law shall forfeit and pay for every such offence a sum not exceeding Five Pounds.

(f) When either of the Tunnels at Harecastle shall be closed for repairs, the Ordinary Rules, Bye-Laws and Regulations and Orders for entering and passing through these Tunnels other than Rule 23, shall be suspended and inoperative, and instead thereof, the following Rules, Bye-Laws and Regulations shall be in force and observed so long as either of the Tunnels be closed.

All boats going Northwards or Southwards shall pass through the Tunnel, open for traffic either way, by turns, as directed by the Tunnel-Keeper or other Officer in charge of the Tunnels.

The Tunnel-keeper or other Officer in charge of the Tunnels shall have power to arrange and marshal boats in such a manner and order as he thinks fit; any Master, Owner or Manager or other person having the care of any boat, who shall refuse to obey the order of the Tunnel-Keeper or Officer, or shall refuse to comply with any of the above rules shall forfeit and pay any sum not exceeding Five Pounds.

Given under the Common Seal of the NORTH STAFFORDSHIRE RAILWAY COMPANY this Eighteenth day of April, 1905.

HARRY LOCKETT, PRINTER, HANLEY.

A notice announcing additional Bye-laws & Regulations made by the NSR as owners of the Navigation from the Trent to the Mersey, purporting to have come into operation on 7th February 1905, but not approved by the Board of Trade until 20th April that year. There are several references to the Harecastle tunnels. *NA MT6/1417/4*

following day.[78] The NSR was not a line that acquired canals and stifled them. In giving evidence on 22nd May 1906 to the Royal Commission on Canals and Waterways of the UK, the NSR's General Manager, William Douglas Phillipps (1839-1932) said the Trent & Mersey Canal *ran parallel with the railway and extended beyond it at each end, and there was, therefore, a certain amount of prejudice in favour of the canal as regards through traffic. There was, however, no exact competition existing between them; the railway not being in a position to carry a large amount of material that was carried by canal.*[79]

By 1905 Brindley's tunnel was beginning to cause more problems. This prompted the NSR to promote additional bye-laws and regulations, which included rules to control the working of boats through the tunnels when either of them was under repair and to prevent boats loitering in the tunnels causing an obstruction to the navigation. The new arrangements took effect from 7th February 1905, although they were not formally approved by the Board of Trade until 20th April that year. The specific requirements relating to either of the tunnels being closed for repairs were as follows:

All boats going Northwards or Southwards shall pass through the Tunnel, open for traffic either way, by turns, as directed by the Tunnel-Keeper or other Officer in charge of the Tunnels. The Tunnel-Keeper or other Officer in charge of the Tunnels shall have the power to arrange and marshal boats in such a manner and order as he thinks fit; any Master, Owner or Manager or other person having the care of any boat, who shall refuse to comply with any of the above rules shall forfeit and pay any sum not exceeding Five Pounds.

The rule relating to loitering stated:

Any boatman or person having the care or command of any boat or vessel who shall loiter in either of the Harecastle Tunnels, or continue any unnecessary time therein, shall forfeit and pay for every such offence a sum not exceeding Five Pounds.

The new arrangements were very timely as the NSR Traffic & Finance Committee (T&FC) minutes of the meeting held on 16th May 1905 recorded that Brindley's tunnel had been closed for repairs following a collapse of the roof. It had been made safe by the end of that month but remained closed for further repairs until March 1906.[80] This was a worrying time for operations on the canal as in November 1905 there was also trouble in Telford's tunnel when two horses fell into the canal inside the tunnel following 30 yards of the towpath failing. No claim was made and the towpath was quickly repaired.[81] By 1907 subsidence had caused the water to creep over the towpath in two areas. Measuring from the north end of the tunnel there was a problem between 766 yards and 1,116 yards and again between 1,250 yards and 1,316 yards. There were further problems with the old tunnel in 1908 as the T&FC recorded that it would be re-opening on 13th July that year.[82]

On 15th July 1909 Ben Tillett, General Secretary of the Dock, Wharf, Riverside and General Workers' Union wrote to the President of the Board of Trade in the following terms concerning safety issues in both canal tunnels.

Dear Sir,
We shall be very glad if you will use your good offices to have remedied a defect which is the cause of a great deal of sickness, and is a hindrance to navigation, insomuch as both men and horses and the steersmen who are sometimes women, are often adversely affected.

A good many complaints are coming to us, which we have investigated, and our investigator reports as follows: *Owing to complaints of Boatmen I have inspected the Harecastle Tunnel, on the North Stafford Railway Company's Trent to Mersey Navigation; and I find:- That from the Chatterley end, between the numbers 12 & 8 the towpath is entirely submerged; the depth of water varying from 1 foot to 18 inches, more or less, for a distance of about 400 yards. Along this stretch also the Tunnel top has sagged and there is very little headway for a loaded boat, whilst the cabin tops of empty boats actually rub the Tunnel roof; and indeed will not in some cases navigate unless all trimmings are taken down and placed in stern of boat to sink her to some extent so that she can swim. Many complaints of horses being crippled have been made to me, and some have actually been killed owing to accidents in the Tunnel. So low is it in fact that taller horses frequently jamb against the roof and are only extricated with great difficulty. In neither Tunnel – horse or legging – are there any ventilating shafts, and especially concerning the latter, men passing through – the leggers – are often overcome by the smoke that practically fills both Tunnels. I unhesitatingly say these Tunnels are unfit to be navigated through and are extremely dangerous to the life & limb of all who use them.*

I shall be extremely glad for you to give this matter, which is urgent, your prompt consideration. The facts as stated speak for themselves and make the work both dangerous and unhealthy for those forced to follow this calling as an occupation.
Thanking you in anticipation, I remain,
Yours faithfully,
Ben Tillett

The Board of Trade were quick to consult the NSR and no lesser person than the General Manager himself, W.D. Phillipps, replied on 26th July 1909. This is what he had to say:

Sir,
With reference to your R. 7881 of the 21 instant, somebody appears to have given Mr. Ben Tillett a very 'picturesque' account of our Harecastle tunnels. The real facts are briefly as follows:-

Under the powers of our Act of 1831 we bought all the minerals under these tunnels and for 40 yards on either side of them, which, according to the best engineering experts of that date, was considered amply sufficient to protect them. In 1903 our Engineer reported that there were some slight signs of subsidence in the centre of the tunnels, and acting on the advice of three of the most expert Mining Engineers

---

78 NA RAIL 532/16. NSR Traffic Committee meeting, 19th June 1860, Minute 2976.
79 *The Railway Magazine*, Vol. XIX, July 1906, p77.
80 NA RAIL 532/22. NSR T&FC meetings: 16th May 1905, Minute 22631; 30th May 1905, Minute 22636 and 20th March 1906, Minute 23136.
81 NA RAIL 532/22. NSR T&FC meeting, 28th November 1905, Minute 22946.
82 NA RAIL 32/22. NSR T&FC meeting, 7 July 1908, Minute 24520.

CHAPTER 4 – NORTH STAFFORDSHIRE RAILWAY

This photograph depicts the opening of Planet Lock on the Caldon Canal in 1909. It was an additional lock created to overcome the ongoing problems caused by mining subsidence. The illustration has been included as it features four NSR directors/officers mentioned in the text. The man on the left wearing the trilby is the Chairman, Tonman Mosley (1850-1933), while the fellow with the windlass is the Canal Engineer, Harry Curbishley (1864-1931). General Manager William Douglas Phillipps (1839-1932) is sitting on the bow of the narrow boat *Planet*, which was the first boat to pass through the lock, giving the lock its name. Opposite Phillipps on the lockside with the umbrella is the company's Engineer, George James Crosbie Dawson (1841-1914).

Basil Jeuda Collection

Left: Benjamin Tillett (1860-1943), Trade Union Leader and Politician.

NSR Trent & Mersey Canal notice dated 14th July 1913, regarding a number of canal closures which includes that of the new Harecastle Tunnel, from 3rd to 16th August 1913 while repairs were undertaken.

NA MT6/2221/1

65

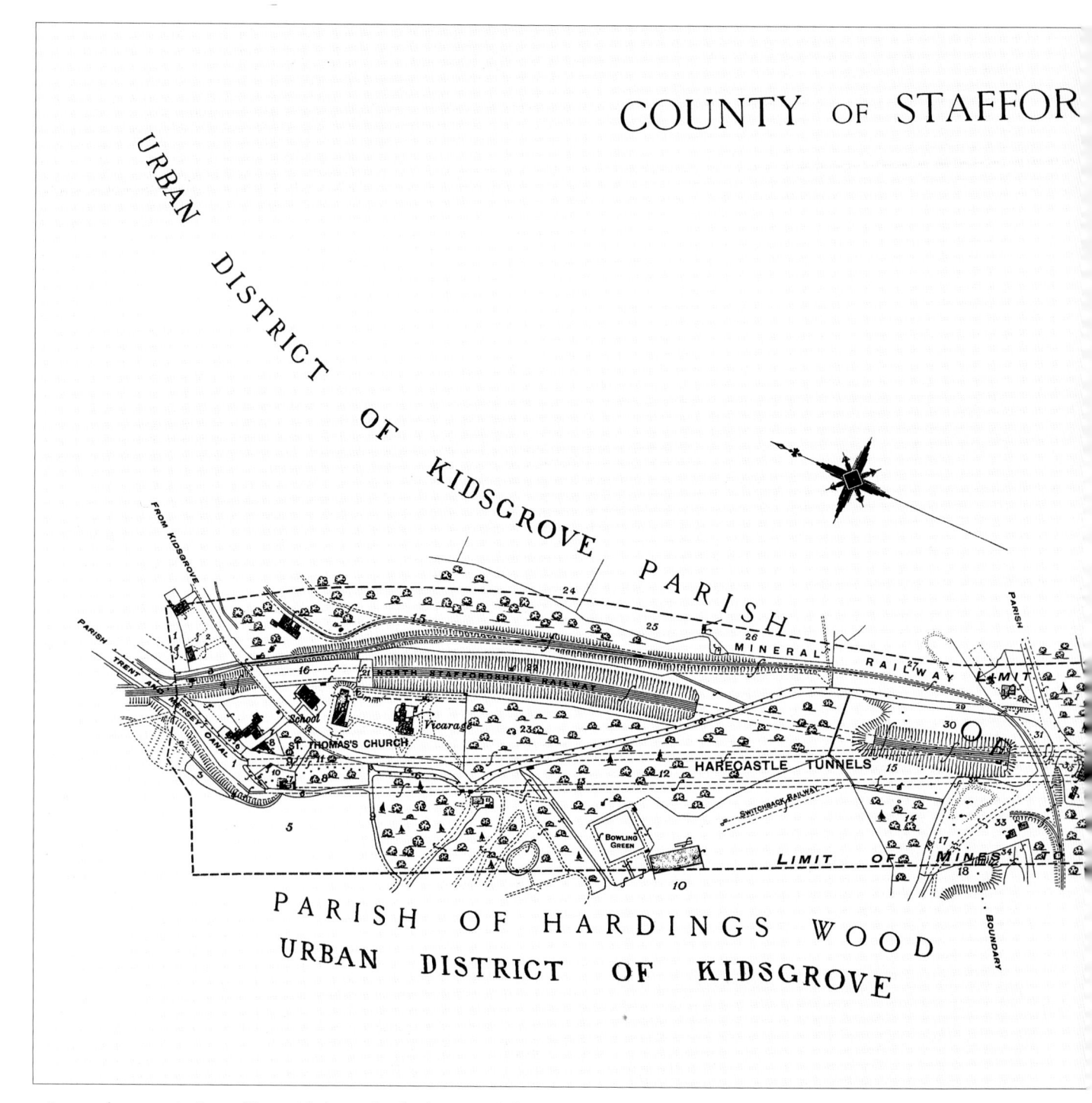

In 1904, due to continuing problems with the canal and railway tunnels from adjacent mining operations, the NSR obtained powers to compulsorily purchase mines and minerals over quite a wide area on both sides of the tunnels. The powers encompassed around 100 yards on each side, with the railway tunnel acting as the centre line, extending for some distance from both ends of the tunnels. While the company had for many years been purchasing mines and minerals in the same area to protect the tunnels, the transactions had been in accordance with the provisions of the Railways Clauses Consolidation Act 1845. As discussed in the text, this allowed for arbitration where agreement could not be reached on the value of such mines. The 1904 Act however, not only gave the railway compulsory powers, it simplified the procedure for agreeing values. The Act, which also embraced a number of other issues, including the use of electric tugs for hauling boats through Telford's canal tunnel, received the Royal Assent on 14th June 1904 (4 Ed VII ch. xliv). Parts of plans accompanying the Bill are included here as they provide an excellent view of the tunnels and their immediate surroundings at that time. The switchback railway and bowling green at the Harecastle end are part of the amusement park and pleasure grounds at Clough Hall, which date from 1890 when the estate was sold by the Heath family, as mentioned in the text.

HLRO HL/CL/BB/6/plan N22 1904

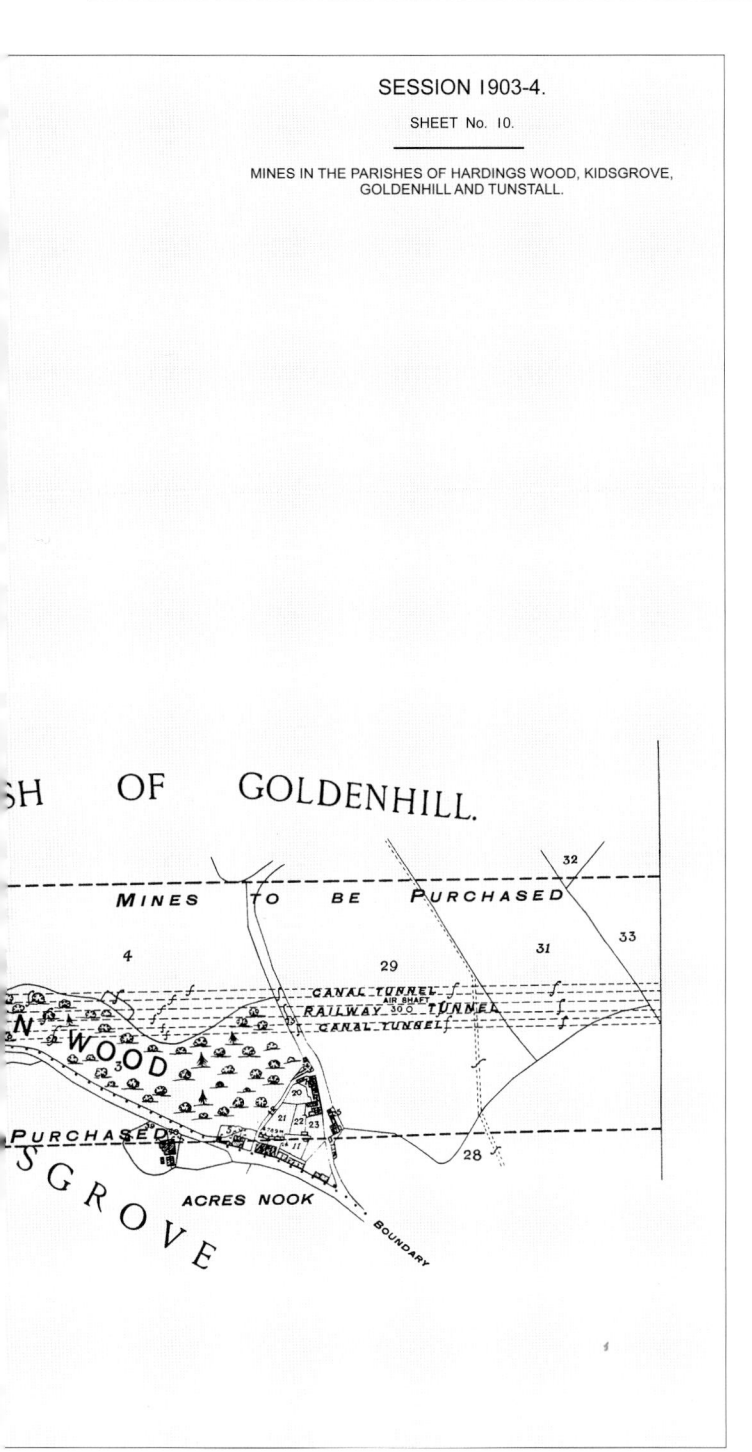

in the district, the Company promptly purchased some additional subjacent minerals for the support of the tunnels. A certain amount of mischief had, however, already been done to the tunnel which is 3,000 yards long, and a length subsided bodily some 11 or 12 inches which brings the towing path under water to a depth of possibly eight inches.

It is a fallacy to think that this has in any way reduced the headway for the horses, as the tunnel having gone down bodily, the same headway remains heretofore, the only difference being that the towing path is a few inches under water as before stated.

There is a stout wooden rail between the edge of the towing path and the water, so that it is impossible for a horse to get into the Canal and if any horses have been killed or crippled, the fame of it has not reached me.

The complaint as to there being a deficiency of headway for empty boats is also a mistake. If the tunnel roof is scratched it is entirely through the bad steering of the boatmen. Who do not take the trouble to keep in the centre of the arch.

The ventilation of the tunnels is good, the only fumes that there are ever in them are occasional instances in which the boatmen have neglected to comply with the bye-law requiring them to extinguish the fires in their cabins before going into the tunnels. I have given special instructions to our Tunnel-keeper to watch this point very carefully and to promptly summon any who are found not complying with the bye-law.

The water will, as usual, be let out of the canals next week for the August Bank Holiday and any small repairs required to the tunnels will be attended to, but Sir John Wolfe Barry who, on the instruction of the Royal Commission on Canals and Waterways, recently inspected our Canal from end to end had nothing derogatory to say about the tunnels.

I am, Sir,
 Your obedient Servant

W.D. Phillipps

On 27th July, the NSR's Solicitor, Mr. Birchell, personally delivered the General Manager's letter commenting that there was an agitation for higher wages among the men working the barges on the canal and the company regarded this as the real reason for the complaint. The trade union repeated its letter to the Board of Trade in February 1910 but complaints about the tunnels from that quarter seem to have gone away only to be replaced by complaints of a different kind from those representing traders using the canal, canal carriers and the Weaver Navigation Trustees.[83]

---

[83] The Board of Trade correspondence with the Dock, Wharf, Riverside and General Workers' Union, Weaver Navigation Trustees, the North Staffordshire Chamber of Commerce and the NSR is preserved at the National Archives – reference NA MT6/2221/1.

The NORTH STAFFORDSHIRE RAILWAY

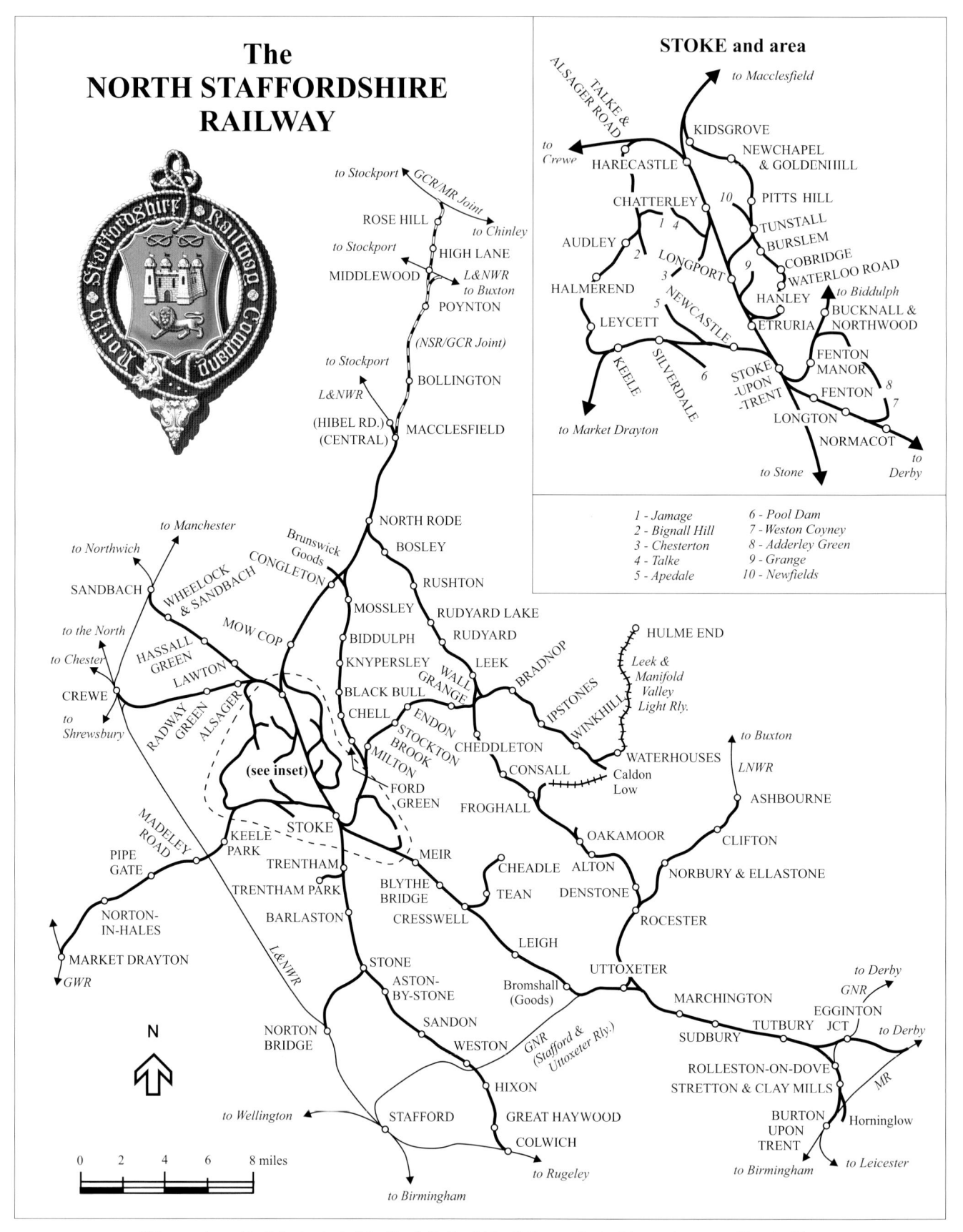

STOKE and area

Key:
1 - Jamage
2 - Bignall Hill
3 - Chesterton
4 - Talke
5 - Apedale
6 - Pool Dam
7 - Weston Coyney
8 - Adderley Green
9 - Grange
10 - Newfields

This map shows the fullest extent of the North Staffordshire Railway prior to it becoming a constituent of the London, Midland & Scottish Railway in 1923.

The late Roger Hateley, courtesy of Susan Hateley

5

AN AVOIDING ROUTE

On 24th October 1911 the NSR's T&FC received a deputation from four canal carrying companies: Anderton Company (Harry Boddington), Fellows, Morton & Company (F. Morton), Mersey Weaver Company (Charles William Shirley) and Potter & Sons (C.P. Walker). Two representatives from the North Staffordshire Chamber of Commerce were also present.[84] The deputation strongly urged the NSR to construct a canal diversion at Harecastle to avoid the tunnels. The Chairman promised that the application would receive sympathetic consideration and requested that G.J. Crosbie Dawson,[85] Chief Engineer and Harry Curbishley,[86] Canal Surveyor, should jointly prepare an accurate cost of a diversion. Pressure mounted in January 1912 when Telford's tunnel had to be closed for further repairs to the towpath. On 1st May 1912 the issue was discussed at a meeting of local authorities held at Stoke and at that meeting John Arthur Saner (1864-1952) was appointed as an independent engineer to go into the matter with the canal engineer of the railway company, Harry Curbishley. Saner could hardly be described as independent as he was engineer to the Weaver Navigation Trustees who, it will be seen, had a vested interest in a diversion. In the record of the NSR's T&FC meeting held on 4th June 1912 there is, in relation to Harecastle tunnels, a reference to a 'Plan C' amounting to over £550,000 which *was not deemed worth considering*; the same minute also stated: *Howley Park decision necessary before any further steps can be taken*.[87] At today's prices £550,000 equates to £57m and so it must have referred to the cost of a diversion. It seems reasonable to assume, bearing in mind the reference to 'Plan C', that there were at least three options under discussion. Indeed the record of the July Committee meeting[88] mentions the approval of a scheme for widening the old tunnel with details to be worked out in time for a Bill to be promoted in the next parliamentary session but this was not proceeded with. Instead Gordon Thomas who was involved in the widening proposal was asked to recommend what was required to put the old tunnel in order.[89] Nothing of any significance was done.

Towards the end of 1912, the Weaver Navigation Trustees entered the fray. On 29th November, Saner, in his capacity of Engineer to the Trustees, wrote to Curbishley saying that one of the Trustees had reported that he had been given notice of closure of Telford's tunnel for something like six months so that repairs could be undertaken, commenting that such an arrangement would be a serious impediment if all the traffic had to pass through Brindley's tunnel. On 3rd December, W.D. Phillipps replied stating that he feared a prolonged stoppage was necessary and could not some part of the Trustees' business be sent by rail! The next day Saner wrote back enquiring whether it would be possible to make arrangements for discharging goods near Harecastle station, running them through the railway tunnel and loading again on the other side where it was necessary to supply premises which did not have railway sidings, all without extra charge. Phillipps replied on 5th December saying that the same idea had struck him but he did not see how it could be worked out. He assured Saner that the old tunnel would not be interfered with, so boats coming up with cargoes of material would still get to their destinations and go back loaded or empty. He then suggested that rather than tranship at both ends of the tunnel, it would probably cost less money to carry the goods throughout by rail, even if it involved cartage at the Stoke end to the consignees' works. Saner immediately copied Phillipps' reply to Charles William Shirley (1870-1942) at Longport who was a manager for the Mersey Weaver Company and whose business interests included the merchanting and milling of pottery materials. Shirley replied instantly saying that the transfer of canal traffic to rail at Harecastle was a very good idea for the goods and grain trade but would be of no use for the raw material and crate trade. He thought the position was very serious, commenting that some of the traffic if transferred to rail might not return to the canal and that he proposed to speak to Harry Boddington (1856-1924) of the Anderton Company about the situation. It will be recalled that Shirley and Boddington were two members of the deputation that met with the NSR in October 1911.

Saner wrote to Phillipps again on 7th December 1912 and his letter casts doubt on his role as an *independent engineer* earlier in the year. The following quotation is taken from his reply to Phillipps: *If I may make an unofficial suggestion, it is that your*

---

84 NA RAIL 532/23. NSR T&FC meeting, 24th October 1911, Minute 26257.
85 George James Crosbie Dawson was born in Liverpool on 30th April 1841 and died in office on 14th June 1914.
86 Harry Curbishley was born on 14th February 1864 and joined the NSR as a pupil in the Engineer's Department in February 1877. He was re-designated Canal Engineer in 1912 and retired from the London, Midland & Scottish Railway on 30th September 1925. He died on 14th February 1931.
87 NA RAIL 532/23. NSR T&FC meeting, 4th June 1912, Minute 26596. The reference to Howley Park refers to Howley Park Coal and Cannel Company *v.* L&NWR Co. heard in the House of Lords. It concerned mine workings in the vicinity of Morley Tunnel and is also known as the Morley Tunnel case.
88 NA RAIL 532/23. NSR T&FC meeting, 30th July 1912, Minute 26717.

89 NA RAIL 532/32. NSR T&FC meeting, 8th October 1912, Minute 26767.

Company should not waste any money on the old tunnels, but at once proceed with a new cutting on the lines suggested years ago by the late Mr. Smith and myself, and more recently brought up to date by Mr. Curbishley. The first cost would no doubt be somewhat more, but the advantages afterwards would be correspondingly greater. I feel it would be more satisfactory to all parties, and would place the canal where it ought to have been originally, as, if tradition is to be believed, the old tunnel was only made out of "bravado" to shew [sic] what could be done, though no doubt the then existence of coal which could be worked direct into the boats, the galleries are still there, may have had something to do with the original decision. However that may be, there is no reason now for continuing the trouble, and I may say I am quite prepared to support the scheme Mr. Curbishley has recommended in our joint report to the Conference, at any rate in principle if not exactly in details of dimensions. Phillipps replied thus on 9th December: *The difficulty is that the "new" tunnel as we call it cannot be kept going without considerable expenditure in repairs during the six or seven years which it will take to construct the proposed converted canal. I do not propose that the money which we shall spend on this new tunnel shall be wasted, as the new section will be sufficiently large to allow a railway train being run through it, so that if and when the diversion is made in future years this tunnel will be available as a relief to our present railway tunnels which are at times badly blocked with traffic.* There was clearly some vacillation going on with NSR policy thinking! Saner still did not give up and set about querying the estimated time it was suggested it would take to construct the diverted canal drawing comparisons with the time it took to construct the Manchester Ship Canal and suggesting that there were plenty of contractors who could undertake the work in less than three years as there was only a short length of tunnel, the remainder being in open cutting. Saner and Phillipps became entrenched with their opposing views.

The next move was rather different and took place on 22nd January 1912 in the House of Commons. The Newcastle-under-Lyme Member of Parliament, Colonel Josiah Clement Wedgwood (1872-1943),[90] had obviously been lobbied by vested interests to ask the President of the Board of Trade the following question: whether he has received any representations as to the condition of the Harecastle tunnels on the Trent & Mersey canal; whether he is aware that at present traffic may be interrupted causing loss to the trade of North Staffordshire; whether the Board of Trade can bring any pressure to bear upon the railway company owning the canal to proceed with the re-construction of this canal; and, if not, will he advise the Development Commissioners as to the state of affairs and leave them to take the necessary steps to secure the permanence of this trade route independently of the railway company. Sydney Buxton (1853-1934)[91] replied that he had received no recent representations with regard to the tunnels but was aware that they were liable to suffer from mining subsidence. He made it clear that he was not in a position to require the railway company to reconstruct the canal and he understood that the case was not one in which an advance could be granted from the Development Fund, the company not being *a company not trading for profit*.

While all this was going on there was a major disagreement between Dawson and Curbishley which reached Board level. The former clearly preferred a cheaper solution whilst the latter clearly backed Saner, no doubt sympathising with the canal carriers and those who sent their goods via the canal. Two independent canal engineers were engaged to report on the condition of Telford's tunnel. They were George Robert Jebb (1838-1927) of the Birmingham Canal Navigation and Gordon Cale Thomas (1865-1921)[92] of the Grand Junction Canal. The row came to a head at the T&FC meeting held on 28th January 1913 when the following resolution was approved: *That the Company's Engineer, Mr Dawson, be requested to make an examination of and report on the Harecastle New Tunnel after considering carefully Mr Jebb's and Mr Gordon Thomas's reports, and for that purpose to make a specific inspection with such assistance as he may require from Mr. Curbishley or any other member of the Engineering staff, and that such report shall make particular reference to any risks that may be incurred, any stoppage of traffic that may be necessary, and any precautions which may be desirable for carrying out the alterations and repairs suggested by Mr Gordon Thomas;* **and further, the General Manager was requested to remind Mr Curbishley that his appointment is not that of an independent Canal Engineer, but of an assistant Engineer on Mr Dawson's staff for canal purposes**.[93] The resolution was actually prepared by the Chairman, Tonman Mosley,[94] the Deputy Chairman, Beville Stanier[95] and Rodolph Fane de Salis[96] who was a director nominated to look after the interests of the canal preference shareholders. Curbishley was clearly being rapped on the knuckles from on high!

The Weaver Navigation Trustees piled on the pressure by passing a resolution on the matter and requesting the Clerk to the Trustees, Ernest S. Inman, to send a copy to the Secretary of the Board of Trade. His letter dated 7th February 1913 not only

---

90 Josiah Clement Wedgwood was the 1st Baron Wedgwood and was sometimes referred to as Josiah Wedgwood IV.
91 Sydney Buxton was President of the Board of Trade from 1910 to 1914.
92 Gordon Cale Thomas was the celebrated engineer responsible for the famous inclined plane, opened in 1900, at Foxton on the Grand Junction Canal. He was probably recommended by Rodolph Fane De Salis, NSR director and at that time also a director of the Grand Junction Canal Company. Thomas dramatically fell from popularity in 1916 when, rightly or wrongly, he was charged with fraudulent behaviour.
93 NA 532/23. NSR T&FC meeting, 28th January 1913, Minute 26974.
94 Tonman Mosley (1850-1933), who became Lord Anslow in 1916, was the NSR's last Chairman. He attended his first Board meeting as a director on 27th January 1891, becoming Deputy Chairman on 26th January 1900 and Chairman on 19th April 1904. In 1914 he became a director of the Grand Junction Canal Company.
95 Beville Stanier (1867-1921) was first appointed as a director in 1903, becoming Deputy Chairman with effect from 22nd June 1909. He was later known as Captain Sir Beville Stanier, 1st Baronet. The baronetcy was created in 1917.
96 Rodolph Fane De Salis (1854-1931) was a director from 1899 until the NSR ceased to exist in 1923. He was also a director of the Grand Junction Canal Company and became its Chairman in 1914. He was also Chairman of the Singer Motor Company of Coventry and a director of the Great Central Railway.

Rodolph Fane de Salis (1854-1931) was one of the NSR Directors elected specifically to look after the interests of the company's Preference Shareholders. These shares had been issued to proprietors of the Trent & Mersey Canal Company who opted to exchange their canal shares for those of the railway company. He was elected Director in 1899 and is seen here in about 1890 with his first wife, Edith Louise Catherine Rousby (1855-1920) and their daughter, Edith Margaret de Salis (1882-1932). He remained a Director until the company ceased to exist in June 1923, following the Grouping of the Railways on 1st January that year.

conveys the Navigation's stance on the issue but also gives a very good insight into the amount of traffic carried on the canal. It was copied to the NSR's General Manager and to the North Staffordshire Chamber of Commerce. This is what Inman said:

Sir,
I have the honour to hand to you the following copy of a Resolution which was passed by the Weaver Navigation Trustees at their last General Meeting, viz.,

> ORDERED – That the North Stafford Railway Co. be informed that the Weaver Trustees view with alarm the interference with their traffic which will be caused by the threatened closing of Harecastle Tunnel; and urge the taking of prompt steps by the Canal Co. to obviate this.

and in doing so, I am desired to place before you the following observations.

The Weaver Trustees, who control, under various Acts of Parliament, the navigation of the River Weaver, have during the past few years spent considerable sums of money in providing and improving accommodation for the traffic passing over their Navigation and destined for Stoke-on-Trent and other places in the Pottery District of North Staffordshire. That traffic which amounts to about 250,000 tons a year consists mainly of grain, and general goods, china clay and raw pottery materials, which after being received and transferred at Weston Point Docks is forwarded from there, and after passing up the Navigation, about 13 miles to Anderton, is there transferred to the Trent & Mersey Canal by means of the Anderton Boat Lift, and thence proceeds by that Canal to Stoke-on-Trent.

The Harecastle Tunnels situated on that Canal a few miles North of Stoke, consist of two tunnels parallel with each other about 2,800 yards long; the old tunnel having been built in 1766-1777, and the new one in 1824-1827. The old tunnel is very small and without a towing path, so that the only means of locomotion through it is that known as "legging". The new tunnel has a towing path, and is in every way more convenient.

The total traffic on the Trent & Mersey Canal at present is so considerable that both tunnels are kept fully occupied, and should the new tunnel which is the one suffering through coal subsidence, have to be closed, as foreshadowed in the enclosed correspondence, even for six months, serious loss will undoubtedly be experienced, not only by the Weaver Trustees, but also by their Traders; and a considerable portion of the traffic would no doubt be permanently diverted from this Navigation, owing to the small tunnel being quite inadequate to deal with anything like the amount of traffic which it would then be called upon to accommodate.

Again, in view of the fact that the Weston Point Docks of the Trustees are situate two miles from the nearest Railway Station, and that they are consequently entirely dependent upon the Waterway for the transit of traffic therefrom, it follows that any interference with that route will inevitably prove a matter of the most serious moment to them.

The Weaver Trustees are fully alive to the difficulty in which the North Staffordshire Railway Co. are placed owing to the subsidence caused by the coal workings, but they are advised that the alternative route alluded to in the aforesaid correspondence is quite a feasible proposal, which can be carried out in from 2½ to 3 years, and, if adopted, would obviate the necessity for spending considerable sums of money in repairing the present tunnels, an expenditure which might very easily be thrown away.

I am therefore instructed to ask that the Board of Trade will be good enough to urge upon the North Stafford Railway Co. the necessity, not only for making adequate temporary provision forthwith for the traffic in the event of the possible sudden collapse of the tunnel, but also for making the necessary preparations with a view to commencing the construction of the alternative route, in view of the fact that there can be no guarantee that any repairs which may now be done to the tunnel will be effective, so long as unworked coal remains in the vicinity.

I have the honour to be,
Sir,
Your obedient Servant,
Ernest S. Inman
Clerk to the Trustees

There were two enclosures: copies of the correspondence that had ensued between Saner and Phillipps during December 1912 and a plan of the Weaver Navigation showing its connection with the Trent & Mersey Canal at Anderton and the route to the Potteries. Phillipps acknowledged receipt the following day: *I have your letter of yesterday which shall be laid before my Directors in due course. Nobody knows better than the Engineer of the Weaver Trustees who has to do with the Anderton Lift that there are times and occasions when it is absolutely necessary to stop traffic in order to effect repairs which cannot otherwise be executed, and I should think that any stoppage that is likely to take place in doing the necessary repairs to Harecastle Tunnels will necessitate a very much shorter stoppage than the Weaver Trustees found necessary when they were renewing the Anderton Lift a few years ago. You may be quite certain that in our own interests we shall not stop the traffic for one moment longer than is absolutely necessary.* In other words keep your own house in order and stop meddling in our affairs! Phillipps was renowned for having a vigorous and forthright character who called a spade a spade.

At the NSR shareholders' half-yearly meeting held at Stoke on 11th February 1913, the Chairman decided to go public on the matter knowing full well that the proceedings would receive a full report in the local newspapers, which indeed they did.[97] He said recent newspaper accounts of public meetings had expressed the view that there was likely to be an interruption to canal traffic through the state of the Harecastle tunnels. He recalled that in Sir John Wolfe Barry's report to the Royal Commission on Canals and Waterways published in 1910[98] reference was made to an *avoiding route* but this was not recommended on account of the great expenditure required, not only in construction, but in maintenance. When, however, the company had reason to fear that subsidence from mineral workings might cause considerable damage and expense, a possible route for a new section of canal had been inspected which would involve the maintenance of a shorter length of tunnel. Soon after, a deputation [this would be the 1911 deputation] joined in discussions on the position and strongly advocated the adoption of an avoiding route. While sympathising with the deputation's desire to increase the trade of North Staffordshire by means of an improved waterway, it was pointed out that the whole proposition had to be carefully examined from both a financial and engineering perspective. It was also made clear that it would not be reasonable to expect the shareholders to sanction a large capital expenditure unless there was a fair expectation of increased profit as a result of the investment. No undertaking was given on either side but the deputation promised to consider whether it would be possible to pay a higher toll to finance the capital expenditure.

The Chairman said the company followed up the meeting by instructing its Parliamentary Agent to prepare a Bill for presentation during the next session of Parliament but it was withdrawn in the autumn of 1912, primarily because of the excessive projected costs. The NSR Canal Engineer, Harry Curbishley and Colonel John Arthur Saner of the River Weaver Navigation Trustees had been asked to make a joint report and their estimates for the avoiding route were so high that it was thought prudent to give more time for consideration of such a bold project. Instead two experts of great eminence and experience [Jebb and Thomas] were engaged to report on the condition of Telford's tunnel and it was now considered that it was better to take steps to improve that tunnel rather than to proceed with an avoiding route. The Chairman concluded by stating that the NSR's engineer, G.J. Crosbie Dawson fully agreed with this course of action. The improvement work concentrated on dredging and renewing parts of the tunnel arch and invert.

However, following the publicity, Harry Curbishley was still proving to be awkward! At the T&FC meeting held on 25 March 1913[99] the Harecastle problem was considered again after which the following minute was drafted by the Chairman, Deputy Chairman and De Salis:

(1) That the amount of Mr Gordon Thomas's account for expenses etc amounting to £68 17s 3d, and the amount of £21 10s 0d for the recording and measuring apparatus be paid to Mr Thomas together with an additional fee of 50 Guineas.

(2) That Mr Crosbie Dawson the Company's Engineer be requested to carry out repairs and alterations in the Harecastle Tunnels on the lines of Mr Gordon Thomas's report, **and that for this purpose one of his Assistant Engineers, other than Mr Curbishley, should be put in charge of the work.**

(3) That all plans, sections, drawings, papers and things relating to the Tunnels are to be handed over to Mr Dawson as and when he requires them.

(4) **That the General Manager be requested to communicate with Mr Curbishley as to the two preceding Minutes, & explain that the Board requires that loyal assistance be given by the Canal staff in the carrying out of this work, and that Mr Curbishley confine himself to the work on other parts of the Canal.**

This time the message seems to have got across as at the next meeting of the Committee held on 8th April 1913 it was decided that Dawson be allowed to make use of Curbishley under his strict supervision, notwithstanding the previous ruling.[100]

However the saga was still not over. This time it was the North Staffordshire Chamber of Commerce that picked up the cudgel and requested a meeting with the Board of Trade which took place on 24th April 1913. The day before *The Times* published an *Engineering Supplement* which contained a special feature on the Potteries. The NSR took full advantage and shared a full page advertisement with the Shelton Iron, Steel & Coal Co Ltd. The NSR advertisement featured both the railway and the canal and extolled the virtues of North Staffordshire for business and pleasure. It bore the name of W.D. Phillipps as General Manager. He was clearly playing one of his masterstrokes as the feature on the Potteries also covered the railway, canal and Harecastle tunnels. This is what was said about the latter: *The old tunnel is, for all practical purposes, as good as ever, but the newer one has subsided, owing to mineral working, over a length of about 600 yards near the middle, the headway being reduced by nearly 2ft. A year or so ago there was a rumour that the tunnel might have to be closed, but there has been no further subsidence during the past nine months, and it is hoped that there is no risk of further injury. It will only be necessary to take advantage of stoppages of the traffic at holiday times to rebuild and raise the subsided part of the roof to its original height. It has been decided to install Bullivant's*

---

97 *Staffordshire Sentinel*, 12th February 1913.
98 The Report focussed on improving the links between the canals and waterways connecting the Midlands with the Humber, Mersey, Severn and Thames estuaries.

99 NA 532/23. NSR T&FC meeting, 25th March 1913, Minute 27064.
100 NA 532/23. NSR T&FC meeting, 8th April 1913, Minute 27087.

NORTH STAFFS. RAILWAY MEETING.

Mr. Tonman Mosley's Statement.

CANAL QUESTION:

Harecastle Diversion Scheme Too Costly.

THE TRADE OUTLOOK.

The 134th half-yearly meeting of the North Staffordshire Railway Company was held at Stoke on Tuesday afternoon. Mr. Tonman Mosley presided, and the other directors present were:—Mr. Beville Stanier, M.P. (deputy-chairman), the Earl of Harrowby, Sir Henry Wiggin, Bart., Sir Thomas A. Salt, Bart., Mr. Rodolph Fane de Salis, and Mr. W. Morton Philips. There was a good attendance of shareholders.

THE CHAIRMAN'S STATEMENT.

The Chairman said that that meeting was the last they would hold under the old system of accounts, and they proposed in future to hold only one meeting annually. That was going to be the rule, he believed, among all railway companies. They proposed to give the shareholders an interim dividend at the end of the half-year, and then give a final dividend after the full accounts had been made up at the end of the year. It was suggested, if they decided on that policy, that the annual meeting should be held one year in Stoke and the next in London. The next meeting, therefore, would in all probability be in February, 1914, in London, and the following year they would meet in Stoke. The accounts and tables under the new Railway Acts would no doubt require a considerable amount of explanation next year. It would take a great deal of careful examination to be able to tell exactly how the Acts worked out in comparison with those now before them. In fact it would be almost impossible to give anything like the same comparisons they had been able to give in the past.

THE COAL STRIKE.

So far as the report under their consideration was concerned, the comparisons had been very much upset by the fluctuations consequent on the great industrial disputes which took place last year, and also in 1911. They had called special attention in one paragraph of the report to the effect the coal strike had had on their receipts. They would notice, however, that in relation to minerals and also merchandise, they had, during the last half year, been making up for the deficiency of haulage on these articles which was experienced in the previous half-year, and which was due to the strike. In other words, although the receipts during the past half-year showed a considerable increase, they were really only making up for the losses sustained during the previous half-year. The only way of making a comparison of any value was by taking the whole of the year 1912, and comparing it with the year 1911, but he did not propose to inflict that comparison upon them, although he would mention a few of the more salient details. Now the receipts totalled £567,185, and showed an increase of £35,476, while the expenditure amounted to £353,974, or an increase of £31,914. That gave them a balance of £213,211, or an increase as compared with the balance a year ago of £3,562. But from the last half-year they carried forward £2,957 less than they did a year ago. On the other hand, they had £2,738 to their advantage in the debit and credit account and bank interest account.

£179,260 FOR DIVIDENDS.

That enabled them to carry forward for dividends a net balance of £179,260, which was an increase of £3,316. They would notice that they had to pay £3,525 more for their preference dividends than they did a year ago, owing to the issue of preference stock which took place in 1912, but they had a balance of £100,247 left, out of which they recommended a dividend for the ordinary stock at the same rate as last year, namely, 5 per cent. That gave them a carry forward of £10,381, as compared with £10,570 the year before. The dividend for the whole year worked out at 4⅜ per cent., as against 4¾ per cent. the previous year. Owing to dearness of money, they had been able to earn a good deal. The £2,738 to which he had just referred, with their balance to credit on capital account, had helped very considerably towards the extra dividend on the Preference Stock. In times of high bank rates like the present, it had been far better for them to have a credit at their bankers than to be overdrawn. They had reason to congratulate themselves indeed, on having got their Preference Stock out at the time they did, and at the price they did.

INCREASED EXPENSES.

Their balance on capital account stood at over £42,000 to credit, but their expenditure gave a total increase of £31,914. This sum contained an increase of £7,000 which they would find in their usual working account reserve, and £8,000 allotted for canal subsidences. The previous year they only allotted £1,000 for this. Now they had a reserve in the balance-sheet for this of £13,000. The other increases were principally in connection with the increased price of coal and increased wages, but he would deal with them separately. Before coming to that he would like to point out some new items of expenditure. There was the sum of £1,461 under Part I. of the National Insurance Act, and the sum of £238 under Part II. The staff had done wonderfully well in carrying out these new duties, and they believed that the system they had adopted had reduced the trouble and expense to a minimum. So far as some of their men who came under Part II. were concerned, they naturally thought at first sight that it would have been better for them not to have come under that section, for as long as they were in the service of the company, they were not likely to be out of employment for any length of time. If they looked at the matter more closely, however, and considered the scheme of the whole Act, they would see how hard it would be upon any of these men if they did leave their (the company's) employment, and afterwards becoming unemployed were unable to take advantage of the Act. As he had told them at one of their meetings, they had appointed a Health Committee, upon which sat representatives of the railway friendly societies, and general shelters had been erected for the use of their consumptive employees. He was very glad to say that they were doing excellent work, and also glad to inform them that the Friendly Society was most generously providing them with some extra ones for use in urban districts.

MAINTENANCE OF WAY.

So far as the maintenance of way was concerned, there had been a decrease in the expenses, but that did not mean to say that their engineer had not been busy. He had relaid with new materials—90lb. steel rails, of course—ten miles of main line, and had resleepered two more. In addition he had laid in and re-laid two miles of sidings. Two new bridges had been built, four old timber and cast iron ones had been reconstructed in wrought iron, and 17 others had been thoroughly repaired. He had also been putting in new sidings at Tutbury and Uttoxeter, and had provided on the incline at Cauldon a very good water supply from a well 220 feet deep. From this they would be able to supply by gravitation almost all their houses in the district, and also all the water required for their limestone quarries. They would notice in the engineering table that they had placed £2,000 more this year to their reconstruction account. Last year they allotted £1,000, but this year they had allotted £3,000, the account now standing in the balance sheet at £1,297 8s. 4d. Dealing with minor items in the balance sheet the Chairman said there was one to which he wished to call their attention, and that was the increase in traffic expenses amounting to £5,338. That was accounted for largely by an increase in salaries and wages amounting to £3,451. Practically all this was due to the concessions made through the Conciliation Board, and it did not cover them all, to many of them did not come into force until the 1st January this year, and therefore did not appear in the account.

THE INCREASED RECEIPTS.

Their increased receipts were made up as follows:—Increase in passengers, £809; in parcels, horses and carriages, £1,881; in merchandise, £13,734; in minerals, £14,835; on the canal, £1,656; for limestone, £733; and under the head of demurrage, £1,275. The passenger traffic was very hard to analyse and compare, for last year they still had the second class running. The total increase, however, was satisfactory. If they took the passenger traffic of 1912, and compared it with 1911, they would find a decrease in the receipts of £9,613, but this could be more than accounted for by the prolonged coal strike last year. Unlike minerals and merchandise, they could not recover passenger traffic once it was lost. The percentage of first-class passengers had increased from .97 per cent. to 1.39 per cent., which was most satisfactory, and which showed that a considerable number of second-class passengers had travelled first under the new arrangement. In merchandise they had an increase of £13,734 for the half-year, or £13,662 for the whole year, showing that, unlike the passenger traffic, they had recovered most of what was lost during the coal strike. Minerals gave an increase of £14,835 for the last half-year, but only £1,887 for the year, the same remark applying to them as to the merchandise. The canal receipts increase for the whole year was £894, although in the last six months the increase amounted to £1,656. He was afraid that they could not expect the canal to take up any traffic which was interrupted on the railway. There was no sign of it being able to appreciably increase its business. The average receipts per ton had slightly increased—for merchandise from 3s. 5½d. to 3s. 8d., and for minerals from 1s. 3d. to 1s. 3½d. The working expenses ratio to gross receipts had gone up, being 60.19 pounds sterling, against 59.32 for the railway alone and 62.24 pounds sterling, against 60.57 for rail and canal together. Train mileage showed an increase of 13,802 miles, goods and minerals giving an increase of 23,897, but passenger trains showing a decrease of 9,012; rail motors a decrease of 533; and light railways a decrease of 550. He would like to allude to their savings bank, which continued to do a very useful work. Deposits showed an increase of £4,900, and the account stood at the end of last year at £35,327.

THE CANAL QUESTION.

Turning to the canal question, the Chairman said they had noticed in the newspapers accounts of public meetings at which there had evidently been expressed a feeling that there was likely to be an interruption of traffic through the state of the Harecastle tunnels. Well, for some time past they had been giving a very great deal of attention to the canal, and more particularly to the Harecastle tunnels. In Sir Wolfe Barry's report to the Railway Commission, an "avoiding route" was referred to, but was not recommended on account of the greater expenditure necessary, not only in construction, but in maintenance. When, however, they had reason to fear that subsidence from mineral workings might cause considerable damage and expense, they themselves inspected a possible route for an open-air canal which would give them a shorter length of tunnel to maintain. Soon after a deputation from the North Staffordshire Chamber of Commerce, introduced by Mr. Boddington, discussed the position with them, and strongly advocated the adoption of an avoiding route. They (the company) were careful to explain, while sympathising with the deputation's desire to increase the trade of North Staffordshire by means of an improved waterway, that the whole proposition must be carefully examined by them (the company) both from a financial and an engineering point of view, and that in all probability they would call in expert opinion. They also pointed out that it would not be reasonable to expect their shareholders to sanction a large capital expenditure unless they could show some early return by way of interest, and a fair expectation of increased profit later on. There was no undertaking given on either side, but the deputation promised to consider whether it would be possible to pay a higher toll, and so give something in return for any expenditure which they might lay out. It was merely a friendly conference.

BILL PROPOSED AND WITHDRAWN.

They (the company) followed this up by instructing their Parliamentary Agent to prepare a Bill, and to take the necessary steps for bringing it in during the last session, but they withdrew it in autumn for several reasons. The question of carrying out the scheme known as "the cross," suggested by the majority of the Canal Commission, was again being actively discussed, especially in Birmingham and North Staffordshire, and a committee was formed to see what could be done in the matter. Their canal engineer, Mr. Curbishley, and Mr Saner, of the Weaver Navigation, were also asked to make a joint report. In the meantime they (the company) found that their estimates of expenditure were so high that the avoiding route would entail on them a very much larger expenditure than they felt justified in contemplating, and to avoid any clashing of interests they thought it better to take more time for consideration. That was the chief reason why they withdrew the Bill. Since then the expert opinions had been received, and the Hanley Park Tunnel case had been decided in the House of Lords. The advice of both the experts was to put the Harecastle Tunnel in order in preference to making an avoiding route, and their fears of further serious subsidences being dispersed by the judgment of the House of Lords, they were now acting on the advice given and had several schemes under consideration for giving better headroom and generally improving the new tunnel. They were led to believe that this could be done without any abnormal stoppage of traffic, and that there would in this way be really less delay and obstruction to the trade of North Staffordshire than if they had undertaken the construction of an avoiding route.

EXPERT OPINION.

Their engineer, Mr. Crosbie-Dawson, had carefully examined the reports of the experts, and saw no reason why the recommendations contained in them could not be carried out. He might say that if they were they would be saved the expenditure of many thousands of pounds, and would give no fewer facilities for navigation than they had given in the past. The engineers whom they consulted were Mr. Jebb, of the Birmingham Canal Navigation, and Mr. Gordon Thomas, of the Grand Junction Canal, both gentlemen of great eminence and experience. An improved waterway, such as was contemplated by the Railway Commission, would involve an expenditure far beyond the resources of a little railway company such as theirs, and would probably also involve a considerable stoppage in trade during construction. The Chamber of Commerce, he was sure, would agree with him that a stoppage in the trade would be a most serious thing for North Staffordshire and they (the company) hoped to avoid that by carrying out their less ambitious but thoroughly practically policy, always providing that no inforeseen accident or fresh development altered their decision.

THE TRADE OUTLOOK.

Concluding, the Chairman said he was afraid the outlook was not so promising. Trade seemed to be rather on the downward grade; in fact, their information led them to believe that what they called the boom had already gone by. Their expenses were increasing, and were likely to increase, owing to high prices at the present time, and also owing to the concessions they had made. The Railway Rates Bill, he was afraid, was not likely to be of much assistance to them. They did not want to get into conflict with traders by trying to force any advantages given to them under that Act. They must spend a considerable amount of money on the canal, and they must not effect economies at the expense of efficiency. Therefore, he thought that they must not look forward to high dividends for some time to come. He assured them, however, that their General Manager had a great deal of grit in him, and all the staff being loyally behind him they could depend upon it that all would be done in their interests which was humanly possible.

The report was adopted and a resolution carried declaring a dividend of three per cent. per annum on the Three Per Cent. Preference Stock and five per cent. per annum on the Ordinary Stock.

Mr. Beville Stanier, Mr. Charles Bill and Sir Thomas A. Salt, the retiring directors, were re-elected, and Mr. William Cash was re-elected auditor.

A vote of thanks to the chairman was heartily carried.

In its issue of 12th February 1913, reproduced here, *The Staffordshire Advertiser* reported on the NSR's 134th half-yearly meeting of its shareholders held on the previous Tuesday. The Chairman, Tonman Mosley, in his address, gave the reasons why the company was not prepared to entertain a diversion scheme for the Harecastle Tunnels *NA MT6/2221/1*

NORTH STAFFORDSHIRE CANAL.

THE CONDITION OF THE HARECASTLE TUNNELS.

A special meeting of the North Staffordshire Chamber of Commerce was held at the North Stafford Hotel, Stoke, on Wednesday afternoon, for the purpose of considering correspondence with the North Stafford Railway Company as to the present condition of the Harecastle canal tunnels and suggested repairs or improvements. Mr. H. Boddington (president) was in the chair, and there were also present Mr. F. W. Morton (of Messrs. Fellows, Morton, and Clayton, canal carriers, of Birmingham), Messrs. J. Ridgway, S. W. Wheatley, Walton Stanley, C. P. Walker, C. Steel, G. Lester, R. L. Johnson, T. Paxton Barratt, J. W. Pickard, G. Ridgway, C. W. Shirley, Spencer Till, F. R. Williams, and W. E. Robinson, with Mr. A. P. Llewellyn, secretary, and Mr. S. H. Dodd, assistant secretary.

The PRESIDENT explained that the canal was formed by local promoters under an Act of 1766, and after the opening years it was highly successful, because the whole of the traffic from London to Manchester and Liverpool passed over the navigation. The difficulty now was the tunnels. The old tunnel was commenced in 1766 and opened in 1777, and it was simply a narrow hole, or what they would to-day describe as a big drain, just wide enough to pass a boat through. There was no towing-path, and boats had to be propelled through by what was known as "legging." The traffic increased, and in 1827 a new tunnel was constructed. It was a considerable improvement on the old one—much wider and with a towing-path for horses. The custom since had been to work the traffic going north through one tunnel and the traffic coming south through the other one. At the time it was constructed Parliament laid down that forty yards of minerals on either side were to be reserved to maintain the tunnel, this being considered at the time to be ample protection. Experience had shown, however, that Parliament was very much out of it, and although the mines had never been worked under the tunnel, the getting of minerals from the immediate neighbourhood had caused a pull from one side to the other; the tunnel had become considerably deteriorated, the roof had crushed in, and the place had got into such bad order that about seven years ago the old tunnel was closed for 15 months and about 200 yards re-built. During that time the traffic was worked through the horse tunnel in turns. Of course, the traffic worked through by horse was much more rapid than the "legging" through the old tunnel, and that being so they managed to get traffic through, although at considerable inconvenience. Now the question had come before them owing to the condition of the new tunnel. It had become considerably deteriorated, and repairs must be carried out. It was suggested there would have to be a long stoppage of the new tunnel. If that were so, it was simply impossible to work the traffic through the old tunnel, and there would be considerable interference with the supply of potters' materials for that district. In 1911 213,000 tons of potters' materials were brought in the district by canal, as against 37,000 by rail. Therefore, if the new tunnel was considerably interfered with, experienced men thought they would not be able to get half the ordinary work through the old tunnel. These potters' materials came from the Mersey from three different ports—Ellesmere Port, Weston Point, and Runcorn. As regards the alternative of putting the materials on the rail, he did not think the railway company at the present time could supply sufficient trucks. But even if they did, they had not the siding accommodation to allow the traffic to be dealt with. Then the ports of the Mersey with the exception of Ellesmere Port, had been laid out chiefly for water traffic, and there would be difficulty in placing the material on rail. If the new tunnel were to be temporarily closed, therefore, he did not see how they could avoid having a considerable interference with the supplies of raw material, and it was of the greatest urgency that something should be done to keep the canal going. Under the Land Clauses Consolidation Act, a railway or canal company was at liberty to buy the minerals under their property with a view to protecting themselves, and if they did not choose to buy sufficient they must take the risk. Under that right the railway company had bought considerably more minerals than 40 yards, with a view to protecting the tunnel, but in the House of Lords recently, in the Howley Tunnel case it was decided that although this Act gave the canal company certain powers of buying minerals it did not take from them the right which every man possessed that his neighbour should not do him injury; therefore the view was taken now that the owner of the minerals must not do anything to injure the railway or canal. Unfortunately, the injury in this case had already been done: therefore, there was no remedy. It might be a protection in the future, but it did not help them as regards the past. They were face to face with the fact that the tunnel was in exceedingly bad order; if it was to be repaired they were likely to suffer great inconvenience to their business, if not a stoppage of a large portion. Mr. Boddington went on to say that in 1911 the Canal Engineer of the North Staffordshire Railway Company had brought out a scheme for the diversion of the canal to take the place of the tunnel—there would only be a short tunnel. A deputation consisting of canal traders and members of the Chamber of Commerce waited on the Railway Company and impressed on them their views that such diversion was highly desirable in every interest of the district. They came away feeling they had made a very favourable impression on the company, and they were told by the Railway Company that they would deal with the matter by that scheme or some other.

The SECRETARY then proceeded to read correspondence which had taken place with the Railway Company. Mr. W. D. Phillipps, the general manager, writing under date of Oct. 11, said:—"With reference to the interview between a deputation from your Chamber and my directors last autumn, I am directed to inform you that my Board, after much consideration, think that it will not be opportune for them to go to Parliament next session for an Act to enable them to construct a diversion of their canal so as to avoid the Harecastle tunnels, as in view of the very influential committee appointed at a meeting of local authorities at Stoke-on-Trent, on the 1st of May last, with regard to improving the waterway between the Mersey and the Potteries, my directors feel that a Parliamentary Committee would be very likely to throw out a bill promoted by them at this juncture, and possibly even consider it an impudent attempt to prejudice, in their own favour, the general question. Mr. Saner, the independent engineer appointed by the Conference of Local Authorities and Associations, in his report to that committee, is very outspoken in his opinion on this point. I am further to inform you that they have determined in the meantime to take such steps as may be necessary to put the existing tunnels in thoroughly good order."

The Secretary of the Chamber replied as follows under date of Oct. 21:—"I am afraid that I do not quite understand your letter, and I shall be glad if you can give me some further information before the next meeting of my Chamber. You refer to Mr. Saner's report to the Conference of Local Authorities. I am informed that the committee has not met since Mr. Saner and Mr. Curbishley were asked to make a joint report, and that, consequently, no report has been given to the committee. I am sure my Chamber will be greatly disappointed if nothing is done during the next session of Parliament, as they do not consider the present canal tunnel capable of proper repair, and even if repaired it would be liable to the present state of affairs again arising if mining is to be continued in the district. You will remember the deputation pointed out to your directors the disastrous consequences of any suspension of the canal traffic to the potting industry of the district, and I trust your directors will not abandon a scheme which not only met the difficulties of to-day, but secured the position of a navigable navigation for all reasonable time to come."

Mr. Phillipps again wrote on the 23rd of October:—"Mr. Saner very courteously furnished us with an 'advauce' copy of his report, and when you have read it you will agree that my directors, having appointed their general manager to represent them on the committee, and having allowed their Canal Engineer to be associated with Mr. Saner as engineering expert, would be stultifying themselves and treating the committee with great discourtesy if they were to go their own way and promote a bill in Parliament, which the committee would be bound to oppose if they accept Mr. Saner's views. As it would probably take 10 years to construct the proposed canal diversion at Harecastle (including the time necessarily occupied in getting an Act of Parliament, preparing working drawings, and letting the contract), the existing 'new' tunnel will have to undergo very heavy repairs *in any case* if it is to be kept open, and my directors have therefore asked Mr. G. R. Jebb, of the Birmingham Canal, who has had more experience in repairing canals subject to mineral subsidence than any man living, to advise them as to what must be done, and you may rely on it that my directors fully realize their responsibilities and will do all that is humanly possible to prevent the possibility of interruption to the canal traffic, which they deprecate quite as unreservedly as your Chamber does."

On Jan. 17, Mr. Llewellyn wrote to Mr. Phillipps that the Chamber had considered the matter and had passed the following resolution:—"The Chamber of Commerce, having considered the correspondence with the North Staffordshire Railway Company, regrets the North Staffordshire Railway Company are not going on, during the ensuing session of Parliament, with their scheme of diversion of the canal at Harecastle, which the Chamber favours as against repairs of the tunnels, during the execution of which, it feels, the Potteries must suffer the gravest inconvenience in any stoppage of their supplies of material; and suggests that a special meeting of the Chamber be called after the meeting of the local committee on the 20th inst. to consider the Engineer's report, when the Chamber will have more information at their command to enable them to arrive at a decision."

On Jan. 28 Mr. Phillipps replied:—"I laid your favours before my directors to-day. They have now been advised by competent engineers that the existing tunnels can be reinstated without any very large expenditure of money or any longer stoppages than would be necessary to keep the existing canal going during the carrying out of the diversion scheme, which your Chamber is advocating. As in view of the decision of the House of Lords in the Howley tunnel case, there is every probability that the mine-owners will in the future be more careful how they do damage to the tunnel, my directors feel they will not be justified in asking their shareholders to spend such a large sum of money as the proposed diversion of the canal would cost. I am to point out that you are under a misapprehension in thinking that the company undertook to go to Parliament for a bill to obtain powers to make a diverted canal. What was said was that in case of its being finally adopted a bill would have to be promoted in Parliament, but that expert engineering advice would have to be obtained and the financial question most carefully considered."

Mr. Llewellyn also read a copy of letter sent by the Mersey Weaver Navigation to the Board of Trade:—"Feb. 7,—I have the honour to hand you copy of a resolution which was passed by the Weaver Navigation Trustees at their last general meeting—namely, 'Ordered, that the North Staffordshire Railway Company be informed that the Weaver Trustees view with alarm the interference with their traffic which would be caused by the threatened closing of Harecastle tunnel and urge the taking of prompt steps by the Canal Company to obviate this.' In doing so, I am desired to place before you the following observations:—The Weaver Trustees who control under various Acts of Parliament the navigation of the river Weaver have during the past few years spent considerable sums of money in providing and improving the accommodation for traffic passing over their navigation and destined for Stoke-on-Trent and other places in the Potteries district of North Staffordshire. That traffic, which amounts to about 250,000 tons a-year, consists mainly of grain and general goods, china clay, and potters' raw materials, which after being received and transferred at Weston Point docks is forwarded from there, and after passing up the Navigation about 13 miles to Anderton is there transferred to the Trent and Mersey Canal by means of the Anderton boat lift, and then proceeds by that canal to Stoke-on-Trent. The Harecastle tunnels, situated on the canal a few miles north of Stoke, consist of two tunnels parallel with each other, about 2,800 yards long, the old tunnel having been built in 1766–77 and the new one in 1824–27. The old tunnel is very small and without a towing-path, so that the only means of locomotion through it is that known as 'legging.' The new tunnel has a towing-path and is in every way more convenient. The total traffic on the Trent and Mersey Canal at present is so considerable that both the tunnels are kept fully occupied, and should the new tunnel, which is the one suffering through coal subsidence, have to be closed as foreshadowed in the correspondence enclosed, even for six months, serious loss will undoubtedly be experienced, not only by the Weaver Trustees, but also by their traders, and a considerable portion of the traffic would undoubtedly be permanently diverted from this navigation owing to the small tunnel being quite inadequate to deal with anything like the amount of traffic which it would then be called upon to accommodate. In view of the fact that the Weston Point docks of the Trustees are situated two miles from the nearest railway station, and that they are consequently entirely dependent upon the waterway for the transit of traffic therefrom, it follows that any interference with that route would inevitably prove a matter of the most serious moment to them. The Weaver Trustees are fully alive to the difficulty in which the North Staffordshire Railway Company are placed owing to subsidences caused by the coal working, but they are advised that the alternative route alluded to in the correspondence is quite a feasible proposal, which could be carried out in from two and a-half to three years, and if adopted would obviate the necessity for spending considerable sums of money in repairing the present tunnels, an expenditure which might very easily be thrown away. I am therefore instructed to ask that the Board will be good enough to urge upon the North Staffordshire Railway Company the necessity of not only making adequate temporary provision forthwith for the traffic in the event of the possible sudden collapse of the tunnel, but also for making the necessary preparations with a view to commencing the construction of the alternative route in view of the fact that there can be no guarantee that any repairs which may now be done to the tunnel will be effective so long as unworked coal remains in the vicinity."

Mr. MORTON mentioned that the traffic which his company dealt with between the Midlands and the Ports of Liverpool had to pass through these tunnels. When the old tunnel was closed, considerable difficulty was experienced, but if the new one was closed it was absolutely impossible for the traffic to be worked through the old one. It was the same thing as trying to make a pint pot hold a quart of water. Their trade was bound to suffer. The North Staffordshire canal was one of the best-kept railway-owned canals in the kingdom, and he reminded the Chamber that the company had without being pushed in the matter improved the canal and also increased their water supply. Therefore, he did not think it was desirable that any of them should take up an antagonist attitude to the railway company. Now came the question of the amount of money to be provided for making this diversion which many of them who had had experience of canals felt persuaded was the only way of dealing with the problem. He was not an engineer, but he felt this diversion could be made for about £250,000 or £300,000, and as carriers on the canal they were not adverse to paying an increased toll to help pay the interest on that outlay. That increased toll and the saving which would be effected in repairs to the old tunnel would, he estimated, be sufficient to provide interest at 4 per cent. on two-thirds of the amount required. That being so, it should do away with the financial difficulty. As an alternative scheme, he suggested that there should be five locks on each side of the hill, and the water pumped to the summit. He thought the Railway Company had been very badly advised to repair the present tunnels. The period of ten or twelve years mentioned for the carrying out of a diversion scheme was absurd. The whole thing could be done in two and a-half or three years, and he would undertake to find a contractor who would do the work.

Mr. J. RIDGWAY said the immediate difficulty was the temporarily carrying on of traffic whilst the diversion was being made or whilst the tunnel was being repaired. It depended largely on the condition of the tunnel itself. The proposal of the Mersey Weaver Navigation Trustees as to temporarily bridging over the difficulty was a little vague.

Mr. BODDINGTON stated that when the Railway Company proposed to close the canal for six or eight months it was with a view of rebuilding the bad portions, but he was told that with a little patching, which could probably be done at week-ends, it could be kept going for some time.

After further discussion, it was agreed, on the motion of the PRESIDENT, seconded by Mr. J. RIDGWAY:—"That this Chamber, having heard read the letter of the Weaver Navigation Trustees to the Secretary of the Board of Trade, under date the 7th inst., respecting the Harecastle canal tunnel and the North Staffordshire Railway Company, entirely agree with the request contained in the last clause of the letter, and urges the Board of Trade under the very important and exceptional circumstances to press the North Staffordshire Railway Company to proceed with the deviation canal, and in the meantime to make such arrangements as will enable the present canal traffic to be carried on until the new works can be ready."

It was decided to send copies of the resolution to the President of the Board of Trade, to the North Staffordshire Railway Company, and to the Weaver Navigation Trustees.

Report of a meeting of the North Staffordshire Chamber of Commerce held on 12th February 1913, as recorded by *The Staffordshire Advertiser* in its issue of Saturday 15th February, regarding the condition of Harecastle Tunnel. This issue is discussed in the text. The underlining in the newspaper clip refers to the Lands' Clauses Consolidation Act 1845, 8 Vic. ch. xviii, which received the Royal Assent on 8th May 1845. Part of its Preamble refers to the acquisition of lands required for undertakings or works of a public nature. The Act does not specifically refer to canals or railways.
NA MT6/2221/1

This joint NSR advertisement with the Shelton Iron, Steel & Coal Company Limited appeared in *The Times Engineering Supplement* on 23rd April 1913. The advertisement accompanied a feature on the Potteries which disclosed, for the first time in public, the NSR's intention to employ electric haulage through Telford's tunnel.

system of rope haulage in this tunnel as an experiment. **As there are no ventilating shafts in the tunnel the towing barge will have to be worked by electric power, and it will be necessary for the company to construct a power station at the Chatterley end of the tunnel.** The last statement appears to be the first time that the plans for electric haulage were made public. What a blow to the Chamber who met the next day.

The Chamber was represented at the Board of Trade meeting by its President, Harry Boddington. He was, of course, Harry Boddington from the Anderton Company, canal carriers and had been campaigning against the NSR in one guise or another since 1911. He was supported by the Vice President, Sydney Malkin (1865-1953), a tile manufacturer. Boddington commenced by stating that the old tunnel was closed seven years ago for eighteen months for repairs, but the possible closing of the new tunnel might, owing to subsidence, have to be closed for six months to enable repairs to be carried out. He said the continued use of this tunnel was vital to the district as most of the clay for the Potteries came through it; the railway could not handle the traffic even if they could load it. He explained that white clay could not be put into ordinary open rail wagons and that, in any case, there were no sidings where the traffic could be handled. He considered that the estimate of £350,000 which the NSR had mentioned, as the cost of constructing a canal diversion, was excessive and that initially a cost of only one third of that amount had been mentioned.[101]

Boddington then referred to the article in *The Times* but was rather dismissive of it. He said that if the article correctly represented the position, the district had nothing to fear, but he doubted whether it was accurate and believed it to be inspired by the railway company, especially because, as far as he knew, this was the first time that a public reference had been made to the possibility of adopting a new system of rope haulage through the tunnel. What the traders felt was that after all that had been said as to the possibility of subsidence there ought to be an authoritative statement as to the condition of the tunnel so that they could know what the facts really were. The NSR now spoke of repairing the tunnel in holiday time and nothing more might in fact be wanted, but the traders ought to know for certain how they stood.

W.F. Marwood, Assistant Secretary, Board of Trade explained the Board's powers for ordering an inspection under section 41 of the Railway and Canal Traffic Act 1888. He pointed out that if the Chamber wished to apply for such an inspection, it would be necessary for them to allege that the canal was actually *in such a condition as to be dangerous to the public or to cause serious inconvenience or hindrance to traffic*. However, he further explained that even if an inspection were made, the Board had no compulsory powers to force the NSR to take any remedial action. Marwood said that he would meet with W.D. Phillipps to see if he could ascertain exactly what the company thought the present condition of the tunnel to be. He added that it was possible that the recent change in the NSR's attitude was due to the decision of the House of Lords in the *Morley Tunnel Case* which laid down that a railway company had a common law right to lateral support for its tunnels outside certain limits to which the Mining Code in the Railway Clauses Act applied, which would diminish the danger of subsidence in future.[102]

Reference was made to the Joint Committee of Local Authorities which was considering the larger question of waterways between the Mersey and the Potteries. According to Boddington, Phillipps' suggestion that the NSR could not make any proposal while this committee was considering this broader issue was only pretence. He proclaimed that the investigations of the committee were really useless and went on to say that it was originally appointed to consider only the issue of Harecastle tunnels and that there was no chance whatsoever that the present idea to take over the Trent & Mersey Canal and the Weaver Navigation would produce any real result. Moreover, in the context of the possibility of any new canal, he pointed out that the NSR, as owners of the Trent & Mersey, had a monopoly of the main water supply, thereby putting the railway company in a commanding position.

Marwood agreed to talk to Phillipps which indeed he did and there were then further exchanges between the Board, the NSR and the Chamber but none of this resulted in a solution that was acceptable to the Chamber. On 30th July 1913 the Chamber sent a copy of the following resolution to the Board of Trade:

RESOLVED (Unanimously):-

That this Chamber having heard and considered the further correspondence which has passed between the Board of Trade and the Secretary of this Chamber, is of opinion that the condition of the (new) Harecastle Tunnel on the Trent and Mersey Navigation is in such a condition as to cause serious inconvenience or hindrance to the traffic of the Staffordshire Potteries, and requests the Board of Trade to direct such Officer or other person as they may appoint for the purpose, to inspect the said (new) Tunnel and make a report thereon to the Board of Trade.

The Board of Trade appointed Lieutenant Colonel Edward Druitt (1859-1922) to carry out the inspection. This is his report dated 18th August 1913:

Sir,
I have the honour to report for the information of the Board of Trade, that in compliance with the instructions contained in your Minute of the 31st July, I have inspected the Harecastle (new) Tunnel on the Trent and Mersey Navigation, under Section 41 of the Railway and Canal traffic Act of 1888.

---

101 These cost estimates conflict with the figure of £550,000 for 'Plan C' under NSR Traffic & Finance Committee Minute 26596, 4th June 1912.

102 Howey Park Coal and Cannel Company v. L&NWR Co concerning mining in the vicinity of Morley Tunnel which was 2m 12ch long and located on the line from Leeds to Batley. The House of Lords ruled that a railway company has a common law right to lateral support for its tunnels beyond the 40 yards distance to which the Mining Code in the Railway Clauses Consolidation Act 1845 applied.

The new tunnel was built by Telford in 1827 and lies 90 [sic] yards to the east of the old tunnel built by Brindley in 1777, and the North Staffordshire Railway Company's railway tunnel runs between the two canal tunnels, at a higher level. Neither the old tunnel, which is a small one 8ft 6ins wide, nor the railway tunnel shew [sic] any signs of subsidence. The new tunnel is 14ft wide of which about 5ft is taken up by the towing path, leaving 9ft waterway, and the average headway above water level in the parts that have not subsided or have done so almost inappreciably is 9ft 6in. The depth of water in this part is 5ft 6in. The most heavily laden boats draw 3ft 9in as a maximum when carrying about 25 or 30 tons load. Their beam is 7ft, and at present where the greatest subsidence has taken place, the masts of lightly laden boats are in close proximity to the roof and are said sometimes to scrape it.

I went through the tunnel from end to end accompanied by Mr Crosbie Dawson, the Engineer to the North Staffordshire Railway, his assistant, the Canal Superintendent, and Mr Malkin, the President of the North Staffordshire Chamber of Commerce.

Assuming the original height of the crown of the arch of the tunnel to be 10ft above the water level (but it may have been some inches lower) then from the Harecastle end of the tunnel to about the 500 yards mark the average subsidence is about 6in. From the 500 yards mark to the 700 yards mark the average is about 1ft 6in and from the 700 yards mark to the 1,500 yards mark the average amounts to from 2ft 3in to 3ft 3in. From the 1,500 yards mark the subsidence diminishes, and from the 1,600 yards mark to the Chatterley end of the tunnel the average subsidence is from 3in to 4in.

A length of 11 yards of the arch at its worst place between the 900 yards mark and the 1,000 yards mark, was rebuilt during the coal strike last year, giving the full 10ft height above water level, and is standing very well. During the holidays at the beginning of this month, a further length of 60ft of the arch was rebuilt, at the lowest part, about the 1,000 yards mark, giving a 10ft headway above water level. As the canal can be closed for only short periods such as the late holidays without interfering with traffic, only short lengths can be dealt with at a time, as the necessary staging has to be erected and subsequently removed, and the old brickwork which is very hard and the shale rock above it cut out, before the new arch can be built. I saw the new work in progress and from my examination of the tunnel, I think the whole of the brick work right through is in a sound condition, but in places the face of the brick work has come away, but these patches can be cut out and rebuilt. From the opening up of the arch of the tunnel where the new work is in progress, it can be seen that the whole surrounding ground has bodily subsided with the tunnel, as the rock is in contact with the outside of the arch and it is not the tunnel alone which has subsided. As far as I could judge there has been no recent subsidence anywhere in the tunnel, and I am informed that the greatest amount took place prior to 1903, and has been little in the last 2½ years, and during the past year almost imperceptible, and although it is impossible to forecast with accuracy what may happen in a district with old mine workings underneath such a tunnel, I do not think there is ground for apprehending any further serious subsidence.

The Company have purchased all the coal underneath all three tunnels and for a space of 40 yards outside the two canal tunnels, and are still purchasing further seams when it appears advisable. I think the course they propose, viz: to go on rebuilding the arch of the tunnel and headway of 10ft above water level as opportunity occurs, is the best method to adopt without unduly interfering with the traffic. This could

This is Lieutenant Colonel Edward Druitt (1859-1922), who in 1913 inspected Telford's tunnel on behalf of the Board of Trade, prior to the installation of the electric haulage system.

be done much more quickly if the traffic through the tunnel could be stopped for a longer period, but this must depend on the local trade conditions.

The traffic is conducted by horse traction and a certain amount of inconvenience is caused by the towing path being under water for a certain length where the subsidence exceeds 2ft, but the Company are intending, I understand, to make a trial of electric haulage, and if this is successful, then the towing path could be removed, and the barges could be kept in the middle of the tunnel under the highest point of the arch, instead of as now over to one side, and a greater headway would be given.

I may say in conclusion that the NSR gave me every facility for inspecting the tunnel, and all possible information regarding its history from an engineering point of view.

Lt. Col. E. DRUITT

Druitt must have inspected the tunnel when it was closed for the annual Wakes Holiday stoppage. The new tunnel was closed for repairs from midnight, Sunday 3rd August 1913 until 8pm on Saturday 16th August. Copies of the inspection report were sent to the Chamber and the NSR and that was that. The skirmishing was over.[103]

---

103 The Board of Trade correspondence with the Dock, Wharf, Riverside and General Workers' Union, Weaver Navigation Trustees, the North Staffordshire Chamber of Commerce and the NSR is preserved at the National Archives – reference NA MT6/2221/1.

RAILWAY DEPARTMENT,

BOARD OF TRADE,

8, Richmond Terrace,

Whitehall, London, S.W.

18th. August, 1913.

SIR,

I have the honour to report for the information of the Board of Trade, that in compliance with the instructions contained in your Minute of the 31st. July, I have inspected the Harecastle (new) Tunnel on the Trent & Mersey Navigation, under Section 41 of the Railway and Canal Traffic Act of 1888.

The new tunnel was built by Telford in 1827 and lies 90 yards to the east of the old tunnel built by Brindley in 1777, and the North Staffordshire Railway Company's railway tunnel runs between the two canal tunnels at a higher level. Neither the old tunnel, which is a small one 8ft. 6ins. wide, nor the railway tunnel shew any signs of subsidence. The new tunnel is 14ft. wide of which about 5ft. is taken up by the towing path, leaving 9ft. waterway, and the average headway above water level in the parts that have not subsided or have done so almost inappreciably is 9ft. 6ins. The depth of water in this part is 5ft. 6ins. The most heavily laden boats draw 3ft. 9 ins. as a maximum when carrying about 25 or 30 tons load. Their beam is 7ft., and at present where the greatest subsidence has taken place, the masts of lightly laden boats are in close proximity to the roof and are said sometimes to scrape it.

I went through the tunnel from end to end accompanied by Mr. Crosbie-Dawson the engineer to the

North

The Assistant Secretary,
Railway Dept.,
Board of Trade.

This is the original version of Lieutenant Colonel Druitt's report on his inspection of the tunnel dated 18th August 1913. *NA MT6/2221/1*

North Staffordshire Railway, his assistant, the Canal Superintendent, and Mr. Malkin the President of the North Staffordshire Chamber of Commerce.

Assuming the original height of the crown of the arch of the tunnel to be 10ft. above the water level, (but it may have been some inches lower), then from the Harecastle end of the tunnel to about the 500 yards mark the average subsidence is about 6ins. From the 500 yards mark to the 700 yards mark the average is about 1ft. 6ins. and from the 700 yards mark to the 1500 yards mark the avaerage amounts to from 2ft. 3ins. to 3ft. 3ins. From the 1500 yards mark the subsidence diminishes, and from the 1600 yards mark to the Chatterley end of the tunnel the average subsidence is from 3ins. to 4ins.

A length of 11 yards of the arch at its worst place between the 900 yards mark and the 1000 yards mark, was rebuilt during the coal strike last year, giving the full 10ft. height above water level, and is standing very well. During the holidays at the beginning of this month, a further length of 60ft. of the arch was rebuilt, at the lowest part, about the 1000 yards mark, giving a 10ft. headway above water level. As the canal can be closed for only short periods such as the late holidays without interfering with the traffic, only short lengths can be dealt with at a time, as the necessary staging has to be erected and subsequently removed, and the old brickwork which is very hard and the shale rock above it cut out, before the new arch can be built. I saw the new work in progress and from my examination of the tunnel I think as a whole the brick work right through is in a sound condition, but in places the face of the brick work has come away, but these patches can be cut out and rebuilt. From the opening up of the arch of the tunnel where the new work is in progress, it can be seen that the whole surrounding ground has bodily subsided with the tunnel, as the rock is in contact with the outside of the arch and

and it is not the tunnel alone which has subsided. As far as I could judge there has been no very recent subsidences anywhere in the tunnel, and I am informed that the greatest amount took place prior to 1903, and has been little in the last 2½ years, and during the past year almost imperceptible, and although it is impossible to forecast with accuracy what may happen in a district with old mine workings underneath such a tunnel, I do not think there is ground for apprehending any further serious subsidence.

The Company have purchased all the coal underneath all three tunnels and for a space of 40 yards outside the two canal tunnels, and are still purchasing further seams when it appears advisable. I think the course they propose, viz. to go on rebuilding the arch of the tunnel and headway of 10ft. above water level as opportunity occurs, is the best method to adopt (without unduly interfering with its traffic). This could be done much more quickly if the traffic through the tunnel could be stopped for a longer period, but this must depend on the local trade conditions.

The traffic is conducted by horse traction and a certain amount of inconvenience is caused by the towing path being under water for a certain length where the subsidence exceeds 2ft., but the Company are intending, I understand, to make a trial of electric haulage, and if this is successful, then the towing path could be removed and the barges could be kept in the middle of the tunnel under the highest part of the arch, instead of as now over to one side, and a greater headway would be given.

I may say in conclusion that the N.S.R. gave me every facility for inspecting the tunnel, and all possible information regarding its history from an engineering point of view.

I am &c.

E. Dunitz

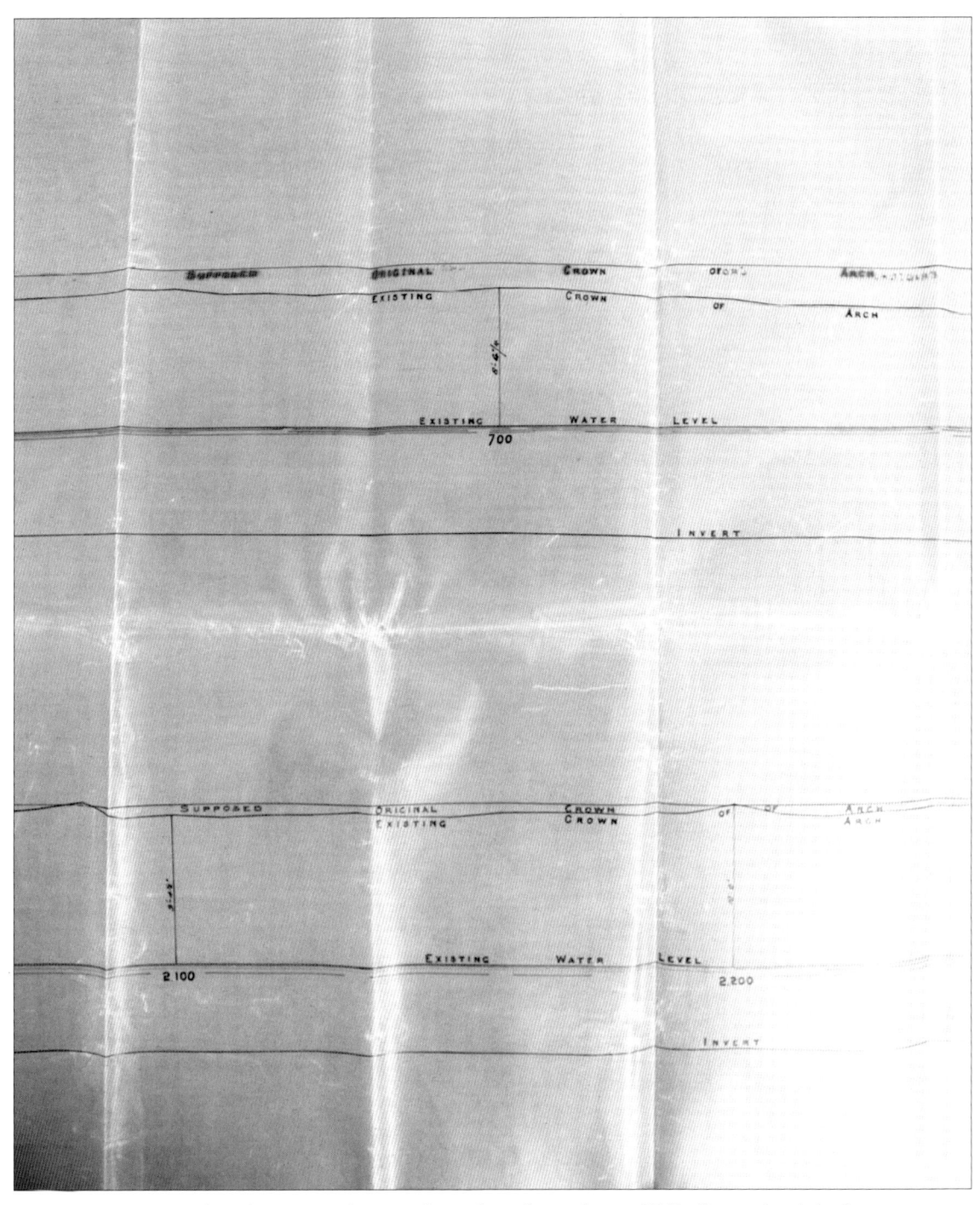

Mention is made in the text regarding complaints about the condition of Telford's tunnel and the damage caused by mining subsidence. The NSR commissioned a detailed plan of the complete tunnel to illustrate how this was affecting the headroom between the normal level of the water and the roof. While the plan is far too long to reproduce in its entirety, this small section is indicative of the general situation with the top line indicating the original level of the top of the arch and the bottom one portraying the situation in 1913 when Lieutenant Colonel Druitt undertook his inspection.   *NA MT6/2221/1*

6

ELECTRIC TUGS

The ultimate solution to the Harecastle tunnel problem had a touch of genius. The NSR was very much a pioneer in the use of electricity for buildings, carriage lighting, the operation of cranes and capstans and other ancillary purposes. The canal was not to be deprived of this new source of energy as, in the North Staffordshire Railway Act 1904,[104] the company obtained powers to provide haulage through Harecastle tunnels by *tugs worked by electricity or mechanical power other than steam* and to levy a charge for the haulage of boats. That charge was actually specified in the Act as 6d for empty boats or boats not laden with more than two tons and 1s 0d for each boat laden with more than two tons. The employment of steam tugs was out of the question because of the poor ventilation; all the shafts used in the construction of both tunnels had been filled in, presumably to avoid the cost of maintaining them.

However, the wording of section 20 of the 1904 Act, refers to the North Staffordshire Railway Act of 1879,[105] where powers had already been granted to employ steam haulage or fixed machinery, although in section 27, only the tunnels at Preston Brook, Barnton and Saltersford are mentioned. Presumably steam tugs and fixed machinery were not at that time considered appropriate for the Harecastle tunnels, probably in view of their length and lack of ventilation. The NSR New Works Act of 1864, section 22,[106] had granted even earlier powers for steam or other tugs or fixed machinery at the above three tunnels, plus Harecastle Old Tunnel, specifying various fees and charges that the company could make for the use of such tugs or machinery. There was no time limit attached to the powers in this case and by clause 14 of the company's 1867 Act,[107] some of the fees and charges were adjusted, in some cases up and in others down. Despite all this, the North Staffordshire Railway Act 1891,[108] which received the Royal Assent on 11th June that year, gave the company powers to remove the towing path in the New Tunnel and provide a towage service by tugs propelled by steam or other tugs or fixed machinery. The company could provide the tugs itself or issue licences for others to do so, but the service was to be free of charge to those using it. It does however seem somewhat strange that while the use of steam tugs at Harecastle was not provided for in the 1879 Act, it was in this and the 1864 Act, although only in the case of the Old Tunnel. This is rather strange as, of course, the same problem of smoke and steam would have been even more serious in its smaller bore. The powers in the 1891 Act were part of a much bigger scheme to improve the western end of the canal by reducing the number of locks and effecting other improvements, possibly prompted by the construction of the Manchester Ship Canal, although in the event the powers were allowed to lapse without anything being done. It is interesting to note that the North Staffordshire Chamber of Commerce petitioned Parliament against the Bill for the 1891 Act on the basis that the railway company was promoting the canal improvements in an effort to forestall the Ship Canal Bill which was then before Parliament. While this was strenuously denied by the NSR and while the Chamber of Commerce wanted a time limit placed if any powers were granted, which of course the railway company did not, the Select Committee appointed by Parliament must have had its suspicions, inserting in the Act a three year limit on the acquisition of any land, along with the removal of the towpath through the tunnel.

Passage of the company's Bill through the 1903-1904 Parliamentary Session must have been far from easy as [predictably!] the North Staffordshire Chamber of Commerce opposed the new scheme on the grounds that traders hitherto using their own horses for towage would, in future, be compelled to pay for the services of a tug.

The solution of providing electric haulage through Telford's tunnel was implemented under the guidance of Andrew Frederick Rock (1859-1930), the NSR's innovative Telegraph Superintendent and Electrical Engineer. How ironic that such a scheme, previously rejected by the Chamber of Commerce, should now find favour as a direct consequence of its more recent intervention and its ineffective support for an avoiding route. Electric haulage had clearly been one of the options being considered to overcome the problems associated with the Harecastle tunnels. At the T&FC meeting held on 8th April 1913, the one where there was a turnabout in allowing Harry Curbishley to participate in what was going on at Harecastle, it was decided to build two accumulator barges in the company's boat yard at Stone. Moreover, it was also decided to install an electric generating station at Chatterley to charge the batteries of the accumulator barges, rather than to purchase electricity from the Birchenwood Colliery Company. Finally it was agreed to accept an offer by Bullivant & Co. Limited to supply a steel tug for hauling boats through Telford's tunnel at a cost of

---

104 4 Edw VII ch. xliv, Royal Assent 24th June 1904, section 20.
105 42-43 Vic ch. ccv, Royal Assent 11th August 1879.
106 27-28 Vic ch. cccviii, Royal Assent 29th July 1864.
107 30-31 Vic ch. cxlii, Royal Assent 15th July 1867.
108 54-55 Vic ch. xxxiv, Royal Assent 11th June 1891.

Andrew Frederick Rock (1859-1930), the NSR Telegraph Superintendent and Electrical Engineer, who masterminded the electric haulage system through Telford's tunnel.
E. Harrison & Son, Newcastle-under-Lyme

£1,563.[109] The total cost of the entire project was £6,227 as approved by the NSR Board at its meeting on 22nd April 1913.[110] The approval of the electric haulage scheme might well have placated Curbishley. The T&FC meeting held on 1st July 1913 approved estimated expenditure of £500 for a 26ft × 56ft brick-built engine room for the suction gas plant, together with £400 for a lay-by for the accumulator barges; the actual tender prices for the work were £345 and £375 15s 0d, respectively.[111] During the 1913 traditional Potteries Wakes stoppage in August, 90ft of improved headway work in Telford's tunnel was completed.[112] On 22nd February 1914 expenditure of £60 was approved for a coal store, closet and water supply at the Chatterley power house.[113] A coal supply seems to indicate that the NSR produced its own gas for the gas suction plant which is perhaps confirmed by the company authorising a gas supply to two railway cottages at Chatterley at a cost of £23 in March 1919.[114]

The overall scheme involved a fixed steel rope being laid on the bottom of the tunnel invert and anchored at some distance from each end. During the Christmas 1913 stoppage 948 tons of mud was dredged from the canal within the tunnel with a further 76 tons from the north end shortly afterwards.[115] This work would be in anticipation of laying the rope which was two inches in circumference and 3,500 yards long. It passed over two five feet diameter winding drums mounted on the tug, one in front of the other in a watertight channel. The drums were operated by two 15hp electric motors so pulling the vessel and its train of narrow boats along.[116] There was no other means of steering. Power for the motors was obtained from one of the two accumulator barges towed immediately behind the tug. The accumulator barges had to be manoeuvred around the tug at the end of each trip through the tunnel. The tug had a length of 40 feet, a beam of seven feet with a draught of three feet. The hull was of steel plate construction but two wooden fenders were fitted to prevent it from rubbing against the brickwork of the tunnel or the towpath. Repairs to the tug were usually undertaken at the company's Etruria depot some four miles to the south of the Chatterley end of the tunnel.

The two accumulator barges were 72 feet in length and each contained 115 chloride cells which were housed in lead-lined teak boxes in order to protect them from rain and drips from the tunnel roof. The reference to chloride cells must refer to alkaline cells as opposed to a lead-acid battery. The former used potassium hydrate as an electrolyte, which is an alkaline, as opposed to sulphuric acid in a lead-acid battery. Alkaline cells only give 1.2 volts per cell, compared with 1.5 volts for lead acid cells. Therefore, the 115 cells on each of the accumulator barges when fully charged must have produced 138 volts with presumably a high amperage. The accumulator barges carried a light at each end. While one of them was in use, the other would be moored outside the generating station at Chatterley so that the accumulator cells could be re-charged, an operation which lasted several days. The barges were used alternately, being changed over at the end of each week. The generating station was located on the piece of land in the fork of the canal by the two tunnel mouths. It housed two 70bhp gas engines and two dynamos which, when turning at 600rpm, produced 45 kilowatts. The electrical equipment was supplied by Campbell (the gas engines), General Electric (the dynamos) and Royce (the tug motors), while the NSR's Electrical Department was responsible for installing the switchgear.

At the T&FC meeting held on 28th July 1914 it was reported that the initial haulage boat trials were quite satisfactory with 62 minutes taken to pass through the tunnel with a tow of fifteen narrow boats and 55 minutes with a tow of eight boats.[117] Extensive repair work to the tunnel was undertaken during the annual Wakes Holiday stoppage with orders placed for 20,000 Staffordshire blue bricks, 20,000 brindled bricks, two trucks of lime, 120 casks of cement, two hundredweights of carbide and a large quantity of timber.[118] The new arrangement became fully operational on 30th November 1914 which is just as well as during the previous month there had been a collapse of a portion of the brickwork in the old tunnel.[119] *The Staffordshire Advertiser* reported that the proposed new arrangement would dispense with the services of the professional leggers in Brindley's tunnel, reminding its readers that *for four hours or more, the slow,*

---

109   NA 532/23. NSR T&FC meeting, 8th April 1913, Minute 27087.
110   NA RAIL. 532/8 Directors' meeting, 22nd April 1913, Minute 4514.
111   NA 532/23. NSR T&FC meetings: 1st July 1913, Minute 27241; 15th July 1913, Minute 27278 and 29th July 1913, Minute 27293.
112   NA RAIL 532/23. NSR T&FC meeting, 9th September 1913, Minute 27314.
113   NA RAIL 532/23. NSR T&FC meeting, 22nd February 1914, Minute 27614.
114   NA RAIL 532/25. T&FC meeting, 18th March 1919, Minute 30292.
115   NA 532/23 NSR T&FC meeting, 27th January 1914, Minute 27560

116   The two motors could be worked singly or together, depending on the load to be towed.
117   NA RAIL 532/23. NSR T& FC meeting, 28th July 1914, Minute 27908.
118   NA RAIL 532/23. NSR T&FC meeting, 11th August 1914, Minute 27950.
119   NA RAIL 532/23 NSR T&FC meeting, 6th October 1914, Minute 27988.

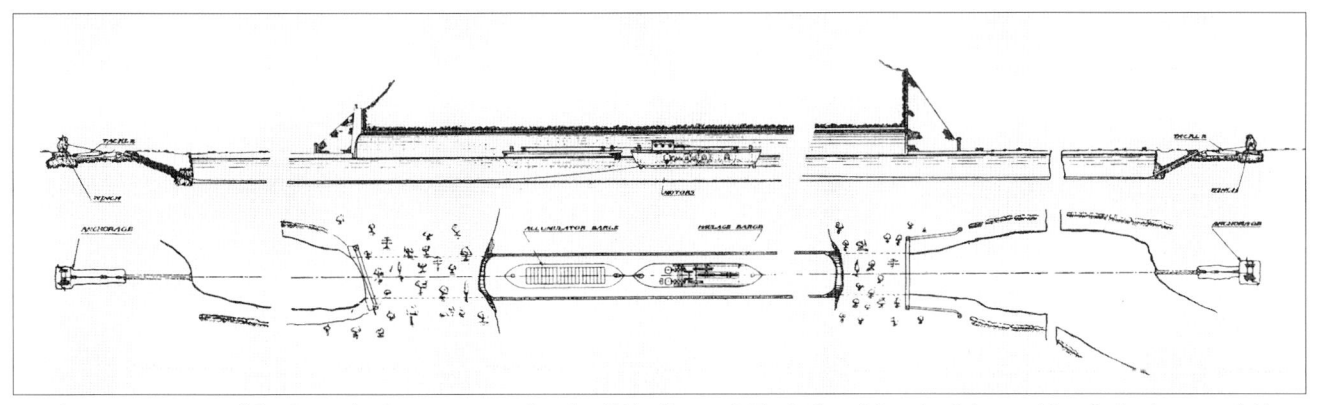

A diagrammatic view of the electric haulage system employed in Telford's tunnel, *The Railway Magazine*, July 1914. Note the haulage rope laid on the canal bed.

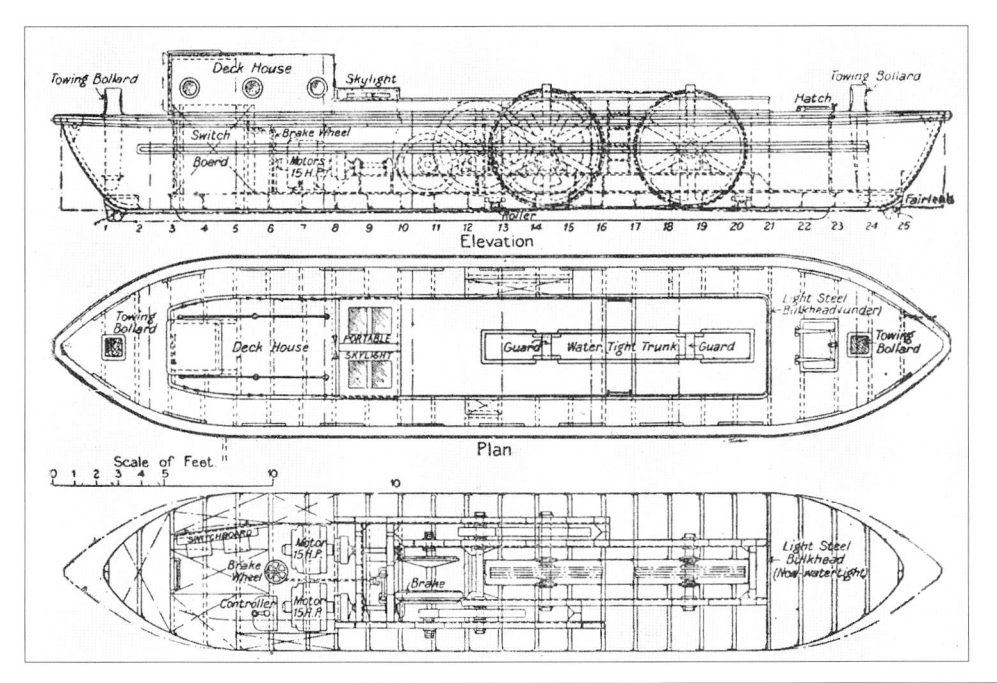

An outline diagram of the electric tug employed on the haulage system through Telford's tunnel. This illustration is from *The Railway and Travel Monthly*, August 1918.

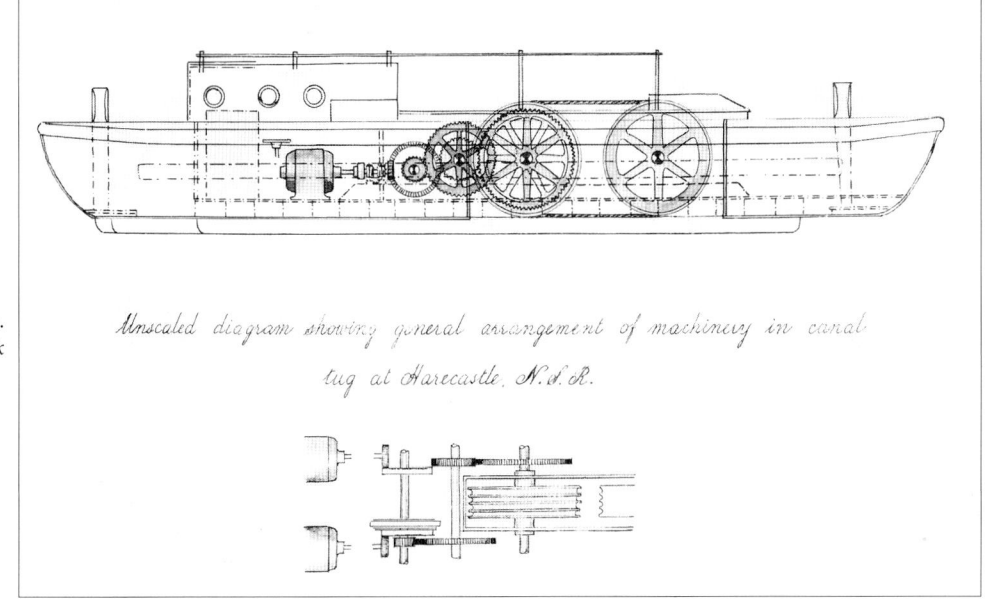

Another diagram of the electric tug.
The late Dr J.R. Hollick

The two accumulator barges outside the generating station at Chatterley in 1914. The tunnel keeper's wife is airing her washing above the entrance to Telford's tunnel.

The interior of the generating house in 1914. It had two Campbell 70 brake horsepower gas engines and two General Electric open frame multi-polar shunt-wound direct current dynamos.

The electric tug awaiting business at the north end of Telford's tunnel in around 1918.

methodical clatter of the leggers' feet coming into contact with the brick and rocky lining of the tunnel echoes through the darkness before the barge emerges once more into the open at Chatterley and continues its course to the Potteries.[120] That was about to be a thing of the past.

During that year the maximum number of boats passing through the tunnels during a 24 hour period was estimated at about 100 in each direction. Initially the tug was available for towing during eighteen hours each day making about six trips in each direction with an average of about seventeen boats in tow, although theoretically it could handle up to thirty boats. Estimated speed was between 2 and 3mph. At the shareholders' meeting held on 23rd February 1915 Harry Boddington (Yes, he was also a NSR shareholder!) congratulated the directors on the success of the electric haulage traction but pointed out that there was considerable delay at either end of the tunnel where the boats were assembled. He suggested that this delay might be obviated by straightening the canal at the ends of the tunnel so that the boats could be drawn straight out enabling the haulage boat to return immediately. The chairman said the company was most anxious to facilitate this suggestion but had been unable to obtain the land necessary to carry out the proposed improvement. At the shareholders' meeting held on 22nd February the following year, it was reported that electric haulage in Telford's tunnel had been working very satisfactorily but there had been an unfortunate breakdown causing the service to be suspended for some weeks. This followed an accident necessitating the tugboat being taken out of service for repairs, which prompted the seeking of a tender for another tug but nothing was done.[121] Full advantage was taken of the summer Wakes holiday stoppage in 1916 to undertake further tunnel repairs; the stoppage lasted from 7th to 26th August.[122] This resulted in a claim from carriers Fellows, Morton & Co. for an allowance of £146 3s 4d to meet the extra tolls paid by them during the stoppage following the diversion of their boats via Wardle lock at Middlewich and the Shropshire Union Canal. The claim was declined.[123] Further stoppages for tunnel repairs took place the following year from 5th to 10th April over the Easter holidays and from 5th to 25th August.[124] Workings by the Birchenwood Colliery Company were causing concern and were

---

120 *The Staffordshire Advertiser*, 7th March 1914.
121 NA RAIL 532/23. NSR T&FC meetings: 25th January 1916, Minute 28703 and 22nd February 1916, Minute 28748.
122 NA RAIL 532/23. NSR T&FC meeting, 25th July 1916, Minute 28950.
123 NA RAIL 532/23. NSR T&FC meeting, 28th November 1916, Minute 29101.
124 NA RAIL 532/23. NSR T&FC meetings: 20th March 1917, Minute 29245 and 10th July 1917, Minute 29400.

The electric tug and an accumulator barge at the Chatterley end of Telford's tunnel with a string of narrow boats in tow. The horses have been walked over the hill via Boat Horse Road and are waiting to take the boats onwards to their destinations. The connection point for recharging the accumulator barges is to the left.
Stephenson Locomotive Society Collection

NORTH STAFFORDSHIRE RAILWAY AND TRENT AND MERSEY CANAL

THE name of the great Josiah Wedgwood is, of course, associated throughout the civilised world with the art of potting, but it is not generally known that he took a very active part in the promotion of the scheme for the construction of what is now known as the Trent and Mersey Canal, which in its day did so much for the development of the resources of North Staffordshire, and for the material progress of the inhabitants. This canal was the forerunner of the railway, and an account of the North Staffordshire Railway, however brief, would be incomplete without some reference to the Trent and Mersey Canal. It is difficult, at the present day, so thoroughly accustomed as we are to the easy and rapid transit of merchandise, to understand what the lack of any means of conveyance, beyond the ordinary pack-horse, meant in the middle of the eighteenth century when this canal was projected. The principal materials used in the manufacture of pottery came from a great distance—flint stones from the South Eastern ports of England, and clay from Devonshire and Cornwall. The flints were brought by sea to Hull, and the clay to Liverpool. From Hull the materials were brought up the Trent in boats to Willington, and the clay was in like manner brought from Liverpool up the Weaver to Winsford, in Cheshire. From these points the materials were conveyed by road, chiefly on the backs of horses, to the towns in the Potteries where they were made into Earthenware and China. The manufactured articles were returned in the same rude way, crates of earthenware and china being slung across the horses' backs, and thus conveyed to their respective destinations. This method of transport was not only difficult, but, in addition, was extremely costly, and when the subject of water carriage came to be discussed in 1765, Josiah Wedgwood entered with great spirit into the movement then set on foot for the construction of what, at that time, was called the Grand Trunk Canal. It is a matter of history that this great inland waterway was commenced in 1766, and the work carried to a successful issue by the famous engineer, James Brindley. A glance at the accompanying plan will shew the course of the canal, and will enable the reader to understand the great impetus given to the commerce of the district by its construction.

North Staffordshire continued to develop, and as the result of its enormous mineral wealth, also indicated on the accompanying plan, became the home of many industries. With the advent of railways in the first half of the nineteenth century came the opportunity for further expansion of trade by the construction of the North Staffordshire Railway, which was opened for traffic in 1848-49. Thenceforward the history of the North Staffordshire Railway is but the history of the progress of the people and the trade of the district which it serves. It would be tedious to set out the extensions in detail. Both mineral and passenger lines have been constructed and acquired as the increase in the trade of the district and the convenience of the public have required, so that at the present time the interests of North Staffordshire, as far as railway and canal accommodation is concerned, may be said to be exceedingly well served. The Grand Trunk Canal constructed by Brindley, to which reference has already been made, is now known as the Trent and Mersey Canal. Raw materials, such as flints, clay, and bone, are chiefly conveyed by the canal from the ports to the Potteries, and both canal and railway are used for the conveyance of the ever-increasing tonnage of minerals and manufactured goods which emanate from the hive of industry radiating from Stoke-on-Trent. As a measure of the development of the district, it may be mentioned that while at the time of the projection of Brindley's Canal the population of the Potteries did not exceed 7,000 souls, at the present day the population of the County Borough of Stoke-on-Trent, which includes in its area the whole of the pottery towns, numbers nearly a quarter of a million people. Notwithstanding the progress so far made, such is the enormous mineral wealth of North Staffordshire that it may be said to be still only on the threshold of its prosperity. Sites for new works and new manufactures are obtainable near to, or adjoining, the North Staffordshire Railway and Trent and Mersey Canal systems, with or without Siding accommodation, as may be required, and full information will be furnished by the General Manager at Stoke-on-Trent, to whom all enquiries should be addressed.

The natural scenery of North Staffordshire is very beautiful, and the industrialism of the coalfield, except in the immediate vicinity, has fortunately failed to spoil it. The people may still point with pride to the scenic charms of the valleys of the rivers Trent, Dane, Churnet, Manifold and Dove, and in connection with the last named, Dovedale has long been known as the most beautiful and harmonious blending of rock, water, wood and dale within the limits of the four seas.

Stoke-on-Trent is an excellent centre either for business or pleasure, and the accommodation at the North Stafford Hotel is very good. It is situated where the Through Services from Liverpool (Lime Street) to Derby and Burton, and London (Euston) to Manchester intercept, and there is consequently an excellent service of trains to and from Stoke in every direction. For visitors who prefer the country there is the very comfortable family Hotel (Hotel Rudyard), near Leek, which is most romantically situated close to Rudyard Lake, where excellent golfing, boating and fishing are obtainable.

This summary of the history of the North Staffordshire Railway and the Trent & Mersey Canal, together with the map shown opposite, is taken from a Stoke-on-Trent Chamber of Commerce publication. The map takes the form of an advertisement emphasising the importance of the railway and canal in attracting new business. Attention is drawn to deposits of coal, gypsum, limestone and salt, all of which generated large bulk traffic movements by both railway and canal.

CHAPTER 6 – ELECTRIC TUGS

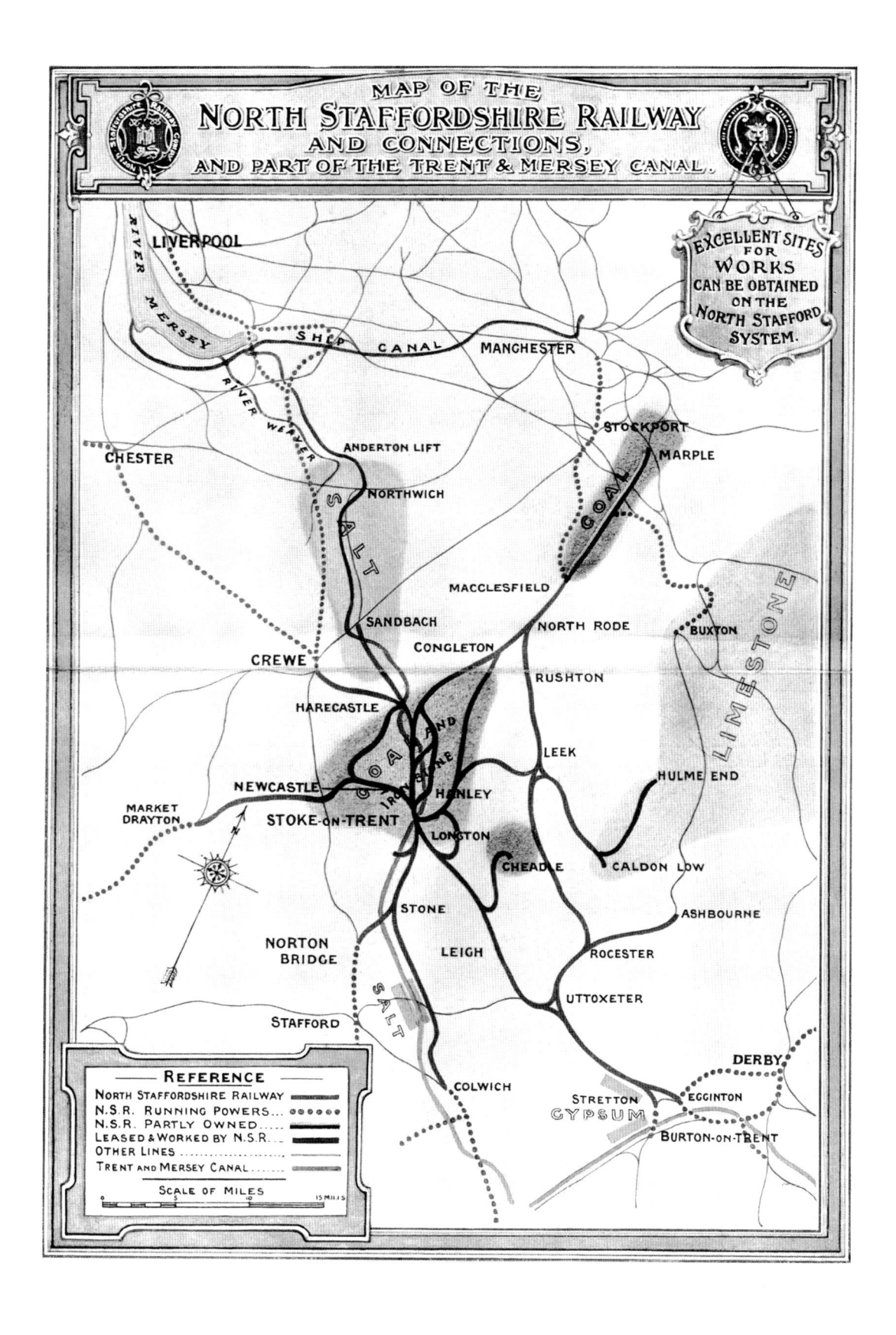

Right: This advertisement also extols the virtues of establishing manufactories and works in North Staffordshire, illustrating examples of existing successful businesses. Those requesting more information are asked to apply to F.A.L. Barnwell, NSR, Stoke-on-Trent. Frederick Arthur Lowry Barnwell (1877-1945) was appointed as NSR General Manager on 1st October 1919, while retaining the position as the company's Engineer, which he had held hitherto. He retained his dual role until 1st January 1921 when Cecil Guy Rose (1877-1962) took over as Engineer, leaving Barnwell to become the last General Manager of the Company.

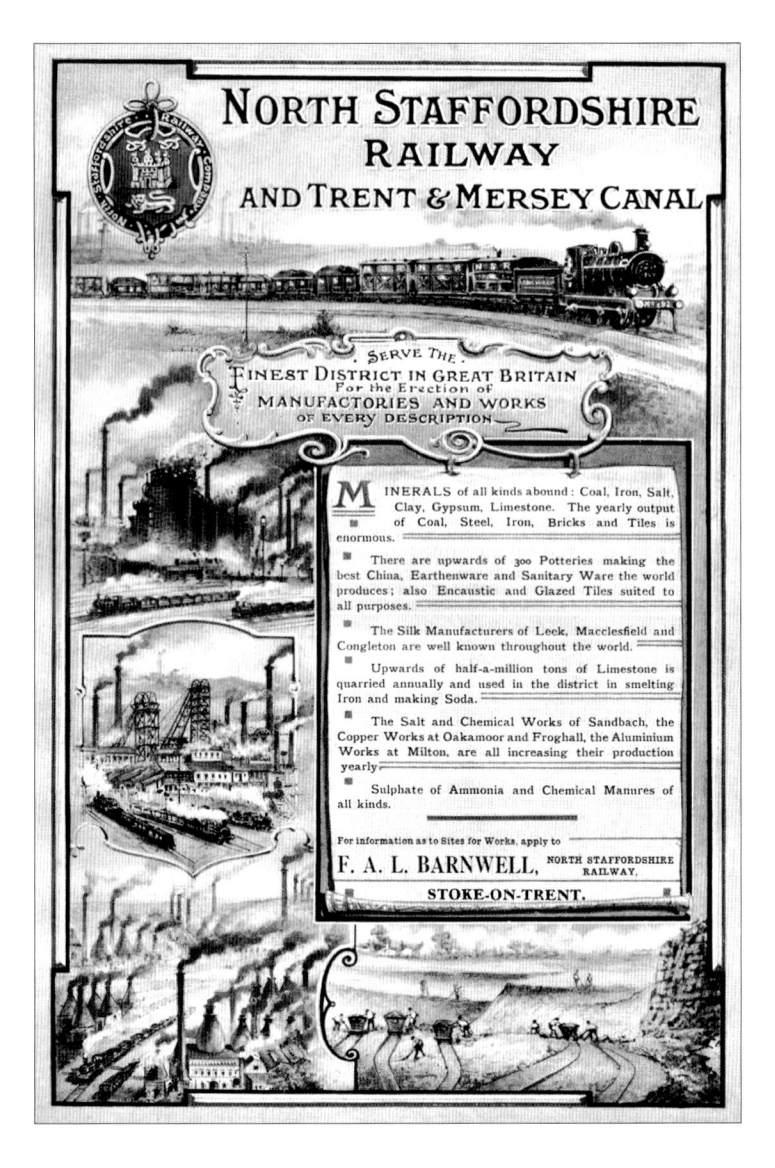

Left: The Railway Year Book for 1921 featured this NSR advertisement promoting railway and canal sites for new business, emphasising that by locating alongside the canal, there would be a plentiful supply of water available for steam or condensing purposes. The NSR certainly did not neglect its canal.

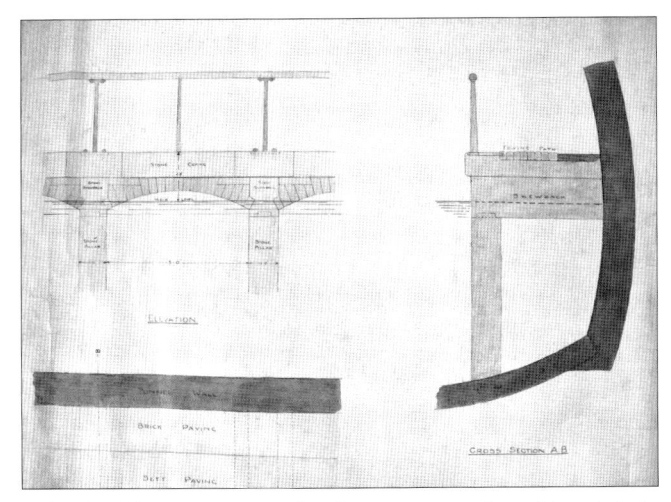

This detail from an LM&SR plan shows a cross section of the original towing path in Telford's tunnel supported by stone pillars with sett paving for the towing path itself. This would provide a better grip for the horses. *National Waterways Museum 86/102*

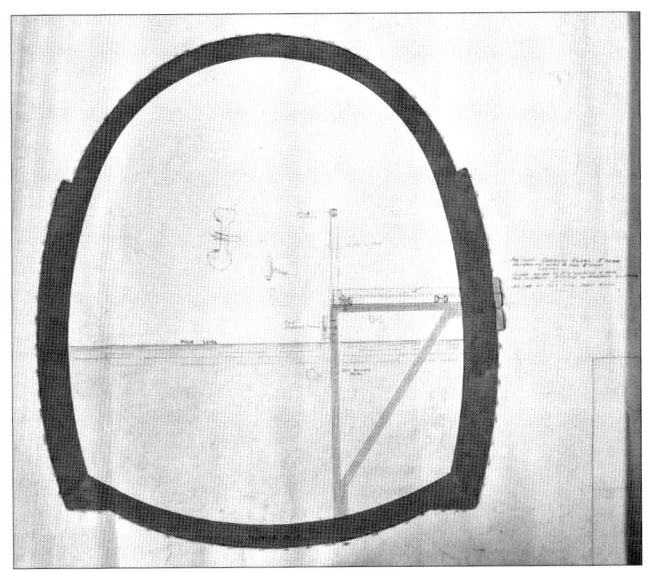

The same plan illustrates a replacement towpath supported by angle iron and old bullhead rails. The towpath was formed of pre-cast concrete slabs three inches thick, reinforced with quarter inch diameter rods spaced six inches apart. The slabs, each of which weighed about four cwt, were to be in three feet lengths with the top surface striped to prevent the horses from slipping. The towpath was to have a replacement handrail and its supports equipped with a nine inch by three inch timber rubbing strake above the water line, running throughout the tunnel. The plan is undated but is probably c.1926 when subsidence had resulted in part of the old towpath being under water. *National Waterways Museum 86/102*

being carefully monitored.[125] By June 1917 the original haulage rope was becoming worn so a duplicate was ordered at a cost of £133 (£1 18s od per cwt) from John & Edwin Wright Limited, Universe Wire Rope Works, Birmingham.[126] It was installed by July 1918 when the original rope was sent to the stores for scrap.[127] Another rope replacement was required in 1920.[128]

For a while Brindley's tunnel remained in use, possibly to cover for the eventuality of further breakdowns in the tug service. In 1915 the canal engineer was authorised to undertake repairs from time to time as men were available.[129] However after several roof falls it was closed to navigation in 1918. A proposal to remove the towpath in Telford's tunnel did not materialise although all craft whether horse drawn or motor were compelled to use the tug service.

The NSR together with all its assets, including the Trent & Mersey Canal, became a constituent part of the London Midland & Scottish Railway (LM&SR) in 1923 in accordance with the grouping of the railways under the Railways Act 1921.[130] The new arrangements came into effect on 1st January 1923 but, in the case of the NSR, the final formalities were not completed until 30th June 1923 when the old company ceased to exist. The delay was caused by the chairman attempting to agree better terms for the directors and shareholders. At a meeting of the LM&SR's Traffic Committee held on 23rd June 1926 it was reported that the original tug was in need of overhaul and that subsidence had resulted in part of the towpath through Telford's tunnel being under water.[131] The cost of repairs was estimated at £16,000 with the cost of an additional tug estimated at £1,300. At that time up to 17,000 boats annually were passing through the tunnel and it was anticipated that higher tolls for tug services would produce additional revenue of £500 per annum. The repairs were no doubt undertaken swiftly but a new tug was not ordered until 1930.

The new tug was authorised by the LM&SR Traffic Committee held on 25th June 1930 at an actual cost of £1,359 plus an additional cost of £45 for 300 *Type B conductors*.[132] This decision heralded the demise of the accumulator barges and a major change in the system of providing electrical power. In 1931 the accumulator barges were abandoned and electricity provided via an overhead wire suspended from the tunnel roof. Fortunately, the 1904 Act was drafted with considerable foresight as this method of current collection was allowed for in the existing legislation so avoiding the need to seek additional statutory powers. The overhead conductor, suspended by wires strung across the canal between wooden poles, continued for a short distance beyond the tunnel mouths and presented the uniformed onlooker with a very curious spectacle. Current, from a mains supply, was collected tramcar-style by means of a trolley pole pivoted at one end of each tug, the original tug being converted to the new method

---

125 NA RAIL 532/23. NSR T&FC meetings: 19th September 1916, Minute 28993 and 9th January 1917, Minute 29144.
126 NA RAIL 532/23. NSR T&FC meeting, 26th June 1917, Minute 29375.
127 NA RAIL 532/23. NSR T&FC meeting, 23rd July 1918, Minute 29941.
128 NA RAIL 532/24. NSR T&FC meeting, 17th February 1920.
129 NA RAIL 532/23. NSR T&FC meeting, 7th September 1915, Minute 28517.
130 11-12 Geo V ch. lv, Royal Assent, 19th August 1921.
131 NA RAIL 418/75 LM&SR Traffic Committee meeting, 23rd June 1926, Minute 1020.
132 NA RAIL 418/78 LM&SR Traffic Committee meeting, 25th June 1930, Minute 2431.

This view at Chatterley taken in November 1935 looks south and captures the scene shortly after the abandonment of the accumulator barges in favour of the overhead wire current collection system. One of the redundant accumulator barges can be seen moored alongside the generating station. The photograph shows the towpath turnover bridge and beyond that is the railway bridge leading to the Goldendale Ironworks. Turnover bridges were designed to enable horses towing boats to cross the canal at locations where the towpath changed sides, but without the need to unhitch the tow rope.

In this scene at Kidsgrove, also from 1935, five narrow boats loaded with raw materials for the pottery industry are waiting to be towed through Harecastle tunnel utilising the new overhead wire system on their way to the pottery towns. *Daisy* was owned by the Anderton Company Ltd. Ahead of *Daisy* is the well-laden narrow boat *Speedwell*, which belonged to Potter & Son of Runcorn (registered as Runcorn No. 1004); the boat is probably loaded with china clay. A railway coal wagon owned by Fenton Collieries Ltd can just be glimpsed to the right.

Cyril Arapoff/National Waterways Museum

A string of narrow boats enters the northern portal of Telford's tunnel behind one of the electric tugs. The sheet draped over the nearest boat establishes its owner as the Anderton Company Limited, one of the oldest canal carriers in North Staffordshire.
*Cyril Arapoff/
National Waterways Museum*

Electric tug and driver/skipper Bill O'Grady emerging from the Chatterley portal of Telford's tunnel. Note the trolley pole making connection with the overhead electric conductor wire. The system employed a somewhat unusual arrangement, whereby the return conductor was the underground haulage cable, which was of course, submerged for most of its length.
Kidsgrove Library Local History Collection

William O'Grady and his tug. He was born at Chell on 7th May 1904 and his death was recorded at Stoke-on-Trent in 1983. *Kidsgrove Library Local History Collection*

This workboat and a similar vessel were towed immediately behind the electric tugs. It is loaded with weights and may have been used to keep the stern of the tugs well down in the water as a substitute for the heavy accumulator barges after they were withdrawn in 1931; this followed the installation of an overhead electricity supply conductor suspended from the tunnel roof. The tugs were propelled by on-board electric motors which, via a gearbox and pulley arrangement, plied in and out a wire rope, that otherwise lay on the canal bed.
Kidsgrove Library Local History Collection

Here is the workboat being attached to the tug at Chatterley.
Kidsgrove Library Local History Collection

The workboat is seen again in this view connected to the tug at the south portal of Telford's tunnel.
Kidsgrove Library Local History Collection

CHAPTER 6 – ELECTRIC TUGS

The Goldenhill schoolboys lead the tow in the well ballasted workboat in readiness to enter the south end of Telford's tunnel.
Kidsgrove Library Local History Collection

Here the boys are inspecting the tug at Kidsgrove, no doubt intently listening to an explanation from their school master.
Kidsgrove Library Local History Collection

This view shows the turnover bridge at the north end of the Harecastle tunnels at Kidsgrove with the *Potteries Line* railway bridge beyond. The string of boats is being assembled for its journey south with the workboat containing the weights in the foreground, next to the tug.
Kidsgrove Library Local History Collection

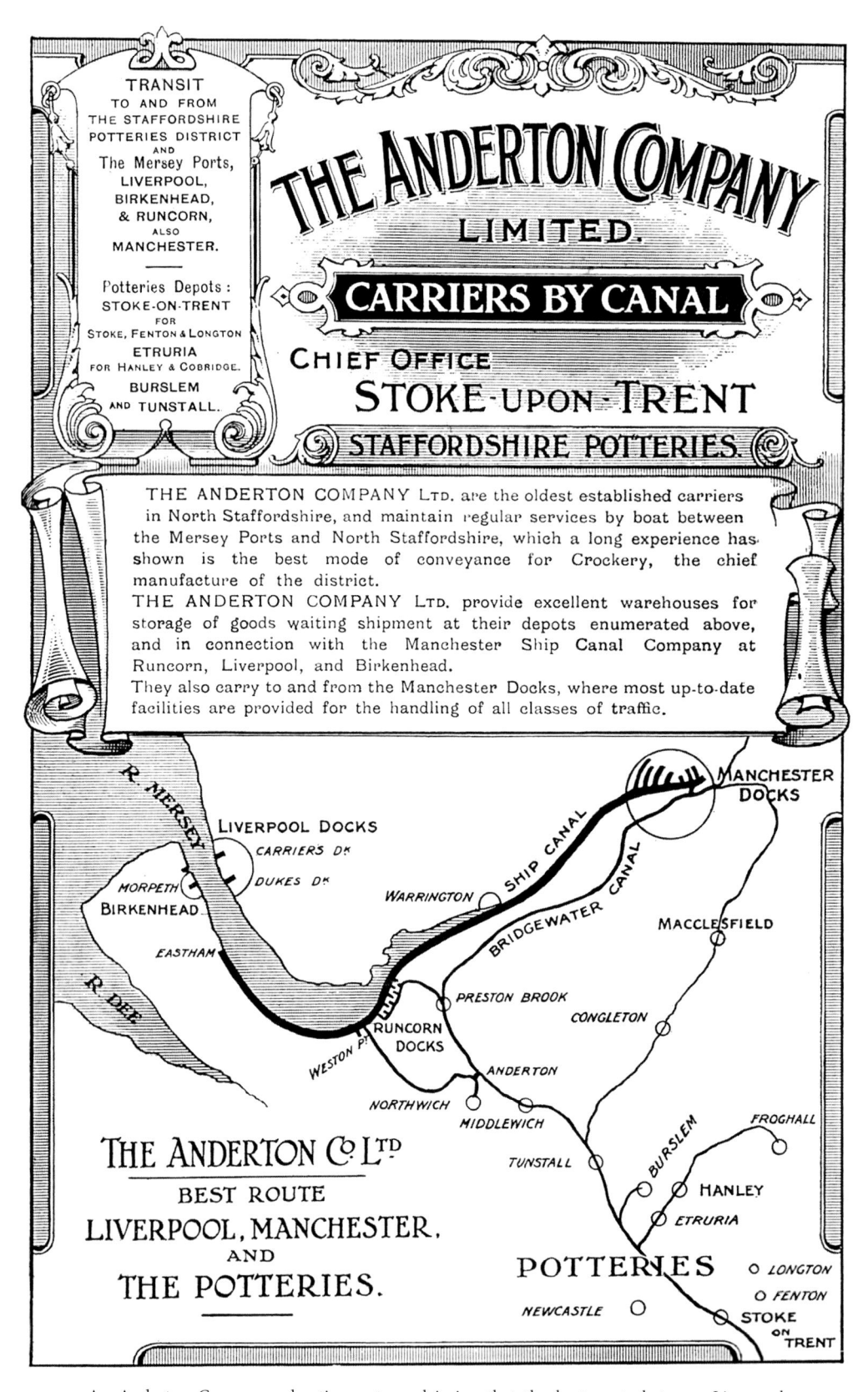

An Anderton Company advertisement proclaiming that the best route between Liverpool and Manchester to the Potteries was by canal which was also claimed to be the best mode of conveyance for crockery, the chief manufacture of the district.

of power supply. At the end of each trip, which took about three quarters of an hour, the tugman had to reverse the trolley pole for the return journey. The old generating station at Chatterley was abandoned.

Vivid blue sparks spluttered from the overhead conductor..... from the dark depths ahead a distant muttering slowly grew to a prodigious groaning and grinding sound, like that of a decrepit tramcar climbing a steep hill. That was the late Tom Rolt's description of one of the tugs in action as he waited for his narrow boat *Cressy* to be towed under the wires in 1939.[133]

During 1940 concern was expressed that pollution in the canal at Harecastle was corroding the ironwork that supported the towpath and the haulage rope on which the electric tug service depended. Samples were sent for analysis at the LM&SR Research Department at Derby. At a point 620 yards from the Harecastle entrance there was a 12in × 12in opening through which surplus water from disused coal mines discharged into the tunnel. The research investigations pointed to the trouble being caused by a chemical or gas undertaking and the Birchenwood Coal & Coke Co. Ltd was the suspected culprit. The problem was raised again in 1944 as the life of the haulage rope had reduced to only thirteen months, compared with three years previously. Further analysis of the polluted water indicated the presence of phenols and a high proportion of ammonium compounds, again strongly suggesting that the chemical works was the source of the pollution.[134] By 1947 there was so much detritus in the tunnel that the LM&SR provided water mains as a means of flushing the canal bed.[135] The density of traffic created difficulties in employing more conventional means of dredging.

After the Second World War, the number of boats using the tunnel greatly decreased and by 1950, after nationalisation,[136] averaged less than 100 a week. The decline continued and, on many occasions, the tug had to run with no boats in tow in order to maintain the advertised service. Six return trips were still made on each weekday. The timetable was later revised to provide for fewer trips on the afternoon shift. The condition of the tugs in the final years left much to be desired and it was not uncommon for both of them to be unserviceable. On these occasions, there is evidence that diesel-engined boats passed through the tunnel unassisted despite the lack of ventilation. On 6th January 1953, the British Transport Commission's Docks & Inland Waterways Executive authorised a scheme, estimated to cost £2,250, to install a system of forced ventilation in the tunnel to enable craft to proceed under their own power on a permanent basis.[137] The contract was awarded to Woods Ltd of Colchester. The firm installed three thirty-eight inch diameter electric fans in a building constructed over the tunnel mouth at Chatterley, these drew fresh air and exhaust fumes through the tunnel from the Harecastle end. The tug service was discontinued in 1954. In fact, the tugs again became unserviceable before the new scheme was completed. The overhead wires were removed and the submerged haulage cable recovered from the canal bed. It was estimated that the capital cost of the ventilation system would be recouped within two years from the savings achieved as a result of the new arrangement.

---

133 *Narrow Boat* by L.T.C. Rolt, Eyre Methuen, 1944.
134 Archived correspondence deposited at the National Waterways Museum, Ellesmere Port.
135 NA RAIL 418/99. LM&SR Works Committee meeting, 29th October 1947, Minute 422.
136 From 1st January 1948 the majority of Great Britain's canals, inland waterways and railways were nationalised under the overall umbrella of the British Transport Commission, under the Transport Act 1947. 10-11 Geo VI ch. 49, Royal Assent 6th August 1947.
137 Docks & Inland Waterways Executive meeting, 6th January 1953, Minute 2682.

One of the two electric tugs moored at Kidsgrove in the early 1950s.
The late William Jack

This 1935 aerial view shows the canal tunnel entrances at Chatterley to the bottom left. The generating house can be seen in the fork of the canal and to the left of that is the white painted tunnel keeper's cottage. The canal can be seen running across the photograph and is crossed from left to right by the towpath turnover bridge and then the railway bridge leading to the Goldendale ironworks with its blast furnaces and complex of railway sidings. At the time of the photograph the sidings were shunted by two outside cylinder 0-4-0 tank engines built by the Yorkshire Engine Company Limited, Meadow Hall Works, Sheffield. They were named *Goldendale* (Maker's No. 285 of 1876) and *Clifford* (Maker's No. 947 of 1907) and had distinctive ogee-shaped saddle tanks which were typical of the builder around the time they were built. At this stage both the canal and the mainline railway seen running below were owned by the LM&SR.

Historic England EPW046737

Goldendale at the ironworks in its final condition, having received a new boiler from Walker Bros of Wigan in 1934 and been repaired by Cowlishaw Walker of Biddulph in 1946. The locomotive, which had 12in. × 20in. outside cylinders and 3ft 3in. diameter wheels, was scrapped in March 1960. *Clifford* was withdrawn in 1960, but not scrapped until 1963.

CHAPTER 6 – ELECTRIC TUGS

Another view of the same tug shown on page 95 showing the trolley pole in its lowered position.
The late William Jack

This early 1950s view is at Chatterley looking north with the disused Brindley tunnel to the left and Telford's tunnel to the right. The mainline railway is to the left, still paralleled with rows of distinctive telegraph poles with their porcelain insulators. The signal to the extreme left, on the bracket, is the Chatterley Junction Down Starter; there was an Advanced Starter by the former station platform just before the tunnel portal. The tall signal with twin sets of arms is the Chatterley Junction Up Home with the Bradwell sidings distant which was repeated on the Chatterley starter – due to the distance from its signal box, it must have been motor operated. The signal's height was necessary so that it could be observed by drivers almost as soon as a train emerged from the tunnel. The distant for this signal was a motor operated banner, located between the middle and south tunnels. The prominent overhead wiring appears to be a mains supply to the old generating station. This means that at some time past the original gas engines were replaced with a mains supply, presumably complete with a transformer and rectifier to drop the voltage and convert to direct current. The white painted tunnel keeper's cottage can be seen behind the generating station.
The late William Jack

A tug and train of boats in 1953 about to enter the south end of Telford's tunnel. The other tug is moored on the right. The overhead pick-up wire can clearly be seen strung between the poles on either side of the canal. The bridges over the canal are the towpath turnover bridge and the railway bridge with the rail connection to the Goldendale ironworks. *The late William Jack*

One of the tugs emerging from the south end of Telford's tunnel with a train of boats under tow. Note the vintage LM&SR sign.

CHAPTER 6 – ELECTRIC TUGS

The fan house at Chatterley in course of erection on 19th June 1954, with the overhead pick-up wire still in position.
The late William Jack

A string of narrow boats leaves Telford's tunnel at Chatterley on 5th November 1960.
Harry Arnold/Waterways Images

This view was taken on 25th June 1962 from the stern of the narrow boat *Margaret*, which was travelling north through Telford's tunnel. It clearly illustrates that the original towpath had indeed been replaced, although by this time it was in a terrible state. Compare this view of the towpath with the drawing on page 89.
Harry Arnold/Waterways Images

Inside Telford's tunnel looking north from the narrow boat *Margaret* on 25th June 1962. The northern portal can just be glimpsed in the distance as one of the crew gingerly checks a part of the towpath that is still intact. In less than a year the newly formed British Waterways Board became responsible for the canal system.
Harry Arnold/Waterway Images

7

BRITISH WATERWAYS BOARD

Under the Transport Act 1962 the British Transport Commission (BTC) was abolished.[138] The ownership of the canals and inland waterways, formerly controlled by the BTC, passed to the British Waterways Board (BWB) with effect from 1st January 1963. On 3rd July 1966 Sir John Hamilton Wedgwood, Bart (1907-1989) re-enacted the cutting of the first sod of the Trent & Mersey Canal by his great-great-great-grandfather on 26th July 1766. A plaque was fixed to the fan house at Chatterley by the City Council of Stoke-on-Trent to commemorate the occasion.

In July 1973 two small areas of roof in Telford's tunnel collapsed and temporary repairs were carried out. Two months later a more serious collapse took place following further movements of the tunnel lining which necessitated the complete closure of the tunnel. The closure was prolonged and lasted until 1977 before it was once more made safe for navigation. Contracts for the difficult repair work were awarded in three separate phases to Rock Services (Midlands) Limited, Mowlem Northern Limited and Shand Midlands, part of the Lehane MacKenzie & Shand Group.[139] Rock Services, the first of the three contractors to commence work were initially engaged to effect temporary repairs but were retained after two further lengths of the tunnel roof collapsed in September 1973 covering an area of 41 yards. In the collapsed areas it proved difficult to stabilise and secure the strata above the tunnel. Work was hindered by the fallen material blocking the channel and the constant heavy flow of dripping water. Stainless steel rock bolts were used to hold back the strata and prevent further collapse; steel mesh was then placed against the face and held in place by stainless steel straps prior to the formation of a new lining in reinforced concrete secured to the rock bolts.

Mowlem Northern Limited was awarded the contract for the second phase which involved three faulty sections, once again with a total length of 41 yards. The firm removed the old brickwork in three foot lengths, reshaped the tunnel where necessary to regain headroom and reformed the tunnel lining with engineering bricks. A drainage layer of large rounded aggregate was packed behind the brickwork with sheets of PVC[140] placed between the aggregate and the brickwork to deflect water away from the tunnel lining towards drainage holes drilled through the brickwork. Early on in the Mowlem contract a roof fall running to a height of 16 feet above the old tunnel lining was encountered. This void was packed with Thermalite blocks. Most of the work was done by hand and the very cramped conditions meant that only five men and a minimum of plant could be accommodated. Mowlem designed a suitable work platform that could be moved easily and the BWB built two workboats to transport bricks, sand and cement into the tunnel and remove the extracted material. Mowlem completed its contract during the autumn of 1975.

Before letting the third contract to Shand Midlands, BWB engineers knew that one unrepaired length was situated vertically below the recorded position of one of the fifteen construction shafts sunk for the building of the tunnel. There was no trace of these shafts on the surface or in the tunnel. In order to locate this shaft, the centre line of the tunnel was marked on the surface of Harecastle Hill and the shaft's position pinpointed. A 30 yard square was then excavated around the site but the shaft was not found. The search was then extended another ten yards to the south which resulted in a nine feet diameter brick-lined shaft being located in-filled with spoil. This shaft was then drilled 165ft to the depth of the tunnel where the tunnel lining was penetrated successfully. The precise position of the shaft when measured within the tunnel showed that it was 17 yards away from its recorded position. This meant that it was just outside the repair length to be undertaken by Shand Midlands, enabling the contract to proceed in January 1976 but with caution when approaching the vicinity of the shaft. Four sections were in need of repair totalling 75 yards. Two sections were worked on simultaneously but, because of the ever-present danger of collapse, the contractor only opened up three foot of damaged brickwork at any one time enabling the new lining to proceed at a pace of 18 inches a day. Almost immediately a very bad section was encountered where an abandoned coal working crossed the tunnel leaving large voids behind the old lining which had to be carefully packed. There was also evidence of considerable instability in the strata and additionally in the structural condition of the tunnel which in places was collapsing ahead of

---
138 10-11 Eliz II ch. xlvi
139 *Waterways News* published by the British Waterways Board, January 1977, Number 65.
140 Polyvinyl chloride (PVC) is a very durable and long lasting plastics material now used extensively in the construction industry.

A group of boatmen's children at Chatterley, typically attired for the early 1950s, some ten years before the British Waterways Board took over from the Docks and Inland Waterways Executive. The view looks towards Longport.
Kidsgrove Library Local History Collection

The north end of the tunnels with Telford's tunnel on the left and Brindley's on the right on 28th June 1970.

Left: The north end of the tunnels with Telford's tunnel on the left and Brindley's on the right.

Right: A string of narrow boats being towed away from the canal bank in readiness to enter Telford's tunnel at the Chatterley end.
Kidsgrove Library Local History Collection

This picture, taken at Chatterley on 21st August 2019, shows from left to right: the closed southern entrance to Brindley's tunnel, the toll keeper's cottage dating from 1827, the listed tunnel retaining walls and the fan house built in 1954.
Barry Knapper

The north end of the tunnels showing the semi-circular fendering used to guide the boats behind the tug into and out of Telford's tunnel. Access to Brindley's tunnel is blocked off by a permanently moored narrow boat used to support a walkway.
Kidsgrove Library Local History Collection

A string of boats towed by electric tug is about to enter the north end of Telford's tunnel assisted by the lady at the tiller of the butty with its bow near the canal bank.
Kidsgrove Library Local History Collection

CHAPTER 7 – BRITISH WATERWAYS BOARD

Left: The plaque mounted on the fan house commemorating the re-enactment in 1966 by Sir John Wedgwood of the cutting of the first sod by Josiah Wedgwood in 1766.

Below: Another view showing the fan house and the tunnel keeper's cottage. The commemorative plaque is just to the left of the tunnel entrance. *(National Waterways Museum)*

This scene depicts the south end of the tunnels in December 1975 during the prolonged stoppage of Telford's tunnel for repairs, as evidenced by the workboats moored by the derelict engine house. The entrance to the closed Brindley tunnel is behind the derelict building as is the route of the old NSR mainline, since diverted.

HARECASTLE'S CANAL AND RAILWAY TUNNELS

This view taken on 2nd August 2018 shows the northern entrances to the Harecastle tunnels, with Telford's tunnel to the left and the long disused Brindley's tunnel to the right. The modern pleasure cruising narrow boat *Kai Tak* is awaiting passage through the tunnel; the other vessel is the Canal and River Trust's workboat *Harecastle*. The orangey-brown canal water from ironstone deposits is very apparent. The Trust's modern building on the right, which comprises the tunnel keeper's office and a sanitary station for boat users, nicely complements its ancient surroundings.

The closed northern entrance to Brindley's tunnel, a photograph taken on 2nd August 2018. Notice that entry is no longer possible, following the intrepid adventure of the canoeists mentioned in the text.

CHAPTER 7 – BRITISH WATERWAYS BOARD

The view from the north end of the tunnels looking towards Kidsgrove on 2nd August 2018 with the Canal & River Trust's workboat *Harecastle* moored in the foreground and the narrow boat *Kai Tak* on the right. The brick-arched turnover bridge can be seen in the near distance followed by the graffiti-disfigured railway bridge carrying the electrified former North Staffordshire Railway's Pottery Line.

From the same viewpoint as the view above from an old post card.
Kidsgrove Library Local History Collection

The present day timings and instructions for passage through Telford's tunnel. Boats pass through in convoys of up to eight and before entering the tunnel the skippers of all the boats in the convoy must attend a safety briefing.

BWB Chairman, Sir Frank Price, cuts the tape at the south end of Telford's tunnel on 2nd April 1977 to mark its reopening. Frank Leslie Price was born in Birmingham in 1922 and knighted in 1966. He was BWB Chairman from 1968 to 1984.
Harry Arnold/Waterway Images

the workface. However, all these difficulties were overcome and the tunnel was formally reopened for navigation on 2nd April 1977[141] by Sir Frank Price, BWB Chairman.[142] The ceremony took place at the northern end of the tunnel after which Sir Frank and his guests sailed through the tunnel on a specially adapted BWB narrow boat. At the southern end of the tunnel Sir Frank was presented with a silver goblet by Roger Lee, Chairman of the Trent & Mersey Canal Society and also given a section of the towpath handrail as a memento.[143] Shortly afterwards, during the weekend of 23rd and 24th April, the Stoke-on-Trent Branch of the Inland Waterways Association held *A Grand Celebration* at Westport Lake, Burslem to mark the re-opening. Following the repairs, which cost in excess of £200,000, the opportunity was taken to remove the long disused towpath which enabled boats to take advantage of the greater air draught in the middle of the tunnel. This was something advocated by Board of Trade Inspector, Lt Col Edward Druitt way back in 1913, but obviously not implemented.

In July 1979 two former Olympic canoeists, Jon Goodwin of Baldwins Gate and the late Robin Witter of Chester attempted to pass through Brindley's tunnel using canoes. They entered the tunnel at the Chatterley end and after travelling some 800 yards, found that the roof had partly collapsed to about three feet above water level with the canal at that point only about four feet wide. At about the halfway point they came across a totally unexpected feature. There was a stretch about 80 yards long where the narrow tunnel suddenly widened to about 13 feet and the roof rose to about ten feet above the water level. Could it have been a hitherto unrecorded passing place? If so, how was the passage of the boats controlled and how did the leggers cope, bearing in mind the wider dimensions of the tunnel. It remains a mystery. After navigating the wider section of the tunnel they encountered a mass of stalactites before coming to an abrupt halt. The way ahead was totally blocked with sand from floor to roof so they returned by travelling backwards until they could turn their canoes in the widened section. Not daunted, they decided to enter the tunnel from the Kidsgrove end, transporting their canoes by road to that location. The entrance to the tunnel was heavily silted and they had to manhandle their canoes for some 500 yards before they could be floated. Shortly afterwards it was discovered that the tunnel was unlined for about 100 yards with the height and width varying widely. After 600 yards there was a section of Staffordshire blue bricks which ran for about 75 yards and was obviously a repaired section as such bricks did not exist anywhere else in the tunnel. At about 700 yards they came across a complete sand blockage which was probably the other end of the same blockage they had experienced earlier. A full report of the findings is included at Appendix 2.

On 30 October 1983 a traditional replacement milepost at the south end of the tunnels was unveiled by Brian Haskins, BWB Northwich Area Engineer, indicating 61 miles to Shardlow and

---

141 On the previous day the narrow boat *Dragon* had sailed from Barlaston and passed through the tunnel, being joined during the morning of 2nd April by the narrow boat *Hampton* which had also sailed from Barlaston. They were owned by John Moss of Newcastle-under-Lyme and Martin Fuller of Barlaston.
142 Frank Leslie Price was born at Hockley, Birmingham in 1922 and knighted in 1966. He was BWB Chairman from 1968 to 1984.
143 *Congleton Chronicle*, 7th April 1977.

CHAPTER 7 – BRITISH WATERWAYS BOARD

On 21st October 1985 a contract was let to Miller Construction Limited to undertake further repair works in Telford's tunnel. The section of canal through the tunnel was drained so that a two-foot narrow-gauge railway could be laid throughout the tunnel to facilitate the works. This view at the south end of the tunnel shows narrow-gauge skips being loaded with cement prior to being propelled into the tunnel by the four-wheel battery electric locomotive seen in the foreground. Four such locomotives were used on the contract, all built by NEI Mining Equipment Limited, Clayton Equipment of Hatton, Derbyshire. *Harry Arnold/Waterway Images*

Right: This view taken on 20th February 1986 shows the temporary railway inside the tunnel with repairs being effected to the roof.
Harry Arnold/Waterway Images

Above: This shows a Miller Construction train at the northern end of the tunnel.
Harry Arnold/Waterway Images

Left: This 1986 view is taken from the same location as the previous photograph but looks in the opposite direction towards Kidsgrove. The bridge beyond the dammed off section of the canal is turnover bridge No. 132 and beyond that is the railway bridge carrying the former NSR mainline. *Harry Arnold/Waterway Images*

31 miles to Preston Brook. A small explanatory plaque explains that the original milepost was located on the horse path above the tunnels, a location no longer available for the replacement. The milepost at the north end of the tunnels is an original cast by Rangeley & Dixson at their Lichfield Road foundry at Stone in 1820.[144] It states 62 miles to Shardlow and 30 to Preston Brook.

In the mid-1980s further repairs were necessary to Telford's tunnel which involved draining a section of the canal so that two-foot narrow gauge four-wheeled battery electric locomotives could be used inside Telford's tunnel.[145] The contractor was Miller Construction Limited with the contract let on 21st October 1985 and completed on 24th March the following year. Many repairs have taken place since but there has not been such a prolonged stoppage as that which took place in the 1970s.

On 22nd April 1988 the northern portals of both tunnels and their retaining walls became Grade II listed structures and the same designation was granted to the southern portals on 31st October 1989, together with the former tunnel keeper's cottage at Chatterley which is now referred to as the Lodge.[146] Telford's tunnel is now the responsibility of the Canal and River Trust which has charitable status, having taken over the former BWB's responsibilities for canals and waterways in England and Wales, with effect from 2nd July 2012. With regard to the tunnel, the latest work has concerned repairs to the washwall at its northern end, involving the underpinning of 50ft of the wall and the re-pointing and repair of 180ft of brickwork, largely making use of original bricks recovered from the canal bed.

---

144 John Rangeley (1781-1842), born in Birkenshaw, Yorkshire married Sarah Dixson (1778-1860) of Stone at St. Michael's Church, Stone on 9th September 1799. Shortly afterwards on 20th September that year, Sarah's brother William Dixson (1776-1834) married Rangeley's sister, Sarah (1778-1850) at St. Peter's Church, Birstall, Yorkshire. Rangeley was an engineer; Dixson from a family of shoe makers provided the capital. The partnership was dissolved on 31st October 1820.

145 The locomotives, all built by NEI Mining Equipment Limited, Clayton Equipment, of Hatton, Derbyshire carried running numbers L18 to L21; their maker's numbers were respectively 5446 and 5481/3 of 1968 and B0987.2 and B0987.1 of 1976.

146 Listing applies to buildings and structures of special architectural and historic interest and gives them protection for future generations to enjoy.

The milepost at the northern entrance to the tunnels is an original, cast by Rangeley & Dixson at their Lichfield Road foundry at Stone in 1820.

Upper right: A traditional narrow boat and butty enters the north end of Telford's tunnel on 22nd May 2007. Note the orangey-yellow ochre hue of the canal water caused by the presence of ironstone.
Harry Arnold/Waterway Images

Right: This picture, taken at the south end of the tunnels on 21st August 2019, demonstrates how popular the canal has become for leisure cruising. A boat is emerging from Telford's tunnel and the mouth of the closed Brindley tunnel can just be seen behind the dog walker. *Barry Knapper*

8

THE RAILWAY TUNNELS

There were at least two abortive schemes for railways that would have passed through Harecastle prior to the NSR building its line. Both involved lines from Manchester running south to, in one case Birmingham and in the other, to join the embryonic Birmingham & Derby Junction Railway (B&DJR), which had received its Act of Parliament on 19th May 1836. The second scheme however, also included a branch that would have given a connection to Birmingham, via the Grand Junction Railway (GJR). Both proposals had different, albeit similar ways of getting round the high ground at Harecastle and in both cases alternative plans had to be developed following objections by a local and influential land owner, Thomas Kinnersly (1782-1855), who we have already met.

First on the scene was the Manchester South Union Railway of which George Stephenson was the engineer with George Parker Bidder his assistant. The plans and sections were deposited with Parliament and the local authorities through whose areas the railway was intended to pass, on 31st December 1836.[147] This was an extremely ambitious undertaking with a mainline of almost seventy-two miles in length from Manchester via Stockport, Macclesfield, Harecastle, Stoke and Lichfield terminating at Tamworth where, as mentioned above, it would have joined the B&DJR. Branches were proposed to Leek, just over nine miles long, with another to Alrewas, almost eight miles long, where another junction would have been made with the B&DJR.[148] Short branch lines, between four and five miles in length, were projected to give connections to Birmingham and Liverpool, leaving the mainline in the vicinity of Stone, south of the Pottery towns, one in each direction to join the GJR near Mill Meece.

---

147 CRO Q/Rum89. HLRO HC/CL/PB/3/plan 1836/174. HC/CL/PB/6/plan 1837/108.
148 The B&DJR amalgamated with the North Midland Railway and the Midland Counties Railway to form the Midland Railway with effect from 10th May 1844.

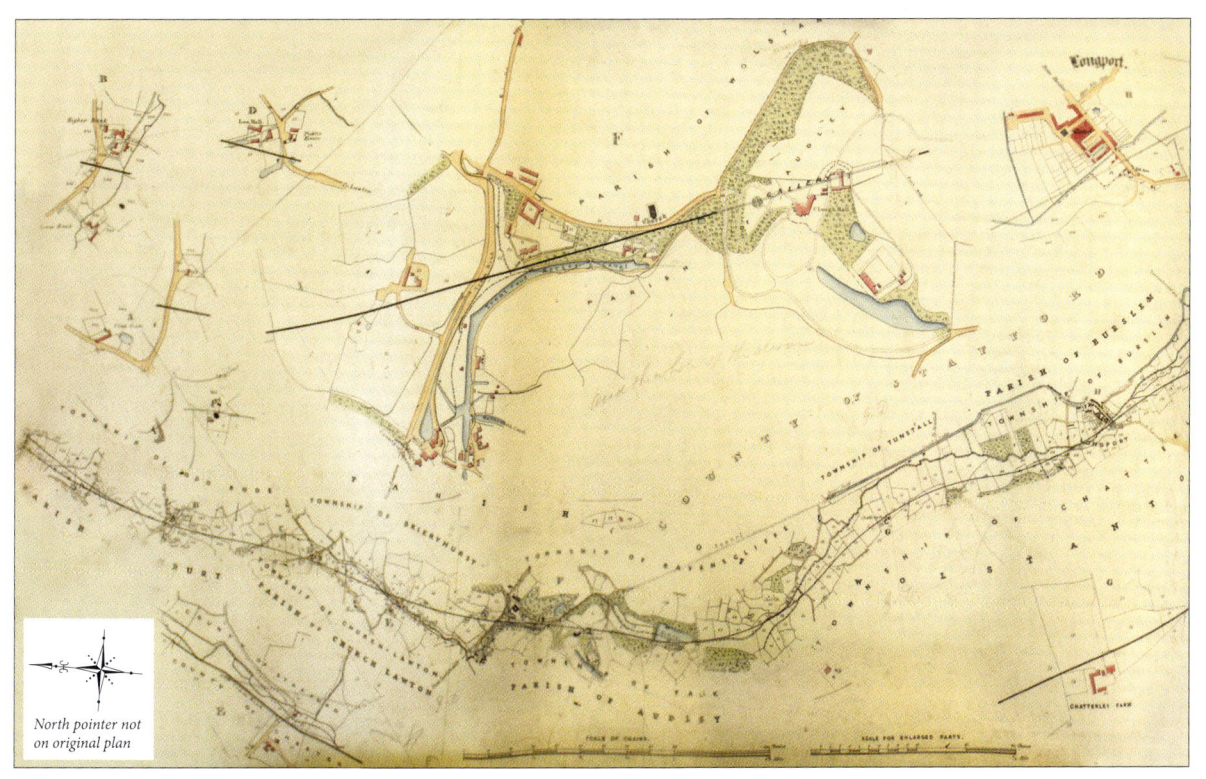

This plan is from the submission made to Parliament by the projected Manchester South Union Railway, as discussed in the text. It was deposited with Parliament on 31st December 1836 and is not only interesting in showing how the railway intended getting round Harecastle Hill, but also in showing the existing canal and surroundings. Notice the line would have passed to the west of the canal tunnels. *CRO QRum/89*

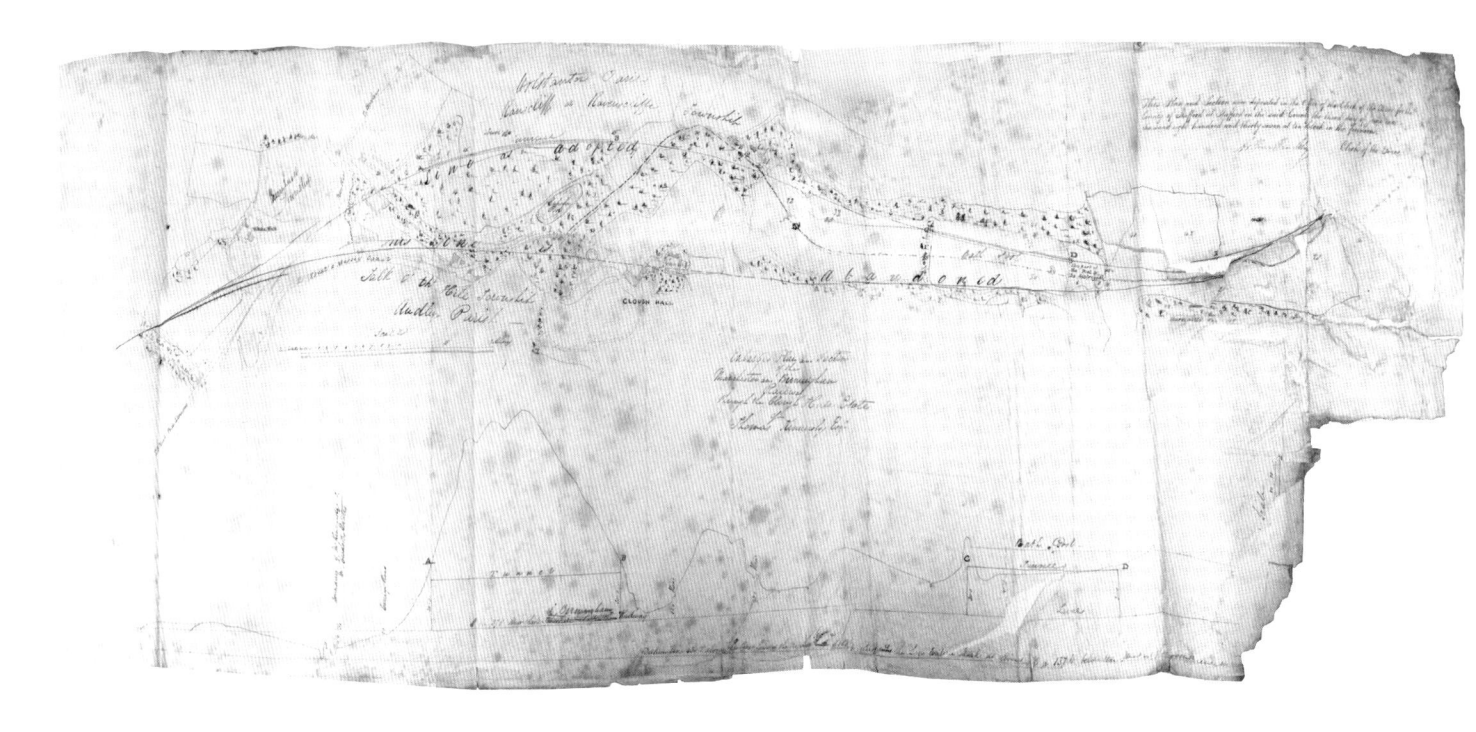

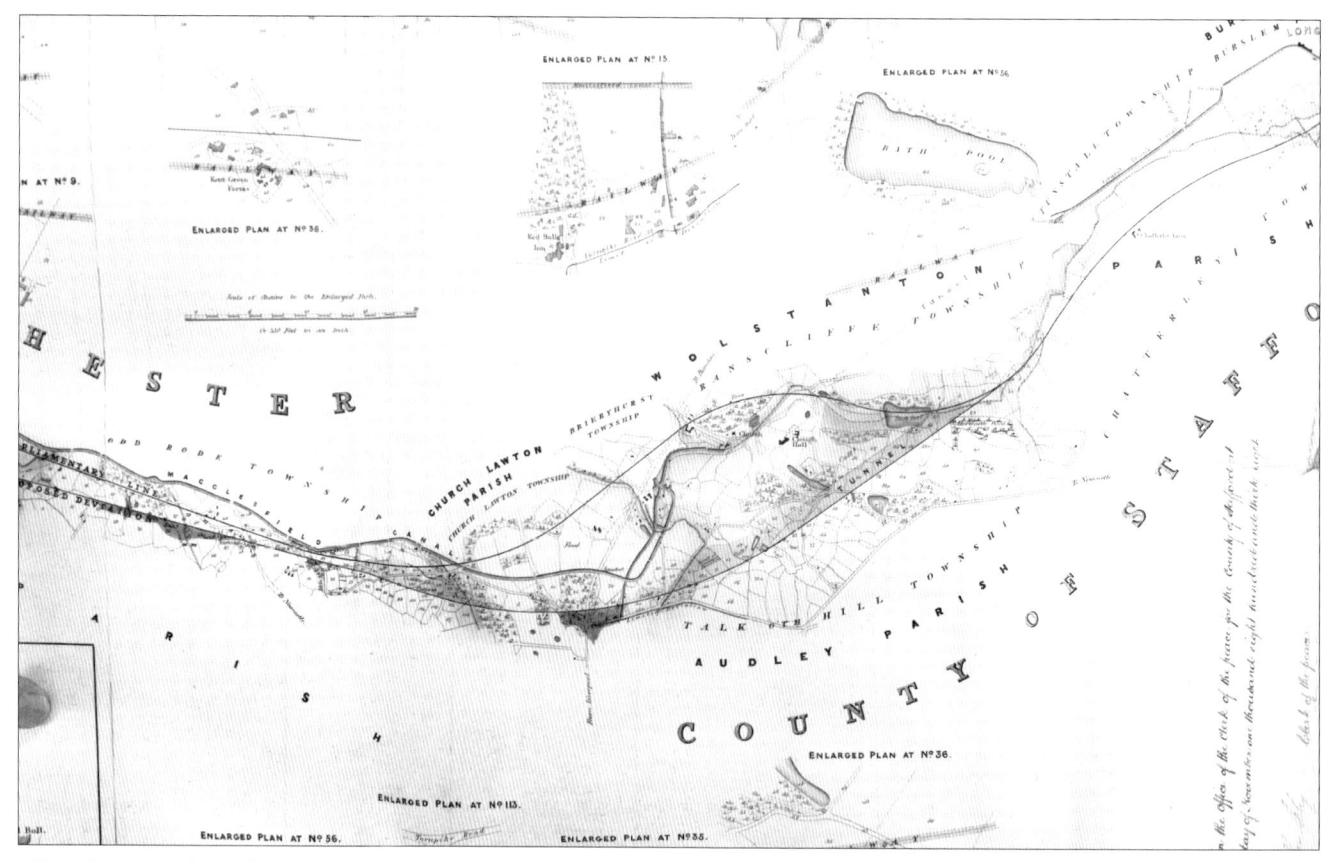

The other 1836 railway scheme was for the Manchester & Birmingham Railway to pass through North Staffordshire, also via Harecastle. Following objections by local land owners as discussed in the text, the proposed route through the area was altered and these plans show both the original projected course and the revised one. Notice that the original line would have passed right through Thomas Kinnersly's Clough Hall estate, tunnelling under the Hall itself. This revised plan of the line in the Harecastle area was deposited with the Clerk of the Peace for the County of Stafford on 3rd June 1837. The section is particularly interesting as it shows the contours of the land along with two tunnels for the proposed alternative route.

CRO QRum/100

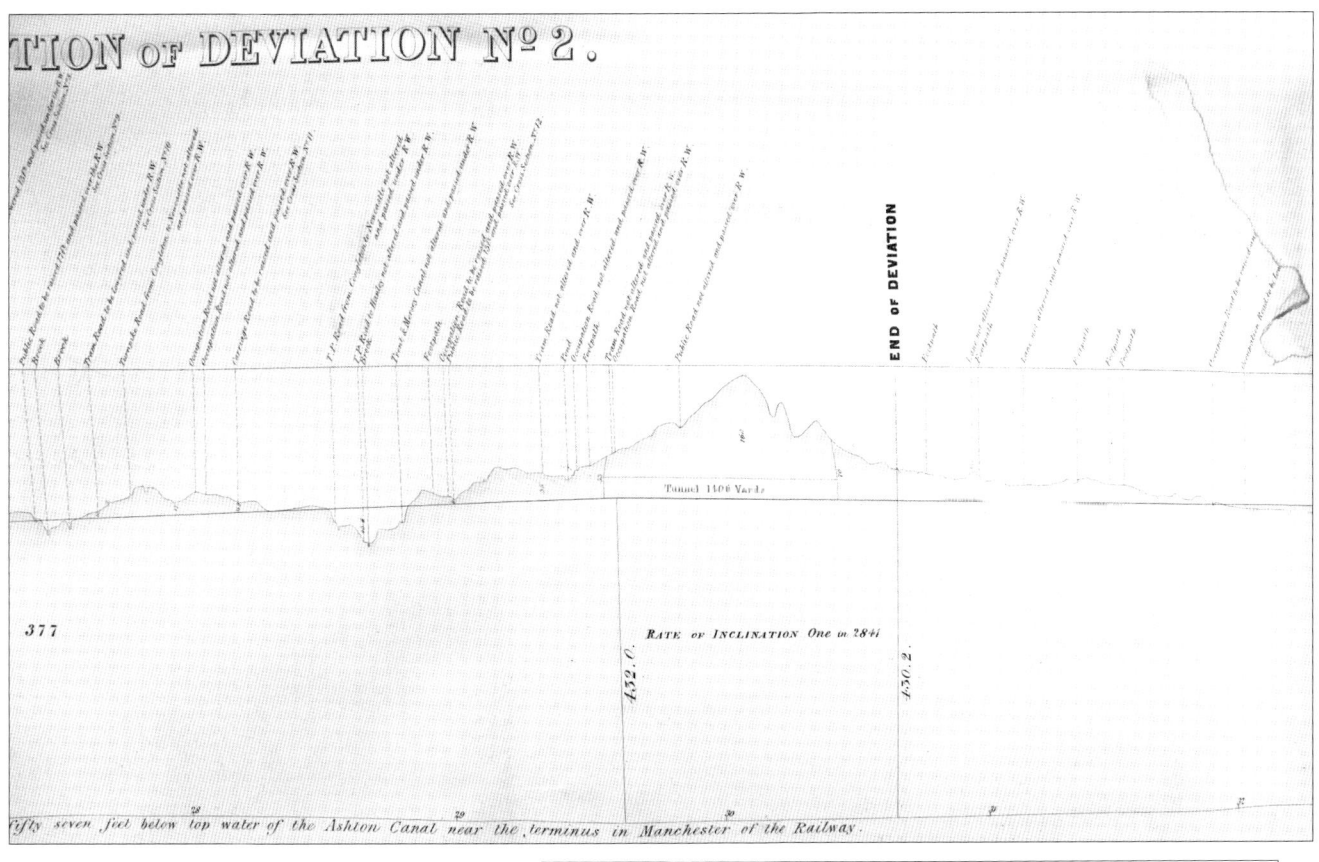

CHAPTER 8 – THE RAILWAY TUNNELS

Further plans of the proposed Manchester & Birmingham Railway, deposited on 1st March 1838, illustrating yet another alternative route to meet the objections of Thomas Kinnersly. This time the course has been moved to the west of his estate, but still involving a tunnel, in this case 1,496 yards long. In the event, this railway built its mainline from Manchester to Crewe with a branch at Macclesfield, which was as near as it got to Harecastle.
CRO QRum/102

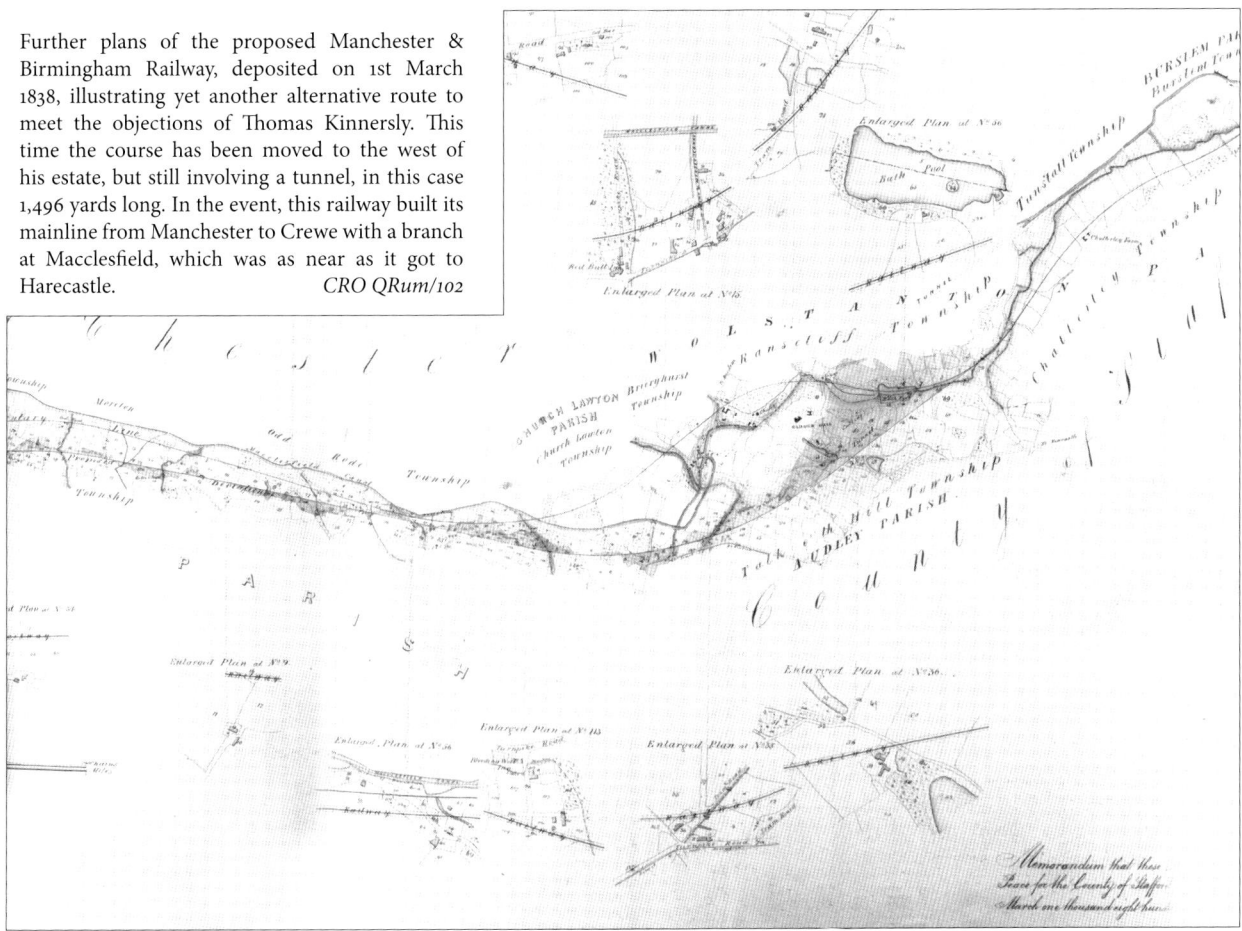

The whole route envisaged enormous engineering works in order to maintain a relatively level formation, running to the west of the later NSR line through Harecastle, with a short tunnel of approximately 440 yards long. This was directly under the site of Thomas Kinnersly's mansion at Clough Hall. The rest of the course through the high ground was for much of its length in a deep cutting. On 6th February the following year the whole scheme was submitted again, with the route through Harecastle diverted to the east, thereby missing the area of Kinnersly's estate. The revision included two additional branches, one from Harecastle to Crewe, where another junction would have been made with the GJR. The other one was from Stoke to Leek where it would have joined the branch in the original proposals from the direction of Macclesfield, both lines terminating adjacent to the basin at the end of the Leek Branch Canal. In the case of the revised plans a total estimated cost was quoted at £2,000,000. In the event, none of these projected railways were built and in fact, no statutory powers were granted.

The other scheme, also in 1836, was for a railway from Manchester to Birmingham that would again have passed through Harecastle – the appropriately named Manchester & Birmingham Railway.[149] This line would have followed much the same route as the other one with a tunnel as it passed through the Harecastle area, once again under Clough Hall, but this time slightly shorter at approximately 375 yards. However, south of Stoke, rather than continuing directly south, it would have joined the GJR around where the later NSR Norton Bridge Junction was situated. A revision to the plans and sections was deposited on 3rd June 1837, again following objections by Thomas Kinnersly as the owner of the Clough Hall Estate. The route of the line at Harecastle was once more diverted to the east, this time entailing two tunnels, another of around the same length as the one originally proposed, with a second of approximately 310 yards under the Bath Pool. This railway did receive its Act of Parliament on 30th June 1837, for a line from Manchester to Crewe where it joined the GJR, but only part of the projected line via the Pottery towns was authorised. This went only as far as Macclesfield and opened on 24th November 1845. As we shall see, it was another three years before the NSR opened its line, which made an end-on junction with the railway at Macclesfield, by which time the Manchester & Birmingham Railway had on 16th July 1846, been vested in the London & North Western Railway.

The contract for the construction of the NSR's mainline from Macclesfield to Colwich – the Pottery Line – which included the three Harecastle railway tunnels was let to the famous railway contractor Thomas Brassey (1805-1870). George Parker Bidder, mentioned earlier, was the man largely responsible for engineering the NSR; he was assisted by John Curphey Forsyth (1815-1879) who was engaged by Bidder in the autumn of 1845 to assist with the preparation of the plans. Early in the following year Forsyth was appointed resident engineer for the Pottery Line and he subsequently remained with the company as its engineer until his retirement in 1864,[150] after which he was appointed consulting engineer and engineer for the construction of new lines until shortly before his death on 15th February 1879.

The longest of the three Harecastle railway tunnels was the south tunnel which was a fraction over a mile in length at 1,763 yards; the length of the middle tunnel was 178 yards and the north tunnel 127 yards. The lengths are taken from the official NSR *Bridge Register* which recorded them as No. 65 (South), No. 64 (Middle) and No. 63 (North). Each of the three tunnels accommodated a double line of railway. Between the northern end of the south tunnel and the middle tunnel was a 350 yard cutting and between the middle and the north tunnels, a cutting of 333 yards. The maximum cover over the south tunnel was 180ft compared to 70ft above the middle tunnel. The cover over the north tunnel was relatively shallow. The railway crossed over the canal between the north tunnel and Harecastle station by means of NSR Bridge No. 61, a cast iron skew girder bridge with a timber floor.

In its issue for 23rd October 1846 the *Derbyshire Advertiser and Journal* reported that the contractors for the NSR's Pottery Line had *entered vigorously upon the various works* and that the sinking of the shafts from Harecastle Hill to the proposed depth of the tunnel had commenced. Some four months later on 27th February 1847, *The Staffordshire Advertiser* explained that the new tunnel would be approached from the south by a deep cutting of some hundreds of yards long and seventy to ninety feet deep. It would occupy the space between the canal tunnels, but at a greater altitude, being seventeen or eighteen feet above the water level. The newspaper continued by saying that to the north there would be another deep cutting and beyond that another short tunnel through the hill behind Kidsgrove church and Parsonage. Already about 500 men and fifty horses were employed, *everything going on with the regularity of clockwork*. It went on to say that the men and the horses would shortly be aided by nine steam engines of 10 to 14 horse power which were being fitted up at stated distances on the hill. Rapid progress was being made with the south cutting, a depth of about twenty feet and proportionate width having already been obtained. The excavation of the tunnel would proceed through nine shafts, 230 yards apart, of about nine or ten feet in diameter, substantially bricked round and sunk to the level of the permanent way. Between some of them communication had already been opened by *drift ways* six feet square. No. 1 shaft from the south was 25 yards deep; No. 2, 36 yards; No. 3, 48 yards; No. 4, 49 yards; No. 5, 40 yards; No. 6, 57 yards; No. 7, 49 yards; No. 8, 15 yards; No. 9, 31 yards. The dip in the strata was from north to south and it was understood that the tunnel would intersect most of the Potteries' coalfield measures. So far little water had been encountered and no pumping had been required, probably because of drainage by the canal tunnels. This was achieved by cutting cross passages from the new workings as drainage channels.[151] Across the summit of the hill a tramway had been

---

149 CRO QRum/100.

150 From 1853 until 1864 he also acted as General Manager.
151 Harecastle South Tunnel: Research Summary, BRB (Residuary) Ltd, 2010.

constructed for the conveyance of materials to and from the various shafts during the progress of the works. The fairly lengthy report on the new railway tunnel concluded by pointing out that stables, carpenters' and smiths' shops had been erected and that two shafts for the short Kidsgrove tunnel had also been sunk with many men likewise employed. At the shareholders' meeting held on the same day, Bidder reported that six of the proposed nine shafts had been sunk to their lowest level and that 843 yards of heading had been driven. The Trent and Mersey Canal proved extremely useful for the transport of materials required for the railway tunnels.[152]

The Staffordshire Advertiser for 24th April 1847 carried this report: *Last Saturday* [i.e. 17th April 1847] *the first brick in the inverse curve at the northern end of shaft No. 1, in the Harecastle tunnel, near Tunstall, was laid by Mr. Till, the resident engineer. The next was laid by Mr. Thomas Jones, and this was followed in succession by Mr. Wilson, principal mason, Mr. Hall, inspector of the works, and each of the sub-contractors of the several shafts. A bumper toast was drank on the laying of each brick, half a gallon of ale being allowed to each navvy for the day's celebration. The festivity was afterwards prolonged, at the Swan Inn, Tunstall.* A month later the navvies were not so convivial! On 29th May 1847, the same newspaper reported on a clash between the English and Irish employed on the tunnel works. *The English labourers had armed themselves with sticks and some of their working tools, but the Irish had prudently declined coming into open warfare. At the precise moment, Mr. Jones, the superintendent of the works, fortunately came up, when order was restored, and directions were given for forty-four of the English labourers to be paid off. Mr. Povey, the superintendent of the constabulary for that quarter, has placed a stronger body of the police in that neighbourhood, to prevent any breach of the peace.*

At the meeting of the directors held on 25th June 1847, Bidder reported that *the whole of the tunnel shafting has been completed, and the tunnelling has commenced at eight of the nine shafts, 60 yards of tunnel are completed with brickwork.* When commenting on the tunnel in his report dated 13th January 1848, Bidder said that *the number of shafts has been doubled, thus ensuring a more speedy completion of this important work; 600 lineal yards of tunnel are completed, 676 yards of mining, and 2,047 lineal yards of headings have been driven; and also 538 yards of shafts have been sunk.* By 15th July 1848 he was able to report that only eighty yards of the tunnel remained to be completed – quite remarkable progress especially when compared with the time it took to construct the earlier and much smaller bore canal tunnels.

---

152 *Ibid.*

George Parker Bidder (1806-1878), the engineer primarily responsible for the construction of the principal lines of the North Staffordshire Railway. *Mary Evans Picture Library*

John Curphey Forsyth (1815-1879) was engaged by Bidder in 1845 to assist with the preparation of the engineering plans for the NSR. He was appointed resident engineer for the Pottery Line and remained associated with the company in various capacities until shortly before his death. *National Railway Museum*

George Wynne (1804-1890) was the Board of Trade Inspector responsible for inspecting the Harecastle railway tunnels on 6th October 1848, prior to their formal opening three days later.
National Portrait Gallery

It is interesting to note that Brassey employed George Findlay (1829-1893), the future the General Manager of the London & North Western Railway (L&NWR), on the Harecastle tunnel contract. He was appointed as chief inspector of mining and brickwork. As such, he was responsible for checking the lines and levels of the tunnels, proving that the centres of the arches were correct and measuring the work of the sub contractors. He was also responsible for the construction of the tunnel portals.

The completed tunnels were inspected by Board of Trade Inspecting Officer Lieutenant George Wynne (1804-1890)[153] on 6th October 1848. In compiling his report Wynne included some interesting detail. He remarked on the tunnels passing through the coal measures and noted that the lining was brickwork in hydraulic lime cement mortar and 2ft 6in thick. He also noted that, where the tunnel passed through a fine stratum of sand, an invert had been inserted in the construction, but not in the rest of the tunnel. In his view the only difference between the south and middle tunnels was that the latter had been constructed with masonry sidewalls instead of brick. The dimensions of the south tunnel were noted as 23ft 9in wide at rail level with a height of 21ft 6in from rail level to crown.[154]

The tunnels were opened for goods and passenger traffic on 9th October 1848. On the following 28th October *The Staffordshire Advertiser* reported that the winding up of the *Tunnel Sick Club* had taken place the previous day when its clerk, Robert Davies, confirmed that upwards of £1,500 had been paid in the past eighteen months to the widows and orphans of deceased labourers and for the relief of fever, small-pox and other sicknesses and accidents of the workmen. The newspaper went on to record that the occasion was followed by a sumptuous supper served to celebrate the completion of the tunnel. Some thirty sub-contractors and clerks were present. Thomas Jones, agent to Brassey, was in the chair with Mr. Wilson, chief master bricklayer, in the vice-chair. *After the usual loyal toasts had received becoming attention, the healths of Mr. Brassey, Mr. John Jones, the Chairman and Directors of the North Staffordshire Railway Company, the engineers, Dr. Field and Mr C. Davenport, surgeons, were next given.*

On 9th November 1848, under Brassey's instructions, forty draught horses were auctioned at the tunnel along with shaft and cart gearing. On the following 14th November another auction was held at Harecastle which included six stationary steam engines, a saw mill and pit frames. The engines had all been purchased new for the tunnel work; two were of 10 horse power and three of 15 horse power. The third of 32 horse power, which had never been erected, was made by Butler & Company of Stanningley, near Leeds and was made available for inspection at Shelton Wharf between Newcastle-under-Lyme and Hanley.[155]

Construction of the main railway tunnel came at a high price. We have been able to identify six fatalities, four in 1847 and two in 1848. Patrick Ford, aged forty-five, died in August 1847 while working at the bottom of No. 7 shaft when a wagon loaded with sand fell down the shaft killing him instantly. The following month John Maclean, aged twenty-six, was at the top of No. 1 shaft when he stumbled on the slippery surface and fell down the shaft to meet his death, eighty feet below. In October William Thaerthan at the No. 5 shaft put a match to a powder charge and retreated to what he thought to be a safe distance but when the blast took place he was hit by a piece of *black bass* and was so severely injured that he died shortly after his rescue from the tunnel. He was thirty-two. There was to be yet another fatality before the year was out. In December David Roberts, aged thirty-five, one of the workmen employed at the No. 6 shaft, was severely injured when his head hit the top of the tunnel. He had been assisting to remove a large timber when it sprang free and projected him upwards with great force. He died five days later. In March 1848 there were two further fatalities. The first and the saddest of all happened to Thomas Edwards, a lad of between ten and eleven years of age, employed at No. 4 shaft. He had just come up the shaft and having landed was in the act

---

153 George Wynne was with the Board of Trade from 1847 until 1858 when he resigned his appointment as Senior Government Inspector of Railways to resume an active military career in China as Chief Royal Engineer. He was present at the storming and capture of Nantow on 11th August 1858 and the attack of Skek-Tsing on 8th January 1859, following which he received the war medal for China. From 1866 to 1870 he served as Chief Royal Engineer in Ireland and was made a General in 1877.

154 Harecastle South Tunnel: Research Summary, BRB (Residuary) Ltd, 2010.
155 *The Staffordshire Advertiser*, 4th November 1848.

CHAPTER 8 – THE RAILWAY TUNNELS

A view looking up a ventilation shaft in the south railway tunnel.
Kidsgrove Library Local History Collection

of getting his powder-flask out of the skip when he missed his footing and fell back down the shaft to a depth of 60 yards. He was killed instantly. At the inquest, the jury in returning a verdict of accidental death asked for a representation to be made to the contractors in reference to No. 4 shaft which they said was so *frequently without a proper banksman*. The last fatality we have been able to identify also occurred in March 1848 when Frederick Renshaw, aged twenty, fell down No. 3 shaft. Fatalities also occurred when the canal tunnels were dug but they do not appear to have been so graphically recorded.[156]

At the meeting of the NSR's Traffic Committee held on 14th June 1853 it was reported that five L&NWR officials had passed from Macclesfield through Harecastle tunnel to Tunstall and back and thence to Crewe with a *Special Engine*, without the NSR's permission. The station just to the south of the longest railway tunnel was originally named Tunstall. It was opened in January 1864 and renamed Chatterley on 1st October 1873 when the Potteries Loop Line reached the town of Tunstall. The company secretary was instructed to convey the company's strong disapproval to the L&NWR which later gave an assurance that such an irregularity would not happen again.[157] Three of the L&NWR officials were identified as Messrs Norris, Cooper and Harrison. We believe that Norris was Richard Stuart Norris (1812-1878), Engineer & Superintendent, L&NWR Northern Division. We wonder what this episode was all about and what was that *Special Engine*?

On 27th June 1854 the 12-noon L&NWR passenger train from Manchester to London was derailed in the main Harecastle tunnel and one or two passengers were slightly hurt.[158] The train, which consisted of five carriages and two brake vans, left Harecastle station at 1.15pm and when it had travelled about one third of the way into the tunnel, the guard observed a second class carriage next to the first brake van off-the-line and before the train could stop, all vehicles behind the locomotive had been derailed. Both lines were closed, the Down line for one hour and the Up line for about four hours, but arrangements were made as speedily as possible to work Up and Down traffic over the Down line between Burslem (renamed Longport in July 1873) and Harecastle & Kidsgrove. Forsyth attributed the accident to a defect in the permanent way.[159]

Right: This is a portrait of Henry Woodhouse (1823-1895) who was responsible for superintending and maintaining the NSR's permanent way from 1st August 1853 until 30th June 1856 when the NSR took over direct responsibility for those tasks. Woodhouse did not approve of the NSR's insistence of using Field and Jeffreys' patent wedges (keys) which brought about the culmination of his involvement with the NSR.

In 1853 the NSR agreed that Henry Woodhouse, L&NWR Permanent Way Superintendent should superintend and maintain the NSR's permanent way under the sole control of the NSR and *on the same footing on which Contractors have hitherto fulfilled that undertaking.*[160] Henry Woodhouse (1823-1895) had joined the L&NWR in February 1843 and on 1st October 1852 had been appointed Permanent Way Superintendent for the whole L&NWR system; he was based at Stafford. At the meeting of the NSR's Traffic Committee held on 26th July 1853 a letter dated 11th July from the L&NWR's Secretary, Charles Stewart, was read out. It stated that after consultation with Deputy Chairman, Robert Benson and General Manager, Captain Mark Huish, the best way of implementing the new arrangement *would be to make Mr. Woodhouse and his Staff for the purpose of the North Staffordshire Line servants of your Company and responsible accordingly.* It was resolved that the suggestion be approved and adopted, the new arrangement coming into effect on 1st August 1853.[161]

In 1856 the new arrangement came under stress when Woodhouse wrote objecting to the use of *Field & Jeffreys' patent Chair Key* on the NSR's permanent way. The NSR's Engineer, John

---

156 The railway tunnel deaths are recorded in *The Staffordshire Advertiser* for 14th August, 11th September, 30th October and 4th December 1847 and 25th March 1848.
157 NA RAIL 532/15. NSR Traffic Committee meetings, 16th June and 28th June 1853, Minutes 1079 and 1094.
158 NA RAIL 532/5. NSR Directors' meeting, 20th July 1854, Minute 864.
159 NA RAIL 532/15. NSR Traffic Committee meeting, 28th June 1854, Minute 1370.
160 NA RAIL 532/15. NSR Traffic Committee meeting, 25th June 1853, Minute 1098.
161 NA RAIL 532/15. NSR Traffic Committee meeting, 26th July 1853, Minutes 1121 and 1122.

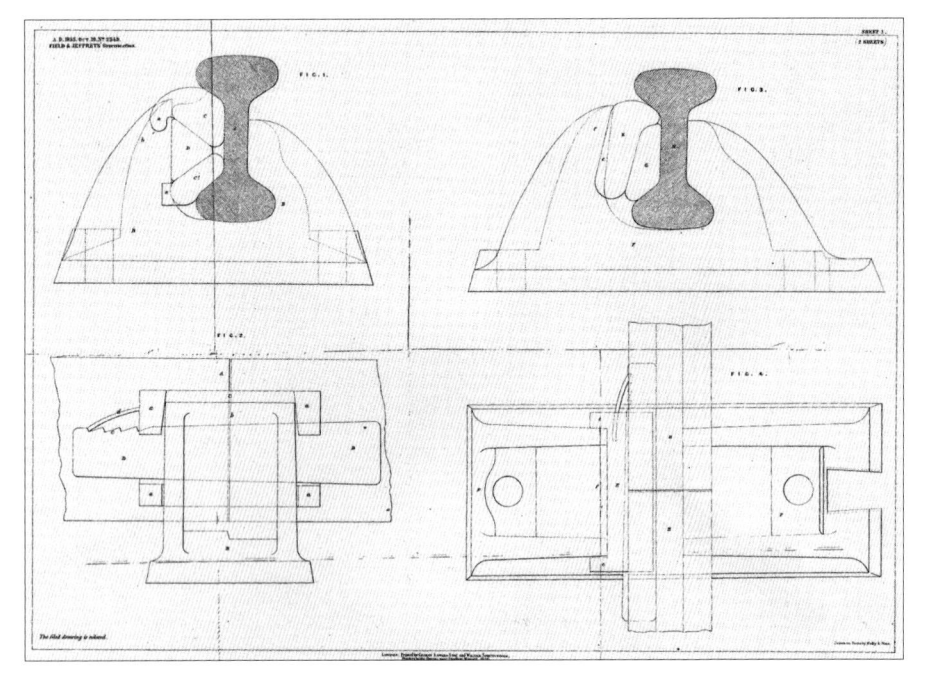

This diagram is taken from the Letters Patent No. 2349 granted to William Field and Edward Jeffreys of Shrewsbury for their invention of an: Improved means for securing the rails of railways in their chairs or bearings. The patented chairs were adopted by the NSR for the relaying of the tracks in Harecastle tunnels in 1856. Variations in the arrangement could be used either as a normal chair or for different sections of rail, as well where two rails were joined together as would be the case with the standard fishplate we are familiar with today. On the drawing, Figs 2 and 4 clearly show the metal wedge and its spring referred to in the text. *British Library*

Curphey Forsyth was asked to investigate and report his opinion of the invention and to communicate with the chairman on the subject.[162] At the meeting of the committee held on 15th April, it was resolved on the strong recommendation of Forsyth to consent to the use of Field & Jeffreys' keys in relaying the permanent way through Harecastle Tunnel.[163] Quite apart from the issue with the L&NWR it is interesting to note that the permanent way in the tunnels needed renewing after only seven years' use. On 24th April Woodhouse wrote to the NSR's Secretary, Jonathan Samuda, in the following terms:

London & North Western Railway
Permanent Way Dept, Head Office
Stafford, April 24th 1856

Dear Sir,

I beg to acknowledge receipt of your note of the 21st Inst from which it would appear that the Directors do not adopt my views respecting the method of Relaying the Harecastle Tunnel. As I strongly object to incur a divided responsibility in a question involving, as I think, the safety of the public, I think it desirable that I should be relieved from the superintendence of the Permanent Way of your Line.

I therefore request, that arrangements may be made to effect this object as early as practicable, & shall be glad to confer on the subject with any person you may appoint.

Yours truly, Henry Woodhouse

The NSR Traffic Committee considered the latter at its meeting on 29th April 1856 and resolved that the Secretary should reply in the following terms:[164]

---

162 NA RAIL 532/15. NSR Traffic Committee meeting, 18 March 1856, Minute 1767. The NSR minutes wrongly record the second patentee's name as Jeffries. This has been corrected as there is no point in perpetuating an obvious error.
163 NA RAIL 532/15. NSR Traffic Committee meeting, 15th April 1856, Minute 1794.
164 NA RAIL 532/16. NSR Traffic Committee meeting, 29 April 1856, Minute 1802.

Stoke 29th April 1856

Dear Sir,

I have this day laid before the Directors your letter of the 24th Inst in which you state that you strongly object to incur a divided responsibility in a question involving, as you think, the safety of the public, & express a wish to be relieved from the Superintendence of the Permanent Way of the North Staffordshire Line of Railway.

In reply, the Directors desire me to state that in authorising the use of Field & Jeffreys Patent Railway Keys in relaying the permanent way through the Harecastle Tunnel on the recommendation of their Engineer, Mr. Forsyth, they had no wish or intention to impose upon you any responsibility for the use of such Keys, which will rest entirely with Mr Forsyth.

Yours truly, J. Samuda, Secretary

Woodhouse was having none of this and wrote back on 5th May 1856 as follows:

London & North Western Railway
Permanent Way Dept. Head Office
Stafford, May 5th 1856

Dear Sir,

I am in receipt of your favour of the 29th Ulto & in reply beg to state that I do not consider that I am thereby relieved from the position to which I objected in my letter of the 24th Ulto. I have hitherto considered that my position on the North Staffordshire Line was that of Head of a Department, holding myself immediately responsible to the Directors.

I cannot consent to act in a subordinate capacity under Mr. Forsyth & must beg of the Directors to place the charge of the Permanent Way of the North Staffordshire Lines in other hands as early as practicable.

Yours truly, Henry Woodhouse

The letter was read out at the meeting of the Traffic Committee held on 13th May 1856 when it was resolved that Woodhouse be told that with effect from 30th June that year the

NSR would undertake the maintenance of its own permanent way.[165] At the same meeting it was reported that on 2nd May a platelayer named Thomas Shuker, in the employ of Messrs Field & Jeffreys, Patentees, had been killed whilst engaged in relaying the permanent way through Harecastle tunnel but that the accident appeared to be attributable entirely to the incautiousness of the deceased.[166] This was confirmed by an inquest held at the Plough Inn, Kidsgrove when a verdict of accidental death was returned. The deceased, aged thirty-one, had been run over by the 2.15pm train passenger train from Macclesfield.[167] It is clear from this report that Forsyth had actually already instructed Field & Jeffreys to get on with the job.

Field was William Field (1812-1894), his partner being Edward Alexander Jeffreys (1824-1889). At the time of the grant of the patent referred to as a *Compound Wedge for Rails* both men lived in Shrewsbury; both men had strong connections with Thomas Brassey, who had been the appointed contractor for the Harecastle tunnels. *The Engineer* for 4th January 1856 carried this announcement:

COMPOUND WEDGE FOR RAILS – *Messrs Field and Jeffreys have lately patented a plan for securing rails in their chairs or bearings, and so making a perfect uniform joint, which is said to be equal to the "fish", at one-fifth of the cost. This invention is being adopted on the whole of the Shrewsbury and Hereford of 51 miles; and with great success on the Shrewsbury and Chester; the Chester and Holyhead; Chester General Station and Shrewsbury Station. It has also been taken into use on the Shropshire Union, and on some of the principal Scotch lines. The utility of this invention consists in its cheapness, and its being applicable to existing lines. The improvement is obtained by a compound wedge, which is thus described by the patentees: "The wedge, on being driven up longitudinally, expands the gibs vertically and laterally, in the four directions; the wedge being cast or wrought-iron, with ratchet teeth, into which a spring drops, and prevents the wedge getting back. The spring can be loose, or cast into the gibs and when fixed, the wedge will not be liable to come out, or loosen, the weather having no effect on it".*

The patent dated 19th October 1855 was sealed on 25th January 1856 and numbered 2349. The Letters Patent summarised the invention as an *Improved means for securing the rails of railways in their chairs or bearings.*

We wonder why Woodhouse was so averse to the new invention. Field acted as partner with Brassey for the construction of many railways and as his agent for others. For example he acted as agent for the Shrewsbury and Hereford contract let in 1851 and as partner when that railway was widened in 1861. He was also in partnership with Brassey for the Nantwich and Market Drayton contract let in 1862 and became contractor in his own right for the Stafford and Uttoxeter Railway opened in 1867. Jeffreys was apprenticed to Bury, Curtis & Kennedy of Liverpool and in 1845 was appointed locomotive superintendent of the Shrewsbury and Chester Railway staying with that company for eight years. In 1853 Brassey secured his services to manage and work the Shrewsbury and Hereford Railway which he did until the termination of Brassey's lease of the line in 1863. Thereafter he became involved with Lowmoor Ironworks at Bradford and the Monk Bridge Ironworks at Leeds, becoming a director of the latter. So these were men of some experience who obviously impressed Forsyth. It is not known how the patented keys performed in service but the next instance of the permanent way in Harecastle tunnels being relaid occurred in 1865 when the Up line was relaid.[168]

There was a fatality in the north tunnel on 26th August 1911 which was shrouded in mystery and captured a lot of local media attention. The fatal accident happened to William Henry Keay, relief station master at Radway Green. On the day in question Keay, who had been employed by the NSR for twenty years and had recently been commended for staying on duty during a strike, was travelling to Etruria on his way home. He caught the 8.50pm train from Radway Green and brought with him some books and the cash he had taken during the day which he intended to deposit at Etruria station. He lived nearby at Basford. At Radway Green he got into the train with the guard and collected the tickets from the passengers alighting at Alsager. He then got into a first class compartment and was last seen alive at Harecastle station where he was spotted leaning out of a carriage window. When the train arrived at Chatterley, the guard noticed that he was not in the carriage but that his hat, books and cash bag were on the seat. The guard assumed that he had gone to another part of the train to see a friend but when the train arrived at Etruria he was still missing. A platelayer was sent to search the line and Keay's body was found inside Harecastle north tunnel about twenty yards from the north end. After the accident, the doors and handles of the carriages were inspected and found to be in perfect order with no indication that anything was wrong.

The inquest was held on 20th August 1911; death had occurred following a fracture of the skull and the jury returned an open verdict. The cause of the accident remained a mystery. Keay's widow decided to claim compensation from the NSR and the case was heard on 10th January 1912 at Stoke County Court.[169] Keay's widow explained that her late husband, aged 34, had no worries, financial or otherwise and enjoyed good health. The guard on the train, William Henry Watson from Uttoxeter, stated that when the train arrived at Chatterley the carriage door was properly shut. It would have been impossible for the deceased to open it whilst in the tunnel as it was only a few inches from the tunnel side and if the door opened it would have been smashed to pieces. At the request of the judge, a train was stopped at exactly the spot where the body was found to prove this very point. On 14th February 1912 judgement was given in favour of the NSR.[170] The judge remarked that it was a very extraordinary and mysterious affair but Mrs Keay had failed to satisfy him that falling from the train whilst the door was closed was occasioned out of any risk arising out of her late husband's employment. However, he

---

165 NA RAIL 532/1. NSR Traffic Committee meeting, 13th May 1856, Minute 1813.
166 NA RAIL 532/16. NSR Traffic Committee meeting, 13th May 1856, Minute 1810.
167 *Staffordshire Sentinel and Commercial & General Advertiser*, 10th May 1856.
168 NA RAIL 532/17. NSR Traffic Committee meeting, 21st March 1865, Minute 4666.
169 *Staffordshire Sentinel*, 11th January 1912.
170 *Staffordshire Sentinel*, 14th and 15th February 1912.

303

North Staffordshire Railway.

Special Arrangements, Train Alterations
AND
Notice of the Running of Special Trains,

From June 21st, to June 27th, 1919, inclusive.

PERMANENT WAY, ETC., OPERATIONS.

Macclesfield to Colwich and Norton Bridge—Harecastle Tunnels—On Sunday, June 22nd, Men will be engaged repairing Brickwork, etc., between Trains—Both Lines affected. There is scaffolding and centreing in the Tunnels which is only just clear of our gauge. Therefore, all vehicles passing through must be kept strictly within this Company's loading gauge.

Harecastle—Bridge at 13 miles 41 chains. This Bridge is being painted during the week, between Trains—Up and Down Lines affected.

Longport Sidings—On Sunday, June 22nd—Renewing No. 5 Siding—Down Side. This Siding to be kept clear of all traffic.

Glebe Street—On Sunday, June 22nd—Repairs to Point and Signal Connections.

Mount Pleasant—Between 20¾ and 21 miles—A New Running Road is being laid in on the Down Side during the week.

Between Barlaston and Stone—26 to 26¾ miles 17 chains—Relaying—Up Line, during the week, between Trains. A Warning Board will be fixed whilst the work is in progress.

Stoke to Willington and Burton—Between Leigh and Bromshall Junction—Bridge at 11¼ miles—Undergoing repairs during the week, between Trains—Up and Down Lines affected.

Bromshall Junction—On Monday, June 23rd and during the week—Repairs to Point and Signal Connections.

This is the front page of an NSR Special Arrangements Notice for the period 21st to 27th June 1919, which among other items, gives details to those concerned of repairs being undertaken to the Harecastle Tunnels.

hoped that the NSR would reinstate its gesture of a £25 payment.

In marked contrast to the attention given to the canal tunnels, the NSR Board and T&FC minutes are remarkably silent on matters concerning the railway tunnels. A significant expenditure of £2,000 was incurred on relining the brickwork in 1906[171] and at its meeting of 9th February 1915, the T&FC authorised the installation of 9-inch socket pipes throughout the south railway tunnel with catch-pits at about every fifty yards. This was to improve the drainage by allowing water seeping into the railway tunnel to flow into the canal.[172] There was a mishap in the railway tunnel on 7th January 1916 when a North Eastern Railway wagon loaded with *pitwood* was derailed by a pit prop[173] and during the following year an Up banner signal was provided at the north tunnel entrance at a cost of £32 10s 0d.[174] The banner signal was a repeater for the Chatterley Up home signal and would presumably be electrically operated even at this early date. Until the line was taken out of use there was also an electric banner repeater between the middle and the main south tunnel for the Chatterley Up home signal and another at the other end for the Harecastle Down home signals. A special arrangement notice in force from 21st to 27th June 1919 gave warning to enginemen and operating staff that men would be engaged in the tunnels repairing brickwork between trains and that both lines would be affected. It went on to explain that there was scaffolding and centering in the tunnels which was only just clear of the loading gauge such that all vehicles passing through must be kept strictly within the company's loading gauge. The LM&SR Works Committee minutes, although surprisingly detailed, are even more silent on the railway tunnels than the NSR equivalents. We suspect that this is because the tunnels were exceptionally well built and not so susceptible to the stresses that subsidence had on the canal tunnels built in earlier times with more primitive methods, especially Brindley's pioneering tunnel which opened some seventy-three years before the railway tunnels. There would, of course, have been occasional relaying of track and other odd repairs but the expense for these would have been accommodated in the local engineers' day-to-day budgets, not requiring higher authority once the overall annual budgets had been approved.

The station immediately to the north of the tunnels was originally named Harecastle. It has been renamed several times: Harecastle & Kidsgrove from 1853;[175] Kidsgrove Junction from 1869; Harecastle from 15th November 1875 following the opening of the Loop Line station at Kidsgrove; Kidsgrove Central from 2nd October 1944, adopting its current name of Kidsgrove on 18th April 1966. It opened on 9th October 1848 concurrently with the three tunnels and served both the mainline to Macclesfield and the branch to Crewe, which it still does. Between 1893 and 1931 it also served as the terminus for the Audley line passenger services and, between 1893 and 1930, for those that ran to and from Wheelock on the Sandbach branch. As mentioned above, the station immediately to the south of the south tunnel was Chatterley, originally named Tunstall prior to the opening of the Loop Line station of that name on 1st December 1873. It survived until closure by British Railways (BR) on 27th September 1948. It is surprising that it stayed open for so long as in 1947 the total number of passengers using the station was only 750 producing revenue of £43 with receipts from parcels traffic amounting to £11. The net annual saving as a result of closing the station was £419, together with an additional saving of £1,789 on immediate essential repairs. After closure the parcels traffic was dealt with by extending the delivery area of Tunstall station on the Loop Line which was only one mile away by road from Chatterley.

Kathleen Murial Allen, née Evans (1913-1997), station mistress at Chatterley.

Chatterley station was unusual in that during the Second World War the person in charge of the station was a lady, station mistress Kathleen Murial Allen, née Evans.[176] She reported to the station master at Longport and remained in charge at Chatterley until the station closed. A longstanding station master at Longport was Cecil Arthur Pye (1886-1968) who completed forty-six years of service with the NSR and LM&SR. He was appointed stationmaster at Longport in June 1927 and retired from that position, also in charge of Chatterley, on 7th June 1946.[177]

---

171 NA RAIL 532/22. NSR T&FC meeting, 2nd October 1906, Minute 23535.
172 NA RAIL 532/23. NSR T&FC meeting, 9th February 1915, Minute 28201.
173 NA RAIL 532/23. NSR T&FC meeting, 11th January 1916, Minute 28684.
174 NA RAIL 532/23. NSR T&FC meeting, 27th November 1917, Minute 29592.
175 NA RAIL 532/15. NSR TC meeting 3rd May 1853, Minute 1053.

176 Kathleen Murial Evans was born at Leek on 1st March 1913. In 1935 she married Edward Allen who was born on 2nd September 1911; he was a blast furnace man at Goldendale Iron Works. They both died in 1997.
177 *The Staffordshire Advertiser*, 1st June 1946.

Chatterley Junction on 3rd April 1958 looking south-west with the Talk & Chesterton branches curving away to the right. The derelict building behind the water tank is the former engine house for the blast furnace blowing engines of the Chatterley Ironworks. It outlasted the furnaces by many years as they ceased production in 1901, but it was not demolished until the early 1970s. The bridge abutments visible on the branch had been part of a bridge that accommodated an internal works railway serving Ashwood Colliery. The building construction on the right was in connection with new messing facilities for the local staff.

View looking north on 4th February 1967 from the footsteps of Chatterley Junction signal box after the deviation line opened. Prior to rationalisation of the arrangements here after the deviation line was brought into use, the former mainlines were still used as part of the local shunting facilities to serve Goldendale Ironworks. The connection to the works is the line curving away to the right, the works itself being just off the picture. On the extreme left is the NCB coal stocking and blending ground with its large mountain of coal, which was also rail-served from the sidings to the left. Notice that the vehicles at the end of the siding on the right, are slag ladle wagons belonging to the ironworks.

Train describer label from Chatterley Junction signal box.

The two-character 'B6' headcode displayed on this train was for the local diesel multiple unit (DMU) service between Derby and Crewe. On 23rd April 1966 a three-car Cravens unit, later Class '105', was working the 5.57 pm train from Derby and is approaching the former station at Chatterley. The Trent & Mersey Canal is to the left with Goldendale Ironworks to the extreme left. The signal on the right is the Chatterley Junction Down Starter and the tall one on the left with the repeating arms, the Up Home, with the Bradwell Sidings Up Distant below. *The late Michael Mensing*

CHAPTER 8 – THE RAILWAY TUNNELS

With the former Chatterley station platforms flanking the mainlines, this photograph was taken somewhat earlier than the previous one, with the 2.15pm train from Derby consisting of a three-car Birmingham Railway Carriage & Wagon Company diesel multiple unit (DMU), later known as Class '104'. *The late Michael Mensing*

A more general view from a similar standpoint taken on 30th May 1966 and looking directly south, with a Cravens DMU approaching; these units were later known as Class '105'. The bridge, No. 67, carried a water trough across the railway. The twin towers reaching to the sky on the left of the tall signal are the winding towers of Wolstanton Colliery and the top of the former Chatterley Ironworks engine house can be seen to the right. The very tall spire of St Margaret's Parish Church in Wolstanton is just visible on the central skyline.

Stoke-allocated Stanier Class '5' 2-6-0 No. 42977, heading south by the former Chatterley station on 28th September 1963, with a goods train. At the time Stoke had several engines of this comparatively small class of only forty, on its allocation.

The late Michael Mensing

123

Metro-Cammell three-car DMU, later Class '101', with a three-car BRCW unit behind, forming the 5.43pm Birmingham New Street to Macclesfield service on 23rd April 1966. The train is in the cutting approaching Harecastle south tunnel after passing the Chatterley Junction Down Advanced starting signal. The distant on the left is the Up for Chatterley Junction. 'B1' was the two-character headcode in force at the time for this route.

The late Michael Mensing

Heading south at Chatterley on 28th May 1960 with a Class H through-goods working is Mirfield-allocated Stanier '8F' 2-8-0 No. 48265. Mirfield engines were regular visitors to the Stoke area, but usually the 2-8-0 ex-War Department *Austerity* type of which the shed had a large allocation. Notice that the points to exit the Down relief line, along with the associated catch points, were operated from a lever frame located in that small cabin. The key to unlock the frame was under the control of the Chatterley Junction signalman and when it was required to be used, one of the local shunting staff would man the frame. Normally trains using the Down relief line would regain the Down mainline via a crossover just to the north of the signal box.

Another view from almost the same point showing very clearly the former station platforms at Chatterley and once again, the cabin housing the ground frame. On the left, Down side platform, is a shunting disc signal, also operated by the ground frame, which controlled propelling movements from the Down mainline to the relief line, although quite why such a movement would be required, is a bit of a mystery, except perhaps, for light engines wanting access to the sidings. The banner signal repeated the position of the Down Advanced Starter which was difficult to sight in view of the road bridge. This bridge, No. 66, carried the Talke to Tunstall road, Lowlands Road, over the railway.

This is a much earlier view of Chatterley station looking north, although unfortunately, not dated. It does however, illustrate some of the station buildings. The station opened at the same time as the mainline and was originally known as Tunstall. It was renamed Chatterley on 1st October 1873 when the Potteries Loop Line opened as far as Tunstall, which of course, served the town much better. Chatterley Station closed on 27th September 1948.

Left: On Sunday 6th March 1966, the Williams Deacon's Bank Railway Club chartered a special train, reporting number 1T70, from Stockport to Derby, where the participants were able to visit the locomotive works. Routed via the North Stafford, here it is passing the old station at Chatterley. The motive power was Eastern Region A4 pacific No. 60019 *Bittern*, the first time an engine of this class had visited North Staffordshire. The ground signal for controlling propelling movements on to the Down relief line is clearly visible. The train returned later in the day.

Right: Class '4F' 0-6-0 goods engine No. 44049, a Derby-allocated engine at the time, has just emerged from the south end of Harecastle Tunnel with a Class H goods on 28th September 1963; a very mixed train indeed. The signal is the Chatterley Junction Down Advanced Starter and the smoke has obscured the tunnel portal.

The late Michael Mensing

Left: Another view from the same vantage point as the previous one with the same train featured on page 123, but this time having just emerged from Harecastle Tunnel. The train is a Class F express goods without continuous brakes. Notice that the Chatterley Down Advanced Starter has a diamond-shaped sign below the signal arm. This told the crew that when standing at the signal the train was occupying a track circuit, which would be indicated in the signal box, as a result of which the crew would not have to observe Rule 55. Without a track circuit the fireman would have been required to go to the signal box to remind the signalman of the train's situation, remaining there until the signal could be cleared.

The late Michael Mensing

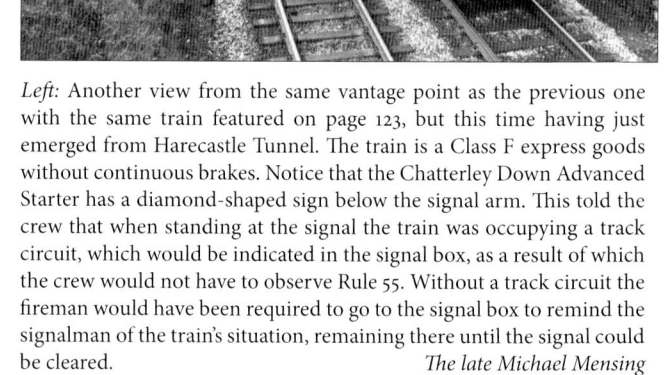

On Saturday 23rd April 1966 the Railway Correspondence & Travel Society chartered a special train, reporting number 1X75, aptly named *St George*, as it was St George's Day. Starting from Nuneaton the six-coach train wandered around the Black Country and Shropshire to arrive at Hartford Junction on the West Coast Main Line, where the train reversed, with this engine, 'Crab' 2-6-0 No. 42727 of Birkenhead North, taking over. The train then proceeded via the former Cheshire Lines Route to Northwich, followed by the branch to Middlewich and Sandbach, then the NSR route via Hassall Green and Harecastle on its way back to Nuneaton via Uttoxeter and Burton-on-Trent. Obviously, Birkenhead had gone to some trouble in preparing the engine, with the train seen here emerging from the south end of Harecastle South Tunnel. The banner signal at the entrance to the tunnel repeated the position of the Harecastle Junction Down Home Signal.

The late Michael Mensing

CHAPTER 8 – THE RAILWAY TUNNELS

Left: The south portal of Harecastle Tunnel on 30th May 1966. The signal on the right is the Chatterley Junction Up Distant. Notice directly above the entrance to the tunnel, one of the ventilating shaft brick surrounds and to the left of the entrance, a signal banner repeater. This repeated the position of the Kidsgrove Junction Down Distant signals. In the Bridge Register this tunnel was numbered 65 and recorded as one mile and three yards long.

This much earlier view of the main Harecastle Tunnel south portal, allows us a sight of the rather photogenic platelayers' cabin that existed there with its very ornate chimney; it looks as if it must have been extended at some time in its life. There are a lot of rail lengths in the six-foot and some chairs in the left hand cess; presumably some relaying had been underway.

Class '4F' 0-6-0 No. 44079 emerges from the south portal of the south tunnel during the spring of 1962 with an Up freight. The platelayers' cabin opposite the banner signal can be seen in its modified form. The locomotive was based at Alsager, Shed Code 5E. It was one of a batch of twenty-five built by the North British Locomotive Company Limited, Glasgow in 1925 and was withdrawn in November 1964 having given thirty-nine years' service. *The late Alan Fozard*

127

We now move to the other end of the main, south Harecastle Tunnel and this is the portal with a much less distinguished platelayer's cabin. Once again a lot of tools and equipment laying around suggesting work in progress, although it is difficult to make out exactly what can be seen in the six-foot.

Below: Approaching the south main Harecastle Tunnel on 26th September 1960, with the Middle Tunnel to the left, is Class '4F' 0-6-0 No. 44352, an Alsager engine at the time, with an Up Class H empty ballast train. The wagons were probably en-route to the quarry at Caldon Low. From Stoke the train would travel via the Biddulph Valley, Leek and Caldon Low lines to the quarry. The banner repeater signal just in front of the engine replicates the position of the Chatterley Junction Up Distant signal.
The late Michael Mensing

Above left: Taken on the same occasion as the previous view, here we have the Down COMET, albeit on this occasion, minus the locomotive headboard. This London Euston to Manchester train was due to depart Euston at 09.35am and Stoke at 12.15pm, with an additional stop at Macclesfield where it was due to depart at 12.46pm. So, if it was running to time, this photograph would have been taken at approximately 12.24pm, the train's booked passing time at Kidsgrove Junction. The diagram this locomotive was working had only recently been allocated one of the new English Electric Type '4' 2,000 horsepower diesel-electric locomotives, in this case D215, allocated to Manchester Longsight Depot. The semaphore signals are the Kidsgrove Junction Splitting Distants, the left-hand one cleared for the Macclesfield line, while the other arm was for the Crewe line.
The late Michael Mensing

This and the next two photographs were all taken on 26th September 1960, showing trains between the Middle and North Tunnels. This first one has Class '4F' 0-6-0 No. 44068, a long-standing member of Stoke's large allocation of this class of engine; in fact this one was at Stoke from when BR was first formed until withdrawn in October 1963. The train is a Down Class J mineral with a train of BR standard 16 ton mineral wagons loaded with coal from the North Staffordshire collieries. It would be heading for Alsager, where in those days a lot of local trains were remarshalled.

The late Michael Mensing

Stanier Class '4' 2-6-4 tank engine No. 42470 of Aston Shed in Birmingham, was in charge of the 10.11am Birmingham to Stockport Edgeley parcels, a Down Class C train which on this occasion, included some empty coaching stock. It was due to have left Stoke at 1.29pm, having spent almost an hour there for remarshalling and was due to leave Kidsgrove at 1.48pm, having work to do there. This was a regular working for an Aston engine. It returned with the 7.30pm parcels from Stockport to Birmingham, due to depart Stoke at 9.20pm. The Middle Tunnel was No. 63 in the Bridge Register and the North Tunnel No. 64. The register records their lengths as 127 and 178 yards respectively.   *The late Michael Mensing*

An Up train in this view with another of the ubiquitous Class '4F' 0-6-0 goods engines, former LM&SR Standard Freight locomotives as they were referred to. This one is No. 44536 of Stoke shed and the train a very short Class J mineral. The signal by the brake van is the Kidsgrove Junction Up Advanced Starter.

The late Michael Mensing

This is the northern portal of the North Tunnel looking south with the Harecastle Junction, as it then was, crossover road in the foreground. At the northern end of the tunnel, Avenue Road crossed over the railway and this section of the tunnel was given a separate number in the Bridge Register as bridge No. 62. The photograph is part of a series embracing bridges and other structures commissioned by the NSR, probably dating from the early part of the last century. They are mounted in albums and form part of the NSR archives in the custody of the National Archives.

NA RAIL 532/44

Between the North Tunnel and what became Kidsgrove Central Junction the line passed over the Trent & Mersey Canal by bridge No. 61. This was located at 13 miles and 68 chains from Macclesfield, where the NSR mile posts started. As can be seen, the bridge consisted of twin spans, with girders of cast iron and skew spans of 34ft and 35ft 6in. The canal was wider at this point, probably to allow for boats waiting to enter the canal tunnels. The bridge was reconstructed with steel girders and concrete in 1926 at a cost of £5,220, which had been authorised by the LM&SR Works Committee at its meeting on 28th July 1926. Widnes Foundry (1925) Limited had been contracted to supply the material. The signals to the top right are the Harecastle Junction Splitting Home Signals. This is another photograph from the NSR albums.

NA RAIL 532/44

As can be seen in this view taken on 26th September 1960, Bridge No. 61 is now constructed of steel girders. The masonry bridge in the foreground crossing over the canal was to allow the towpath to transfer from the west to the east side and presumably, dates from when the new canal tunnel was built as it was situated to the east side of the old tunnel. The Down goods train is in the charge of a Hughes/Fowler *Crab* Class '5' 2-6-0 engine No. 42888, one of several members of this class allocated to Stoke at the time and unusually, running tender first. Part of the town of Kidsgrove can be glimpsed between the trees, which form part of Kidswood.

The late Michael Mensing

This photograph, looking north, probably dating from early in the LM&SR period, was taken from Avenue Road which passed over the northern end of the North Tunnel. Harecastle Station is in the distance with the junction signal box to the left. The water tank on the right was for locomotive water supplies, as provision was made on both the Macclesfield and Crewe lines for engines to take water, the supply coming from the Bath Pool. Locomotive water supplies were important here as a lot of shunting took place in connection with Birchenwood and other collieries and additionally, engines working the Audley and Sandbach branches would have required supplies.

A view in the opposite direction to the previous one but taken at around the same time and looking south towards the North Tunnel. There is a train emerging from the tunnel heading for the Crewe line, which is the one to the right, hauled by what appears to be a tank engine running bunker first. Although it is not very clear here, on the original print, just to the left of the water tank and above the end of the fence on the left, is the Birchenwood Colliery Company's railway that served the Kidswood and Bath Pool areas. The level crossing gates protecting The Avenue from the railway are immediately to the left of the bridge parapet. There is quite a bit of activity at the end of the Up Macclesfield line platform, with contemporary advertisements for Bass Ale and Player's Navy Cut cigarettes.

Harecastle Junction signal box which had a McKenzie & Holland frame with 32 levers. Although undated the photograph is from the NSR period, as evidenced by the fellow standing in the six foot who is wearing the railway company's uniform. The left-hand signal is cleared for a train to proceed on the Macclesfield line.

Looking due north again with the Crewe line platforms to the left and the Macclesfield ones to the right. Bridge No. 61 is on the left with the canal towpath and flight of steps to give access. Notice the tall signals to assist sighting and the Up passenger train from the Macclesfield direction just departing. The engine is NSR No. 75, one of the Class 'E' 0-6-0 inside-cylinder tender engines and in the case of this one, built by the company at Stoke in 1871. It was transferred to the duplicate list as 75A in 1919 and became LM&SR 2321 at the Grouping; it was withdrawn in 1926. The coal wagon on the right in the railway company's goods yard belonged to Joel Settle, a local coal owner, distribution and shipping agent with a number of interests in local collieries, coking plants and railway wagon building activities.

A similar view to the previous one and dating from around the same time. On this occasion the train is an Up one from the Crewe line hauled by a member of the NSR Class 'B' 2-4-0 tank engines although this one, No. 21, was one of a few that were rebuilt with a 2-4-2 wheel arrangement. It had been built by the company at its Stoke Works in 1882 and rebuilt in 1901, surviving to become LM&SR No. 1457 and not withdrawn until 1932. The train consists of a rake of six-wheel coaches which were the standard on these local trains at the time. Notice the signalman is operating one of the block instruments, probably sending the train entering section signal to Chatterley Junction. Notice too, that to assist sighting not only are the Starting Signals tall, but the one for the Up line from Crewe was located on the Down side.

CHAPTER 8 – THE RAILWAY TUNNELS

The complete station at Harecastle looking north, Crewe line to the left and Macclesfield to the right. The footbridge is bridge No. 60, made of wrought iron lattice girders on cast iron columns. The signal box at the end of the Macclesfield Down platform is Harecastle Goods Cabin which at the time the photograph was taken, was a block post. This is another photograph from the NSR Albums which probably date from early in the last century.
NA RAIL 532/44

This rather nice view looks due east from the rising ground to the west of the Crewe line platforms at Harecastle. There are trains in both the Crewe line platforms, both of which appear to consist of six-wheel coaches; notice the bowler hatted gentleman sitting in the middle First Class compartment with his newspaper, oblivious of all that was going on around him. The two small boys on the platform are standing by a large hand roller suggesting that some work was in progress on the platform surface. The station signage is interesting in connection with passengers changing trains, along with the advertising boards. To the extreme left is the Harecastle Hotel, still there today, selling beers from the local Parker's Burslem Brewery. One of the wagons in the goods yard beyond the Macclesfield line platforms belonged to Borax Consolidated Limited, a company with a factory in the town; a substantial part of Kidsgrove provides the backcloth. Meadowcroft & Company, whose office in the goods yard can be prominently seen, were local coal merchants. The chimney above the clock tower on the Town Hall to the right, belongs to Trubshaw Colliery, situated on the high ground towards Newchapel, while the one on the extreme right is at Speedwell Colliery.

Signalman Fred Hayles in April 1937, operating a block instrument in Harecastle Junction signal box. The instrument is a single wire three-position one of Tyer's manufacture, which were standard equipment on the NSR.

Below: Early in BR days on 12th June 1948 is a Stoke-allocated Stanier Class '4' 2-6-4 tank with the engine still in LM&SR livery, albeit with its new number 42585. The train is an Up local passenger train from the Macclesfield direction, about to depart from what by this time had been renamed as Kidsgrove Central Station. This train had probably started its journey at Manchester London Road and may have been heading for Birmingham New Street as several of the Manchester trains did. The building to the extreme right is the goods yard office.

Stephenson Locomotive Society Collection No. 6395

A second photograph taken at Kidsgrove Central on 12th June 1948, an Up train again, but on this occasion from Crewe, with another of the Stanier Class '4' 2-6-4 tank engines in charge. This one too, while still in LM&SR livery, has its BR number 42544 and was at the time allocated to Carnforth. Its appearance on this train was probably following a recent visit to Crewe Works as it was not unusual, for the Crewe sheds to borrow engines after they had visited the workshops, prior to sending them home. Stoke did however, have a large allocation of engines of this class, along with some of the earlier ones from the Fowler period and they were in charge of most of the local passenger trains.

Stephenson Locomotive Society Collection No. 2259

A view of Kidsgrove Central in early BR days by which time the platforms had been numbered, notice the number 3 sign on the Up Crewe line platform. The numbers ran from 1 for the Up Macclesfield to 4 for the Down Crewe.

Kidsgrove Central Junction looking north in October 1957; notice the signal box is now designated as Kidsgrove Central Junction and that the Up Crewe Starting Signal has a repeater lower down. The former NSR goods shed survives to the extreme right.

The main station buildings at Kidsgrove Central, formerly known as Harecastle, in 1952, taken from the driveway and car park. The rather imposing classically styled entrance doorway with triangular pediment reflects the station's importance when the lines first opened. Not many cars around in those days; the Standard on the left has the registration number ACA 4 – that would be worth a tidy sum these days!

The DMUs used on the Birmingham to Manchester services via Stoke had the two-character B4 headcode and unlike the Derby to Crewe trains which generally consisted of a three-car unit, these trains usually comprised of two three-car units to make a six vehicle train. On 26th September 1960 the 3.30pm Stoke to Manchester London Road train is entering Kidsgrove Central Station, comprised of two of the Birmingham Railway Carriage & Wagon Company three-car units, later known as Class '104'. At morning and evening peak travelling times, along with lunch times on Saturdays, some of these trains ran via the Loop Line between Kidsgrove and Etruria, rather than the mainline as seen here. The diesel units were based at Cockshute Depot at Stoke, which had been purpose built when they were first introduced; it opened in October 1957.

The late Michael Mensing

Shunting at Harecastle and Kidsgrove was the preserve of one of the engines allocated to Alsager shed which opened in 1890. On 26th September 1960 shunting is being performed by a member of the LM&SR Fowler Class '3F' 0-6-0 tank engines, No. 47596, one that alternated between Stoke and Alsager sheds for the whole time of its BR ownership, until withdrawal in July 1965. In this view it has propelled a train from Harecastle goods yard prior to crossing over onto the Down Crewe line and proceeding in that direction. It has probably completed its days' work and is heading back to Alsager with a few odd wagons destined for the marshalling yard there. The wagons are loaded with coke from the Birchenwood Coking Plant, while the tank wagon belonging to ICI would have probably been loaded with one of the chemical by-products from the coke making process. Notice one of the wagons is of wooden construction; there were not many wooden bodied coal/coke wagons still in use by this date, largely replaced by the ubiquitous BR standard 16 ton mineral wagons, like the other one in the train. The 55 sign by the engine's bunker is the speed limit on the Up line through the North Tunnel; it was raised to 60 mph through the other two tunnels. Notice that due to the radius of the curve, the Down Crewe line has a check rail, the speed restriction over this junction was and still is, 15 mph.

The late Michael Mensing

On and from Sunday 25th July 1965 the signalling arrangements at Kidsgrove were altered from Absolute Block to Track Circuit Block, employing multiple aspect signals. A new signal box was commissioned and the old one demolished, the work being in connection with the forthcoming electrification of the route from Colwich and Norton Bridge via Stoke to Macclesfield and Cheadle Hulme. At the same time the deviation line was brought into use and the former NSR line from Chatterley to Kidsgrove, including the South and Middle Harecastle Tunnels, was taken out of use. This photograph was taken on 30th May 1966 and looks south with a distant view of a DMU through the opened out former North Tunnel, climbing the 1 in 80 grade of the deviation line.

Right: Taken at the same time as the previous photograph but looking in the opposite, north direction, with the Crewe line on the left and Macclesfield on the right. On the left is the 15 mph speed board for the Crewe line, along with the remains of the foundations of the earlier signal box.

Below: A much later view of the new signal box taken on 22nd December 2001 with a Class '156' new generation DMU No. 156417, on a train from Crewe to Derby. This signal box did not have a very long life, not that is, compared with its predecessor as it was replaced during signalling rationalisation works in May 2002, control passing to the existing power signal box at Stoke.

As Birchenwood Colliery and the earlier Clough Hall Ironworks feature so prominently in these pages, a photograph of the colliery seems appropriate. This one dates from around the early 1920s, taken from a standpoint of the Liverpool Road, or Kidsgrove Bank as it is locally referred to. The headgear belongs to the No. 18 pit shaft which was the principal coal winding one. The large building on the right is the Luhrig coal washing plant with the storage bunker alongside. The by-product recovery coking plants of which there were two, along with the associated chemical plant, were further south and beyond the colliery complex.

In 1938 a new battery of seventeen Simon-Carves coke ovens were erected at Birchenwood to replace the last of the older ones and this photograph, taken on 8th September 1938, shows them under construction with part of the earlier battery in the foreground.

Clough Hall c.1910, with its ornamental lake in the foreground. Dating from around 1800, the Hall was built for the second John Gilbert and acquired after his death by Thomas Kinnersly (1782-1855). The Kinnersly family occupied it between 1817 and 1874. In 1890 the Hall was purchased by a Manchester firm which turned the grounds into a pleasure park, with ornate gardens, rides and fetes. During the First World War the Hall became a hotel and at one time housed Belgian refugees. After the war the Hall fell into disuse and was unfortunately demolished in May 1927. However, the twin lodges that formed the entrance to the driveway from the Newcastle to Talke road, the present A34, remain as a reminder of this splendid building.

This photograph, taken on 26th April 1900, is part of Kidswood colliery which was used primarily for ventilating the main Birchenwood Colliery underground workings. The two buildings to the upper right house the two fans and their steam engines with the boilers and associated chimney to the left. Behind the fence is the railway line which was a back-shunt from the Bath Pool line, its main purpose to deliver coal for the boilers. This photograph was taken shortly after the fans were installed, part of significant developments at the colliery after Robert Heath & Sons Limited acquired control.

The Nelson Pit in about 1900, a very old one which probably dated from around the time the first canal tunnel was being built. It was used, at least latterly, by both the Kinnersly and Birchenwood Companies for drainage purposes. Served by a siding from the Bath Pool line which can just be seen in the distance, a small beam pumping engine was located here, along with associated boiler plant. The engine however, would not have been the same one that John Gilbert had installed. Notice the coal wagon on the siding to the left with the chute for the coal; as at Kidswood, the main purpose of the rail connection was to deliver coal for the boilers.

The remains of the Nelson Pit surface buildings in about 1959; water was still being pumped from the shaft, electric pumps having replaced the steam engine. The water was used at Birchenwood for quenching the newly made coke. Large quantities of water were required as soon as the coke was withdrawn from the ovens as otherwise, it would continue to burn.

The roadway in this view is the former route of the Birchenwood Colliery railway line from Kidsgrove to Ravenscliffe. It looks south with the Bath Pool visible to the right. Taken in about 1959, the scene here was completely obliterated by the railway deviation scheme.

Mention is made in the text of a company being formed in 1922, Tarmac (Kidsgrove) Limited, to exploit the slag from the former Clough Hall Ironworks that had previously been dumped. Some of it was located around the site of the Nelson Pit and the main Harecastle Tunnel and this was where a reduction and processing plant was established. This photograph and the one following were taken at the site, which was served by the private Birchenwood Colliery and later coking plant line from Harecastle Goods Yard. While the normal motive power was the second of the colliery company's locomotives named *Alexander*, when this engine was under repair, one was loaned from Robert Heath & Low Moor Limited and later Norton & Biddulph Collieries Victoria Colliery at Black Bull. This was one of the collieries, formerly part of Robert Heath & Sons Limited, which was connected with Birchenwood by a private mineral railway. As mentioned in the text the Heath family had been the owners of the Birchenwood Colliery and were shareholders in Tarmac (Kidsgrove) Limited. The locomotive shown here is Norton & Biddulph Collieries No. 8, a standard four-coupled saddle tank design of Heaths with 14 × 20 inch outside cylinders. A number of this type were built by the company in its workshops at Black Bull. However, this is the prototype of the design, which had been built in 1885 by the Falcon Engine & Car Works at Loughborough and rebuilt by Heaths in 1891 and again by Cowlishaw Walker & Company in 1931. This company had acquired Heath's workshops at Black Bull after the firm went into liquidation in 1929. As can be seen in the photographs the locomotive is in excellent condition and as it carries the design of works plate used by Cowlishaw Walker when it overhauled the colliery locomotives, the photographs are assumed to have been taken shortly after the 1931 overhaul. With operations here finishing when all the economically viable slag had been recovered around 1932, these photographs would have been taken towards to end of operations. This locomotive finished its life at another of the former Heath collieries, Norton Colliery at Ford Green, where it was scrapped in 1957.

H.W. Robinson Collection, Industrial Railway Society

Although this photograph was taken much later and on the main Birchenwood site, it is appropriate to illustrate the second locomotive named *Alexander*. It was built by W.G. Bagnall Limited, maker's number 2107 and is seen here busy shunting on 20th July 1966. Although this locomotive was completed in late 1919, it had been built for stock and when in 1922, the original engine of the name was sent to Bagnall's Castle Engine Works in Stafford for overhaul, it was found to be in such bad condition that a new locomotive was offered and accepted in part exchange. Arriving at Birchenwood in September 1922, it carried the nameplates from the earlier locomotive. It was scrapped in October 1973 shortly after the Coking and By-Product plant closed.

NORTH STAFFORDSHIRE RAILWAY LINE SURVEY

The detailed plans on the following pages reflect an official survey undertaken for the NSR at the turn of the 19th Century. They cover the line from Harecastle North signal box through the Harecastle railway tunnels to Chatterley Junction signal box. The plans also clearly show the two canal tunnels. Particular points of note in order from north to south are the industrial line from Moss Coal Pit closed in 1894, Kidsgrove station on the Loop Line, Harecastle station and the northern entrances to the tunnels. The Clough Hall Gardens are shown as converted in 1890 from part of the Thomas Kinnersly Clough Hall estate. There then appears the industrial railway line over the mouth of the north end of the south tunnel leading to the Nelson engine house with its chimney and pond. This is followed by The Line Houses village which is located about half way above the longest (south) railway tunnel. The series concludes with the south end of the south railway tunnel, Chatterley station, the south portals of both canal tunnels, Chatterley signal box, the Goldendale Iron Works accessed by a railway bridge over the canal and the branch to Talk o' th' Hill Colliery and Chesterton opposite Chatterley Junction signal box and close by the Chatterley Iron Works. The plans were originally printed at a scale of two chains to an inch. The scale is not valid for these reduced reproductions.

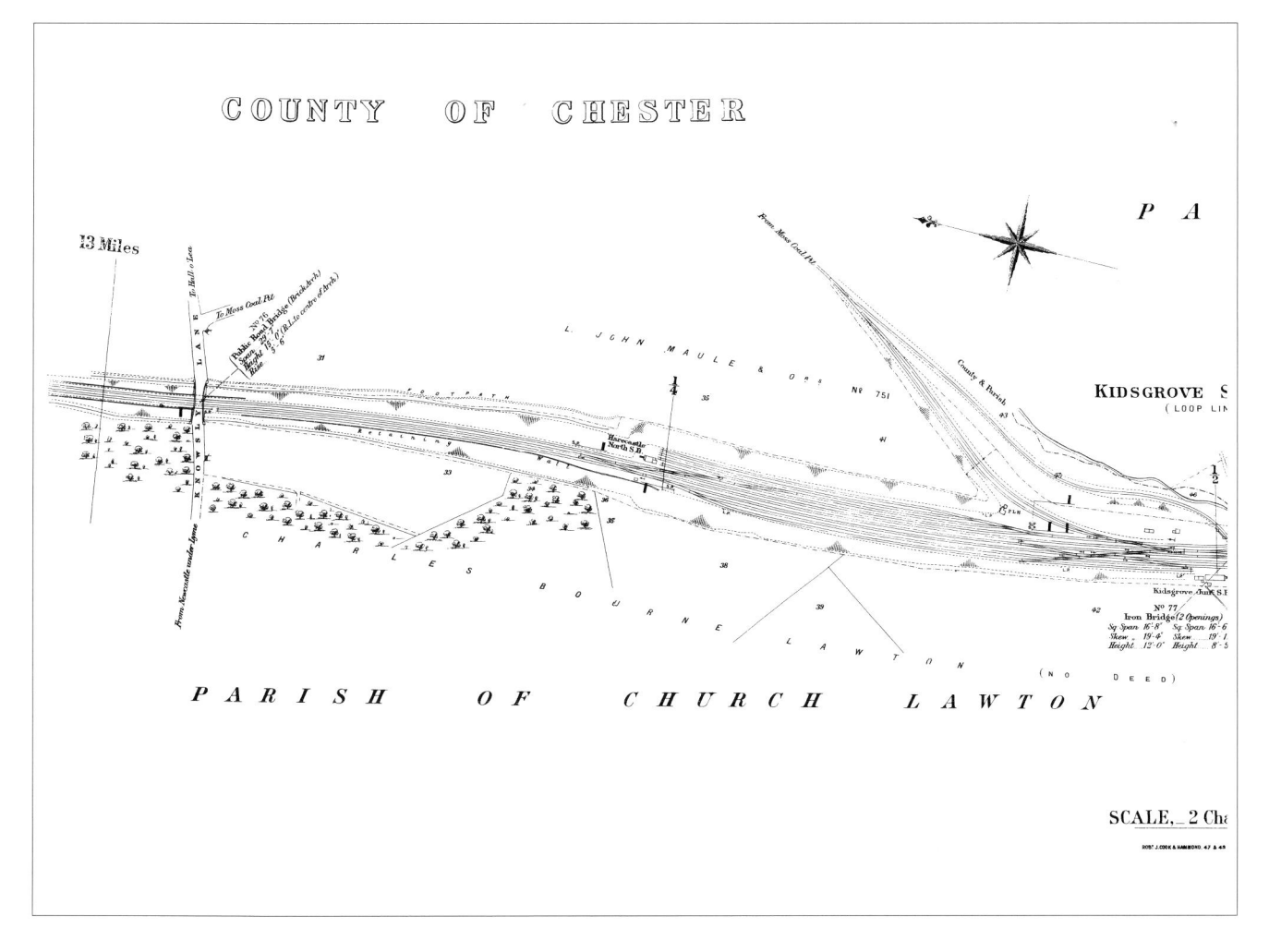

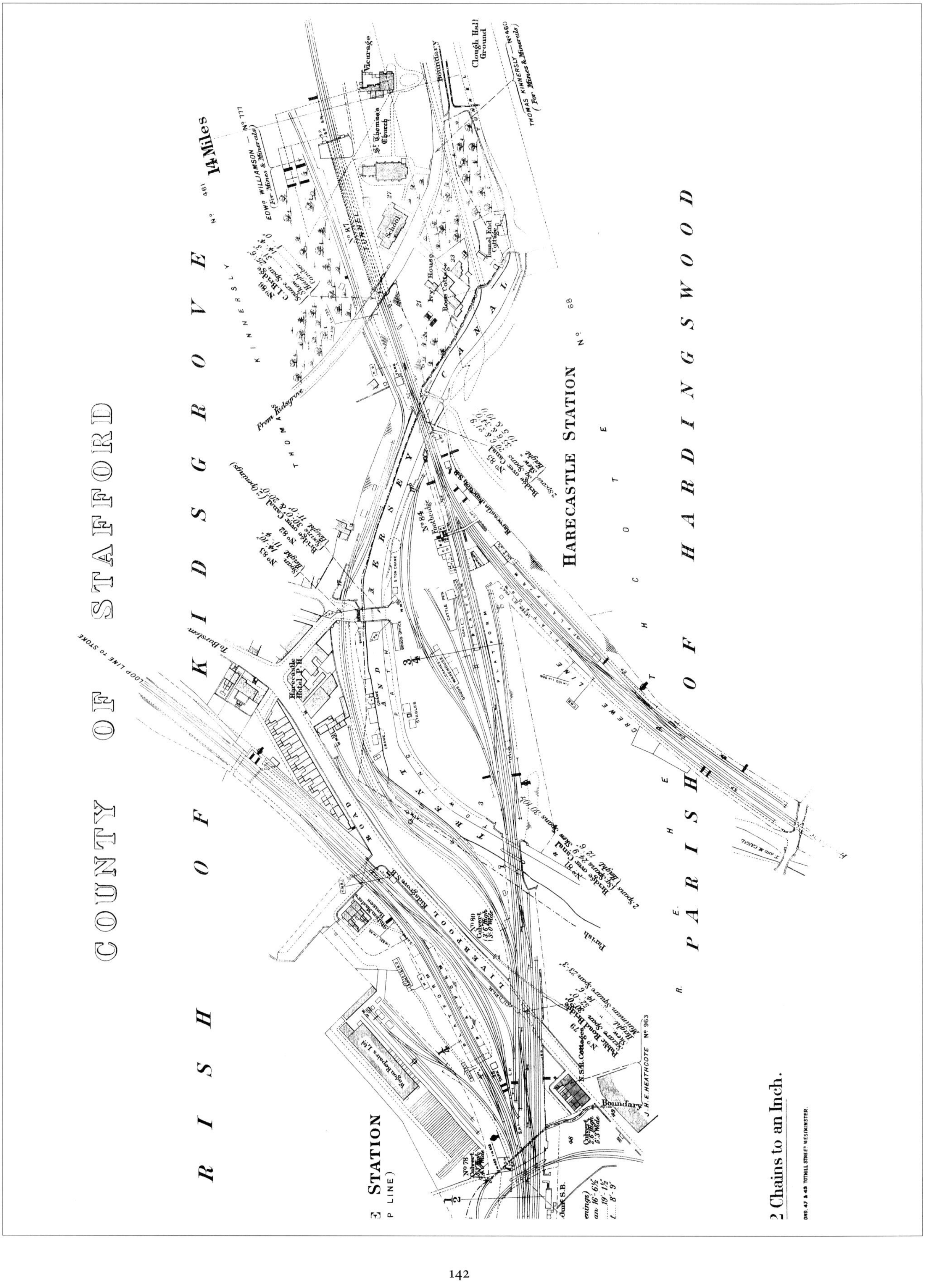

CHAPTER 8 – THE RAILWAY TUNNELS

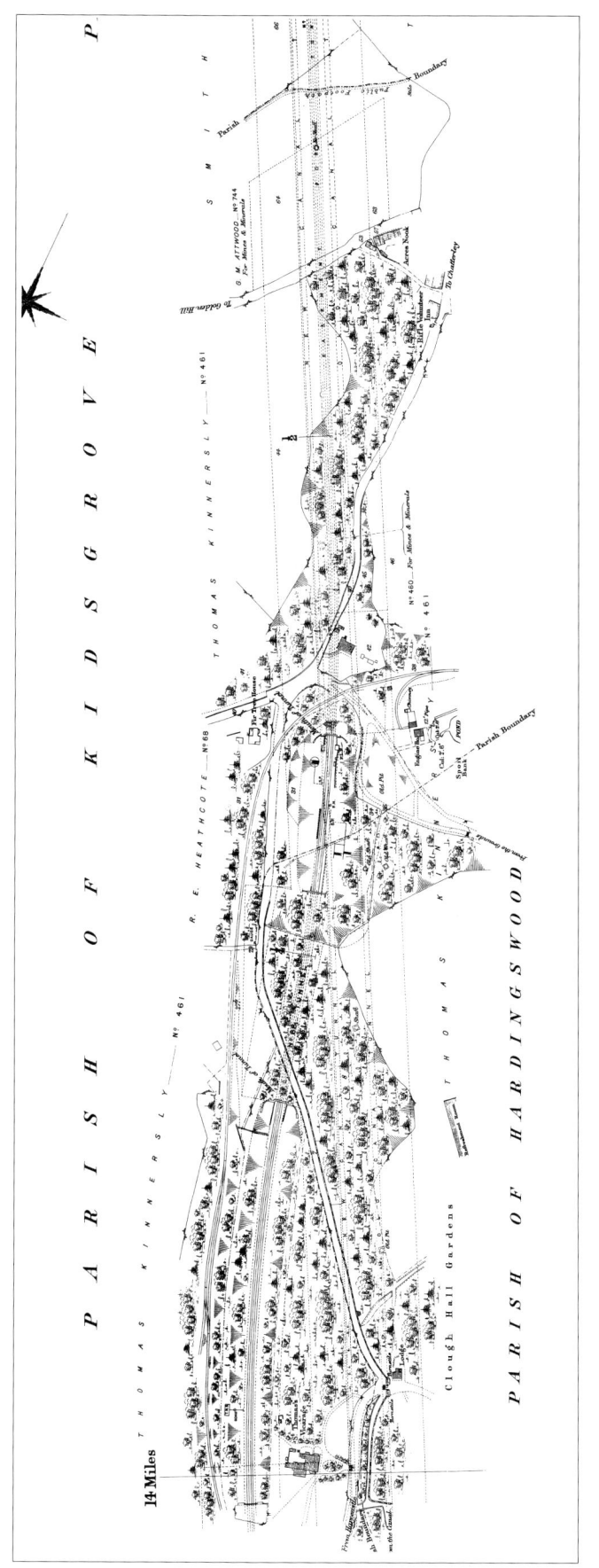

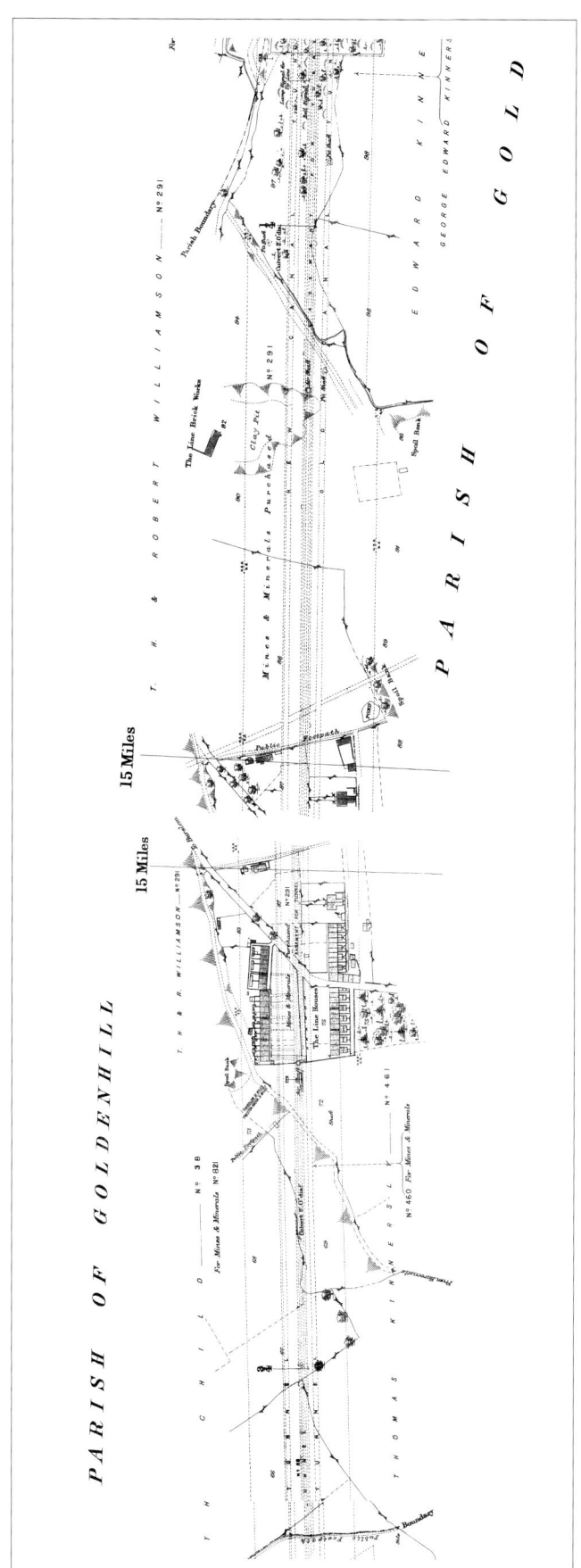

143

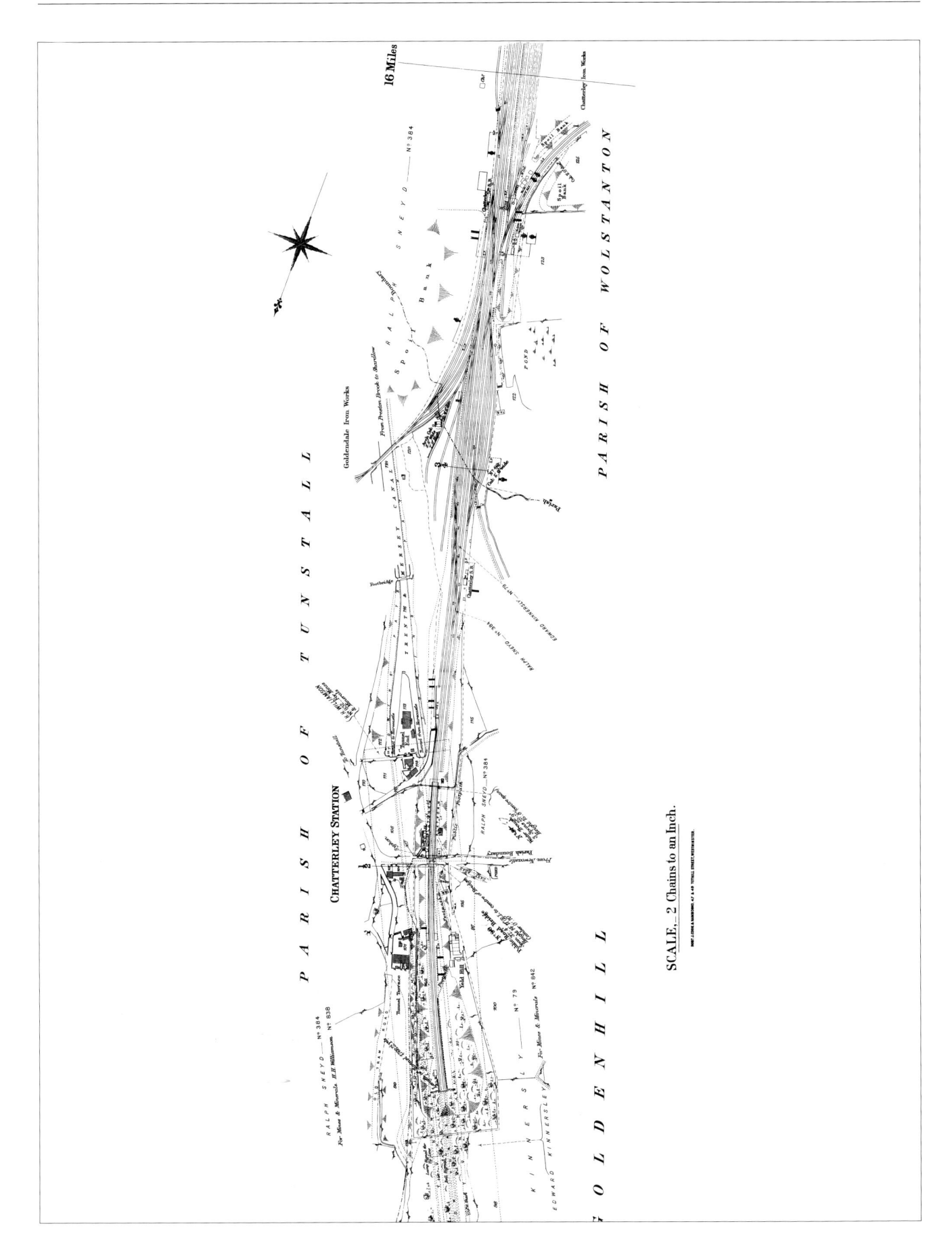

9

THE HARECASTLE DIVERSION

Throughout their operational lives the tunnels served trains travelling from Crewe to Derby and trains from Manchester via Macclesfield to Colwich and Norton Bridge on the West Coast Main Line. This pattern of working continued throughout the LM&SR era and into the days of the nationalised British Railways (BR) but that all came to an end on 27th June 1966 when the new diversionary route to the west of the tunnels was opened for traffic.

The diversion was a direct result of London Midland Region's mainline electrification scheme. This embraced the route from London Euston to Manchester and Liverpool, including the line via Birmingham and Wolverhampton, along with the former NSR lines from Colwich and Norton Bridge to Macclesfield; thereafter joining the line from Crewe to Stockport and Manchester at Cheadle Hulme. As with the canal tunnels, the railway tunnels became increasingly difficult to maintain as time and subsidence took their toll. The arch in the main tunnel was under increasing pressure from movements in the strata above and constant renewals of the masonry became necessary. In addition the main tunnel was very wet in two places and all three tunnels had reached the stage when extensive repairs were necessary requiring an anticipated average *engineering possession* on forty weekends in every year and entailing an expenditure of some £20,000 per annum. This deterioration and the difficulty in accommodating the overhead wires because of the tight tunnel parameters led to consideration being given to five distinct options. These were:

1. Open out the tunnels entirely.
2. Enlarge the bores by relining so as to give the required clearances.
3. Construct entirely new tunnels alongside.
4. Interlace the tracks through the tunnels or convert the railway to a single line with bi-directional signalling.
5. Construct an avoiding line around the tunnels.

The single line proposal was the cheapest option but, given today's intensive level of traffic, how fortunate it was discarded.

The new route around the tunnels involved abandoning the south and middle tunnels and opening out the north tunnel which had a relatively shallow cover. Site work on the project began in June 1964. The new route was two miles 850 yards long and involved alterations to the layout at Chatterley sidings, the diversion of the Chesterton branch[178] from a north to a south facing junction and the construction of a new short tunnel of 272 yards in length under a 73ft high ridge near to Kidsgrove. The new line limited the space previously occupied by the Bath Pool reservoir. This involved extending the reservoir to the north and damming its eastern side to provide space for the new railway which was in a cutting at a lower level than the normal water line in the reservoir. In order to deal with surplus water in times of flooding, arrangements were made to pipe it away via an underground five feet diameter culvert to the disused Brindley canal tunnel. The original Bath Pool, on the Clough Hall Estate, was so named because it was shaped like a bath. There were streams at both ends: the one at the south end joined the Fowlea Brook and found its way to the River Trent, whereas the flow from the stream at the north end eventually found its way to the River Mersey. So, in effect, Bath Pool breached the Trent/Mersey watershed. The pool had always served as a reservoir for the canal. The railway diversionary works also impacted on another smaller reservoir, known as Nelson Pool, which was replaced by a closed reinforced concrete structure. The new works involved the provision of two road bridges, two foot bridges and a road under-pass.[179]

The most interesting feature on the diversion is the new tunnel constructed to the west of the old middle tunnel. Driving started at the north end on the up gradient immediately behind the new Boat Horse Road bridge which rests on a deck of pre-stressed concrete beams. This is a skew bridge and the space between the last beam and the start of the tunnel bore is covered with a flat reinforced concrete deck, so that there is no portal to the north end of the tunnel in the normal sense. Rock of a very poor and shattered quality was soon encountered. This caused considerable delay and changed the more traditional method of construction from the bench and heading technique to the side-heading method. There are no refuges as the width at the waist is sufficient to give protection to permanent way staff who might happen to be in the tunnel while trains are passing. The south portal of the tunnel was cast in the open and a concrete saddle formed over the bore on the inside against the rock face to prevent the spillage of loose rock into the excavated tunnel when the final breakthrough took place.[180]

During the driving, two old shafts were encountered. One was an original construction shaft over Telford's canal tunnel which

---

178 The new connection for the Chesterton branch became operational on 18th October 1964. It was still used at that time for traffic to and from Parkhouse Colliery but the new connection was short lived as the branch was officially closed on 21st June 1968, following the cessation of coal winding at the colliery during the previous month.

179 NA MT14/529 British Railways London Midland Region press release dated 27th June 1966.
180 *The Railway Gazette*, 6th May 1966.

had to be bridged by a reinforced concrete beam to support the new railway tunnel floor. The other was an old mine shaft which was filled with rubble and topped with a concrete plug. The break through between the north and south headings occurred on 24th February 1966, *The Times* reporting that the first man to see light at both ends of the tunnel was Thomas McGoohan of Donegal.[181]

The old north tunnel consisted of vertical masonry walls with a brick roof. The walls were found to be in very good condition such that it was possible to bridge across between the walls with reinforced concrete portal frames, the legs of which were dowelled into the tops of the existing walls. These frames were placed 10ft apart with the cross members slightly above surface ground level. Concrete retaining walls were then built up between the frames to complete the construction. A diesel locomotive-powered mono-rail system was employed using side-tip wagons. The line remained open throughout the operation except for six weekends when complete possession was required for the demolition of the old tunnel roof using explosives. During these possessions some passenger trains were diverted over the Potteries Loop Line which had closed to regular passenger traffic on 2nd March 1964. If the diverted trains consisted of BR Mark One coaches, they had to travel over the Pinnox branch from Tunstall Upper Junction to gain access to the mainline at Longport Junction, as the curvature at Hanley station was too tight for the BR Mark One standard 64ft length coaches. Just prior to closure, traffic on the old mainline through the tunnels totalled about 210 trains on each weekday.[182] From photographic evidence, it appears that the south and middle tunnels remained open for a short while for construction traffic after the old line had been severed at the Kidsgrove end.

The person with prime responsibility for the diversion was William Fitzgerald Beatty MBE (1909-1995) who was the Chief

---

181 *The Times*, 25th February 1966.
182 *The Railway Gazette*, 6th May 1966.

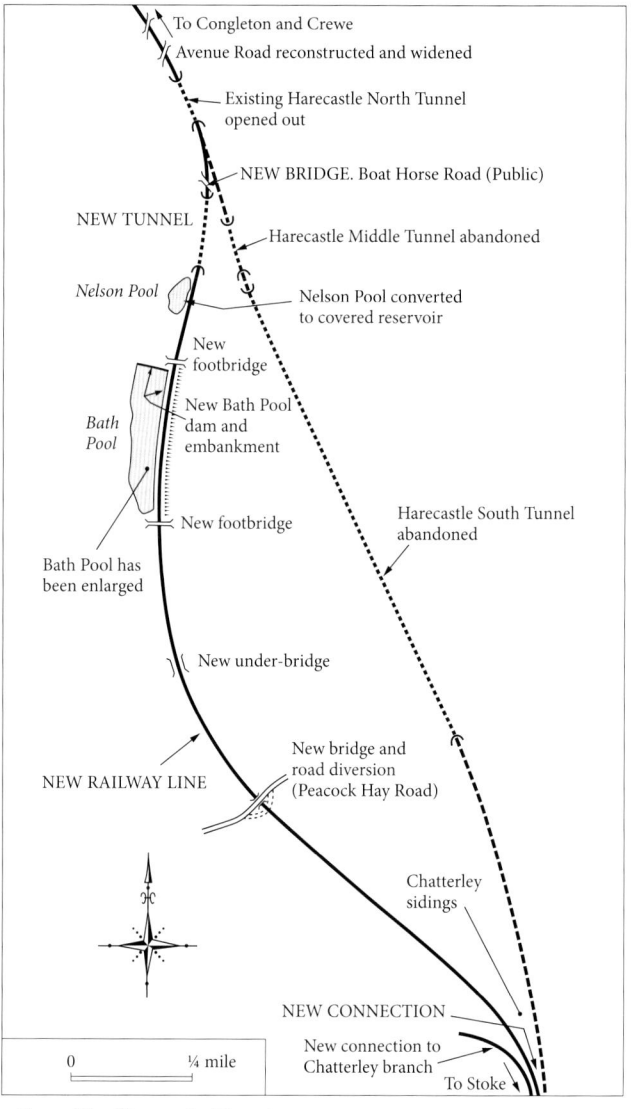

Plan of the Harecastle Diversion.

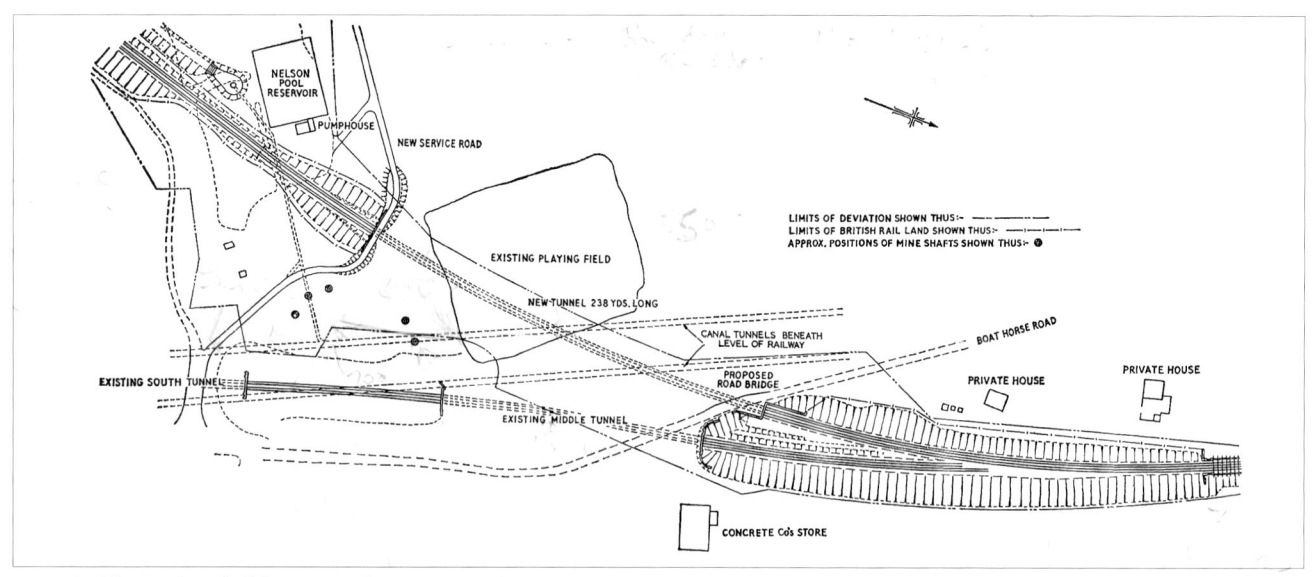

Detail of the north end of the Harecastle Diversion.

CHAPTER 9 – THE HARECASTLE DIVERSION

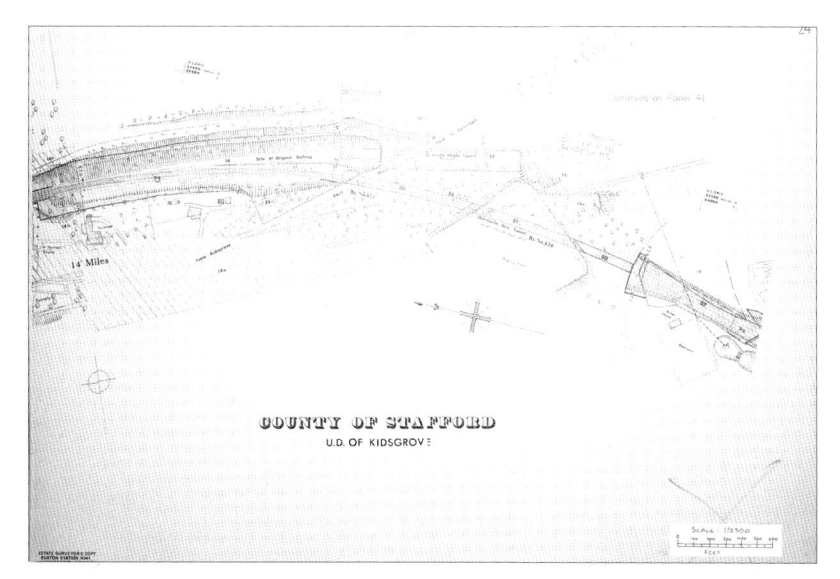

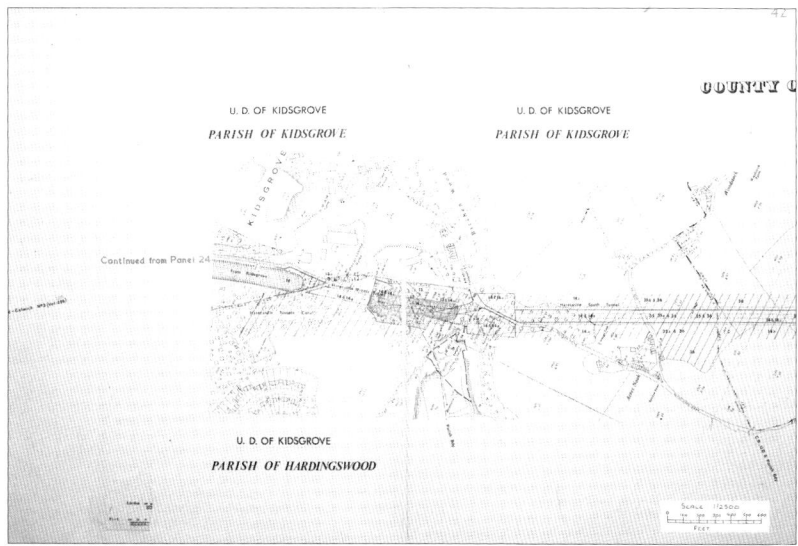

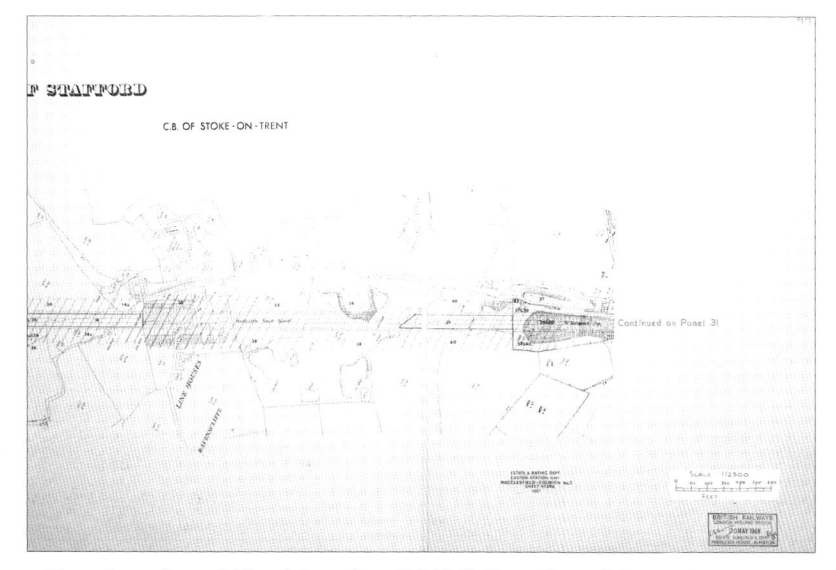

These three plans which originate from British Railways Estate & Rating Department, have a date of 1967. They show the northern end of the Diversion Scheme, along with the route of the old after it had been taken out of use. *Historic Railways Estate*

This view, featuring the final stages of the reconstruction of the Bath Pool, looks north, taken after the deviation line had opened. The folly at Mow Cop can be seen on the skyline to the left and the Gill Bank housing estate is on the horizon to the right. A three-car diesel multiple unit bound for Crewe is passing a splitting banner signal for Kidsgrove Junction and is about to enter the southern portal of the new Harecastle tunnel.
Kidsgrove Library Local History Collection

The route of the Harecastle Diversion line can be seen to the right curving through the Bath Pool valley into the new tunnel at the extreme top right of the photograph. The road running across the photograph is Peacock Hay Road which crosses the new railway at centre right. The line of trees to the bottom left of the photograph marks the route of the old Talk o' th' Hill branch which closed between High Carr and Talk o' th' Hill colliery in 1931 and between High Carr and Chesterton Junction in 1955; its route was later occupied by part of the A500 Potteries D Road.
Kidsgrove Library Local History Collection

CHAPTER 9 – THE HARECASTLE DIVERSION

Early site works for the Harecastle Diversion commenced in June 1964 and the new line was opened two years later on 27th June 1966. This scene showing part of the construction site looks south towards the Chatterley valley. The first chimney to the left is part of the former Ashwood Colliery; the more distant chimney and building are part of the former Chatterley Ironworks and the church in the far distance is St. Paul's at Burslem.

Kidsgrove Library Local History Collection

This photograph was taken from the new Peacock's Hay road overbridge and looks south. Track laying has commenced but there appears to be a problem with the construction train which has derailed. The smoke and steam in the left distance is from the Goldendale Ironworks.

Kidsgrove Library Local History Collection

The southern portal of the new tunnel features prominently in this view with the erection of the overhead line equipment nearing completion. To the left can be seen the concrete top of the re-sited and sunken Bath Pool.
Kidsgrove Library Local History Collection

This view looks north towards Kidsgrove Central station on the site of the old north tunnel which has been opened out. The vertical masonry walls of the old tunnel were found to be in very good condition, such that it was decided to bridge across them with reinforced concrete portal frames which can be seen under construction here. The frames were placed ten feet apart and their legs were dowelled into the tops of the existing walls. The two skips used for tipping concrete are working on a monorail system. A semaphore home signal can just be discerned in the right distance which will be the Crewe line Up starter. The building to the left is the former Wade School which was named after the Reverend Frederick Tobias Wade (1809-1884), incumbent at St. Thomas', Kidsgrove from 1837 to 1880.
*Kidsgrove Library
Local History Collection*

CHAPTER 9 – THE HARECASTLE DIVERSION

This view looks south from inside the partly dismantled north tunnel which was completely opened out. The signal seen through the tunnel mouth is the Kidsgrove Up advanced starter.
Kidsgrove Library Local History Collection

A view looking south in the opened out north tunnel well illustrating the newly installed concrete portal frames. Presumably taken during a weekend civil engineering occupation, with the traffic diverted via the Loop and Pinnox lines. *Kidsgrove Library Local History Collection*

151

Freshly ballasted track, together with the recently installed overhead line equipment, as seen at the south end of the diversion, looking south, with Goldendale Ironworks in the distance towards the top left of the photograph. Note the new wire fencing with concrete posts.
Kidsgrove Library Local History Collection

The construction of the new footbridge at Bath Pool looking south and well illustrating the use of the contractor's narrow gauge railway.
Kidsgrove Library Local History Collection

CHAPTER 9 – THE HARECASTLE DIVERSION

A Ruston Bucyrus 22 RB crawler crane is being utilised to lift the bucket containing the concrete prior to pouring it into carefully placed shuttering. There was nothing pre-fabricated about the new footbridge at Bath Pool!
Kidsgrove Library Local History Collection

The main contractor for the Harecastle Diversion was Tarmac Civil Engineering Limited whose staff are seen here constructing the new footbridge at Bath Pool. A tiny narrow gauge industrial locomotive is being used to convey concrete pouring buckets on flat wagons to the site. The view looks slightly south with the remains of the screens of a later privately owned Ravenscliffe Colliery to the top right. No hard hats in those days but perhaps even more risky is the absence of fall protection guards to the working platform. Today's Health & Safety Executive would, no doubt, take a dim view of it all.
Kidsgrove Library Local History Collection

This view looks south towards the northern portal of the old middle tunnel. The Ruston Bucyrus dragline crane on the embankment to the right is starting to excavate the route towards the new tunnel that bypassed Harecastle hill to the west. The signal is the Kidsgrove Up Advanced Starter.
Kidsgrove Library Local History Collection

A construction scene showing the north end of the middle railway tunnel to the left. The cut and cover work in the foreground had to be undertaken at the north end of the new railway tunnel on the diverted line in order to reinstate Boat Horse Road over the railway.
Kidsgrove Library Local History Collection

CHAPTER 9 – THE HARECASTLE DIVERSION

This view looks north from the middle railway tunnel and illustrates the start of work to create the diverted route to the left. The north tunnel in the distance had yet to be opened out and the short home signal seen in the distance to the right is the Kidsgrove Up advanced starter.
Kidsgrove Library Local History Collection

Civil Engineer, British Railways, London Midland Region;[183] Dobbie & Partners were engaged as consulting engineers and the main contractor was Tarmac Civil Engineering Limited, Wolverhampton. The contractor made quite extensive use of a temporary two-foot gauge railway during the works with at least one Motor Rail *Simplex* four-wheel diesel-mechanical locomotive as motive power with a fleet of both side-tip and other designs of specialist wagons. As previously mentioned the new route was opened to passenger and freight traffic on 27th June 1966 but was not fully energised for electric traction until 30th October that year, following which some electric hauled revenue earning traffic began to flow from 5th December, with the proposed full electrified passenger service commencing in January 1967. However, an unanticipated operating problem quickly manifested itself in that for some inexplicable reason the circuit breakers controlling the section of the Up line between Kidsgrove Central and Bradwell Sidings kept tripping out and on occasions when no electric trains were in that section. The problem was quite acute as the breakers were not designed to trip out so frequently and were literally burning up! After dismissing the errant *Ghost of Harecastle Tunnel* as the culprit, it was eventually discovered that every time a steam hauled train passed through the new tunnel in the Up direction, out came those breakers! The new line after leaving Kidsgrove climbed for nearly a mile at 1 in 80 through the new tunnel. The exhaust from the steam engines climbing hard reverberated from the tunnel roof causing such vibration to the contact wire that the circuit breakers tripped out. There were still several diagrammed steam workings at the time but not enough diesels around to replace them. The steam workings

183 He was born in Belfast on 12th February 1909, the son of Joseph Nicholson Beatty (1868-1939) who in 1896 joined the staff of Naylor Bros as engineer for the construction of the L&NWR line from Ashbourne to Buxton. William Fitzgerald Beatty was awarded his MBE in the 1950 New Year's Honours when he was Assistant District Engineer, Railway Executive, Watford. He served with the Engineers and Railway Staff Corps achieving the rank of major, resigning his commission on 31st December 1974.

Aerial view of the Chatterley, south end of the deviation line under construction, curving away to the top right and heading for Bath Pool. The road running across the scene towards the top of the photograph is Lowlands Road, from where the photograph to the left was taken. The line curving away to the left middle is the realigned Chesterton branch, the original formation of which can be discerned having been cut by the deviation line. The former Chatterley Ironworks engine house was still standing at the time; it can be seen between the new and old Chesterton branch formations, as can the old bridge abutments over the original branch, just to the left of the deviation line. The NCB coal stocking and blending ground with its railway sidings are to the right upper, with Harecastle Farm to the left middle.

Although this is not a very good photograph, it has been worth including as it shows the deviation line under construction on 22nd April 1965. The view looks south from Lowlands Road, which runs via Chatterley from Talke to Tunstall. At the point where the photographer was standing, a bridge was constructed to take the new line under the road.

This view of Peacock's Hay looking south is taken from an almost identical position as the opposite view but at a slightly lower level. It portrays the tranquillity of the countryside before the commotion of constructing the deviation.

Right: Looking north showing the deviation line curving away to the left, with the former Up relief line to the right, which had been left in situ to give access to the sidings serving Goldendale Ironworks and the NCB facility. The loaded coal train from Parkhouse Colliery is on the realigned section of the Chesterton branch, hauled by 350 horsepower diesel-electric shunting locomotive D4109, later designated as Class '09' and renumbered as 09021. Once again the former engine house of Chatterley Ironworks is prominent. The building alongside the deviation line just to the right of the overhead catenary support in the centre of the view, is the NCB locomotive shed for the coal stocking ground although in the event, a locomotive was never stationed there as the shunting was undertaken by BR engines and men.

A second aerial view of the deviation line construction works, this time at the north end. At the bottom is the existing mainline with the entrance to the Middle Tunnel and on its right, the formation of the new line and the short tunnel entrance portal. To the upper right is the formation of the new line after it emerged from the south end of the tunnel, no track having yet been laid. To the right is the new covered reservoir and below, the cricket ground. The road running from the bottom of the photograph by the new tunnel entrance, crossing the existing line and continuing through the trees to disappear top left, is Boat Horse Road. This road was constructed at the time of the original canal tunnel and so named as it was the means of taking the horses used for hauling the canal boats from one end of Brindley's tunnel to the other, while the boats were legged through.

included BR Standard Class '9F' 2-10-0 heavy freight engines based at Birkenhead North bringing iron ore from Bidston Dock to the iron and steel works of Shelton Iron & Steel Limited at Etruria. As a means of overcoming the problem, the decision was taken to employ diesels on the steam workings through the tunnel in accordance with the following instructions – unique among the plethora of *Weekly Notices* issued to footplatemen:

Working of Steam-hauled Freight Trains over the Up-Line
Between Kidsgrove Central & Longport Junction

To prevent damage to the overhead line equipment in the Kidsgrove area, steam locomotives must not haul trains under their own power over the Up line between Kidsgrove Central (signals KC 28 or KC 31) and Bradwell Sidings (signal BS 106). Steam-hauled Up trains will be hauled complete with steam locomotive by a 2,000hp Type '4' diesel locomotive between Alsager East Junction or Lawton Junction or Kidsgrove Central and Longport Junction. Where the load of the train exceeds 60 BWUs (Basic Wagon Units), the steam locomotive may assist the hauling diesel locomotive except between the signals mentioned above, providing permanent and/or temporary speed restrictions are observed. The vacuum brake pipes between the diesel and steam locomotives must be coupled. It is essential that the regulator of steam locomotives working trains is closed between the signals mentioned above and drivers of light steam locomotives must keep the emission of smoke and steam to an absolute minimum.

What a palaver and something completely unforeseen by the planners! A selection of English Electric Type '4' (later Class '40') diesels was kept at Alsager for the operation, travelling light to either Lawton Junction or Kidsgrove, if required to assist from these points; they returned from Longport light engine or two or more light engines coupled together. This interesting debacle came to an end with the closure of Stoke Motive Power Depot on 7th August 1967 and the elimination of steam working in North Staffordshire.[184]

The diversion rendered the old tunnels redundant. As explained above, the short tunnel at Harecastle North was opened out but the other two: Harecastle Middle and the longest one at

---

184 The line from Kidsgrove to Crewe was not electrified until 2003 when it was thought expedient to carry out the work as part of a diversionary route for traffic off the West Coast Main Line. The electrified line was opened on 28th September 2003.

This photograph was taken in the spring of 1966, just a few weeks prior to the new route being brought into use on Monday 26th June 1966. The Cravens DMU is on a Crewe to Derby service and about to enter the Middle Tunnel, with the new short tunnel on the deviation line to the right. Notice the difference in levels, the new line climbing at a grade of 1 in 80 as it left the old formation. The road passing over the tunnels is Boat Horse Road and the trees form part of the Birchen Wood.

Left: This view dates from shortly after the deviation line opened and looks north with the opened out former North Tunnel in the distance. The train is one from Crewe to Derby, formed by another of the Birmingham Railway Carriage & Wagon Company three-car DMUs, which were later designated as Class '104'. The former mainlines are of course, to the right.

Right: After the new line opened there was still a significant amount of goods and mineral traffic worked by steam locomotives. Problems were encountered with the blast from the locomotives' chimneys reverberating from the new tunnel roof as they climbed the steep 1 in 80 incline through the tunnel. To address this issue a procedure was introduced for a small number of English Electric 2,000 horsepower Type '4' diesel-electric locomotives to assist the trains between Alsager on the Crewe line and Bradwell Sidings. This was the first convenient uncoupling point south of the deviation line, just north of Longport. The diesels were stabled at Alsager as the vast majority of the trains were from the Crewe direction, although if there was one on the Macclesfield route, one of the diesels would run light and attach at Kidsgrove. From Bradwell Sidings the diesels went back to Alsager light-engine; on occasions two or more coupled together. Light steam locomotives, or with just a brake van attached, were allowed to operate without assistance. This photograph was taken on 30th June 1967 and shows an Up oil tank train on the deviation line at Lowlands, with D305 assisting a BR Class Standard Class '9F' 2-10-0, the number of which has unfortunately not been recorded.

Lower right: Taken on the same occasion as the previous view, this time a Down empty iron ore train with another '9F', No. 92088 from Birkenhead shed; Down trains of course, did not need to be assisted. At this time most of the iron ore used at the Shelton Iron & Steel Works at Etruria, was imported through Bidston Dock on the River Mersey near Birkenhead and moved to Shelton by rail. As the turntables at Stoke were not long enough to turn one of these engines, the empty trains had to return as far as Crewe with the engines running tender first. The layout of the connection to Basford Hall Sidings from the North Stafford line at Crewe however, automatically turned trains round so that after the engine had run round its train, it was smokebox leading back to Birkenhead.

One of the BR Swindon-built three-car Cross-Country DMUs, later designated as Class '120', working the 12.39pm Nottingham to Crewe service on 26th April 1975. On the deviation line at Ravenscliffe, the view looks south with the town of Tunstall on the skyline.
The late Michael Mensing

This image was taken at around the same time and at the same location as the previous view, but looking in the opposite, north direction. The train is the 2.10pm from Manchester to London, reporting number 1A53, hauled by Class '86/2' Bo-Bo electric locomotive No. 86253. From almost the inception of the NSR a number of the direct trains connecting London with Manchester have used the North Stafford route and today there are two trains every hour in each direction. While they all call at Stoke, one each hour also calls at Macclesfield.
The late Michael Mensing

Harecastle South remain intact. In 1969 the BBC televised *The Last Train Through the Harecastle Tunnel* for its *Wednesday Play* series. The play, written by Peter Terson,[185] followed a trainspotter's curious encounters during a weekend trip which embraced a ride on the last train through the condemned tunnels. Twenty years later there was a bizarre proposal to turn the disused tunnels into a mausoleum as a means of resolving a shortage of burial space in the nearby towns. The idea did not find favour with the local residents and was squashed by Newcastle-under-Lyme Borough Council and Kidsgrove Town Council.[186] So the two tunnels remain, having been devoid of trains for just over half a century. On 22nd April 1988 the two portals of the middle tunnel became listed structures with Grade II status, as did the northern portal of the south tunnel.

In 2010 BRB (Residuary) Limited[187] decided to undertake a survey of all the former railway tunnels in its charge and they employed Kenneth Heywood, former Eastern Region Bridge Engineer, to undertake the work. He found Harecastle South Tunnel very badly silted-up and flooded in parts, making access through its entire length impossible. Those involved had great difficulty removing the silt so as to allow the water to drain away and it was allowed to go into the canal. The presence of methane gas hampered the work as it had to be dispersed. It was, apparently, the biggest redundant asset project ever undertaken by BRB (R).

The reference above to an errant ghost is worthy of explanation. The earliest written account of the ghostly *Kidcrew Buggat* can be found in an entry dated 10th September 1816 in the journal of local Methodist preacher Hugh Bourne (1772-1852). Colliers and boatmen took reports of sighting the ghost as a forecast of foreboding. L.T. Meade's[188] novel of canal life *The Water Gipsies or The Adventures of Tag, Rag and Bobtail* published in 1879 also refers to the ghost, which, by that time, had become the *Kitcrew Buggut*. However, a long article appearing in the *Staffordshire Sentinel and Commercial & General Advertiser* for Saturday 6th December 1879 has the ghost as the *Kitcrew* or *Kidcrew Boggart*! In *The Lighter Side of A Parson's Life*, published privately in 1933, the Rev Frederick George Llewellin (1880-1941), Vicar of Kidsgrove (which is what Kidcrew or Kitcrew had become), preferred *Buggut*. Nowadays the ghost is known as the *Kidsgrove Boggart* and, who knows, the apparition may well still linger in those long-closed tunnels and mine workings under Harecastle Hill.

---

185 Playwright Peter Terson was born as Peter Paterson on 16th February 1932 in Newcastle-upon-Tyne.
186 *Newcastle Herald*, 27th July 1989 and *Staffordshire Evening Sentinel*, 24th August 1989.
187 BRB (Residuary) Limited was created in 2001 as successor to the British Railways Board responsible for discharging a variety of residual functions, including the continuing disposal of non-operational land. It was abolished with effect from 30th September 2013.

188 L.T. Meade was a pseudonym of Elizabeth Thomasina Meade Smith (1844-1914).

This and the next two photographs were taken on 15th February 2018 showing three of the disused railway tunnel portals. As can be seen, they present a pretty sorry sight. This one is the south end of the south, long tunnel, with its approach cutting. It presents an interesting contrast with the earlier views in Chapter 8 taken from almost the same vantage point when the line was still in use.
Barry Knapper

The portal here is the one at the opposite, north end, of the south tunnel; once again a sorry sight with nature having taken over. During the spring and summer months, it would be impossible to see the portal from this vantage point.
Barry Knapper

In this view we can see the south portal of the middle tunnel which, once again, is only visible from this position during the winter months. Both portals of the middle tunnel are Grade II listed structures as is the north portal of the south tunnel.
Barry Knapper

10

COAL AND IRONSTONE MINING

This chapter discusses the coal and ironstone mining that once took place in and around the Harecastle tunnels. The tunnels and the mining activity are in many ways inseparable, the mining having had an enormous influence on the tunnels, while the tunnels have had an influence on the mining. Inevitably therefore, this approach, exploring in greater detail the mining activities in one chapter, has entailed some duplication with what has gone before. This has nonetheless been felt essential, to assist readers to a better understanding of issues discussed earlier, by placing them in their appropriate context. The high ground of Harecastle Hill is a continuation of the Pennine Chain, which divides the valley of the River Trent from the great spread of the Cheshire plain, extending south-west into Shropshire. Within the hill can be found all the coal and ironstone measures of what became known as the North Staffordshire, or more colloquially, the Pottery Coalfield.

No story about Harecastle and its canal tunnels, along with the associated coal and ironstone mining, can be complete without mention of the Gilbert family of Cotton and in particular Thomas (1720-1798) and his younger sibling John (1723-1795). The industrial and political achievements of this family are both extensive and impressive, although only a few need be explored here. However, for those wanting to find out more about these two quite remarkable entrepreneurs and their family, we can do no better than recommend Peter Lead's excellent study, *Agents of Revolution*.[189]

The family hails from the Staffordshire Moorland village of Cotton, located in an area surrounded by the town of Cheadle and the villages of Ipstones, Cauldon, Ellastone and Alton. From humble beginnings members of the family became prominent land owners and in 1701 or 1702, George Gilbert, the brother's grandfather, became an Alderman of Cheadle Corporation. This is probably why some years later, Thomas and John became involved with the Leveson-Gower[190] family and in particular, their industrial interests as in 1720, John, Lord Gower, was elected Mayor of Cheadle.[191] The Leveson-Gower and by marriage the Sutherland families, were large and very influential land owners with extensive industrial interests, not least at Lilleshall in Shropshire and Trentham in North Staffordshire. Thomas, who went to London to study law, was admitted to the Inner Temple in 1740 and called to the Bar four years later. John meantime, the more practical of the two, was apprenticed to Matthew Boulton, a buckle maker in Birmingham and father of Matthew Boulton of Boulton & Watt fame, the well-known early designers and builders of steam engines. However, on the death of his father, Thomas (1688-1741), John returned to Cotton to manage the family's estates which included part ownership of Cloughhead Colliery near Ipstones which, among its customers, supplied fuel for the extensive lime kilns at Caldon Low. The family also had interests in local copper and lead mines, along with associated smelting operations.

Francis Egerton (1736-1803), the 3rd Duke of Bridgewater, owned among his many and varied assets, an estate at Worsley, to the west of Manchester, which included one of his residences, Worsley Old Hall. This rich mineral estate tapped a significant number of coal measures with vast reserves, situated as it was, at the eastern extremity of the Lancashire Coalfield. Moving the coal to its obvious markets in Salford and Manchester had exercised the minds of many, including the Duke's father, Scroop Egerton (1681-1745), 4th Earl of Bridgewater, who in 1720 was created the 1st Duke of Bridgewater. It was for this purpose that the original part of the Bridgewater Canal, as it became known, was born. This canal is often referred to as The Duke's Canal and sometimes cited as the first man-made waterway in this country, although this is not strictly correct. Thomas Gilbert had taken on the role of agent and legal advisor to Granville Leveson-Gower (1721-1803), the 2nd Earl Gower and later, the 1st Marquis of Stafford, who in 1748 married as his second wife, Lady Louisa Egerton, sister of the 3rd Duke of Bridgewater.[192] It would have been through this family connection that the 3rd Duke became aware of the Gilbert brothers with Thomas taking on the role of his general land agent and chief legal advisor. This appointment was additional to similar responsibilities he undertook on behalf of the 2nd Earl Gower.

The Duke, well aware of the financial loss his coal mining activities were incurring due to a lack of economical transport facilities, was also conscious of earlier unsuccessful schemes to make the Worsley Brook navigable southwards to the River Irwell at Barton. Had this been successful, it would have made movement of the coal to the Manchester markets profitable. It was almost certainly Thomas Gilbert who suggested a canal as the

---

189 University of Keele, 1990. ISBN 0-9513713-1-2.
190 Pronounced Lousum-Gore.
191 John (1692-1794), created 1st Earl Gower and Viscount Trentham of Trentham, 8th July 1746.
192 John Egerton, the 2nd Duke, the 3rd Duke's younger brother, died in 1755 when only seventeen years old.

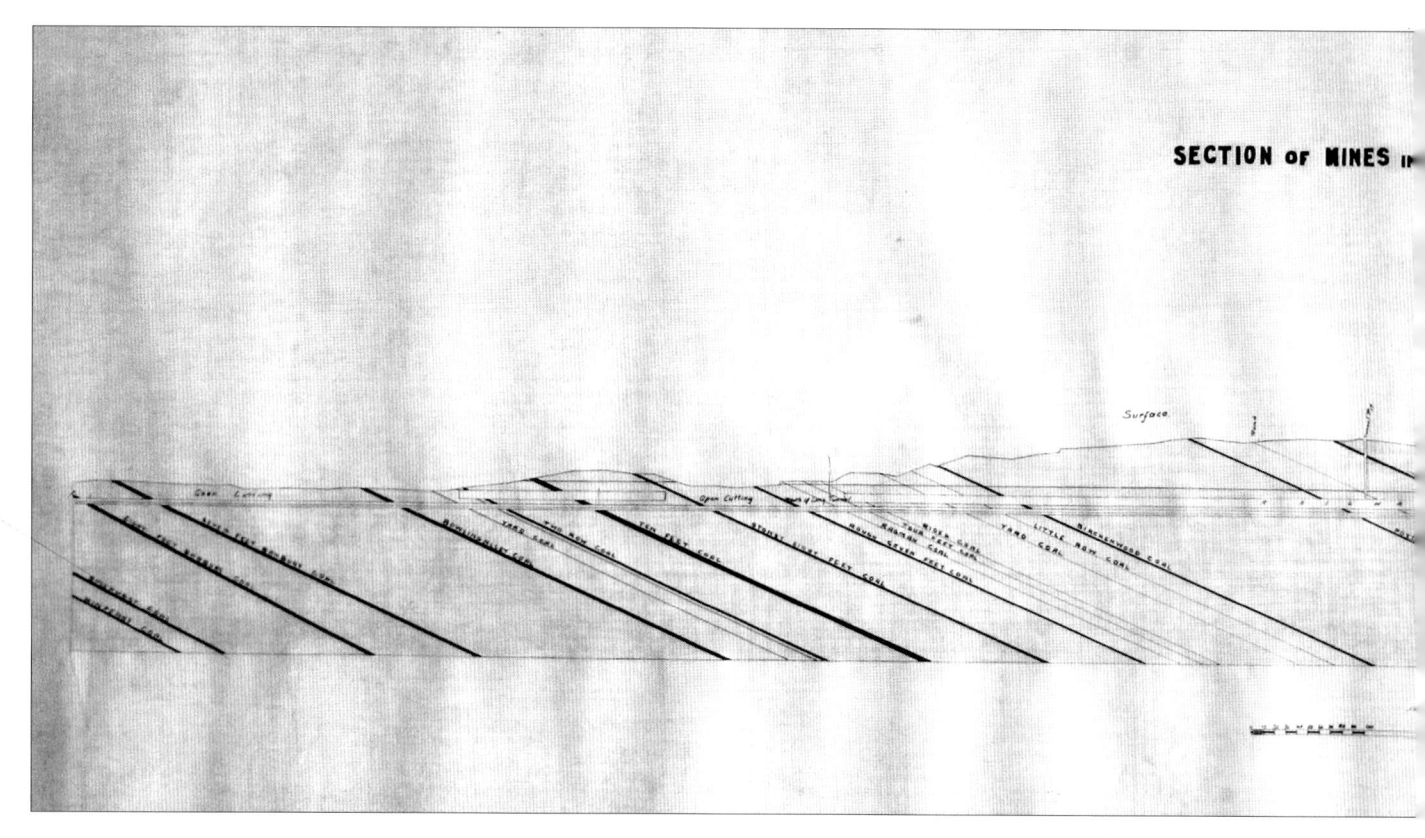

answer to the problem and in 1757, the Duke appointed Thomas's brother John, to investigate the possibility of building a canal from Worsley to Manchester. There is some doubt as to how the Duke became acquainted with James Brindley, who entered his employment in May 1759, to assist in the construction of the canal, the first Act for which had been passed by Parliament in March 1759.[193] The Gilberts were certain to have at least known of Brindley, if they were not already acquainted with him, in view of his engineering achievements in and around the Staffordshire Moorlands. The Duke too, must have been aware of him, following the work he had undertaken between 1752 and 1756, in draining Wet Earth Colliery at Clifton in the Irwell Valley, which was only a couple of miles north-east of the Worsley estate.[194] Whatever the case, the three of them, the Duke, John Gilbert and James Brindley, formed what Hugh Malet describes in his book, *Bridgewater, The Canal Duke 1736-1803*, as *The Canal Triumvirate*.[195] However, this sobriquet was originally bestowed on the trio by the famous pottery manufacturer Josiah Wedgwood. Although Brindley is generally credited as the engineer of what became the Bridgewater Canal, there is considerable evidence that John Gilbert was the directing mind in its conception, design and construction. We do know that whatever else he achieved in connection with the canal, John Gilbert certainly acted in the role of what today, we would identify as the Consulting Engineer.

The first part of what became a relatively extensive group of waterways was originally intended to head directly east, staying to the north of the River Irwell, to terminate at a wharf in Salford. However, after work had started from the Worsley end, the Duke came to the view that if the terminus was in Manchester rather than Salford, not only could he tap the Lancashire markets, but the Cheshire ones too. Therefore, he went to Parliament again and by a second Act of March 1760, a revised scheme was agreed.[196] A particular problem with the new plan was a requirement to cross the River Irwell and rather than joining the river by locking-down and then leaving again by locking-up, with the attendant problems that would introduce, not least with the Proprietors of Mersey & Irwell Navigation, an aqueduct over the river was proposed. Thus came about what was in its time, an outstanding civil engineering achievement, the famous aqueduct at Barton for which Brindley has historically been given the credit. It is not the intention of the present authors to denigrate this famous engineer's reputation; rather to acknowledge the role that John Gilbert played in the conception and construction of the Duke's canals and in particular, this aqueduct. As the first of its kind in the country, it became somewhat of a tourist attraction, standing for over a 100 years until it had to be replaced as part of the late 19th century Manchester Ship Canal project, as the new canal at this point, followed the original course of the River Irwell. The ship canal was officially opened throughout from Eastham on the south bank of the Mersey to Trafford Park in the city, on 1st January 1894.

The original section of the Bridgewater Canal, eight miles long from Worsley to Stretford, was constructed between 1761

---

193 32 Geo II ch. ii, Royal Assent 23rd March 1759.
194 *Brindley at Wet Earth Colliery*, A.G. Banks & R.B. Schofield. David & Charles, 1968.
195 Manchester University Press, 1977. ISBN 0-7190-0679-1.

196 33 Geo II ch. ii, Royal Assent 14th March 1760.

CHAPTER 10 – COAL AND IRONSTONE MINING

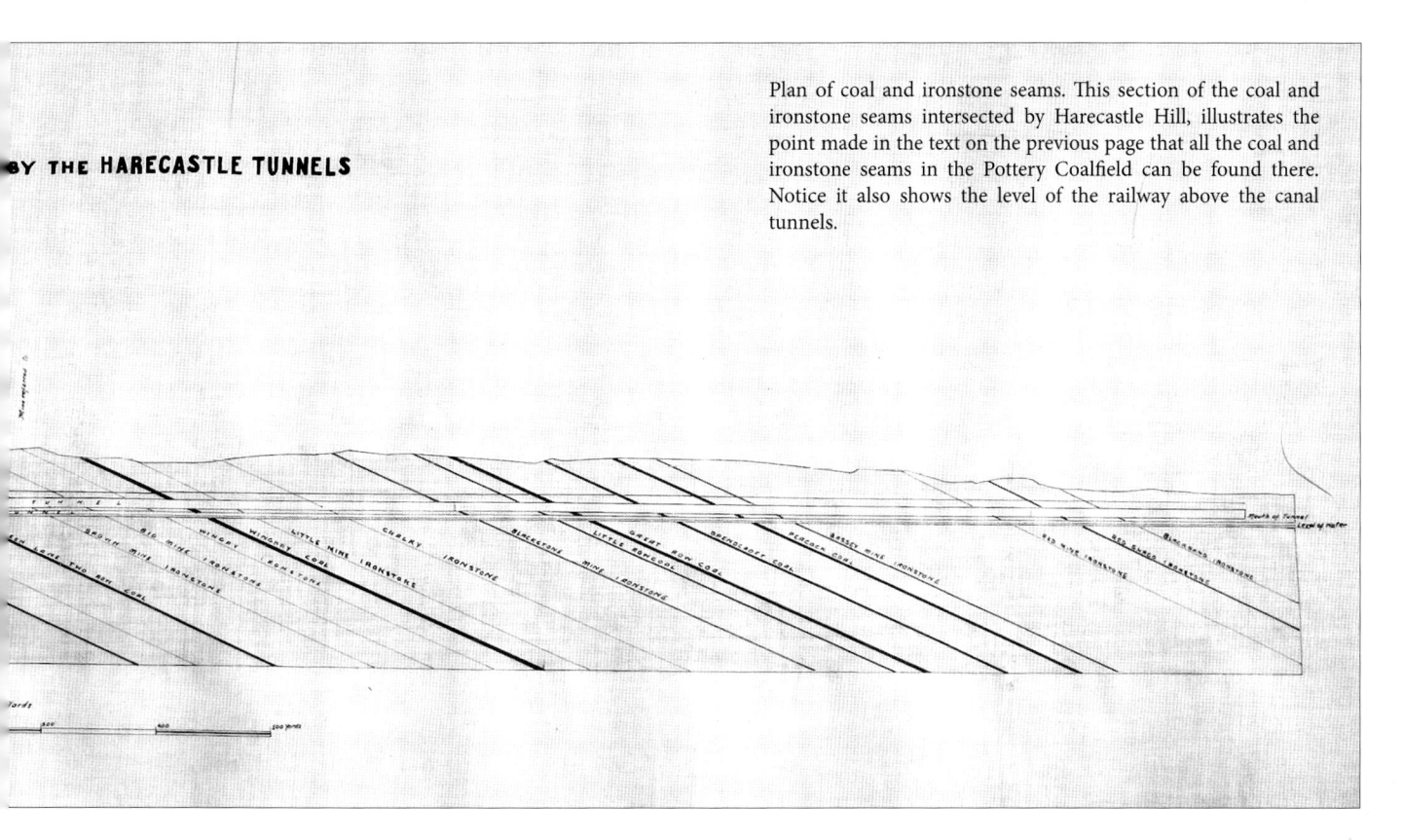

BY THE HARECASTLE TUNNELS

Plan of coal and ironstone seams. This section of the coal and ironstone seams intersected by Harecastle Hill, illustrates the point made in the text on the previous page that all the coal and ironstone seams in the Pottery Coalfield can be found there. Notice it also shows the level of the railway above the canal tunnels.

and 1762, terminating at a basin alongside the later location of the Manchester Ship Canal's Salford Docks. Most of the coal at Worsley was mined underground, using tributary canals to access the coal seams and transport the coal to the main canal basin. This is without doubt how the Gilbert brothers and Brindley came to the view that in driving a tunnel under Harecastle Hill, similar opportunities might present themselves for underground coal mining and as events turned out, ironstone too, direct from the canal. It is pertinent to remind readers that while all the coal measures of the North Staffordshire coalfield are present in the Harecastle area, whether or not the trio were aware of this at the time, is not clear. Under John Gilbert's guidance the Bridgewater Canal was gradually extended and along with several branches, eventually reached the River Mersey at Runcorn. Although the locks to enable the canal to join the river were completed in December 1772, it was not until March 1776 that the waterway was complete between Runcorn and Manchester. It was on this last section that connection was made at Preston Brook with the Grand Trunk Canal, thus completing the route between the Rivers Trent and Mersey. In 1893, as part of the Manchester Ship Canal project, a completely new set of locks had to be constructed for the Bridgewater Canal at Runcorn, which thereafter, joined the Ship Canal rather than the River Mersey.

Before closing this brief résumé of the remarkable Gilbert brothers prior to their involvement in the Grand Trunk Canal, it is worth mentioning that John Gilbert was also involved with various extensions to the Bridgewater Canal network. In the case of one that ran westwards from Worsley to Leigh, where connection was made with the Leigh branch of the Leeds & Liverpool Canal, it involved draining a significant part of the infamous Chat Moss. This is the same area that later caused so much trouble to George Stephenson in building the Liverpool & Manchester Railway. Connections were also established in Manchester with the Rochdale Canal and later still, with the Manchester Ship Canal, the Ship Canal Company having in 1887, acquired the Bridgewater Undertaking. The underground canals built to tap the coal seams at Worsley eventually reached a remarkable total of no fewer than forty-six miles, including an underground inclined plane where boats were moved from one level to another, the loaded boats on the way down, balancing the empty ones on their way up.[197]

In 1762 Thomas Gilbert married Ann Phillips, gifting her as a wedding present a lottery ticket which fortuitously, rendered a prize of no less that £10,000; an enormous sum in those times.[198] Along with Earl Gower he was one of the leading protagonists of the embryonic Grand Trunk Canal, Chairman of the original Committee and for several years after it was formed, holding a similar position for the Company of Proprietors. As a substantial shareholder too, it is likely some of his wife's money was used for this purpose. In later life he became a Member of Parliament, representing Newcastle-under-Lyme between 1763 and 1768 and Lichfield between 1768 and 1794. The Gilbert brothers and Brindley would have become aware of the potential for mining

---

[197] *The Duke of Bridgewater's Underground Canals at Worsley*, Frank Mullineux. Transactions of the Lancashire & Cheshire Antiquarian Society Vol. 71, 1971. *The Canal Duke's Collieries*, Worsley 1760-1900, Glen Atkinson, Neil Richardson, undated. ISBN 0-9506257-7-9.

[198] About £2m at today's value.

163

coal and ironstone under Harecastle Hill and surrounding areas during the initial canal surveys. In 1760 a partnership was formed of Hugh Henshall, Robert Williamson, John Brindley (younger brother of James) and Thomas & John Gilbert (one share). The purpose of the partnership was to purchase from Sir Nigel Gresley for the sum of £2,175, the nearby Turnhurst, Newchapel & Goldenhill Estates.

Henshall we have already met, while Robert Williamson (1743-1799), a member of a family with a number of other local mining interests along with the Goldendale Ironworks, had, on 30th December 1775, married Brindley's widow Anne, who was Hugh Henshall's sister. These estates lie to the east of Harecastle on an extension of the same high ground between the Pottery town of Tunstall and the Biddulph Valley villages of Whitfield and Fegg Hayes.[199] There is a point of view that had it not been for the problems associated with lining the roof and the severe flooding when driving the soughs, as they were called, to tap the coal seams direct from the tunnel, Harecastle tunnel could have been completed in less time. The accusation being that Brindley and the Gilbert brothers in wanting to exploit their mining interests, did so at the expense of the Canal Company Proprietors. In other words, how much time was being taken driving the side tunnels, as opposed to work on the Canal Company's tunnel? In this connection it is worth quoting from the minutes of a General Assembly of the Proprietors of the Canal, held at Stone on 26th December 1775. The complete minute refers to: *what things were wanting to render the Navigation as useful to the Public and as beneficial to the Proprietors*, while the part we are interested in reads:

That an additional supply of Coals of a superior quality to that now got at Harecastle, to be conveyed on the Navigation, are much wanted.

Note that this meeting was after parts of the canal had been opened, including the tunnel at Harecastle. Mention of coals *now got at Harecastle*, might perhaps, refer to coal being mined from seams via the side tunnels that we know had already been constructed, as noted on the Duke of Bridgewater's trip into the then partly completed tunnel on 27th October 1773, described in Chapter 1. This minute is particularly interesting as it might suggest that is was the canal company that was extracting the coal, rather than anybody else. An interesting issue to speculate over?

Whatever the case, regarding the extraction of minerals via the tunnel, the canal finally opened for its entire length in May 1777. In 1782 John Gilbert acquired the Clough Hall Estate at Kidsgrove, often referred to locally as Kid Crew, which at that time, was a relatively small hamlet. The estate eventually consisted of some 700 acres and while legend suggests it was given to Gilbert by a grateful Duke of Bridgewater for services rendered, in fact the Duke helped Gilbert purchase the estate by issuing a mortgage in his favour.[200] However, as this was for a period of 1,000 years, clearly the Duke was not looking to make a great profit! On the east side of the estate Gilbert built a modest mansion for his family – White Hall – and in view of the vast mineral wealth under the estate, he embarked on vigorous developments. While John Gilbert did not create for his employees and their families what became the town of Kidsgrove, as Josiah Wedgwood had built the village of Etruria for his, there are similarities. Like his brother Thomas, he was aware that as the pace of what we now know as the industrial revolution quickened, the facilities, such as they were, for supporting the sick and destitute had to change. In 1782 Thomas had introduced and steered through Parliament *The Relief of the Poor Act*, colloquially known as *Gilbert's Act*,[201] which introduced the concept of Work Houses. While this was by no means the complete answer, or indeed anywhere near one, it was a great improvement on what existed hitherto. On John's death on 3rd August 1795, which occurred while he was staying with the Duke at Worsley, the Clough Hall estate passed to his son, also John (1757-1812), who continued to work and develop the estate, if anything even more vigorously than his father. He even managed to upset and get into awkward and expensive disputes with some of his coal-owning neighbours. In particular Sir John Edensor Heathcote (1757-1822), who owned the adjacent Hardings Wood, Hollins and Woodshutts estates.[202]

In 1805 the younger John Gilbert replaced White Hall with the much larger and grander Clough Hall, on the opposite, west side of the northern part of Harecastle Hill. Readers will notice on the plan of Telford's tunnel reproduced on page 47, the *Nelson Engine*. John Gilbert was a great enthusiast of the famous Admiral and there were several paintings of his battles hanging on the walls of the hall. Viscount Lord Nelson's famous victory at Trafalgar on 21st October 1805, although resulting in his death, may well have been the reason for this pit being so named, combined with the installation of a new steam beam engine in 1804 and 1805. This was supplied by the Coalbrookdale Company and erected by one of that company's engineers, John Rose.[203] Previous to this the pit was known as the Tunnel Pit,[204] with a shaft 79 yards deep to the Ten Feet coal seam which was at the same level as the water in the canal tunnel. There is evidence that some coal seams that were below the level of the canal tunnel were also worked from this shaft. By 1812 the *Nelson Engine* was described as running at fifteen strokes a minute and lifting twenty gallons of water per stroke. Quite why it needed to lift the water however, rather than it being discharged into the canal, is a mystery. Unless that is, the water was being drawn from workings below the level of the canal. The name Tunnel Pit was in view of an underground connection with Brindley's canal tunnel which suggests it was sunk while the canal was being built. This is explored later in this chapter.

The younger John did not live long to enjoy his new opulence and on his death in September 1812 the estate, which consisted

---

199 *North Staffordshire Collieries On The Hill North Of Chell*, Allan C. Baker. Lightmoor Press, 2014. ISBN 3: 978-1899889-84-6.
200 CRO D997/1/22. In D3098/8/11 there is a copy of the Duke's Last Will and Testament which confirms that Gilbert was not a beneficiary.
201 *The Relief of the Poor Act*, 22 Geo III, ch. lxxxiii
202 John Edensor Heathcote of Longton Hall was knighted in 1784.
203 Peter Lead and John Robey in a private paper, *Steam Power in North Staffordshire 1750-1850*, claim that the original engine here was installed in 1797 by the second John Gilbert and was also named *The Nelson*.
204 On some plans it is shown with just a number, 51.

of some 700 acres, was sold by auction. This took place on 30th December that year at the Roe Buck Inn in Newcastle-under-Lyme, the sizable sum of £64,000 being realised. It was purchased by Thomas Kinnersly (1751-1819), a banker from Newcastle-under-Lyme,[205] the price probably reflecting developments undertaken by the Gilberts, father and son, for the extraction of the minerals. Actually, on Gilbert's death, the estate had been placed in trust with three of his relations, Nathaniel Gould of Salford, David Birds of Hadley near Wellington in Shropshire and James Royds of Rochdale, to dispose of as best they could.[206] Both Gould and Birds had previously acted as Gilbert's agents and managers at Clough Hall and at one period Birds lived in the hall. However, there was provision in the will for his wife, Elizabeth, to retain the hall and its associated grounds for the rest of her life, although in the event, she elected to live in London with an address in the Edgware Road.[207] Kinnersly and his descendants continued to work and develop the coal mines and in 1833 blast furnaces were introduced as many of the seams being mined were ironstone. The furnaces were soon complemented by puddling furnaces for wrought iron production, forges and rolling mills. There is a note in the sale particulars of the estate relating to some of the mineral rights being leased from John Jervis, with a commitment to deliver to him at the *tunnel mouth*, coal slack for his own purposes. This confirms that coal was coming from mines accessed underground via the canal side tunnels. John Jervis incidentally, was the famous Admiral (1734-1823), elevated to the peerage on 23rd June 1797, as Viscount and Earl St. Vincent, following his victory on 14th February that year, over the Spanish fleet at Cape St. Vincent. Nelson by the way, was with him on that occasion as Commander of HMS *Captain* and while he disobeyed orders, in doing so is credited with being instrumental in the final victory. The Jervis family, with a seat at Meaford, to the south of the Potteries near Barlaston, owned considerable areas of land in North Staffordshire and South Cheshire.

When Thomas Kinnersly died on 3rd November 1819 the estate passed to his son, also Thomas (1782-1855) and when he died on 4th February 1855, to his wife Mary (née Barnston) and his sister Elizabeth. These two ladies employed as their manager William Matthews and when Elizabeth died on 4th January 1865, her share in the estate passed to her late brother Thomas's niece, Georgina Mary Attwood (1821-1885) and when Mary died on 21st July 1877, Miss Attwood became the sole owner. Through all these changes the business continued to trade as Kinnersly & Company. Miss Attwood was the daughter of Thomas's sister Mary (1779-1823), who on 21st February 1818 had married George Attwood (1777-1854) of Edgbaston, Birmingham, a coal and iron master in his own right, with interests in the Black Country. Miss Attwood did not enjoy very good health which may have contributed to a decline in the business as it became less profitable during her tenure. This is probably why her cousin, Edward Williamson, came to her rescue as on 17th December 1879; the estate was sold to him, the business continuing to trade as Kinnersly & Company.[208] However, there is evidence that Miss Attwood continued to spend some of her time at Clough Hall, as well as at the Attwood family estate at The Priory in Edgbaston.[209] Edward Williamson was a partner with his brothers in a number of other local coal mining and iron making operations, including Stonetrough Colliery near Scholar Green, Brown Lees Colliery at Black Bull and Ravenscliffe Colliery, of which more anon, along with the Goldendale Iron Works at Chatterley. This ironworks was situated just to the south of the Harecastle Tunnels on the east, Tunstall side of the canal.

The depression in the iron trade in the mid-1880s, along with a strike by the men at Clough Hall in early 1886, when they refused to accept a wage reduction of 10 percent, resulted in the works standing idle with over 1,880 men out of work. By this time Williamson had advanced almost £42,000 in underwriting losses, along with funding a few improvements to the plant and equipment. Added to this was a guarantee of £13,000 outstanding with the National Provincial Bank, such that the total unsecured creditors were in debt to the tune of almost £98,000. This was an enormous sum in those times which eventually placed the Williamson family in bankruptcy proceedings with the collapse of their other business interests.[210] The Clough Hall Estate was offered for sale by auction in March 1886 and again in June, but as there were no takers on either occasion, the whole plant remained idle. Further efforts were made but it was not until late in 1886 that part of the estate was sold, with the remainder in 1888. In both cases the sale was on extremely favourable terms to Robert Heath of Biddulph (1816-1893). Heath's father, also Robert (1779-1849), had for many years and until his death, been Thomas Kinnersly's manager, during which time he was responsible for introducing the hot-blast system to the Clough Hall blast furnaces. He was also responsible for other improvements in the mines, iron works, forges and mills.[211]

In April 1888 a group of local iron and coal masters with existing mining and engineering interests in the Potteries area, formed a new limited liability company, the Kidsgrove Steel, Iron & Coal Company Limited. A lease from Robert Heath of part of the estate embracing the iron works and some of the coal and ironstone mines was agreed, with the intention of restarting operations. While some coal and probably ironstone mining was

---

205 Kinnersly is often spelt Kinnersley and while there is evidence that the latter spelling was often in use, there is no-doubt from both legal and family documents that the correct spelling is as rendered here. Thomas Kinnersly had other mining interests in the Newcastle-under-Lyme area.
206 Richard Gould, Thomas Birds and John Royds had respectively married John (the 1st) and Thomas Gilbert's sisters, Elizabeth, Mary and Ann.
207 CRO D997/1/16.
208 Another of Thomas Kinnersly's daughters, Anne, had married Robert Williamson, Edward's father.
209 CRO D997/III/5; D997/I/18; D997/I/22: D2372/1/9/13.
210 It is worth noting too, that when Miss Attwood sold the estate she took on a mortgage with her cousin for £9,000, but on her death the interest payments were in arrears such that her estate was considered as bankrupt.
211 It should be pointed out that the various changes of ownership of the Clough Hall Estate were not quite as simple as outlined here. For example, in some cases mortgages were involved to provide funds for developments and on occasion, they were transferred with the changes of ownership.

undertaken, it is doubtful if the blast furnaces or any other part of the iron works was reactivated and in any event, this company was in liquidation by March 1891. Robert Heath then started to work the minerals with direct labour, around the same time acquiring a small colliery undertaking under another lease he had granted. This lease, which had been signed on 24th March 1891, was for a term of twenty-eight years on behalf of another group of local mining engineers who, on 15th September 1892, formed the Birchenwood Colliery Company Limited. This was another attempt to make a profitable business out of some of the minerals under the estate. The Heath family, consisting of Robert's sons, as he died in 1893, acquired this company in December 1897.[212]

In January 1890 Robert Heath had sold that part of the estate consisting of Clough Hall, its park, gardens and the Bath Pool, minus any mineral rights, to a group of Manchester businessmen who were involved with the well-known amusement and pleasure park at Belle Vue in Manchester. The group had developed a plan to create a similar venture on the Clough Hall Estate, which was considered ideal with its close proximity to the Pottery towns, along with good transport links. Clough Hall Park & Gardens Limited was registered on 30th October 1890 and the park, which included the Bath Pool as a boating lake, opened to the public the following spring.[213] The enterprise was relatively successful, attracting crowds from a wide area, although there were two financial reconstructions of the debt before it became profitable. In 1897 ownership passed to a company of local brewers, Parker's Burslem Brewery Limited, based in the Pottery town of Burslem. While the park and gardens survived the First World War, the depression in the early 1920s saw its popularity decline with closure in about 1925. Subsequently parts of the estate were acquired, although not all at the same time, by the local council for use as a recreation area. With no use for Clough Hall itself, in May 1927, this remarkable building was most unfortunately demolished. However, the twin lodges at the entrance to the drive which ran from the Newcastle to Talke road, the Liverpool Road and present A34, still stand as a poignant reminder of this once great estate.

It is perhaps worth mentioning that prior to the opening on 15th November 1875, of the final section of the NSR Potteries Loop Line between Newchapel & Goldenhill and Kidsgrove, which gave the Clough Hall site direct mainline rail access, the principal transport outlet was via a narrow-gauge tramway. This ran from the northern end of the site in a straight line for around half a mile and partly in tunnels, to a wharf alongside the canal at Harecastle. The wharf was immediately to the north of the present bridge over the canal that carries the access road to the railway station – Station Road. Due to the steep incline between the works and the canal the line was rope-hauled and known as the *Dragon Incline*, *Dragon* being the name bestowed on the steam haulage engine. During the last war a section of this tunnel where Valentine Road branches from the main Liverpool Road, just to the north of the Clough Hall Colliery site, was opened out for use as an air-raid shelter. This was also the location of one of the former Clough Hall pit shafts. Known as the Valentine, its principal function was mine drainage, the steam beam pumping engine being colloquially known as the *Valentine Engine*. A cinema built on the same site many years later, although long-demolished, was appropriately known as the *Valentine*. In the spring of 1978 when a new water main was being constructed in Liverpool Road, which involved excavating part of the former pit and cinema site, a section of the old tunnel was uncovered and found to be in excellent condition. The height to the centre of the arch was around six feet, the tunnel being only some four feet below the surface of the road and bearing in mind this is the main thoroughfare between Tunstall and Kidsgrove, the present A50, the tunnel had withstood the ever increasing weight of road traffic for well over 100 years. It is a shame that a section of it could not have been saved for posterity, as not only was it part of one of the first industrial railways in North Staffordshire, but in all probability, the first one in a tunnel. The short road leading off the A50 to its east, connecting with Market Street and The Mount, is still known as Valentine Road, although how the Valentine name came about in the first place appears to have gone unrecorded.

Mining from the Side Tunnels
Moving now to the coal and ironstone mining that took place from the side tunnels driven from the original canal tunnel. There exists in the Staffordshire & Stoke-on-Trent Archives, a note book of: *Rentals & Accounts of Estates of Moreton Walhouse & Philip Bulkeley in the Parishes of Wolstanton & Audley from Lady Day 1775*.[214] Covering the period from March 1775 to 1781, it was compiled by George Gibbons, a solicitor practicing in the Cheshire market town of Nantwich, who acted as their agent. Moreton Walhouse (1731-1838) lived at Hatherton Hall, just to the north of the village of Hatherton, which is about half a mile west of Cannock in the southern part of the county; in 1790 he was the county's High Sheriff. The family had lived there for several generations. In July 1760 he married Frances, daughter of Fisher Littleton of Pipe Ridware,[215] a sister of Sir Edward Littleton 4th Bart. His grandson, Edward John Walhouse (1791-1863), inherited the Littleton Estates at Teddesley Park on the death of Sir Edward, who was of course, his great uncle, but as he died without issue, the Baronetcy became extinct. However, in May 1835, Edward was elevated to the Peerage in his own right, as the 1st Baron Hatherton. Teddesley is south of Bednall and about two miles south of the county town of Stafford. We are fairly certain that Walhouse's partner must have been the Philip Bulkeley (1721-1802) who was born at Huntley Hall, Cheadle, and the son of James Bulkeley (1669-1729).[216] Philip was a member of the Worshipful Company of Wheelwrights and was granted Freedom of the City

---
212 NA BT31/15257/37179.
213 NA BT31/4978/33274.

214 Lady Day falls on 25th March. It is a Christian custom to celebrate the intimation of the incarnation made by Gabriel to Mary. In those days the 25th March, cited as Lady Day, was often established as the commencement of an accounting period.
215 This was and still is a very small village to the east of Rugeley and about two miles west of King's Bromley.
216 This is the Cheadle in Staffordshire, a few miles south-east of the Pottery towns.

of London on 14th October 1746. He married Catherine Robins (1735-1803) in London on 24th December 1754 and they had nine children, most of whom were born in London. However their seventh and ninth children were born in Cheadle in 1770 and 1772 respectively, so it appears that in later years he returned to the Bulkeley ancestral home. He died at Huntley Hall on 21st December 1802 and is buried at St. Edward's Church in Leek.

Walhouse and Bulkeley, either jointly owned or had on lease, some of the minerals around the canal tunnel, along with other minerals on the Clough Hall Estate. The accounts provide us with details of the tonnages extracted, who was responsible and the sums of money involved. In all cases it would appear contractors were employed to mine the coal, paying Walhouse & Bulkeley for the privilege and then presumably, selling the output to their own accounts. Described as *Coals Gotten in the Tunnel*, listed below are the relevant entries which, in view of the scarcity of information available on this issue, have been quoted in full. Above and below are assumed to refer to whether the coal was above or below the water level of the canal. This is particularly interesting as previous writers on the subject appear to have assumed that all the workings were either in line with, or above the water level of the canal.

Period	Contractor	Tonnage	Receipts
12/4-28/8/1777	Dan Lowe	433t 3cwt	£32 9s 6d
12/4-28/8/1777	Dan Lowe	550t above; 509t below	£123 11s 3d
1/5-5/7/1778	Messrs Stubbs	87t 12 cwt above; 271t below	£20 2s 3d
29/9/1777-30/3/1778	Messrs Stubbs	not stated	£128 8s 6d
30/3/1778-27/9/1778	Messrs Stubbs	958t	£67 18s 0d
27/9/1778-10/4/1779	Messrs Stubbs	884t above; 144t below	£72 12s 0d
16/4/1779-14/9/1779	Messrs Stubbs	237t above; 260t below	£29 13s 6d
17/9/1779-25/3/1780	Messrs Stubbs	190t above; 310t below	£31 15s 0d
25/3/1780-25/9/1780	Messrs Stubbs	112t above; 781t below	£61 19s 6d
25/9/1780-24/3/1781	Messrs Stubbs	57t above; 559t below	£44 15s 0d

Some earlier entries for 1777 do not mention who the contractor was. Clearly however, production was quite spasmodic with perhaps, other operators active in different parts of the tunnel at the same time. Messrs Stubbs is a reference to Thomas Stubbs of Gawsworth, just over the county boundary in Cheshire who was in the case of some other mineral workings, in partnership with a Thomas Moss. Not dissimilar tonnages were being extracted at what was referred to as Clough Hall Meadow, the contractors being variously Messrs Winkle & Company, Winkle & Hancock and a Mr Clowes. In all these cases sizeable sums were paid by Walhouse and Bulkeley as contributions to the cost of *gutters*. These would be underground drainage channels driven to lower levels providing outlets for water to assist in keeping mine workings dry. It was of course, in the interests of the mineral owners and or lease holders, to have adequate drainage, hence contributing to the contractor's costs of what would have been comparatively expensive undertakings. For example in October 1777, £58 14s 0d was paid to Winkle & Company and Mr Clowes and in April the following year, £30 to Winkle & Hancock. On Walhouse and Bulkeley's behalf, Gibbons was also collecting rents regarding a number of other nearby properties, as well as authorising money for repairs to buildings.

Accompanying the note book are a number of letters addressed to Moreton Walhouse, dated between 31st January and 15th December 1781, variously from George Gibbons, Philip Bulkeley and the second John Gilbert, regarding the latter's interest in acquiring Walhouse & Bulkeley's estates and mineral rights. In all cases Gilbert's letters are from his Worsley address. The correspondence covers a range of options including a lease for twenty-one years rather than an outright purchase, along with a suggestion that Walhouse & Bulkeley retain a half interest. On the 22nd February 1781 when John Gilbert happened to be in London, he called on Bulkeley for further discussions, little progress being made as both Bulkeley and Walhouse relied very much on Gibbons' advice, as to the best course of action they might take. On 23rd February 1781 in a letter from Gibbons to Bulkeley, mention was made that Gilbert had proposed to: *be at the expense of a fire engine and all the tunnels and mines about the works and that you and Mr Walhouse will receive annually £300 at least and more if they get a good sale of the coals of which there is no-doubt as they are of very good quality. Mr Walhouse and I think this offer too low.* Obviously, at this point a lease was under consideration. The reference to a fire engine would be a Newcomen atmospheric beam pumping engine, while mention of the tunnels and mines was presumably, in connection with their maintenance and upkeep. Eventually, agreement was reached early in 1782 to sell the estate and underlying minerals to John Gilbert.[217]

Moreton Walhouse was as might be expected, a shareholder in the Trent & Mersey Canal and in a shareholders' return of 24th June 1804, he had an allocation of ten shares. However, a return of 28th September 1782, when we know he was involved with mining in the tunnel, surprisingly shows that he did not have any.[218] His partner incidentally, never seems to have had any shares in the canal company. By the time of a canal shareholders list dated 1829, his eight shares are shown as allocated to his executrix, Anne Craycroft Walhouse and executors, Colonel John Walhouse and M.A. Whyte.[219] The Gilbert brothers by the way, in the 1782 shareholders' return, are credited with thirty-six shares, twenty-six with Thomas and ten with John, while the

---

217 CRO D260/M/E/418/4.
218 Walhouse attended a General Assembly of the Company of Proprietors of the Trent & Mersey Navigation, held in Stone on 27th September 1796, so it would appear he was a shareholder by that time. The meeting was in connection with the sponsors of the projected Commercial Canal, objecting to the Trent & Mersey Canal Company Bill for a branch from the Caldon Canal to Leek and a reservoir at Rudyard. NA. Rail 1019/15/40.
219 NA RAIL 878/4-5-7-10-20-64. CRO D3098/8/11. In 1782 650 shares had been issued, but by 1804 the figure had risen to 1,300 and by 1829, it was 2,600.

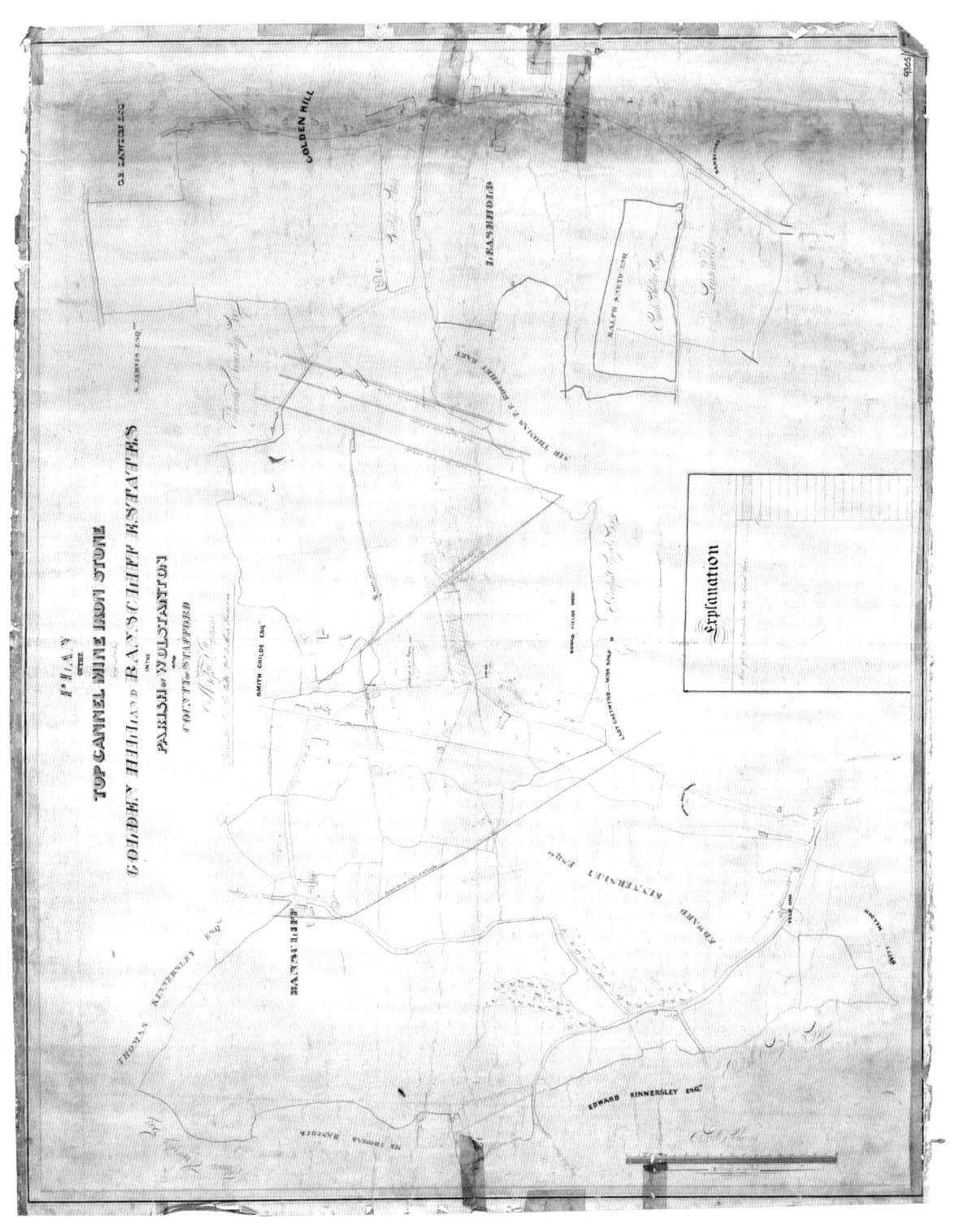

This and the following three plans are of mining activity in the vicinity of the canal and later railway tunnels, included here as they all show the side tunnels constructed to tap the coal and ironstone seams. This enabled the minerals to be loaded directly into boats and transported via the main tunnels to wherever the markets were. They all postdate the building of Telford's tunnel. This first plan shows the Top Cannel Ironstone under the Golden Hill and Ranscliff Estates belonging to Messrs Williamson and is unfortunately undated. However, it has been annotated: Copied by John Wyatt December 1856 and is also marked, mine got to December 1856. Mine being the name given to the ironstone. However, the particularly interesting aspect from our point of view is the side canal tunnel which can be seen in the centre of the plan, with the main canal tunnels running almost vertically. The main side tunnel can be identified by the description: Boat Level.

Keele University, Special Collections & Archives, Derek Wheelhouse Collection.

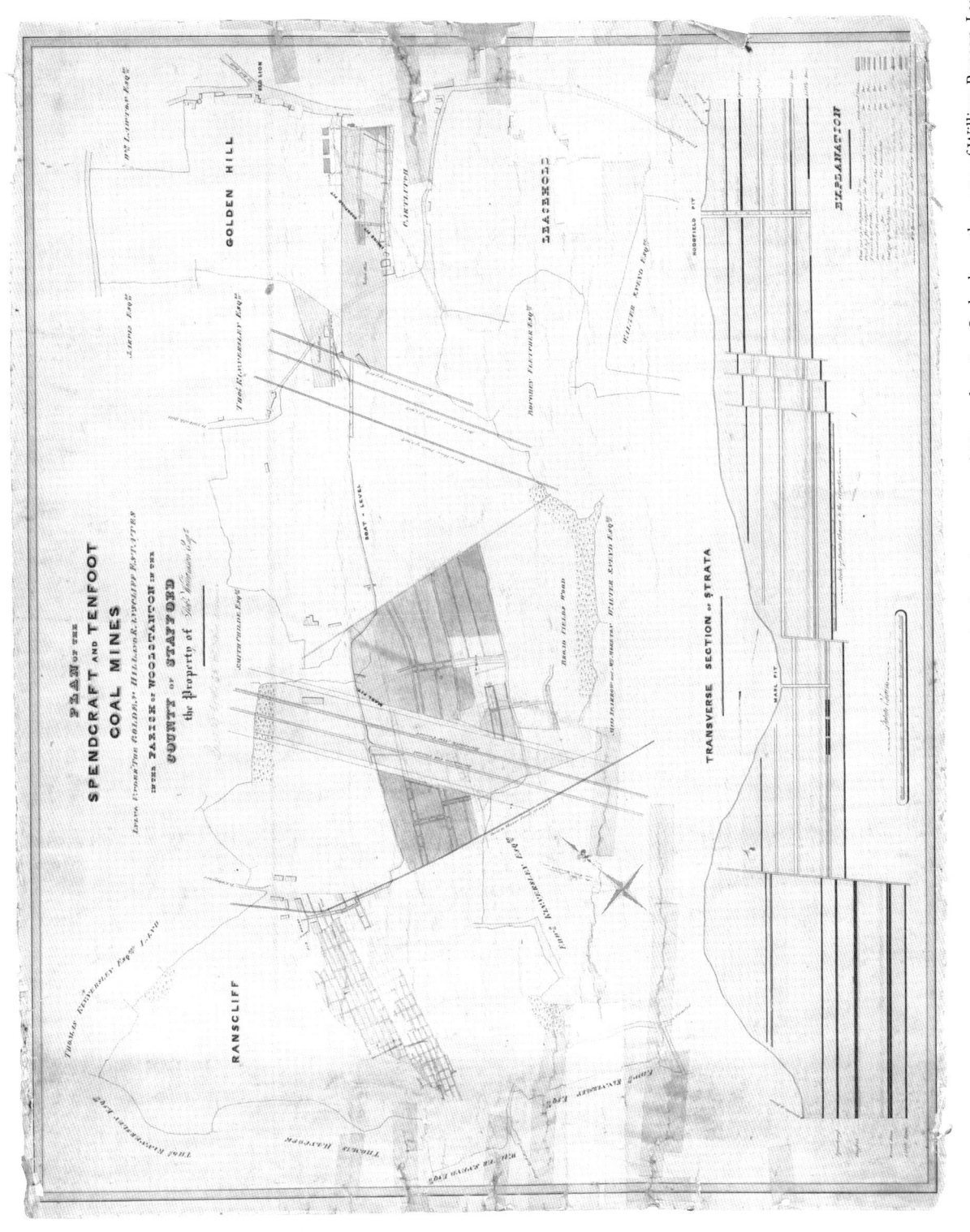

CHAPTER 10 – COAL AND IRONSTONE MINING

In the case of this plan, a section is also included and while it too, is undated, it has been marked with: coal got up to 25th December 1840. It also bears the name of William Benson, Land & Colliery Surveyor of St Helens in Lancashire who was responsible for its preparation. The mines illustrated, in this case the Spendcraft and Tenfoot Coal under the Golden Hill and Ranscliff Estates, of the Williamson family, are specifically identified with Robert Williamson. The canal tunnels are much clearer on this plan, as are the side canals, again identified by the words Boat level. Notice that Spendcraft incidentally, is incorrect and as well as the longer side canal heading to the right towards the Engine and Hodgfield Pits at Golden Hill, there is a shorter one in the opposite direction. Spendcraft incidentally, is incorrect and should read as Spencroft.

Keele University, Special Collections & Archives, Derek Wheelhouse Collection.

This plan is dated 1831 and is also part of the work of William Benson, although in this case with an address at Bury. It shows the Great Row coal mines to the south-east of Golden Hill as worked by Robert Williamson. It has also been annotated with the Great Row coal got up to December 1840. Although in this case the canal tunnels are off the plan to the left, the side tunnel, again annotated as Boat Level, can be seen to the top left. Presumably the short tunnels leading off the main Boat Level to the north, gave access to other coal and ironstone seams, which are not part of this plan. If so, it gives some indication of what must have been an extremely intensive series of mining operations.

Keele University, Special Collections & Archives, Derek Wheelhouse Collection.

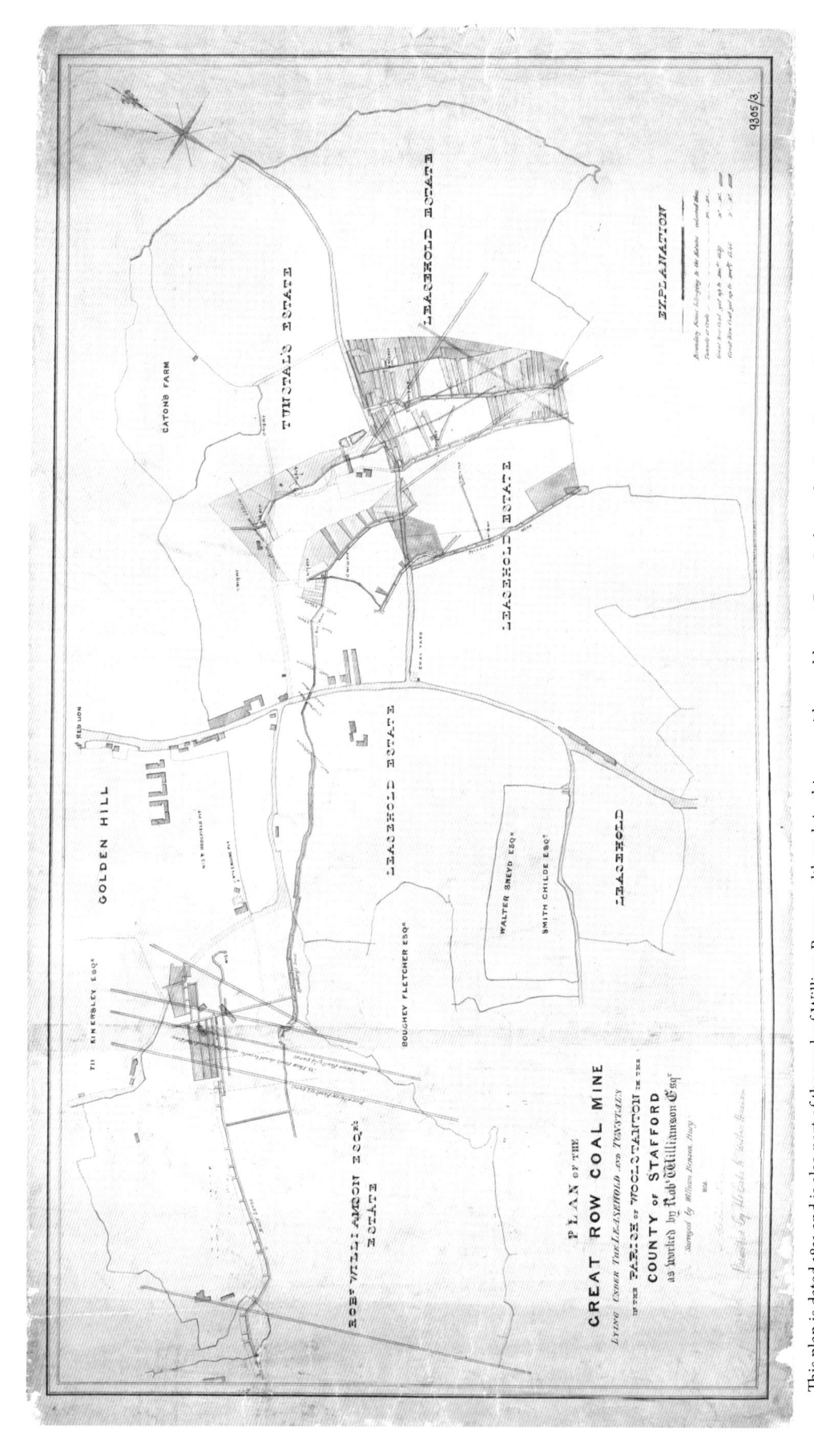

Yet another undated plan but one obviously compiled after the railway tunnels were constructed. While in the case of the three previous plans, the side tunnels would seem to be one and the same as Gilbert's Hole, in this case we are near the north end of the tunnels. The side canal that can be identified to the top left is only connected to Brindley's tunnel and at a sharp angle. It served what is shown as the No 51 Pit, which is the one discussed in the text and more familiarly known as the Nelson Pit. Notice it is connected to the Nos 4 and 10 pits to the top right, which were both on the Clough Hall Estate and part of Clough Hall and later Birchenwood Colliery.
Keele University, Special Collections & Archives, Derek Wheelhouse Collection.

This is part of the Accurate Table of Distances from the River Trent to the River Mersey with a date of 1795, referred to in the text. This of course predates the construction of Telford's tunnel. Notice reference to the Birchenwood Coal and the Turnrail Coal at locations within the tunnel as discussed in the text.   NA Rail 1878/117

Duke of Bridgewater had twenty. Worth a note is a holding of ten shares by Hugh Henshall, as an executor of James Brindley.

An Accurate Table of the Distances on the Navigation from the River Trent to the River Mersey dated 1795, shows within Harecastle tunnel, two of what can only be locations where coal was being extracted by side tunnels.[220] The first, called the *Turnrail Coal* at 880 yards from the south end of the tunnel and the second, the *Birchenwood Coal*, a further 880 yards, or exactly one mile from the southern end. Presumably, the location referred to as the *Turnrail Coal*, is one and the same as *Gilbert's Hole*, mentioned below. Plans reproduced here illustrate the Great Row, Spendcroft and Ten Foot coal seam workings under the Golden Hill and Ravenscliff Estates, the property of Robert Williamson. Both plans show coal mined to December 1840 and in both cases, the surveyor was William Benson of St. Helens in Lancashire. These plans also show side tunnels from Brindley's tunnel underneath the village of Line Houses and while the plans do not extend to either end of the tunnel, with the help of large scale Ordnance

Survey maps, the junction can be established at approximately 980 yards from the southern portal. We are inclined to the view that this is in fact, one and the same as the *Turnrail Coal* mentioned above, bearing in mind that the distance table is only graduated in sixth of a mile distances. The side tunnel headed east for approximately 620 yards to the Ten Foot coal under Goldenhill and just on the west side of the Tunstall to Kidsgrove Road, the present A50.[221] It seems to have terminated by faults in the coal seams, but whether this was the reason for its termination, is not clear. The workings were also served by a number of shafts which would have also been used for drawing coal and ironstone, along with man-riding and ventilation. As well as transport of the coal and ironstone mined, another advantage of the canal side tunnels was drainage. Water in mineral workings above the water level in the canal, would naturally drain into it, saving the expense of pumping. This would not only be the case for seams directly connected to the side tunnels, but in other cases of more distant workings where roadways had been constructed to connect with the side tunnels. From a study of the plans reproduced here, the workings on the east side of the canal tunnels, part of Williamson's Golden Hill Estate, were served by No. 3 Hodgfield, No. 4 Engine and Nos 5 and 22 pits, with all their operations in direct communication with the canal side tunnel. Moving further east, over the main Tunstall to Kidsgrove road, the present A50, are the Tunstall and Leasehold Estates of Williamson, mining the Great Row coal, also served by a number of shafts; numbers 1, 2, 6, 7, 9, 11, 12 and 16 can be seen on the plans. It would appear from the plans that there was an underground connection from these workings with the canal side tunnel and it is possible that some of the coal was moved via roadways, perhaps equipped with tramways, to the canal side tunnel.

The side tunnel in the other, west direction was much shorter, only about 22 yards, to where the Spencroft coal seams were located.[222] From there a roadway continued to further Ten Foot workings underneath the present village of Ravenscliffe, rendered on the plans by its earlier name of Ranscliff. Notice that the tunnel heading east is shown as simply bisecting the later Telford tunnel, while the junction with the earlier tunnel is quite wide on both sides. It is possible this indicates room provided for both holding boats as well as turning them, which seems to confirm that the location is one and the same as the *Turnrail Coal* and *Gilbert's Hole*. Nevertheless, it is interesting to note that at the time the plans were made, the only mines shown were either belonging to, or on lease to, Robert Williamson.[223] There are a couple of minutes in the NSR *Trent & Mersey Navigation Minute Book* of the Canal Traffic Committee, in relation to Williamson's operations. A minute

---

220 NA RAIL 878/117.

221 The Ten Foot coal seam referred to here is probably what was colloquially referred to locally as the *Pottery Ten Foot*, one and the same as the Spencroft. It should not be confused with the Ten Foot seam proper, which occurs much lower down in the coal sequence.

222 This coal seam is incorrectly shown on the plans as Spendcraft. Originally it was known as Spendcroft, later shortened to Spencroft.

223 Keele University, Special Collections & Archives, Derek Wheelhouse Collection.

of 12th July 1853 refers to the Williamson Brothers having an outstanding account for the movement of refuse from Harecastle Tunnel to Longport. When this issue was aired again at the next meeting on 23rd August, a letter was discussed from the Goldendale Iron Company, which Williamsons owned, objecting to the damage caused to their boats when moving refuse from their mines between the *Turnrail* in the Harecastle Tunnel and Tunstall. These two entries would appear to refer to the same issue and clearly, Williamsons were moving, by canal, refuse from mining operations accessed from the tunnel. As there is no mention of coal being moved in this way, presumably either there were no issues in that respect, or the coal was being drawn up one or more of the various shafts. Unfortunately there are no further minutes on the issue, the NSR Solicitor, Mr Keary, being deputed to deal with the matter.[224]

We have not found any evidence as to the dimensions of the side tunnels or how they were lined, but presumably, except areas where hard rock was penetrated, they were brick-lined like the main tunnels. Regarding the type of boats used, one of the only references we have been able to find is by Simeon Shaw,[225] where he refers to *small boats are seen approaching the tunnel by means of a small subterraneous canal*. The tunnel referred to being of course, the main tunnel. This would suggest that the boats used for the coal mining activities were much smaller than those used for the main canal traffic, which to make best use of the canal, would have been 70 feet long, or very near that length. However, exactly how small they were is unclear, bearing in mind they would have had to negotiate the angle between the side tunnel and the main tunnel which would have imposed a restriction. No more do we know if these smaller boats were used to take their loads through the main tunnel or whether there were facilities underground to transfer the coal and ironstone to larger boats. Just to confuse the issue, references to the *turnrail*, suggests that the main canal boats could be turned within the tunnels, which leads one to question if in fact, perhaps at a later date than Shaw's visit, it was possible for the larger boats to access at least some of the side tunnels. The obvious benefits of avoiding any transhipment might well have been the catalyst for such a development. Having said that, any coal for local consumption would not have had to be moved very far from the ends of the main tunnels and we do know for example, that John Gilbert and later Thomas Kinnersly, along with the Heathcote family, had their own wharves at the Harecastle end. Likewise the Williamson family's Goldendale Ironworks was only a few hundred yards from the south end. There were no towpaths in the side tunnels.

Before leaving this issue it is worth quoting from the late L.T.C. (Tom) Rolt's classic book *Narrow Boat*, which describes his journeys round the Midland canals along with his first wife, just prior to and during the first year of the Second World War.[226]

Arriving at the southern end of the tunnel late one evening in the summer of 1939, his narrow-boat *Cressy*, was joined by a pair of working boats to be hauled through the tunnel by the electric powered tug. Below is his description of the passage.

At one point the tunnel was intersected by another at right angles, a relic this of a system of subterranean canals which Brindley drove direct to the coal-faces of his collieries at Golden Hill, thus not only draining the pits, but enabling the coal to be hauled away without having first to be drawn to the surface. These ingenious underground waterways have not been explored within living memory, for the coal-seams at canal level have long been exhausted, but the guard could remember in his early youth an old boatman who had worked through them. The boats, which were drawn along by means of staples fixed in the walls, were necessarily very small and finely built, of only ten tons capacity, in order that they could negotiate the sharp right angle turns between one tunnel and another.

This is particularly interesting and would seem to confirm that the boats using the side tunnels were quite small and that the method of propelling them was by the men gripping staples, as he describes them, fixed to the tunnel walls, thereby pulling the boats along. While this may well have been the case, the presence of the *turnrail*, as described above, would suggest that in at least some cases, these small boats may have transhipped their cargos into larger ones. The *turnrail* could not only have allowed the larger boats to leave the tunnel in the same direction they entered, but also provide space for mooring, so as not to interfere with through traffic.

It is worth exploring the small village of Line Houses which largely dates from when the railway tunnel was being built, the rows of cottages having been constructed to house some of the workers and their families. It takes its name as the cottages were built in straight rows and in line with the tunnels. However, a smaller number of properties probably date from when one or other of the canal tunnels were built and for the same purpose. Boat Horse Road, which was built contiguous with Brindley's canal tunnel to enable the horses that hauled the boats to be moved from one end of the tunnel to the other, while the boats were legged through, passes by the village. Whatever the case, when the Williamson Brothers were in financial trouble, much of their property was sold including most, if not all, the buildings in the village. On 13th June 1887, there was an auction on behalf of the brothers at the North Stafford Hotel in Stoke, which included farms and mineral rights at Ravenscliffe, Latebrook and Line Houses. One lot comprised of fifty-two houses and shops at Line Houses, all of which were occupied under various leases. The 1879 25 inch scale Ordnance Survey map shows a school there too, which apparently, was in existence as early as 1854.[227] Also in the sale was a colliery at Ravenscliffe, noted as recently worked by Williamson Brothers, which must have been a sizable operation

---

224 NA RAIL 878/1. The minutes are not numbered.
225 *Op cit.*
226 Eyre Methuen 1944. It has been reprinted many times and is still available.

227 *The Victoria History of the County of Stafford*, Volume VIII, Oxford University Press, 1963.

Mention is made in the text of a field survey undertaken sometime in the 1930s, by members of the North Staffordshire Field Club, embracing sites of forges, foundries and bloomeries. This is the photograph taken at the time of the visit to accompany the report regarding the furnace at Broadfields, or Latebrook. No slag was discovered, just the remains of later coal mining, as the slag had been lowered down the mine shaft and loaded into boats on the canal side tunnel. Notice the top of a gas street lamp and telegraph pole by the group, indicating the lower level of the Goldenhill to Acres Nook Road.

William Salt Library – 78/2005

as it included: *pumping plant and colliery engines, the minerals comprising the coal measures below the Bassey Mine Ironstone.* There is an interesting note in the documents to the effect that the sale of one of the lots was subject to a conveyance to the NSR dated 1 December 1849, *as to the use of the canal tunnels in connection with the working of mines and otherwise*. This infers that in conveying some mineral rights adjacent to the canal tunnels to the railway company, provision was made for the continued use of the tunnels for mining purposes.[228]

In around 1930 F.W. Dennis, President of the North Staffordshire Field Club, along with a few colleagues, undertook a field study of the sites of bloomeries, forges, furnaces and steel works in North Staffordshire. The comprehensive results of the study were later published in the Club's Transactions, a copy of which is held in the William Salt Library in Stafford.[229] One visit was to a location referred to as Latebrook or Broadfields, the latter more usually referred to as Broadfield, a few hundred yards east of the former. This site is on the south side of the road from Goldenhill to Latebrook and at the time of the visit was locally known as Furnace Bank, although partly obliterated by two small coal mining footrails. Local residents interviewed at the time, after the group had established the lack of any ironworks slag, usually found lying around such sites, mentioned that it had all been taken away. They said it had been lowered down an adjacent pit shaft and loaded into canal boats in the branch canal, for movement to Cheshire for road building. Apparently, a few years previously, this shaft had been filled in. There had been a tramway between the Goldendale Ironworks and this site, presumably built and owned by the Williamson family, suggesting that some of the coal and the pig iron from the furnace may have been moved by this means to Goldendale. The tramway continued beyond the Broadfield site, eastwards to cross the Tunstall to Kidsgrove Road, the present A50, to serve Goldenhill Colliery which, as we have seen, was part of the Tunstall and Leasehold Estates of the Williamsons. The Broadfield furnace had doubtless been erected where it was, despite the brothers' other furnaces being at Goldendale, due to the proximity of the coal and ironstone workings, including the Goldenhill Colliery.

The furnace at Latebrook is also mentioned by Simeon Shaw[230] who says: *at Latebrook there is a large furnace for reducing the iron ore found in the neighbourhood in considerable quantity.*

On the 15th & 16th of December 1826, an auction took place at the Wheat Sheaf Inn in Goldenhill, of leasehold mines and other properties, which included the Goldenhill Iron Works and estates known as Latebrook and Ranscliffe. The surface acreage of the Latebrook estate was 32 and Ranscliffe 44. Of particular interest is the description in the auction notice of the iron works which consisted of a blast furnace, casting house, bridge house, blacksmith's shop, sharpening smithy and store room, along with five houses for the men and their families. The auction notice also mentions the mineral area which consisted of 112 acres, an incoming lessee having powers to get ironstone lying under the land and to make use of coal pits already in existence with powers to mine coal to a depth of 20 yards from the surface. The lease had thirty-seven years to run and the various rents payable for the ironstone and coal raised are outlined. The most interesting part of the sale details however, so far as we are concerned, relates to the canal tunnel as mention is made of a *cross tunnel*. It reads: *The Harecastle Tunnel of the Grand Trunk Canal runs under the estate by which means as well as a cross tunnel which has been driven at immense expense beyond the furnace, the mines are not only laid dry to the depth of from 45 to 70 yards, but coals, ironstone and limestone are conveyed to the furnace and the manufactured iron carried to market at very light expense. The carriage to Manchester by canal is 10/-, to Liverpool 10/- and to Gainsborough 15/- per*

---

228 CRO D997/1/19. NA RAIL 532/122 is also relevant regarding this issue. It is an Indenture between the NSR and the T&M Canal Company dated 7th August 1848.

229 Ref 78/2005.

230 *Op cit.*

A rich looking coal seam inside the side tunnel that was explored during the 1951 Festival of Britain trips into Telford's tunnel. One is left wondering why this seam of coal had not been mined.
Kidsgrove Library Local History Collection

A group of intrepid explorers armed with a miner's safety lamp explore mine workings off Telford's tunnel in June 1951. This was probably an official inspection party assessing the situation prior to the commencement of trips through the tunnel for members of the public, as part of the Festival of Britain Celebrations. These trips are described in the text. *Kidsgrove Library Local History Collection*

Above: A smaller inspection group in June 1951 in an even more confined space. Notice again, the unmined coal seam.
Kidsgrove Library Local History Collection

A narrow boat with a school teacher and her pupils enters the northern end of Telford's tunnel towed by one of the two electric tugs on 30th June 1951, as part of the Festival of Britain celebrations.
Kidsgrove Library Local History Collection

A boatload of passengers about to enter Telford's tunnel at Kidsgrove during the 1951 Festival of Britain celebrations. The gentleman at the front end of the narrow boat appears to be issuing instructions to the passengers facing him.

Kidsgrove Library Local History Collection

ton.[231] *The works are situate within a mile of the great collieries of R.E. Heathcote and Thomas Kinnersley [sic] and are near other extensive collieries to which there is communication by the Grand Trunk Canal. The lessees have an unlimited power of making roads, canals, tunnels and railways; there are several adjoining mines which may be materially enhanced in value, by means of this privilege.* The successful bidder had the right on termination of the lease, *to take away all steam engines, mills, forges, foundries and other buildings, except dwelling houses.* This suggests that in their day, the works were quite extensive.

John Ward in his monumental history – *The Borough of Stoke-upon-Trent*, published in 1843 – mentions that at Latebrook, *a blast furnace formerly worked here, was discontinued about ten years ago.*[232] Despite the lease running until 1863, if Ward was correct, operations, along with dismantling of the plant, had already occurred when his book was being researched. This would suggest that whatever happened at the auction, the ironworks did not survive for very long. In the various official and semi-official records made over the years regarding blast furnaces, Latebrook appears in the statistics only once.[233] In a survey dated 1849, two furnaces are listed, both in use, although no owner or operator is shown. However, in earlier listings for the years 1805, 1810 and 1825, furnaces are recorded at Goldenhill, which we are inclined to assume is one and the same location as Latebrook. In fact, in the auction notice referred to above, Goldenhill is referred to in connection with the Latebrook estate. In 1805 one furnace is shown, owned by Barker & Company, increased to two under the same ownership in 1810, but reduced to one again in 1825. On this occasion the owner was W. Banks, although the furnace was not in use. This fits in nicely with the sale particulars and while the auction notice gives no clue as to who the lessee was at that time, if Goldenhill and Latebrook are in fact one and the same, it would appear to have been W. Banks. Presumably, to provide the blast for the furnace, there must have been a steam engine of some sort, or perhaps an earlier atmospheric engine worked on the Newcomen principle. According to the *Victoria County History of Staffordshire*,[234] there were also five workmens' cottages on the site.

In June 1951, during the Festival of Britain celebrations, arrangements were made by the Urban District Council of Kidsgrove and the Docks and Inland Waterways Executive for the public and schoolchildren to visit Telford's tunnel. The *Souvenir Programme* contained the following announcement:

June 28-30th Waterway trips through Harecastle Tunnel each day. Depart from Hardingswood Lock at 7.45pm on 28th and 29th and at 10am, 12.30pm, 3.45pm and 7.45pm on 30th June. The trip

---

231 CRO SP867 – this document is held at the Stoke-on-Trent Record Office as opposed to the main one in Stafford.
232 Lewis & Son, Finch-Lane, London. There have been a number of subsequent facsimile reprints.
233 *British Blast Furnace Statistics 1790-1980*, Philip Riden & John G. Owen. Merton Priory Press 1995. ISBN 1-898937-05-2.

234 *Op cit.*

will include an inspection of the old mine workings in the tunnel. Return fare 1/-. The last day of the trips was on a Saturday when presumably there would be less commercial traffic about.

The so called *Hardingswood Lock* would have been Red Bull Top Lock No. 41, just to the north of the junction with the Macclesfield Canal, no doubt a convenient place for boarding. From photographic evidence it appears that a dumb barge was used for the trips; it was probably horse drawn from the lock to the mouth of Telford's tunnel where the electric tug took over. The *Souvenir Programme* referred to the old mine workings as *Gilbert's Hole* which had been so called for as long as anybody could remember. Prior to the public being allowed to visit the mine workings, an inspection was made on 18th June, led by the Council's Chief Sanitary Inspector, Norman Roche. He was accompanied by, among others, the Chairman of the Council, Councillor John Cooney and Albert Birchall, the proprietor of the nearby Dales Green Colliery, along with his Fireman. Birchall and his Fireman went along to examine the old mine workings to ensure they were safe for the public to visit, the National Coal Board having warned of the possibility that *Black Damp* might be encountered. In the event, the ventilation, it was said at the time, was in perfect condition, suggesting there was still a passage of some description between the canal tunnel at this point and the atmosphere on the top of Harecastle Hill.[235]

The late William (Bill) Jack and his two sons made one of these trips and we cannot do better than let Bill tell the story in his own words, as related in a letter to the late Dr J.R. (Jack) Hollick, of 28th September 1959.

During my many trips through Harecastle tunnel I have seen Gilbert's Hole and the turnrail which, as far as I can see it, are more or less at the same point. Gilbert's Hole is the tunnel to the coal seam workings and the turnrail is the point where the boats turned round, if necessary, after loading. So naturally these two points must have been very close to each other. The original connection would be in Brindley's old tunnel and looking towards Kidsgrove, Telford's new tunnel would automatically intersect any on the Goldenhill side and consequently, leave untouched any on the Bath Pool side. As I have never been through the legging tunnel, I do not know whether or not there are any connections to old colliery workings but, I do have it on very good authority that the Nelson Pit was the last pit which loaded coal direct from the face to the boats. In Telford's tunnel Gilbert's Hole was the only visible connection to any underground workings and if there were any more, they had obviously been built up long ago. I surmise that why Gilbert's Hole was left open was that it

---

235 *Staffordshire Evening Sentinel*, 18th June 1951. *Black Damp* is a variable mixture of carbon dioxide and nitrogen, sometimes pure nitrogen. When coal oxidizes it takes up oxygen from the air to form carbon dioxide which, along with the residual nitrogen, forms the mixture miners refer to as *Black Damp*. It is a suffocating gas and can be poisonous if carbon monoxide is present. The term Fireman as used in the context here (often also referred to as the Deputy) is the position of a qualified mining official responsible for underground shot-firing to release coal measures, along with the general safety of those working underground, with special reference to the detection of any *Black Damp* or other dangerous gases.

drained the coal seams on that side [presumably, Birchenwood Colliery workings – authors]. However, for many years it could have served no useful purpose because the channel was so choked up with an accumulation of years of deposit from the ironstone seam workings. I think that the boys and I were the last to visit the workings reached from Gilbert's Hole and no one can ever visit them again as they have been completely blocked off to make the fan ventilation system as efficient as possible. As you know during the Festival of Britain, the tunnel was open for boat trips, the channel at Gilbert's Hole having been specially cleared out as far as the first dip. How far the branch tunnel was I have no idea. Armed with powerful electric torches we stood at the furthest point we could get to and shone the lights along the tunnel, but the beams were lost in the distance The channel was not at right-angles to the main tunnel, but at an angle in the direction of Late Brook [that is north-east and usually referred to as Latebrook – authors] and as Gilbert's Hole is about 1,000 yards on from the Chatterley end, this will give you some idea of the general direction. From canal level we climbed a steep, twisting incline and were soon able to see the coal seams and the timbering left by those miners very many years ago. It was a very humid atmosphere and I distinctly recall that the breath from our mouths was carried upwards, proof that this working at least, had an outlet on the surface. As we sat resting for a while, we heard the rumble of a train approach, thunder above us and then die away again in the distance. I can see now that we were quite foolish because pockets of black damp can linger for long in those old workings. After picking ourselves up we made our way down to the tunnel which had now completely filled with a thick mist. As we could not hear the electric tug, we made our way out via the towpath to the Chatterley end.

As the trips started from Hardings Wood, which is at the Kidsgrove end, presumably Bill and his boys alighted at *Gilbert's Hole* and then, after their visit, rather than waiting for the tug on its next trip, or walking back to the end they had entered the tunnel, elected to go the other way. It is interesting to note that Bill and his boys also established that good ventilation of the area was still apparent. The ironstone incidentally, is why the canal water in the vicinity of the tunnels was and, still is, orangey brown in colour. Bill's reference to the direction of the side tunnel leaving the main waterway fits in with the plans discussed above, as does the distance from the southern end at about *1,000 yards*. Jack and Bill were also in contact with Chris Beech, a retired railway signalman at Newchapel & Goldenhill, who lived at Pitts Hill. Chris was a fund of information on local industrial archaeology. Having discussed the issue of the canal mine workings with a number of his contemporaries, as well as others of an older generation, Chris provided a plan with notes from which the sketch included here has been compiled. The description below should be studied in connection with the sketch:

Shafts A, B, C & D were all sunk on the Great Row coal seam. A & D are definitely known to be connected to the canal tunnel and there is reason to believe that B & C are too. The canal widens a little in the basin and one end is known as Gilbert's

This view looks south on 3rd March 1958 and shows the small village of Line Houses, sometimes rendered as Linehouses, which largely takes the form of two straight lines of terraced cottages parallel with the Harecastle tunnels. Opinions vary as to how the name came about. One version relates it to the rows of cottages being in straight lines, while another dates their construction as accommodation for men building the railway line. However, there is evidence that at least some of the dwellings date back to when Telford's tunnel was being driven. A ventilation shaft, which probably originated as a construction shaft for the south railway tunnel, is prominent in the left foreground and the gas lamp seen in the distance marks the site of Boat Horse Road which crossed the village from east to west.

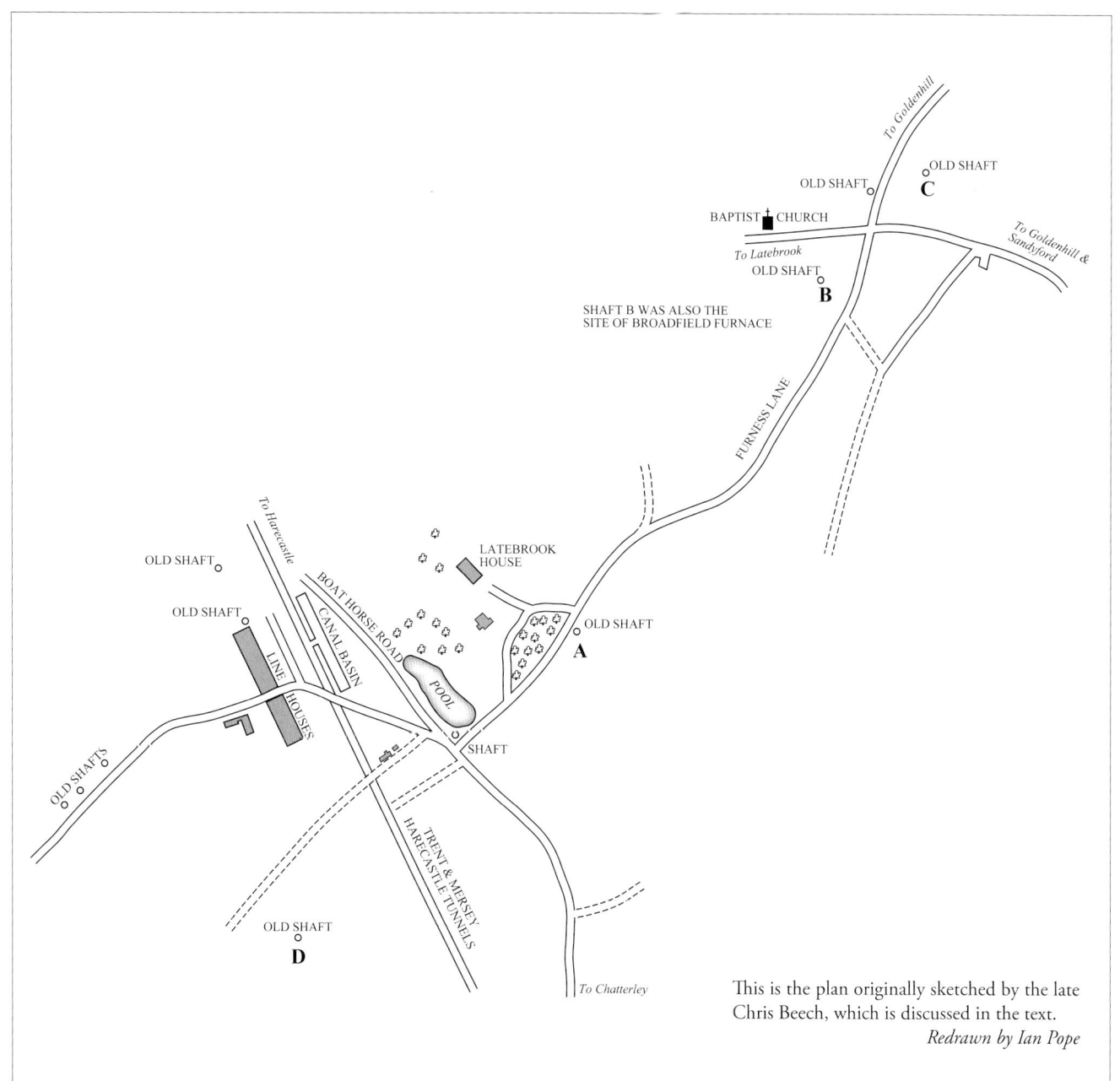

This is the plan originally sketched by the late Chris Beech, which is discussed in the text.
Redrawn by Ian Pope

Hole, the other end as the *Turnrail*. This is where the canal boats were loaded. There was a road from shaft A to the basin in the tunnel along which pit tubs used to travel. The shaft by the pool, not numbered, had iron railings down the side so the workmen could get down to the canal basin. One day a dog fell down shaft B and two weeks later emerged, swimming, from the Kidsgrove end of the old legging tunnel. Shaft A was also known as the Nible & Klink. They all belonged to the Williamsons.

By comparing the sketch with the mine plans discussed above, the location of the basin at Line Houses is an exact match. Shaft A appears on the plans as the Marl Pit, but as can be seen on the plans, it does go down to the Great Row coal seam. Shaft B is No. 22 on the plans, while C is probably No. 16. It is unlikely that either B or C were connected directly to the canal, rather via the mine workings and associated roadways. Shaft D is interesting as it is not obvious from the plans exactly where it was although old Ordnance Survey maps do show old shafts in the same general location. If it was connected directly to the canal and there is no reason to doubt Chris's informant, the plans we have do not help in establishing the underground arrangements.

When those intrepid Olympic canoeists Jon Goodwin and the late Robin Witter ventured into Brindley's tunnel in July 1979, as discussed in Chapter 7, the only evidence they found of the side tunnels was at approximately 800 yards from the south, Chatterley end and on the west side. This is interesting as the only other personal reports we have of any side tunnels, from Bill Jack's notes and the *Staffordshire Evening Sentinel* article referred to above, place a side tunnel – referred to as *Gilbert's Hole* – at around 1,000 yards from the Chatterley end and on the opposite, east side. However, we do have evidence from the mining plans that there were side tunnels on both sides of the tunnel and, of course, there may well have been others that we know nothing about. In this connection too, the next paragraph is pertinent. One other issue is worth a mention before we leave this subject. Could the widened section of the tunnel as discovered by John and Robin, have been another *turnrail*, where boats employed in mining operations from the side tunnels, could have been turned, allowing them to leave the tunnel from the same direction they entered?

One of the photographs included here, which was taken on 20th February 1986, shows part of the inside of Telford's Tunnel during the extensive repairs being undertaken at that time, as described in Chapter 7. The view looks north, with a bricked-up arch being visible on the east side. There are also signs of a similar arch on the opposite side, which would suggest a connection at this point, between the two canal tunnels. According to the engineer involved with the repair work this was the site of *Gilbert's Hole* and if correct, this is where the side tunnel to the Goldenhill area left the main bore. Unfortunately however, no record appears to have been made as to the exact location in the tunnel where the photograph was taken, so it is impossible to say if this is in fact the same place as indicated on the mining plans.

A diagram has recently come to light, referenced as from the Area Planning Department, so doubtless from a local North Staffordshire National Coal Board source. It is reproduced here,

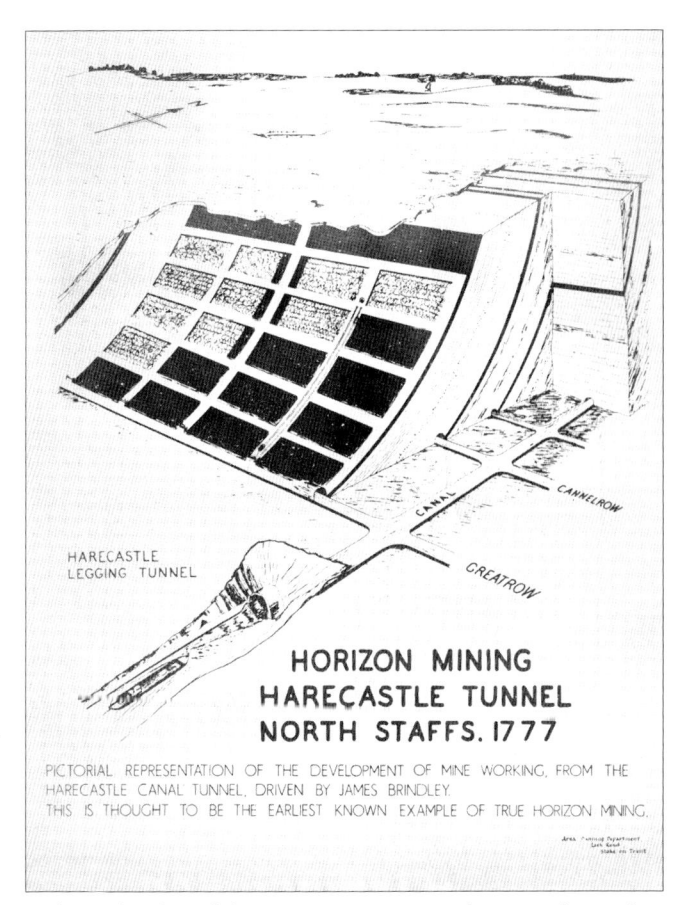

This is the plan of the Horizon, or Horizontal Mining from side tunnels, as discussed in the text and while it undoubtedly displays a large amount of artistic licence, it does show how this particular type of mining was undertaken. For this reason it has been felt appropriate to include it here as there is evidence, that in some areas, this was the method of extracting the minerals. The provenance of the plan is unknown. *Collection Lloyd Boardman*

illustrating workings in the Great Row and Cannel Row coal seams by the Horizon method. The extract below from the *Dictionary of Mining*, describes this method of mining.[236]

Horizon Mining, or Horizontal Mining, or Continental Mining. A system of mine development which is suitable for inclined and perhaps faulted coal seams. Main stone headings are driven at predetermined levels from the winding shaft to intersect and gain access to the seams to be developed. The stone headings, or horizons, are from 100 to 200 yards vertically apart, depending on the seams available and their inclination. The life of each horizon varies from 10 to 30 years. Connections between horizons at inbye points are by staple shafts or drivages in the coal.[237]

Referring to the diagram, the Harecastle canal tunnel represents one main stone heading, intersecting and gaining access to the seams to be developed. The coal workings, in this case, are connected to the canal tunnel by drivages in the coal

---

236 George Newnes Limited 1964.
237 Inbye is a mining term for a direction away from the shaft, or other entry into the workings, while a drivage is a term for a roadway, heading or tunnel in course of construction. It may be horizontal or inclined, but not vertical.

CHAPTER 10 – COAL AND IRONSTONE MINING

This view, taken inside Telford's tunnel on 20th February 1986, looks north. It illustrates the whole width of the tunnel after the removal of the towpath and clearly indicates a considerable seepage of water through the tunnel lining. More importantly, according to the BWB engineer responsible for the tunnel repairs, the bricked-up arch on the right once gave access to the mines within the hill. Is this the site of Gilbert's Hole and are there traces of another bricked-up arch on the left that once led to Brindley's tunnel? The person wearing the hard hat is standing in the middle of the temporary narrow gauge railway used to facilitate repairs.
Harry Arnold/Waterway Images

seams. Reference to winding shafts in the case of the canal side tunnels, should be taken to refer to the side tunnels themselves, while the stone headings are those at right-angles to the tunnels raising vertically and curving. While we do not know how many side tunnels there were, the diagram shows a total of six, three on each side with those to the east, having to intersect the second, Telford's Tunnel, when it was constructed. The diagram points north, so the tunnel entrance is the southern one and the workings are to the west of the tunnel. The diagram does not tell us the distance into the tunnel where the coal seams were. It would appear that an amount of artistic licence has been involved in compiling this diagram such that its accuracy has to be in doubt. There is nevertheless, every possibility that at least some of the mining was broadly of the method shown.

The Railway Clauses Consolidation Act 1845, prevented railway companies under their individual Acts, from compulsory acquiring ownership of minerals under land purchased in connection with constructing railways.[238] However, mine owners, or those working mines within 40 yards on either side of the railway, had to give at least thirty days' notice of any intention to work such minerals. The railway companies on such notice being given, then had powers under the above Act, within thirty days, to give notice of their intention to purchase the minerals at a figure to be agreed between the parties. In other words, to compensate the owner or lessees for the loss of such minerals. Where a price could not be agreed, provision was made in the Act for arbitration. The NSR rarely exercised its right to purchase minerals in these circumstances, except in the case of tunnels like those at Harecastle, along with a few other specific cases. From the plans included here, it can be seen where minerals had been left unworked, to protect both the railway and the canal tunnels. In fact, over a period of time, by around 1890, the NSR had already purchased all the coal and ironstone seams within the 40 yard area, although there were ongoing problems as a result of mining that had taken place in the same area in earlier times. However, acquiring the minerals to protect the tunnels was not always a simple matter, as will be seen as our story unfolds.

During the years 1865 and 1866 there was a long running dispute between the Williamson Brothers, Hugh William, Edward and William Sheppard, regarding minerals they owned under

---
238 8 Vic ch. xx. Royal Assent 8th May 1845.

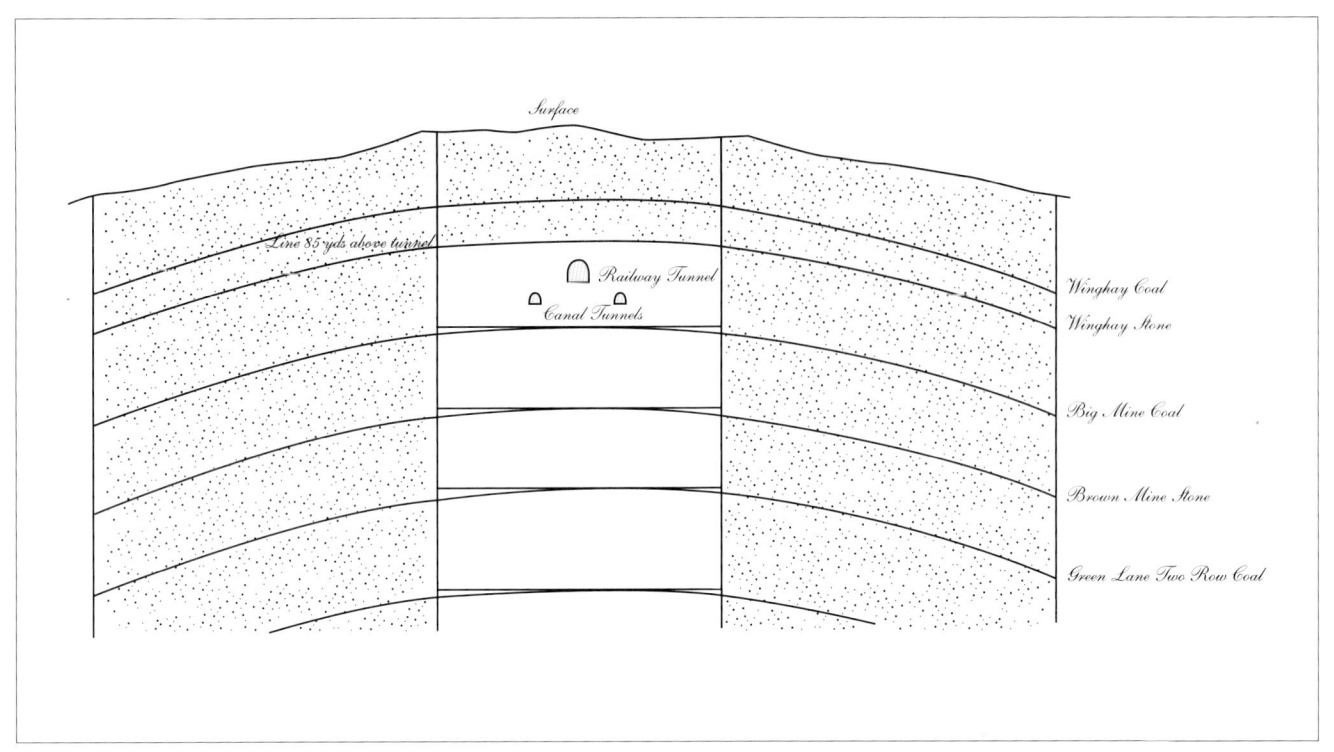

[Diagram: Geological cross-section labelled "Surface" at top, with "Line 85 yds above tunnel", "Railway Tunnel", "Canal Tunnels", and seams labelled on the right: "Winghay Coal", "Winghay Stone", "Big Mine Coal", "Brown Mine Stone", "Green Lane Two Row Coal".]

This plan, redrawn from the original, shows a section of the coal and ironstone seams being worked by the Clough Hall Colliery and their relationship with the railway and canal tunnels. The author was W.S.Cope of Longport, a local mining surveyor and the date, 1866. The two vertical lines illustrate the extremity of the area of the minerals left unworked to prevent damage to the tunnels. This was 40 yards on each side; presumably from the outer wall of each tunnel. However, the mineral owners were allowed, under the provisions of the Canal Company's 1831 Act, to cut and drive such gateways or levels and such headings, airways or waterways as may be necessary for working the other part or parts of such mine or mines. The dimensions of these means of access were not to exceed 4ft 6in wide and 6ft in height.

the Harecastle tunnels. The brothers wrote to the NSR on 22nd February 1865 giving notice of their intention to mine the Red Mine coal and ironstone adjacent to parts of both the canal and railway tunnels. The railway company in its reply dated 29th May 1865, asked that certain of the minerals, within seven yards of the top of the tunnels, be left ungotten. As a price for these mines could not be agreed, an arbitrator was appointed. This was Rupert Alfred Kettle, who eventually awarded a sum of £10,054, with the NSR paying both its own and Williamson's costs. There was a later claim too, which on 19th July 1866 went to Stafford Assizes, when £3,427 was awarded to Williamsons, with the same arrangements for costs.[239] Some of this mining, by the way, was by Kinnersly & Company, although Williamsons were the Royalty owners. There was a later dispute with the brothers, the NSR Traffic & Finance Committee (T&FC) noting at its meeting on 3rd May 1881, acceptance of an umpire's decision regarding their claim, awarding the sum of £1,352 14s 0d.[240]

On 27th June 1874 the NSR received a report it had commissioned following a dispute involving the powers of the 1845 Act, on this occasion with Kinnersly & Company. This was again in connection with the value of coal and ironstone to be left to protect the railway and canal tunnels. John Woodhouse, a Mining Engineer of Derby, in his report valued three acres, three roods and three poles of New Mine coal and ironstone at £4,439, which included Royalty payments.[241] These minerals were part of the estate of Sir Smith Child Bart (1808-1896), of nearby Newfield Hall, who had leased his rights to extract them to Kinnersly & Company against a Royalty payment. Both parties agreed with the report and the NSR made the payment.[242] Woodhouse incidentally, seems to have been called on quite often to give his opinion on these sorts of issues. The NSR T&FC recorded in its minutes back in the period February to July 1862, his involvement in a long running dispute regarding Kinnersly's minerals in the vicinity of the tunnel. On that occasion in conferring with the railway company's engineer and William Matthews, Kinnersly's manager, an agreement was reached regarding the value of mines to be left, without recourse to an umpire. The NSR appears to have realised in this particular case that it would almost certainly have cost the company even more had the issue gone to a completely independent umpire.[243]

---

239 NA RAIL 532/113; 532/114 & 532/115.
240 NA RAIL 532/19. NSR T&FC Minute 11026.
241 One rood is 40 rods, poles or perches, which are all equal to 5½ yards.
242 NA RAIL 532/120. Smith Child had another seat at Stallington, south of the Potteries near Blythe Bridge. The family were significant land owners in the area. Smith Child was Member of Parliament for the Northern Division of Staffordshire from 1851 to 1859 and for West Staffordshire between 1868 and 1874. He was High Sheriff for the county in 1865. Ironically, he was a Director of the NSR between July 1851 and January 1875.
243 NA RAIL 532/17. NSR T&FC Minutes 3619, 3732 and 3744.

CHAPTER 10 – COAL AND IRONSTONE MINING

Extract from 1900 edition of the six inch Ordnance Survey map annotated by the Private Sidings Department of the Railway Clearing House. It shows the canal and the mainline railways in the vicinity of the Harecastle tunnels but highlights, in particular, all the industrial railways in the locality. This is particularly relevant as it shows the private line from Harecastle Goods Yard to the Nelson Pit and the Bathpool area.

Clauses in the 1886 sale documents for the Clough Hall estate are also relevant and of interest in this connection. They are quoted below:

Part of the Eight-Foot Banbury coal seam, containing about 3 roods, 19 perches, in part number 821 [on the plan of the estate – authors] and part of the adjoining railway, has been sold to the North Staffordshire Railway Company under the provisions of the Railway Clauses Consolidation Act for the support of Harecastle North Tunnel. The North Staffordshire Railway Company have acquired the right of using the Nelson Pit and Nelson Bye-Pit and other pits and shafts on the property and certain other rights in connection with the working of the mines in the event of their obtaining powers to work such mines.

The freehold property is sold subject to these rights and also those of the North Staffordshire Railway Company acquired under the Trent & Mersey Navigation Act 1831; the North Staffordshire Railway (Pottery Line) Act 1846; The North Staffordshire Railway Act 1847 and other Acts of Parliament that have been passed from time to time, so far as they affect the mines below and adjacent to the lines of railway passing over the Clough Hall Estate.

The NSR did not acquire these mining rights at that time. The clauses referred to in the 1846 and 1847 Acts concerned an obligation to honour clauses in the earlier Trent & Mersey Canal Act of 1831,[244] also referred to. The area covered in part number 821, mentioned in the first paragraph, was in the Kidswood area over the top of the north tunnel. The adjoining railway should more accurately be described as a tramway; it connected the Nelson Pit and surrounding area to the main Clough Hall site, crossing the Liverpool Road – the present A50 – in the process. The NSR, despite owning part of this tramway, locally known as the Gill Bank Tramway, does not appear to have prevented Kinnersly & Company having use of it.

Despite declining to acquire the mining rights mentioned above, in 1904, following continuing problems with the canal and railway tunnels due to mining operations, the NSR obtained powers to compulsorily purchase mines and minerals over a much wider area on both sides of the tunnels, 100 yards on each side, with the railway tunnel acting as the centre line. The powers also extended for some distance from both ends of the canal tunnels. While we have already seen how in order to protect the tunnels, the company had been purchasing mines and minerals in this same area, albeit somewhat piecemeal over many years, in the case of the railway tunnels, each case had been in accordance with the provisions of the Railways Clauses Consolidation Act 1845. This Act, as we have seen, allowed for arbitration where agreement could not be reached on the price to be paid. The new powers not only extended the area, but also gave the railway company far more power when it came to agreeing values. The Act embraced a number of other issues, including the use of electric tugs for hauling boats through Telford's canal tunnel which has already been discussed in Chapter 6. It received the Royal Assent on 14th June 1904.[245] Parts of the plans accompanying the Bill are included here as they provide an excellent view of the tunnels and their immediate surroundings.[246]

One or two other issues are worth exploring as they too, relate to coal and ironstone workings accessed from the canal tunnels. In late 1935 Norton & Biddulph Collieries Limited (N&BCL), a company that in 1929 acquired the former Robert Heath & Low Moor Company collieries at Black Bull near Biddulph, had concerns regarding water encroaching its underground operations. The problem was water rising in the former Birchenwood Colliery (Clough Hall) workings following the November 1931 abandonment of the Birchenwood pits, after which pumping had ceased. The water was in danger of finding its way from the abandoned operations to those at Black Bull. To address the problem the colliery company proposed starting to pump water at the otherwise abandoned Birchenwood No. 4 shaft. This had been the principal pumping shaft when the colliery was working. The London Midland & Scottish Railway, as owner of the Trent & Mersey Canal, was not completely happy with this as in its view, the water would find its way into the canal. Correspondence survives on this issue, the new owners of the Birchenwood site, the Birchenwood Coal & Coke Company Limited, of which N&BCL was a part owner, claiming there was no connection between the No. 4 shaft and the canal tunnel. In the course of the discussions, J.R.L. Allott, a consultant to the new Birchenwood Company and the former Managing Director and General Manager of the original one, raised the question of the Nelson Pit. He mentioned that at the *Ten Feet* inset of this old pit, which was 79 yards below the surface, there was an underground connection to the canal level. Further investigation, which included studying some old plans of the underground workings, confirmed that this was indeed the case and that there had also been a connection in the *Stoney Eight Feet* coal seam between the workings at Birchenwood and the Nelson Pit. This it was considered, could be used to allow the water to flow from Birchenwood, via the Nelson Pit, into the canal. It would however, involve around 1,200 yards of underground roadways being restored. Mention was also made of what was referred to as *Hackneys Level*, at 58 yards from the surface at the Nelson Pit, which also connected with the canal tunnels, presumably in connection with one of the other old shafts. Hackney would in all probability be the surname of the head miner who originally developed and worked this particular level in the mineral workings. It was quite a common practice for parts of mines to be so named. Quite why the railway company was concerned about water finding its way into the canal is interesting, as most owners of canals were only too glad to receive increased supplies of water! What if anything was done as a result of this

---

244 1-2 Will IV ch. lv, Royal Assent 22nd April 1831. This Act, inter alia, gave the Canal Company and therefore the later NSR, powers to purchase mines and minerals within 40 yards from each side of the canal tunnel. The mine owners/lessees, being obliged to give notice of their intention first. The value of the mines to be left if not agreed mutually, to be determined by recourse to the law.

245 4 Ed VII ch. xliv.
246 HLRO HL/CL/BB/6/plan N22 1904.

issue has however, gone unrecorded.[247]

Evidence of the underground connection between the Nelson Pit and the canal tunnel, only Brindley's in this case, appears on a plan of the Ten Foot and Little Mine coal reproduced here, along with the New Mine Ironstone workings. As can be seen on the plan on page 171, the short branch canal left the main tributary at a sharp angle on its west side and headed south for approximately 30 yards to the foot of the Nelson shaft. On this plan, which unfortunately is not dated, the pit is shown by its number, 51, as opposed to its name.[248]

Some years later, between 1940 and 1944, another issue arose between the Birchenwood Company and the railway company, in this case involving pollution of the canal. This was in the form of ammonium compounds, sulphide, free sulphuretted hydrogen and traces of phenols which it was considered, must have originated from the coking and chemical by-product plants on the former colliery site. The interesting aspect from our point of view, was the discovery that the polluted water was entering Telford's tunnel from old workings situated on its east side, 620 yards from the north end. However, a plan accompanying the correspondence shows the connection pencilled in at 600 yards. Despite the difference, as the Nelson Pit was at approximately 620 yards, both references are assumed to refer to the same place although as we know, the Nelson shaft was on the opposite, west side of Brindley's tunnel. This seems to confirm that at some point in time, the two canal tunnels at this location, had been joined together by a short connecting tunnel.

Also worth a brief mention are two railways, perhaps better described as tramways, which crossed over the canal tunnels. The first, as briefly referred to above, probably dates from early in the Kinnersly period of ownership of the Clough Hall estate and was known as the Gill Bank Tramway. Heading west from the site of the ironworks to the Nelson Pit and onwards to another colliery at Hollins Wood, it passed through the wood known as Birchen Wood and was in all probability, at least when built, a narrow-gauge horse-worked tramway. There was a branch from where this line crossed over the tunnels, running due south and parallel with the tunnels, to further pits towards Bath Pool and beyond. As the ironworks developed, parts of this tramway may have been converted to a standard-gauge locomotive worked line, as a site just to the east of where the tramway crossed the route of the tunnels, was used for dumping slag from the blast furnaces. From 1892 coal mining activities on the Clough Hall site were further expanded by Heath's Birchenwood Colliery Company Limited, improving and deepening several of the shafts, while adding modern facilities for grading and washing the coal. In addition, by-product recovery coking plants were constructed along with chemical works to process the various by-products. By the time of the First World War, the plant was reckoned to be one the most modern by-product recovery coke oven and chemical plants in the country.

In the mid-1890s a standard-gauge railway was constructed by the Birchenwood Colliery Company, from sidings on the east side of the canal at Harecastle, to serve the Bath Pool area. It ran directly south, roughly parallel and on the east side of the NSR mainline, albeit at an increasing higher level, to cross over the railway and canal tunnels almost immediately above the northern portal of the southernmost railway tunnel. This was alongside the Nelson Pit and where the earlier Gill Bank Tramway passed from east to west. The new line then turned south again and continued, probably following the route of the old tramway mentioned earlier, to serve what became known as the Bathpool Pit, as it was near the pool of that name and onwards to the Harecastle Colliery. In later years after these pits closed, the line remained in use to serve a sand pit and small brick works on the site of the Harecastle Colliery. Shortly after leaving Harecastle there was a back-shunt to serve the Kidswood Pit, which by this time had been developed as a pumping and ventilation shaft for the main Birchenwood colliery workings. A second siding, just after the line crossed over the tunnels, replaced the former Gill Bank Tramway to serve the Nelson Pit, which was by this time used as a pumping shaft to help drain the underground operations. An important task of this railway was the transport of coal for the boilers along with other materials, for the Kidswood and Nelson shafts.

In 1922 arrangements were made for removing and processing some of the former Clough Hall Ironworks slag that had been dumped around the site. Some of it as mentioned above, was near the Nelson Pit having been brought there via the Gill Bank Tramway. This was during a period when a market was developing for slag, which hitherto had been considered virtually worthless. Used as hard-core, it was ideal for road foundations, a steady demand having arisen for both improving existing roads as well as building new ones. The enormous post-war increase in road traffic was the main catalyst of this high demand, dumped slag from ironworks all over the county being recovered in similar ways. Where phosphorus was present in the slag, it could also be processed to produce fertilizers. A new company was formed to recover and process the slag, Tarmac (Kidsgrove) Limited,[249] a plant being established near the Nelson Pit and served by the railway described in the previous paragraph. Slag was also brought to the site via the LM&SR and Harecastle Goods Yard from another area where it had been dumped on the east side of the Potteries Loop Line. In 1932 after all the slag considered economically viable had been removed, the plant was dismantled. Although by this time Birchenwood Colliery had closed, the Nelson Pit pump equipment was retained to pump water from the old workings, as well as from the Bath Pool, to the Birchenwood site as the coke ovens remained in production with a significant requirement for water to quench freshly made coke. Until the steam beam pumping engine was replaced by electric pumps, coal was required for the boilers,

---

247 This correspondence is held by the National Waterways Museum at Ellesmere Port and while not specifically referenced can be found in a general file on the Trent & Mersey Canal.
248 Keele University Local History Collection; Derek Wheelhouse Collection.

249 NA BT31/32544/185264. This company was registered on 25th October 1922. It was a joint enterprise between the Heath family, Tarmac Limited and the Hickman family, who were involved with the Springvale Furnaces & Ironworks at Bilston, in the Black Country.

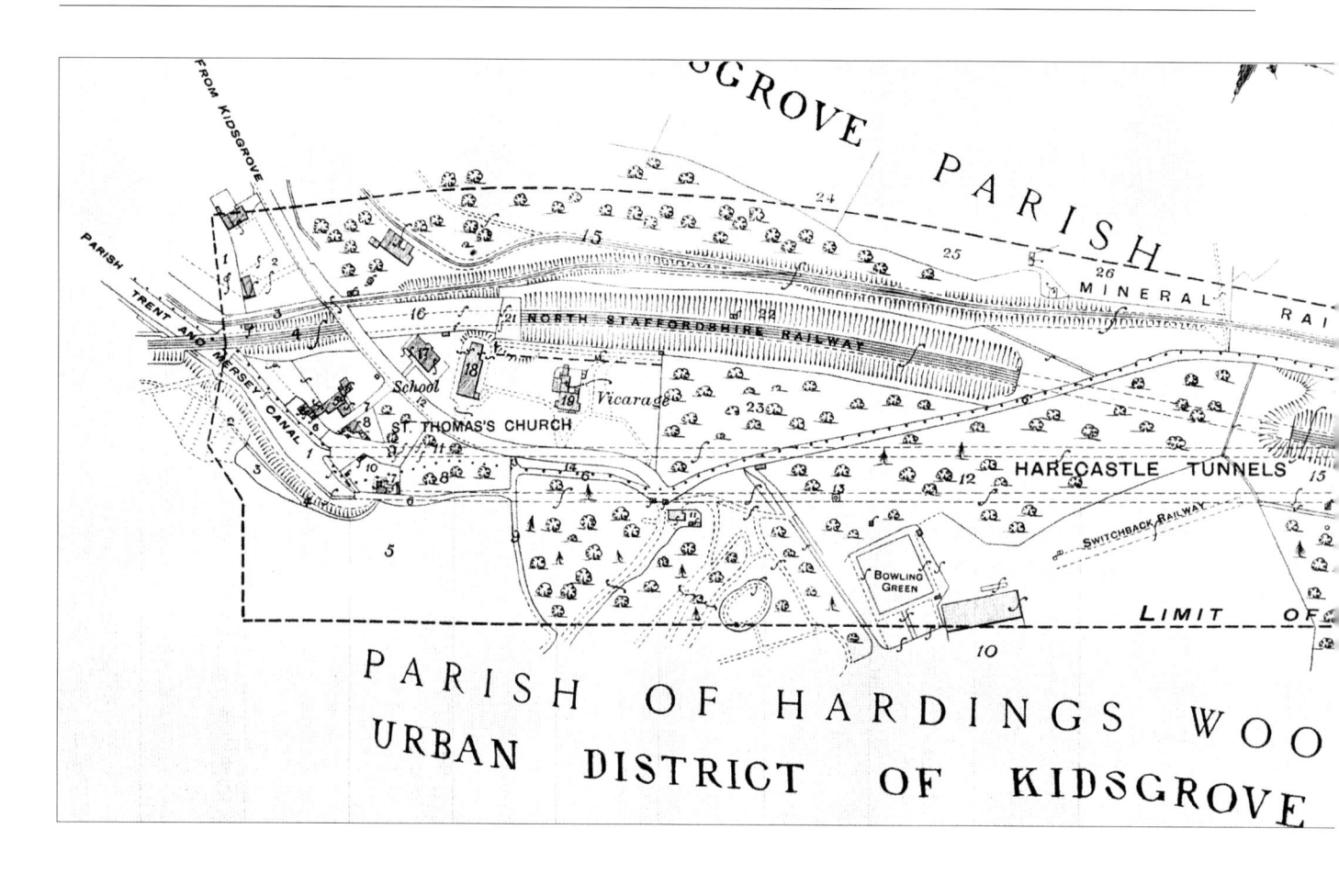

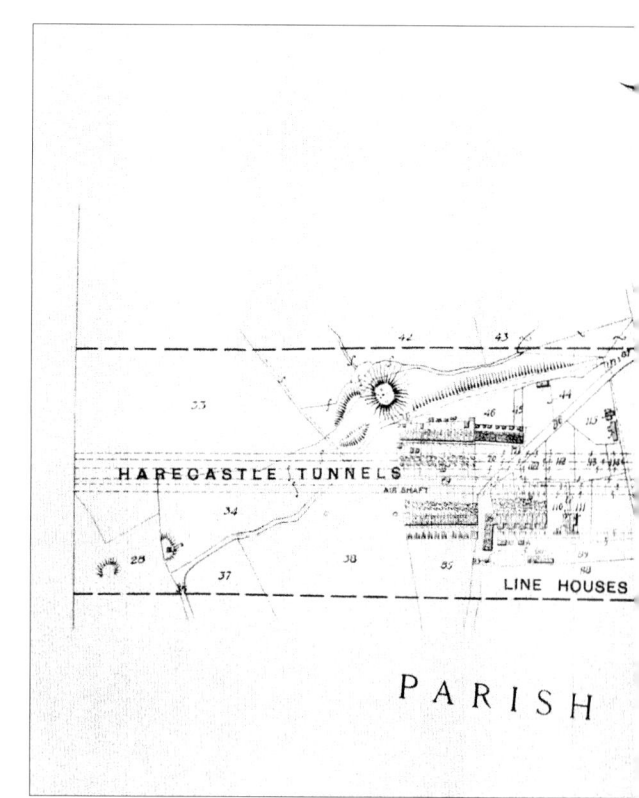

This is the southern part of the NSR 1903-1904 Parliamentary Plan referred to in the text.
HLRO HL/CL/BP/6/plan N22 1904

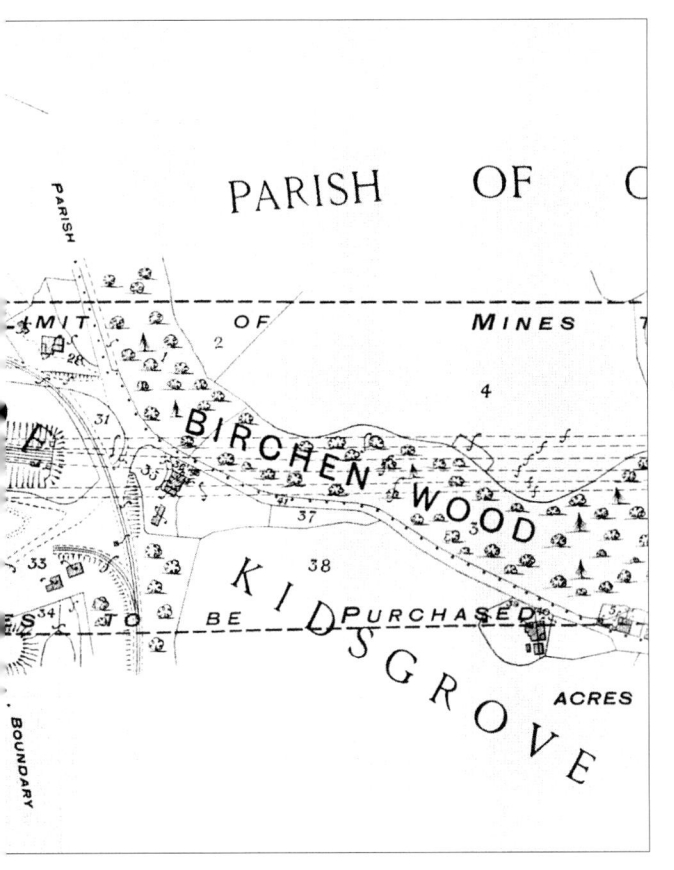

This is the northern part of the Parliamentary Plan that accompanied the NSR 1903-1904 Bill, to compulsorily purchase all the remaining mines and minerals in the vicinity of the canal and railway tunnels, as described in the text. The other southern part is shown below. *HLRO HL/CL/BP/6/plan N22 1904*

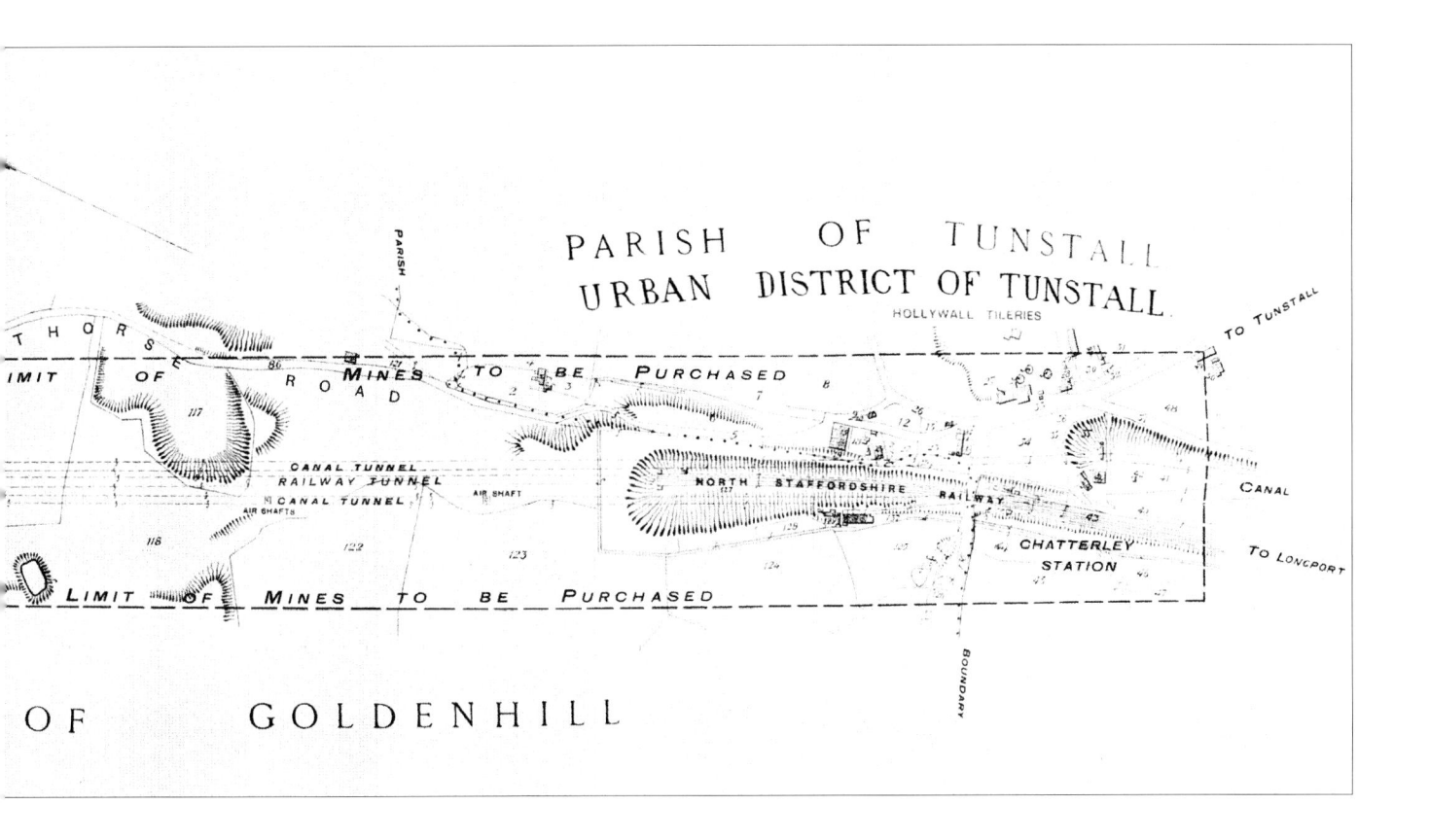

This photograph of the Goldendale Ironworks was taken in August 1972, after pig iron production had ceased in April the previous year. While there had originally been four blast furnaces on the site, as can be seen, at the time of closure there was only one. The view looks north-west with the canal and railway situated in the distance just below the raising ground, with the tunnels to the extreme right.

which continued to be delivered by rail via the goods yard at Harecastle, the line remaining in use as far as the pit. It probably fell out of use just before or in the very early part of the last war.[250] Much of the route of this railway, along with the Nelson Pit, was obliterated by the works in connection with the railway Harecastle Tunnel Deviation Scheme, covered in Chapter 9. The coke ovens at Birchenwood were taken out of use in April 1973, after which the entire Clough Hall site was cleared, with much of it in more recent times, developed for domestic housing.

---

250 *Industrial Locomotives of North Staffordshire*, Allan C. Baker, Industrial Railway Society, 1997, ISBN 0-901096-97-0. *Birchenwood and its Locomotives*, Allan C. Baker, Industrial Locomotive Society, 1974.

Before closing this chapter it is worth mentioning that parts of Kidsgrove still recall its early industrial past, as one of the first integrated coal mining and iron producing operations in North Staffordshire. There are for example, Attwood and Heathcote Streets, along with a Gilbert Close and in the Clough Hall area, a Kinnersley Avenue, albeit the family name is spelt incorrectly. The Parish Church of St. Thomas which is situated in The Avenue was built at Thomas Kinnersly's expense, as was the adjacent Rectory and school. The church was consecrated on 7th May 1837. On the opposite side of the main Tunstall to Kidsgrove Road, the present A50, to the site of the former shaft of the Valentine Pit, can be found the Nelson Buildings.

ACKNOWLEDGEMENTS

It is always a great pleasure to sit down at the conclusion of research and prior to putting a manuscript to bed, so to speak, to recall all those individuals and organisations that have helped in one way or another. In this connection we would like to acknowledge access to the Caldwell Diaries via the Internet and Jeremy James Heath-Caldwell. We also appreciate the assistance kindly given by fellow members of the North Staffordshire Railway Study Group: Basil Jeuda, Barry Knapper, Roland Machin, Derek J. Wheelhouse and Dr. David J. Woolliscroft. Other individuals who have helped us greatly with geological information and local knowledge are Harry Arnold of Waterway Images, Lloyd Boardman, Richard Dean and Martin O'Keeffe.

A very special thank you is due to Philip Leese – The Kidsgrove Historian. Philip was for many years the Librarian at Kidsgrove Library and instrumental in establishing a local history collection which is second to none in its coverage. Through his kindness, we have been able to make extensive use of the collection, not least in the amazing collection of photographs which include those of the construction works in connection with the railway tunnels deviation scheme. We are also very indebted to Jon Goodwin who in 1979 with the late Robin Witter attempted and almost succeeded in passing through the long disused Brindley tunnel in canoes. Their exploits are recorded in the text and, with Jon's kind permission, a full report of their findings complied from notes made by Robin can be found at Appendix 2.

Susan Hateley, widow of cartographer Roger Hateley, kindly granted her permission for us to use her late husband's excellent map of the North Staffordshire Railway. We would also like to acknowledge the cartography skills of Ian Pope and the ephemera images kindly made available to us by David Kitching. About forty-five years ago when the Birchenwood Coking Plant at Kidsgrove closed, Bernard Blake, the Assistant Manager, placed a large number of documents, plans and maps at the disposal of one of us that would have otherwise have gone on to the bonfire and for this we are extremely grateful. We also acknowledge information passed on to us by the late Dr. Jack Hollick and William (Bill) Jack. For information on recent research undertaken on the original railway tunnels we are grateful to John Clarke, Robert Davies and Peter Trewin of the Historical Railway Estate, Department of Transport, as successors to British Railways Board (Residuary) Limited. We have consulted records held by the Coal Authority; the House of Lords Record Office (HLRO); the Institution of Civil Engineers (ICE); the National Archives (NA); the William Salt Library at Stafford and the National Waterways Museum at Ellesmere Port whose archivists, John Benson and Linda Barley have been particularly helpful. Two Staffordshire-based archivists have also been extremely helpful – Helen Burton, Archivist, Keele University, Special Collections & Archives and Liz Street, Archivist at the Staffordshire & Stoke-on-Trent Archives, County Record Office (CRO) at Stafford. Julie Boadilla, Information Specialist at the British Library kindly sourced a copy of Field and Jeffreys' patent referred to in Chapter 8. Except where otherwise credited, all the photographs and illustrative matter are from the authors' own collections. In this regard we would like to place on record the kindness of the late Michael Mensing who was always very generous to both authors in providing copies and allowing the reproduction of examples of his excellent work. Michael travelled the country far and wide, but particularly in the Midland Counties, such that his photographs often appear in our works. Once again in this book, we are grateful for his past generosity as his photographs add so much to our story.

As is the case in all our writings, we are both very conscious of the help, support and very often wise counsel, given so willingly from our dear wives Angela and Darral. Spending countless hours tucked away in our studies, or away for days on end conducting research, their forbearance is nothing short of magnificent. The occasional intervention with a welcoming cup of tea or coffee, or even the odd glass of wine as a sign it is time to give up for the day, is highly appreciated as is their recognition of the tasks we have set ourselves.

Finally and very importantly, we are most grateful to Lightmoor Press for publishing our work and especially to their book designer, Stephen D. Phillips. Stephen has studied our manuscript in great detail and taken a keen interest in our work enabling him to make several useful suggestions, which we have been very pleased to adopt. This book is much the richer for his graphic design skills and diligence.

APPENDIX 1

Estimate of a Line of Locks to pass the Summit of the Grand Trunk Canal in place of a new Tunnel through Harecastle Hill

Canal to be 14 feet wide at bottom – 30 feet 8 inches at top and 5 feet deep

	£	s	d
To cutting at South end for Two Ponds – 40,473 @ 9d	1,517	14	9
To cutting to Summit – 20,908 @ 6d	522	19	0
To 94,167 deep cutting – @ 1s 6d	7,062	10	6
To 97,684 deep cutting – @ 1s 3d	6,105	5	0
To 13,491 deep – cutting @ 9d	505	18	3
To 23,850 cubic yards cutting in north range – @ 6d	596	5	0
To 55,551 cubic yards cutting in north range – @ 1s 0d	2,777	11	0
To 16 Locks @ £900 including puddling	14,400	0	0
To 5 Bridges	1,000	0	0
To 4,117 running yards towing path and fencing @ 3d	617	10	0
To 48 acres of land @ £100	4,800	0	0
To 500 yards of Tunnel to Steam Engines	1,575	6	6
To Feeder	500	0	0
To 2 Steam Engines of 65 horses each	15,000	0	0
To Engine Men £1 1s 0d – Repairs £2 2s 0d – coals 13 tons @ 8s 0d per ton – making £3,066 @ £5 per ft. Capital	31,080	0	0
TOTAL	**88,061**	**0**	**0**

To Raise 500 Locks of 3,240 cubic feet each
= 1,620,600 cubic feet in 20 hours 50 feet high
= 2 Engines of 65 horses each
Lawton, August 18th 1820.

Authors' comments

Rennie's reports and estimates were clearly written by his clerk(s). The copy at the Staffordshire CRO actually contains his signature which is in a very different hand to the rest of the report. This estimate (from the ICE papers) actually referred to 'Horncastle Hill' which we have corrected – no point in perpetuating obvious errors. The rest of the transcript is as near to the exact copy as we can get it. The unexplained figures are cubic yards. The last entry in the table where daily costs for engine men, repairs and coal is said to equate to an annual sum of £3,066 is a puzzle as we make the calculation to be £3,047 15s 0d. We are also at a loss to see how the capital sum of £31,080 was derived. The estimate ends with the calculations to justify the two steam engines required to feed the summit level, presumably based on anticipated traffic levels.

APPENDIX 2

Inspection of Brindley's Tunnel – 1979

Preamble

As previously mentioned we are especially grateful to Jon Goodwin and the late Robin Witter who in 1979, as very adventurous Olympic canoeists, braved the depths of Brindley's canal tunnel. Using their canoes, they discovered that the tunnel was partly blocked. With Jon's kind permission their amazing exploits are described here using Robin's comprehensive report on the condition of the tunnel at that time as a basis. Although the canoeists at first entered the tunnel from the south end, Robin's report describes the condition of the tunnel from north to south, which is how the tunnel's distance markers were numbered. We have decided to undertake some editing of his report to make the narrative flow better, at the same time correcting minor typing errors etc., while being careful not to have interfered with or misinterpreted any of the facts. Jon has been party to this exercise and feels sure Robin would not have had any objections. The exploration of the tunnel was a unique achievement from which we have learnt so much that would otherwise have gone unrecorded. In all probability, nobody had ventured inside the tunnel for a very long time prior their adventure and it is certain that nobody has since, or is ever likely to. Whatever the case, no records other than what is recorded here appear to have survived to describe what was to be seen long after the tunnel became disused. After brief details of their exploits were published in the *Staffordshire Evening Sentinel*, the British Waterways Board erected substantial steel fences around both tunnel mouths such that any further entry is impossible. It was after all, a potentially dangerous escapade now recognised as such by Jon, not least as the photographs taken during the trip used conventional flash bulbs with the resultant possibility for sparks that could have ignited any lingering methane gas, so often found in old underground workings. We are indebted to Jon for relaying his unique experiences and for giving us unfettered access to Robin's report and the photographs taken during the trip. This book is much the richer for their findings.

Condition Report – July 1979

The northern portal is in good condition with the pointing to the brickwork reasonable. The 100 yard channel to the tunnel mouth from the canal mainline, while blocked off and unused, is relatively weed free and full of water. At the tunnel mouth planking has been inserted which has the effect of raising the internal level of silt and water by about two feet above the summit level of the mainline.

The first hundred yards are almost an entirely thick, cloying silt of unknown depth, with only a six inch wide channel draining off the excess water – itself only inches deep. At about 20 yards from the entrance there does seem to be a variation in the type of brickwork, indicating the possibility of a later extension. After about 100 yards the silt layer gradually gives way to water. Along the eastern wall are distance markers at 100 yard intervals, starting at 1, which is, 100 yards from the northern end. At about both 200 and 300 yards inside the tunnel, there are adits on the eastern wall. These are about three feet above the present water level, which is about five feet above the normal summit level of the mainline of the canal. As far as could be seen, some 30 feet inside, they are unlined and while it is not known if they connect to the Telford Tunnel, if they do, being five feet above the water level in that tunnel, they cannot have any effect in water transference between the two tunnels and may have been used for the removal of spoil

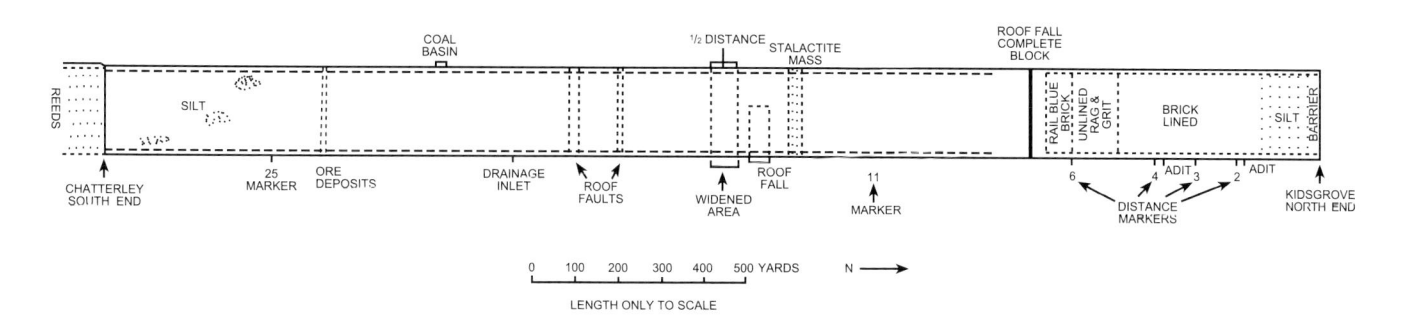

Diagram, redrawn by Ian Pope, from an original by the late Robin Witter, following his and Jon Goodwin's trip by canoes through Brindley's Canal Tunnel. It illustrates a number of issues discussed in Robin's description of the trip.

during construction of the later tunnel.

Up to about the 500 yard mark, distance marker 5 appears to be missing, the water depth increases to about three feet and the whole of the arch and surrounds are uniformly brick-lined, there being no evidence of subsidence or any falls of brickwork from the roof. The height to the roof arch from this artificially raised water level is, in the main, six feet; that is, eight feet from the summit level. There are some bulges in both the roof and walls and there are a few stalactites and *curtains* both of calcite and of ochre-coloured ironstone.

About 500 yards from the northern entrance up to just beyond the 600 yard marker, the tunnel is completely unlined, the natural rock being first dark *Rowley Rag* for some 60 yards, giving way to brownish millstone grit for a further 40 yards and with both the width and height varying considerably through this unlined portion. Just beyond the 600 yard marker, brick lining over the roof arch and walls recommences, but for about 75 yards this is of *railway-blue brick type*, leading to the speculation that this portion of the tunnel as originally constructed was also unlined, the brickwork having been added later. Certainly this brick is quite unlike any other encountered throughout the whole length of the tunnel. At 675 yards from the northern entrance, a five feet diameter precast concrete pipe enters at an oblique angle on the western wall. This connects to numerous drainage tunnels, all of recent construction and at varying levels, which are connected to the present railway tunnel, trains through which could easily be heard and a blast of air down the drainage pipe was felt after each passing train. Presumably, for this reason, this portion of the tunnel is gas free.

At about 700 yards, distance marker 7 not being apparent, there is a total blockage up to roof level. The material forming the blockage, a high grade sand apparently foreign to the area, is of a uniform consistency without apparently any debris or other rubble mixed in. This gives credence to the view that it is not a roof collapse, but rather a deliberate opening up in the tunnel roof of one of the original construction shafts and filling from above with sand to cause the blockage. Further progress along the tunnel line is impossible. Up to this point, about 700 yards, there is no serious subsidence – the roof height from the water level at the blockage remaining at six feet and the width at water level eight feet. The bore is straight and the exit visible. Throughout this length of the tunnel there is very little leakage through the roof and the water colour is not markedly ochre-stained. A water mark, some six inches above the present water level, indicated the height to which the water rises. Along the eastern wall there are small gaps in the brickwork at regular three feet intervals. These might have been mountings for a rail which could either have been for pulling boats through, as opposed to legging, or they might have supported a rubbing strake.

At the south entrance, the water level from the main line to the tunnel mouth – about 100 yards – is weired, raising the water level at this end some one foot above the mainline. The channel is, however, completely overgrown with weeds which cease at the tunnel mouth where the channel becomes just water. The brickwork of the entrance portal is once again in fair condition.

The water at the southern tunnel entrance is mixed with some layers of silt, but nothing like the extent of the northern portal and is more deeply ochre-stained. A water mark along both walls clearly indicates the level to which water can rise within the tunnel. The height from the water level to the roof at the entrance is about five feet and the internal brickwork appears not to be in as good condition as at the northern end; there are substantial bulges in both the walls and the roof arch. Within 200 yards from the entrance the roof height from water level decreases to about four feet, in places being even lower. The water for a short stretch becomes deep crimson in colour, indicating the presence of chromium salts and at about 500 yards from the south entrance there are small stalactites, deposits and *curtains* in an array of white, gold, ochre and crimson colours, across the whole of the tunnel and walls.

Along the eastern wall are distance markers, though not all are present. The first one observed is number 25; that is, about 400 yards from the south entrance. At 800 yards from the south entrance the roof height to water level decreases to about three feet and the width is much reduced, being about four feet. At this point is the entrance to a coal tunnel on the western side, its roof arching being at the same height as the main tunnel. At about 10 yards distance inside this channel, the roof has collapsed and the whole area beyond is silted up. The potential change in water level at this point – as seen from the ochre-stained high water mark – is about 18 inches. The main tunnel continues onwards at about three feet in height with the brickwork in very poor condition. The southern entrance is just visible at about 900 yards; thereafter it is lost as there are considerable variations in straightness of the bore of the tunnel. No distance markers are visible along this length of the tunnel, presumably having sunk beneath the water level. At about 1,100 yards there occurs the first collapse within the tunnel, the roof and eastern wall having fallen in for around 20 feet, with further brickwork in the roof looking precariously positioned and liable to collapse. The water channel is however, uninterrupted. There is a further similar fall at about 1,200 yards from the south entrance, which gives a very good indication of the cross-section of the original brick lining, the nature of the rocks through which the men had to bore and the amount of subsidence that has occurred over the years in this part of the tunnel. It also clearly shows the amount by which the water level can vary.

At an estimated 1,400 yards from the south entrance, approximately the middle of the tunnel, from a headroom of only three feet and a width of four feet, the tunnel opens out dramatically into a comparatively cavernous area of an estimated 80 yards in length, 13 feet wide and 10 feet high. The whole area here is brick lined, but deeply stained with ochre and limestone deposits together with numerous stalactites. Equally dramatically the continuation northwards resumes at three feet in height and four feet wide. Despite speculation that this area represents a passing point, no mooring rings were seen on either wall. At about 1,600 yards from the southern entrance, there is the third and most serious roof fall including the eastern wall, being some 40 feet long and up to 20 feet high. Though the water channel is impeded, it is not completely blocked. Fifty yards beyond this roof fall there is an array of ironstone stalactites in red and orange, completely covering the roof and walls of the tunnel, some two and a half feet from the water level. Stretching down to the water level they totally block the passage. In a sense there are also stalagmites as there is an accretion of deposited material at the lower extremities, clearly picked up from the water when it has risen. The largest of these stalactites is of an order of four inches in diameter and the whole mass stretches for some 20 yards. Beyond this stalactite mass the tunnel width begins to increase, varying between three and five feet above the water level.

Distance marker 11 at 1,800 yards from the southern entrance is in situ and the water from here on is less deeply ochre-stained. No further distance markers were seen, but an estimated 300 to 400 yards were explored before a total blockage up to the roof, consisting of material similar to that seen from the north end was encountered. The roof height at this point was some four feet above water level. Therefore, due to an inability to obtain an exact distance travelled from the south end up to this blockage, it is not possible to be certain whether this is the same blockage as encountered at 700 yards from the northern end of the tunnel, no more its exact length. However, only a maximum of 100 yards of the tunnel is unaccounted for.

It remains to ascertain why the water level in the tunnel varies. This is not necessarily due to rainfall as on one occasion it was noted to have risen by more than a foot within an hour without any rain. It cannot be due to lockage on, or release of water into the mainline of the canal, nor the passage of craft in Telford's tunnel, even supposing the two tunnels are interconnected as has been suggested. The two tunnels are not at the same water level, the Brindley tunnel water is at least two feet above the mainline of the canal, with no known feeders leading directly into the old tunnel other than mine drainage, the flow of which would only be expected to vary substantially after rainfall. Finally, it remains to be stated that because of these unexplained variations in water level, giving not more than 18 inches clearance from the top water level to the roof arch in places, also the precarious nature of the brickwork in other parts, along with the potential presence of toxic gases, particularly at the southern end, the tunnel should under no circumstances be entered without the most stringent safety precautions. There can of course, be no question of restoration of this old tunnel, with all the construction shafts bricked over in the roof, the position of none of them being visible.

Robin Witter
July 1979

The following photographs (pages 194-202), with one exception, were all taken by Robin Witter in July 1979 during the exploration of Brindley's tunnel; the exception was taken by fellow canoeist Jon Goodwin and is credited to him. They start at the north end of the tunnel and the sequence closely follows the condition report that was compiled shortly after the inspection and now forms part of Appendix 2. The captions are based on the report including, where appropriate, direct quotes and from the notes that accompany each individual photograph. The yardages are given from the north portal for the first ten photographs and from the south portal for the remaining photographs, which reflects the measurements as calculated by Robin.

HARECASTLE'S CANAL AND RAILWAY TUNNELS

North - 0 yards
View from the north entrance looking south. *The first hundred yards are almost an entirely thick cloying silt of unknown depth, with only a six inch wide channel draining off excess water – itself only six inches deep.*

North - 300 yards
Distance marker 3 at 300 yards from the northern entrance as fixed to the east wall.

North - 400 yards
Looking south at 400 yards from the northern entrance.

194

APPENDIX 2 – INSPECTION OF BRINDLEY'S TUNNEL – 1979

North - 500 yards
About 500 yards from the northern entrance up to just beyond the 600 yard marker, the tunnel is completely unlined, the natural rock being first dark 'Rowley Rag' for some 60 yards, giving way to brownish millstone grit for a further forty yards and with both the width and height varying considerably through this unlined portion.

North - 580 yards
The natural rock lining looking south at about 580 yards from the north end.

North - 600 yards
Just beyond the 600 yard marker, brick lining over the roof arch and walls recommences, but for about 75 yards this is of 'railway-blue brick type', leading to speculation that this portion of the tunnel as originally constructed was also unlined, the brickwork having been added later.

North - 600 yards Distance marker 6 at 600 yards from the north end and fixed to the natural rock on the east side of the tunnel.

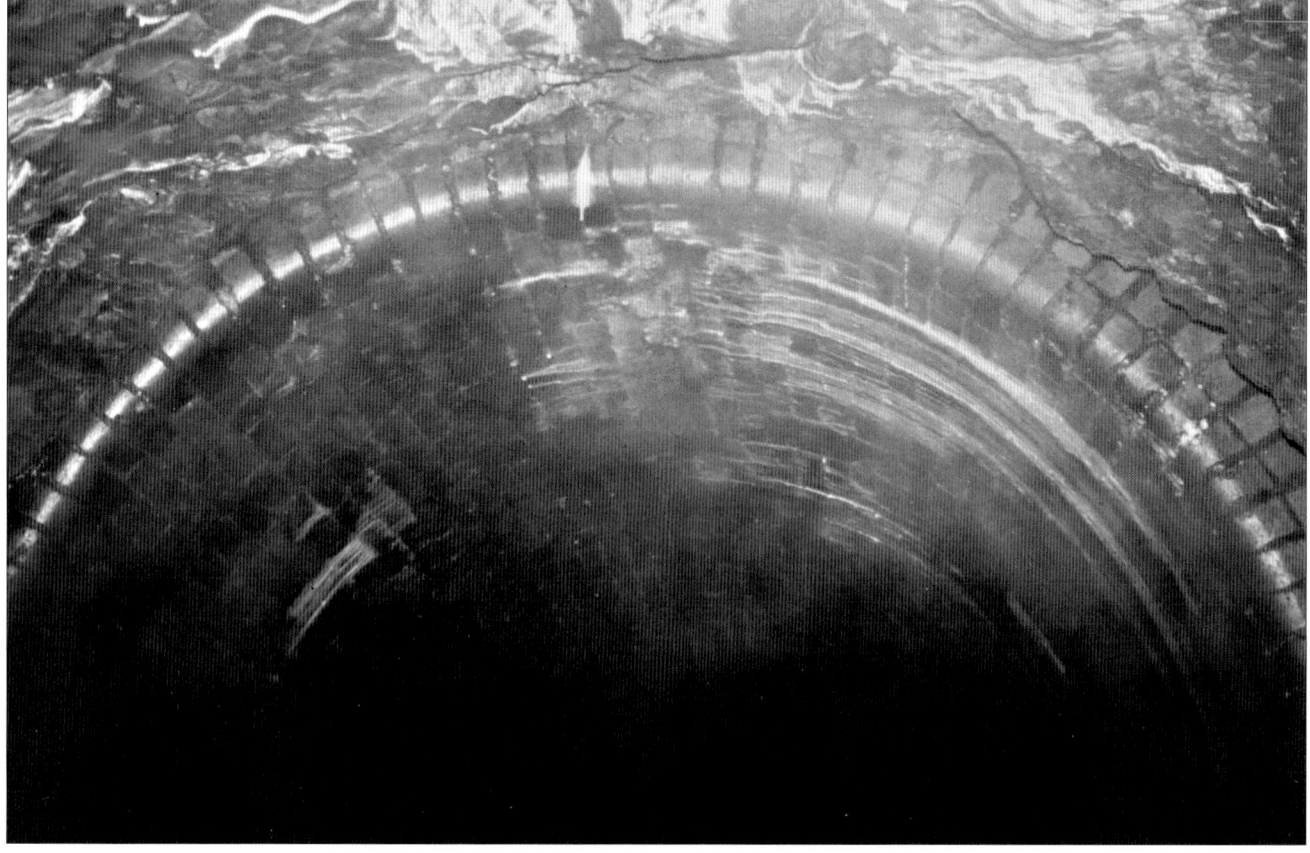

North - 620 yards The start of the blue brick lining at 620 yards from the northern entrance, looking south.

APPENDIX 2 – INSPECTION OF BRINDLEY'S TUNNEL – 1979

North - 670 yards A view in the opposite direction at 670 yards from the northern entrance at the south end of the blue brick lining. Note the change in roof height.

North - 680 yards The blockage looking south at 680 yards from the north end. *The material forming the blockage, a high grade sand apparently foreign to the area, is of a uniform consistency.* This gave the impression that it was a deliberate act.

HARECASTLE'S CANAL AND RAILWAY TUNNELS

South portal - 0 yards
This is the south portal of Brindley's tunnel exactly as it was when the canoeists commenced their exploration in July 1979.

South - 350 yards
View looking north about 350 yards from the south end.

South - 400 yards
Looking in the opposite direction towards Chatterley from 400 yards inside the tunnel.

APPENDIX 2 – INSPECTION OF BRINDLEY'S TUNNEL – 1979

South - 800 yards Former entrance to a coal tunnel in the western wall of Brindley's tunnel at 800 yards from Chatterley.

South - 1,100 yards This view looks north at the first roof collapse at 1,100 yards from the south entrance. Note the structure of the brick lining and the loose bricks.

South - 1,250 yards The second roof collapse at 1,250 yards from the south end, looking north.

South - 1,440 yards Robin Witter in his canoe entering the widened and heightened section of the tunnel, looking south *Jon Goodwin*

South - 1,440 yards The widened and heightened part of the tunnel looking north. This section was equidistant from both ends at 1,440 yards giving credence to it once being a passing place at the half way stage. It could also have been used for transhipping coal and ironstone from smaller boats used in the mine workings accessed by the side tunnels.

South - 1,600 yards Beyond the widened area at about 1,600 yards from the southern end, *there is the third and most serious roof fall including the eastern wall.* Jon Goodwin is seen here paddling his canoe through the collapsed section.

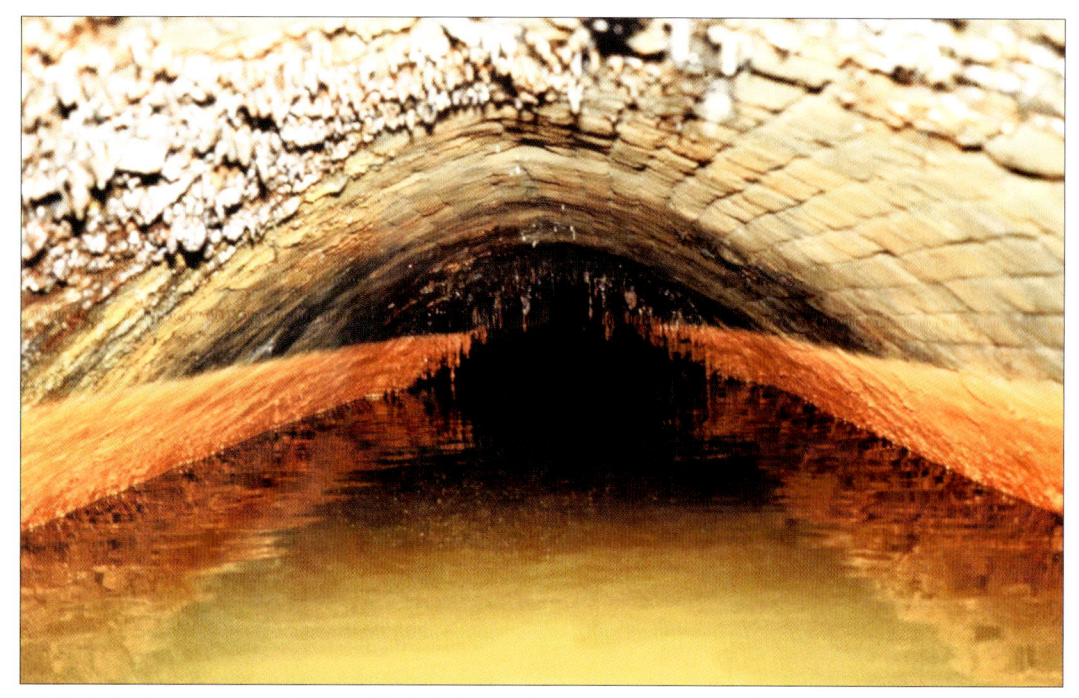

A little further on a stalactite mass blocked the way but the canoeists were able to get by until they came to the total blockage beyond distance marker 11 which was still in situ. They then had to paddle backwards with some difficulty to the widened area before their canoes could be turned around.

Authors' Observations

Readers will doubtless have noticed in studying this fascinating report, that evidence of only one side tunnel was discovered. Also, no evidence was located of where any of the construction shafts, sunk to assist the construction of the tunnel, were located. As discussed in Chapter 10, we do know that there were other side tunnels to access coal and ironstone measures which, combined with the lack of evidence of the construction shafts, suggests that over the years, not inconsiderable replacement of the tunnel lining had taken place. Bearing in mind that the tunnel was in constant use for the best part of 150 years, this is perhaps not surprising. Once the second tunnel was completed, the opportunity was probably taken, as occasion demanded, to undertake work of this nature. In view of the historical importance of this very early civil engineering achievement, in its day the longest tunnel of any sort anywhere in the world, we have included the above selection of the photographs taken during the expedition. As far as we know these are unique and form an extremely valuable and very important record.

It is also worth discussing the reason for the considerable variations in the straightness of the bore at 900 yards from the southern end, as mentioned by Robin. This could be the result of repairs having been undertaken following damage due to adjacent mine workings. As described in the text, we do know that irrespective of the underground mining from the side tunnels, damage was on occasion, caused to both Brindley's and Telford's tunnel by the extraction of coal and ironstone from both above and below their levels; similarly the railway tunnels. This was why at a later date, the NSR purchased the minerals in these areas.

At 675 yards from the northern entrance Robin mentions a pre-cast concrete pipe. This was installed as part of the railway deviation works to deal with surplus water from the Bath Pool reservoir in times of flood. It is a great shame that the tunnel had been completely blocked by the time of the canoeists' expedition as this seems to have been done deliberately. If Robin's 700 yards from the north end of the tunnel is approximately correct as the position of the blockage, this would place it underneath the new railway tunnel, part of the railway deviation scheme, described in Chapter 9. This raises the possibility that the opening up of an old construction shaft leading to the deposit of the high grade sand took place during the railway works. According to *The Railway Gazette* for 6th May 1966 two old shafts were encountered during the driving of the new railway tunnel. One was a construction shaft over Telford's tunnel which was bridged by a reinforced concrete beam to support the new railway tunnel floor. The other was said to be an old mine shaft which was filled with rubble and topped with a concrete plug. We wonder if the *old mine shaft* might have been one of Brindley's construction shafts with its fill now causing the blockage in the tunnel that Robin and Jon discovered.

The reference in the report to the possibility that the northern end of the tunnel might at some point in time have been extended, we consider can be discounted as there would not appear to be any reason why this should be so. The lie of the land thereabouts, shows no indication that its natural form may at any time have been interfered with. The original tunnel keeper's cottage used to stand just above the northern entrance and it probably dated from about the time the tunnel was constructed.

BIBLIOGRAPHY

ANONYMOUS. *The North Staffordshire Railway's Use of Electricity for Shunting and Towing*, Railway and Travel Monthly, Vol. XVII, No. 100, August 1918.

ANONYMOUS. *Victoria History of the County of Stafford*, Vol VIII. Oxford University Press, 1963

ATKINSON, Glen. *The Canal Duke's Collieries, Worsley 1760-1900*, Neil Richardson, undated, ISBN 0 9506257 7 9

BAKER, Allan C. *Birchenwood and its Locomotives*, Industrial Locomotive Society, 1974
The Potteries Loop Line, Trent Valley Publications, 1986, ISBN 0 948131 20 9
Industrial Locomotives of North Staffordshire, Industrial Railway Society, 1997, ISBN 0 901096 97 0
The Iron, Steel and Coal Industry in North Staffordshire, A Brief Account, Irwell Press, 2003, ISBN 1 903266 35 1
North Staffordshire Collieries On The Hill North of Chell, Lightmoor Press, 2014, ISBN 13 9781899889 84 6

BANKS, A.G. and SCHOFIELD, R.B. *Brindley at Wet Earth Colliery*, David & Charles, 1968

BOLTON, John M. *Canal Town, Stone,* Private Publication, 1981

BOUCHER, Cyril T.G. *James Brindley, Engineer 1716-1772*, Goose and Son, 1968

CARDEN, David. *The Foxton Inclined Plane*, Black Dwarf Publications, 2012, ISBN 9781903599 20 4

CHRISTIANSEN, Rex & MILLER, R.W. *The North Staffordshire Railway*, David & Charles, 1971, ISBN 0 7153 5121 4

COCKIN, Tim. *The Staffordshire Encyclopaedia*, Malthouse Press, 2nd Edition, 2006

CORBIE, Nick. *James Brindley, The First Canal Builder*, Tempus, 2005, ISBN 0 7524 3259 1

DEAN, C. *Electric Machinery and Appliances on the North Staffordshire Railway*, The Railway Magazine, Vol. XXXV, No. 205, July 1914

FELL, Mike G. *Harecastle Tunnel Electric Tugs*, Waterways World, Vol. 6, No. 6, June 1977

FOXON, Tom. *The Trent & Mersey Canal, Trade and Transport 1770-1970*, Black Dwarf Lightmoor Publications Ltd, 2015, ISBN 9781903599 22 8

GIBB, Sir Alexander. *The Story of Telford*, Alexander Maclehose & Co., 1935

GIBSON, Walcot. *The Geology of the North Staffordshire Coalfields*, HMSO, 1905

HADFIELD, Charles. *The Canals of the West Midlands*, David & Charles, 1966, ISBN 7153 4660 1

HADFIELD, Charles and BIDDLE, Gordon. *The Canals of North West England*, Volumes 1 and 2, David & Charles, 1970, ISBN 0 7153 4956 2 and 0 7153 4992 9

LEAD, Peter. *Agents of Revolution, John and Thomas Gilbert – Entrepreneurs,* University of Keele, 1989

LEESE, Philip R.*The Kidsgrove Boggart and the Black Dog*, published privately, 1989
The Best of Kidsgrove Times, Vols. II to VI, Good News Publishing, Kidsgrove, 1996-2004

LEWIS, C.G. *Hugh Henshall 1734-1816*, Transactions of the Newcomen Society, No. 76, 2006

LEWIS, Christopher. *The Canal Pioneer, Brindley's School of Engineers*, The History Press, 2011, ISBN 10 0752461664

LINDSAY, Jean. *The Trent & Mersey Canal*, David & Charles, 1979, ISBN 0 7153 7781 7

LLEWELLIN, Rev. Frederick G.*The Lighter Side of a Parson's Life*, published by the author, Kidsgrove, 1933
Kidsgrove & North Staffordshire, published by the author, Kidsgrove, 1936

MALET, Hugh. *The Canal Duke*, David & Charles, 1961
Bridgewater The Canal Duke 1736-1803, Manchester University Press, 1977, ISBN 0 7190 0679 1

MANIFOLD. *The North Staffordshire Railway*, J.H. Henstock, Ashbourne, 1952

MATHER, F.C. *After the Canal Duke*, Oxford University Press, 1970

MEADE, L.T. *The Water Gipsies or The Adventures of Tag, Rag and Bobtail*, 1879

MULLINEUX, Frank. *The Duke of Bridgewater's Underground Canals at Worsley*, Transactions of the Lancashire & Cheshire Antiquarian Society, Vol. 71, 1971

NELSON, A. *Dictionary of Mining*, George Newnes, 1964

NOCK, O.S. *Britain's New Railway*, Ian Allan, 1966

OWENS, Victoria. *James Brindley and the Duke of Bridgewater*, Amberley, 2015, ISBN 978 1 4456 966 5

RICHARDSON, Christine. *James Brindley, Canal Pioneer*, Waterways World Ltd, 2004, ISBN 1 870002 95 4

RIDEN, P. and OWEN, John G.*British Blast Furnace Statistics 1790-1980*, Merton Priory Press, 1995, ISBN 1 898937 05 2

ROLT, L.T.C. *Narrow Boat*, Eyre Methuen, 1944. *Thomas Telford*, Longmans, 1958

SHAW, Simeon. *History of the Staffordshire Potteries*, privately published 1829

SHILL, Ray. *Silent Highways – The Forgotten Heritage of the Midlands Canals,* The History Press, 2011, ISBN 978 0 7524 5842 7

TELFORD, Thomas. *Atlas to the Life of Thomas Telford*, Payne and Foss, 1838

WARD, John. *The Borough of Stoke-upon-Trent*, W. Lewis & Son, 1843

INDEX

No attempt has been made to comprehensively index the main subjects of this book, as to have done so, would have occupied an enormous amount of space which, in the authors' view, would not have greatly added to its value. With the various tunnels given individual chapters, along with the electric tugs, the railway diversion scheme and the coal and ironstone mining, readers should not have too much difficulty in finding their way around. There is a measure of cross-referencing, but it is by no means exhaustive. Where the page numbers appear in *italics*, the reference is to an illustration; however, where the reference refers to the main text on the page as well as an illustration caption, italics are not used.

Acts of Parliament
    Birmingham & Derby Junction Railway 1836, 111
    Grand Trunk Canal 1766, 13
    Land Clauses Consolidation Act 1845, 74
    North Staffordshire Railway Acts 1846, 61, 184
    North Staffordshire Railway Act 1847, 184
    North Staffordshire Railway Act 1879, 81
    North Staffordshire Railway Act 1904, *66, 67*, 81, 89, 184, *186, 187*
    Railways Act 1921, 89
    Railway & Canal Traffic Act 1888, 76
    Railway Clauses Consolidation Act 1845, 66, 181, 184
    Relief of the Poor Act 1782, 164
    Transport Act 1947, 95
    Transport Act 1962, 101
    Trent & Mersey Canal Act 1823 (Telford's Tunnel), 30
    Trent & Mersey Canal Company, summary of Acts, *16*
    Trent & Mersey Canal Company Act 1831, *39-41*, 64, *182*, 184
    Weaver Navigation Act, 71
Allen, Kathleen Murial, Station Mistress, Chatterley, 121
Allott, J.R.L., General Manager, Birchenwood Colliery, 184
Anderton Company, Canal Carriers, 69, 76, 85, *90, 91, 94*
Anderton Boat Lift – River Weaver, 71, 72
Alsager, 119, 157, 158
    Diesel haulage of trains due to problems in new tunnel, 156, 157, *158*
    Locomotive Shed, *127, 128, 129, 136*
Attwood, Georgina Mary, one time owner of Clough Hall Estate *59*, 165
    George, her father, 165

Bache, Thomas & Company, Canal Carriers, Coventry, *33*
Bagnall, W.G. Limited, Locomotive Builders, Stafford, *62, 140*
Barnwell, Frederick Arthur Lowry, NSR Engineer, later General Manager, *88*
Barry, Sir John Wolfe, Consulting Engineer, giving evidence before Royal Commission on Canals & Waterways, 67, 71
Beatty, William Fitzgerald, Civil Engineer, Harecastle Tunnel Diversion Scheme, 146, 156
Benson, William, Land & Colliery Surveyor, St Helens, *169, 170*, 172
Bent, William, Brewery Owner, 26
Bentley, Thomas, Partner of Josiah Wedgwood, *5*
Bidder, George Parker, NSR Civil Engineer, 61, 111, 114
Birchell, William, NSR Solicitor, 67
Birchenwood Coal & Coke Company Limited, 95, 184
Birchenwood Colliery, 19, *62*, 81, 85, 95, *131, 136, 138, 139, 140*, 166, *171, 172*, 178, *184*, 185
    Allott, J.R.L., General Manager, 184
    Coke Oven By-Product Recovery Plant, 136, *138*, 185, 188
    Dickinson, Alexander, Managing Director, 62
    Locomotives, 62
    Settle, Joel, Colliery Manager, 62
Birmingham, Railway, Carriage & Wagon Company:
    Diesel Multiple Units, *123, 136, 158*
Board of Trade, 64, 67, 70, 72, 76, 78
    Buxton, Stanley, President, 70
    Druitt, Lieutenant Colonel Edward, Inspecting Officer, 76, 77, *78, 80*, 108
    Marwood, W.F., Assistant Secretary, 76
    Wynne, George, Inspecting Officer, 116
Boddington, Harry, Anderton Company, Canal Carriers, 69, 76, 85
Borax Consolidated Limited, Kidsgrove, *133*
Boulton, Matthew, Engineer, 161
Boulton & Watt, Manufacturers of Steam Engines, 161
Bourne, Hugh, Methodist Preacher, 159
Brassey, Thomas, Contractor, Harecastle Railway Tunnel, 114, 116, 119
    Auction of construction equipment, 116
BRB (Residuary) Limited, Survey of Old Railway Tunnels, 159
    Heywood, Kenneth, Civil Engineer, 159
Bridgewater, Duke of, 13, *14*, 15, 17, 16, 161, 162, 164, 172
    Portrait, 13
Brindley, James, 13, 14, 15, 23, 46
    Anne, his Wife, 164
    Bridgewater Canal, 161, 162
    Death at Turnhurst Hall, *5*
    Grand Trunk Canal, *5*
    Gravestone, St James Church, Newchapel, *22*
    Harecastle Tunnel 13, *et seq*, 23, *25*, 26, 28, 29, 31, *33, 37*, 44, 46, *53, 58, 60*, 61, 64, 69, 77, *82*, 89, *97, 103, 104, 105, 106, 108*, 121, 145, *157*, 162, 163, 164, *171*, 172, *173*, 178, 180, *181*, 185, 189, 191, 193, *194-202*
    Proposals to By-Pass Tunnel 1807, *24*, 25
    Telford's Description of Tunnel, 19, 20
    Turnhurst Hall & Estate, *5*, 163
Brindley, John, brother of James, 17, 164
British Railways, 145 *et seq*
    Electrification Scheme Euston-Manchester, 145
        Problems with Steam Locomotives operating Through New Railway Tunnel, 156, 157, 158
    Stoke-on-Trent Motive Power Depot, 157
    Swindon-built Diesel Multiple Units, 159
British Transport Commission, 101
    Docks & Inland Waterways Executive, 95
British Waterways Board, *100*, 101 *et seq*, *181*
    Haskins, Brian, Northwich Area Engineer, 108
    Price, Sir Frank, Chairman, 108
Broadfields, Blast Furnace near Goldenhill (also known as Latebrook), 174, 177
    Barker & Company, 177
    Bates, W., 177
Brunel, Marc Isambard, Civil Engineer; Examination of Telford's Tunnel Construction Works, 49
Brunel, Isambard Kingdom, 49
Brunton, William, Eagle Foundry, Birmingham, 31
Bulkeley, Philip, Harecastle Estate Owner, 166, 167
Bullivant & Company, Supply of Steel Tug for Electric Haulage in Tunnel, 81
Burslem, *5*, 14, *52*
    Parker's Brewery, 133, 166
    Railway Station renamed Longport, 117
    St Paul's Church, *52*, 108, *149*
    Wedgwood Pottery Factory, *5*, 13
Bury, Curtis & Kennedy, Engineers, Liverpool, 119
Butler & Company, Leeds, Stationary Steam Engine on Tunnel Works, 116

Caldon Low Limestone Quarries, *38*, 161
Campbell Company, Cardiff, Gas Engines for Electric Tug, 82, *84*
Canals
    Birmingham Canal Navigations, *33*, 70
        Jebb, George Robert, Engineer, 70, 71
    Caldon, 17, *18*, 27, *38*, *57*, *65*
        Leek Branch, *39*, 114
        Norton Green Branch, 17, 30, 37, 38
    Coventry, 26
    Duke of Bridgewater's, 13, 14, 20, 161, 162, 163
    Ellesmere & Chester, *50*
    Grand Junction, 70
        Thomas, Gordon Cale, Engineer, 70, 71
    Gresley, *57*
    Leeds & Liverpool, *20*, 163
        Leigh Branch, 163
    Macclesfield, *56*, 178
    Manchester Ship Canal, 70, 81, 162, 163
    Newcastle-under-Lyme, *57*
    Newcastle-under-Lyme Junction, *57*
    Oxford, 52
    Rochdale, 163
    Shropshire Union, 85
    Staffordshire & Worcestershire, 15
    Thames & Medway, 30
Canal & River Trust, *106*, *107*, 110
Caldwell, James, Trent & Mersey Canal Shareholder, 26, 27
    In connection with Telford's Tunnel, 29, 30, 42, 44, 45, 46, 48, 49, *50*, 51, 54
    Chetwynd, Sir George, in connection with diaries, 48
    Lister, Thomas, in connection with diaries, 48
Chatterley, *18*, *22*, *25*, *34*, *58*, 64, 76, 77, 99, 101, *102*, *103*, 108, 110, 117, 119, *127*, *128*, *132*, *137*, *141*, 178, 180
    Electric Canal Tugs, 81, 82, *84*, 85, 90, *91*, *92*, 95, *96*, *97*
    Harecastle Railway Tunnel Diversion Scheme, 145, *149*, *156*, *157*, 165
    Ironworks, *121*, *123*, *141*, *149*, *156*, *157*
    Station, 121, *122*, *123*, *124*, *125*, *126*
Cheadle, Staffordshire Moorland Town, 167
    Gower, Lord, Mayor of, 161
    Huntley Hall, 166
Cheadle Hulme, Cheshire, *137*, 145
Child, Sir Smith, Bart, Newfield Hall, Coal Royalty Owner, 182
Clough Hall Collieries & Ironworks (*see also under Kidsgrove*), *59*, 60, *171*
    Attwood, Georgina Mary, onetime owner, *59*, 165
    Blast Furnaces, 165, 166
    Dragon Tramway Incline and Engine, 166
    Valentine Pit, 166, 188
Clough Hall Estate, 29, 60, *112*, 114, *138*, *141*, 145, 147, 164, 165, 166, 167, *171*, 184, 185
Clough Hall Park & Gardens Limited, 166
Clowes, Josiah, assistant to Henshall, when building original Canal Tunnel, 15, 167
Coalbrookdale Company, Shropshire, Manufacturers of Steam Engine, 164
Coal Seams:
    Birchenwood, 19, 172
    Cannel Row, 180
    Eight Foot Banbury, 184
    Great Row, *170*, 172, 178, 180
    Little Mine, 185
    Spendcroft, *169*, 172
    Stoney Eight Foot, 184
    Ten Foot, *169*, 172, 185
    Turnrail, 19, 172
    Section of Mines in Harecastle Hill, 162, 163
Collieries
    Apedale, *57*
    Ashwood, 122, *149*
    Bath Pool, 185
    Birchenwood Colliery, 19, *62*, 81, 85, 95, *131*, *136*, *138*, *139*, *140*, 166, 178, 184, 185
        Simon Carves Coke Ovens, 138
    Brown Lees, 165
    Clough Hall, *59*, 60, *138*, 165, 166, *171*, 184, 185
        No. 1 Pit, 171
    Cloughhead, near Ipstones, *161*
    Dale Green, 178
    Engine, Golden Hill, *169*, 172
    Fenton Collieries Limited, 90
    Golden Hill, 17, 46, 172, 174
    Harecastle, 185
    High Carr, *148*
    Hodgfield, Goldenhill, *169*, 172
    Hollins Wood, 185
    Kidswood, *62*, *139*, 185
    Moss Coal Pits, Kidsgrove, *141*
    Nelson, *34*, *36*, 42, 60, *62*, *139*, *140*, *141*, *147*, *164*, *178*, *183*, *184*, 185
    Nelson By-Pit, 184
    Norton, *140*
    Norton & Biddulph, *140*, *184*
    Parkhouse, *157*
    Ravenscliffe, *153*, 165, 173
    Speedwell, Kidsgrove, *133*
    Stonetrough, 165
    Talk o' th' Hill, *141*, *148*
    Trubshaw, Kidsgrove, *133*
    Tunnel Pit, 164
    Valentine, 166, 188
    Victoria, Biddulph, 140
    Wet Earth, Clifton, 162
    Wolstanton, *123*
    Worsley, on the Bridgewater Canal, 19, 163

Contractors
    Brassey, Thomas, Contractor, Harecastle Railway Tunnel, 114
    Dutton & Buckley, Knypersley Reservoir & Tunnel Cuttings, 30, 31
    Greys & Bancks, Supplying Bricks for Telford's Tunnel, 42
    Haywood's Brickyard, Supplying Bricks for Telford's Tunnel, 42
    Lehane, MacKenzie & Shand Group, Tunnel Repairs, 101
    Miller Construction Limited, Tunnel Repairs, 101, 110
    Mowlem Northern Limited, Tunnel Repairs, 101
    Peake & Shufflebotham, Supplying Bricks for Telford's Tunnel, 42
    Pritchard & Hoof, Telford's Tunnel, 30, 42, 44, 46, 48
    Rock Services (Midlands) Limited, Tunnel Repairs, 101
    Tarmac Civil Engineering Limited – Harecastle Tunnel Diversion Scheme, 153
Cooney, John, Kidsgrove Council Councillor, 178
Cowley, Hickin, Batty & Company, Canal Carriers, Birmingham, 33
Cowlishaw Walker & Company, Engineers, Biddulph, *96*, *140*
Cravens Limited, Diesel Multiple Units, *123*, *158*
Crosbie Dawson, George James, NSR Engineer, *65*, 69, 70, 71, 77
Curbishley, Harry, NSR Canal Engineer, *65*, 69, 70, 71, 81, 82

Darwin, Charles, 13
Darwin, Dr Erasmus, Supporter of Josiah Wedgwood in Building Grand Trunk Canal, 13
Darwin, Robert Waring, Married Wedgwood's daughter Susannah, 13
Dennis, E.W., President North Staffordshire Field Club, 174
Dickinson, Alexander, Managing Director Birchenwood Colliery, *62*
Diesel Multiple Units, *122*, *123*, *124*, *136*, *148*, *158*, *159*
    British Railways Class '156', *137*
Dobbie & Partners, Consulting Engineers, Harecastle Tunnel
Docks & Inland Waterways Executive, Ventilation of Canal Tunnel, 177
Donkin, Bryan, Sponsor of Telford for Membership of Institution of Civil Engineers, 31
Dock, Wharf, Riverside & General Workers Union, 64
    Tillett, Benjamin, General Secretary, 64, *65*
Druitt, Lieutenant Colonel Edward, Board of Trade Inspecting Officer, 108
    Inspection of the Canal Tunnels, 76, *77*, *78*, 80
Dutton & Buckley
    Contractors for Knypersley Reservoir, 30
    Contractors for cuttings in connection with Telford's Tunnel, 31

Egerton, Scroop, 4th Earl of Bridgewater, later 1st Duke of Bridgewater, 161
Etruria, 27, 28, *33*, *38*, 48, 82, 119, *136*, *157*, *158*
    Etruria Hall, 5
    Shelton Iron, Steel & Coal Company Limited, *55*, *157*, *158*
    Village, Created by Josiah Wedgwood, 164

Wedgwood Factory, 13, *55*

Falcon Engine & Car Works, Loughborough, Locomotive Builders, *140*
Fane de Salis, Rodolph, NSR Director, 70, *71*
Fellows, Morton & Clayton, Canal Carriers, 69, 85
Festival of Britain 1951, Trips through Harecastle Canal Tunnel, *175*, *176*, 177, 178
Field & Jeffrey's Patent Railway Chair Key, 117, 118, 119
Field, Joshua, Sponsor of James Potter, Membership of Institution of Civil Engineers, 31
Findley, George, Civil Engineer engaged in construction of Railway Tunnels, 116
Forsyth, John Curphey, NSR Engineer, 114, 117, 118, 119

General Electric Company, Dynamos for Electric Tug, 82, *84*
Gibbons, George, Solicitor acting for Walhouse & Bulkeley, Mining Coal in Harecastle Tunnel, 166, 167
Gilbert, George, father of John & Thomas, 161
Gilbert, John, 14, 17, *60*, *138*, *139*, 161, 162, 163, 164, 165, 167, 173
    Birds, David, Executor, 165
    Gilbert's Hole, mining from canal tunnels, *171*, 172, 178, 180, *181*
    Gould, Nathaniel, Executor, 165
    Royds, James, Executor, 165
    Stables, *25*
Gilbert, Thomas, 14, 17, 161, 162, 163, 164, 167
    MP for Newcastle-under-Lyme, 163
    Relief of the Poor Act, 164
Goldendale Ironworks, Chatterley, *58*, *90*, *96*, *122*, *141*, *149*, *152*, *157*, *163*, *164*, 165, 173, 174, *188*
Golden Hill & Ranscliffe Estates, Coal Mining, *168*, *169*, *171*, 172
Goodwin, Jon, Canoe Trip through Brindley's Tunnel, 108, 180, 191 *et seq*
Gower, Earl, 15, 161, 163
Gresley, Sir Nigel, Owner of Turnhurst, Newchapel & Goldenhill Estates, 163

Hamilton, George Ernest, Civil Engineer, reporting on Knypersley Reservoir, 52
Haskins, Brian, British Waterways Board, Northwich Area Engineer, 108
Hayles, Fred, Signalman Harecastle Junction, 134
Heath, Robert, 29, 165, 166
    Thomas Kinnersly's Agent and Manager, 29
Heath, Robert & Sons Limited, *62*, *66*, *139*, *140*, 185
Heath, Robert & Low Moor Limited, *140*, *184*
Heathcote, Sir John Edensor, Land Owner at Kidsgrove, 164, 173, 177
Henshall, Hugh, 14, 15, 17, 58, 164, 172
Henshall, Anne, 14, 164
Heywood, Kenneth, Civil Engineer, Harecastle Railway Tunnel Inspection, 159
Hill, Reginald Clarke, Stallington Hall, 48
Horizon Mining, Harecastle Tunnel, 180
Howley Park Coal & Cannel Company, 69, 76
Huish, Captain Mark, L&NWR General Manager, 114
Hull, City of Kingston-upon, 13, 15, 17, 42

Inland Waterways Association, 108
Institution of Civil Engineers, 27
    Thomas Telford, First President, 29
    James Potter's Membership, 31
    John Rennie, 190
Ironstone Mining, 14, 43, *45*, *106*, *110*, 161, 164, 165, 166, *168*, *170*, 172, 174, 178, 182, 183
    Bassey Mine, 174
    New Mine, 182, 185
    Seams in Harecastle Hill, *163*, *164*

Jebb, George Robert, Engineer, Birmingham Canal Navigations, 70, 71
Jervis, Admiral John, Viscount & Earl St Vincent, local land owner, 165

Keary, William, NSR Solicitor, 173
Keay, William Henry, Relief Station Master Radway Green: fatality, 119
Knypersley Reservoir, 17, 27, 28, 29, 30, *37*, *39*, *42*, 45, 46, 48, 49, 52
Kidsgrove, 17, *18*, 19, *23*, *52*, *56*, *90*, *107*, *108*, 115, 116, 117, 188, *130*, *131*, *135*, *136*, *139*, *141*, 172, 174, 180
    Cooney, John, Kidsgrove Council Councillor, 178

Boat Horse Road, *18*, *23*, *85*, 145, *146*, *154*, *158*, *159*, 173, *179*
Borax Consolidated Limited, *133*
Clough Hall Collieries & Ironworks, *59*, *60*, *138*, 140, *182*, 184, 185, 188
    Blast Furnaces, 165, 166
Clough Hall Estate, 29, 60, *112*, 114, *138*, *141*, 145, 147, 164, 165, 166, 167, *171*, 184, 185
    Bulkeley, Philip, 166, 167
    Nelson, Viscount Lord, paintings of, 164
    Sale by Auction, 165
    Worsley, Duke of, staying there, 164
    Walhouse, Moreton, 166, 167
Clough Hall Park, *23*, 66, 141
Electric Canal Tug, *93*, *95*
Festival of Britain 1951 – Trips through Harecastle Canal Tunnel, 177, 178
Harecastle Railway Tunnel Diversion Scheme, 145, 146, *148*, *150*, *151*, *154*, *155*, 156, 157, 158, 159, 164, 165, 166
Hardings Wood, 25, *90*, *93*, 164, 177, 178
    Proposed Tramway to Kinnersly's Works, 25, 26
Hollins Estate, 164
Kidcrew Buggat, Harecastle Canal Tunnel Ghost, 159
Llewellin, Reverend Frederick George, Vicar of St Thomas, 159
Macclesfield Canal, *56*
Nelson Buildings, 188
Railway Signalling, 127, 128, 129, 137
Roads – *see under Roads*, 188
Roche, Norman, Kidsgrove Council Chief Sanitary Inspector, 178
St Thomas Church, The Avenue, *23*, 60, *114*, *150*
    Llewellin, Reverend Frederick George, Vicar of St Thomas, 159
    Wade, Reverend Tobias, Vicar of St Thomas, 23, 60, 150
Station Names, 121, *134*
Town Council, 159, 177
Tarmac (Kidsgrove) Limited, *140*
Wade School, 150
White Hall, one time home of John Gilbert, 164
Woodshutts Estate, 164
Kidsgrove Steel, Iron & Coal Company Limited, 165
Kinnersly, Thomas, 25, 29, 31, *35*, *59*, *60*, 111, *112*, *113*, 114, *138*, *165*, 173, 177
Kinnersly & Company, *59*, *139*, *141*, 165, 182
    Clough Hall, *138*
    Gill Bank Tramway, 184, 185
    Matthews, William, Manager, 165, 182
    Nelson Pit, *139*
    Newcastle-under-Lyme Bank Owner, 165
    Proposed Tramway from Harding's Wood, *25*, *26*
    St Thomas, Parish Church, 188
    Williamson, Edward, ownership of Estate, 165
Kinnersly, Elizabeth, 165
Kinnersly, Mary, née Barnston, 165

Latebrook, Mining, 173, 174, 178
    Blast Furnace (also known as Broadfields), 177
Lehane, MacKenzie & Shand Group, Contractors on Tunnel Repairs, 101
Lawton, 25, 27, 29
Lee, Roger, Chairman Trent & Mersey Canal Society, 108
Leveson-Gower family, 161
Line Houses, Village on Harecastle Hill, *4*, 9, 12, *59*, *141*, 172, 173, *179*, 180
Littleton, Sir Edward, 4th Bart, 166
Liverpool, 11, 13, 18, *15*, *20*, 26, 42, 48, *94*, 111, 119, 145, 163, 166, *174*
Llewellin, Reverend Frederick George, Vicar of St Thomas, 159
Locomotives:
    Bagnall *Alexander* at Birchenwood Colliery, *62*, *140*
    British Railways:
        Class '86/2' AC Electric, *159*
        Class '09' Diesel-Electric Shunter, *157*
        Class '9F' 2-10-0, *157*, 158
        English Electric Type '4' Diesel-Electric, *128*, 157, *158*
    Eastern Region Class 'A4' 4-6-2, *126*
    Falcon Engine & Car Company, Robert Heath No. 8, *140*
    Motor Rail Limited, Simplex, Locomotives used on Harecastle Tunnel Diversion Scheme, *156*
    NEI Mining Equipment Limited – Clayton Equipment, Battery-electric locomotives, *109*, 110
    NSR Class 'B' 2-4-0 Tank, *132*

NSR Class 'E' 0-6-0, *132*
LM&SR Fowler Class '3F' 0-6-0 Tank, *136*
LM&SR Fowler Class '4F' 0-6-0, *126*, *127*, *128*, *129*
LM&SR Hughes/Fowler Class '5' 'Crab' 2-6-0, *126*, *131*
LM&SR Stanier Class '4' 2-6-4 Tank, *129*, *134*
LM&SR Stanier Class '5' 2-6-0, *123*, *126*
LM&SR Stanier Class '8F' 2-8-0, *124*
Yorkshire Engine *Clifford*, Goldendale Ironworks, *96*
Yorkshire Engine *Goldendale*, Goldendale Ironworks, *96*
Longport, 31, *33*, *52*, 69, *102*, 146, 157, *158*, 173
    Pye, Cecil Arthur, Station Master, 121
    Station, formerly named Burslem, 117
Low Moor Ironworks, Bradford, 119

Manchester, 11, *20*, 52, *62*, 70, 81, *94*, 111, *112*, *113*, 114, 127, *128*, *134*, *136*, *138*, 145, *159*, 161, 162, 163, 166, *174*
McKenzie & Holland, Worcester, NSR Signalling Contractors, *132*
Meakin, J. & G., Hanley, Pottery Manufacturers, *17*
Mersey & Irwell Navigation, 162
    Barton Aqueduct, 162
Mersey Weaver Company, Canal Carriers, 69
Metro-Cammell Diesel Multiple Units, 124
Miller Construction Limited, Contractors Repairing Tunnel, 101, 110
Mosley, Tonman, Chairman NSR, *65*, *70*, *73*
Motor Rail Limited, Locomotive Manufacturers, 156
Mowlem Northern Limited, Contractors Repairing Tunnel, 101

National Coal Board (NCB), 122, 178, 180
    Harecastle Coal Stocking Ground, *156*, *157*
NEI Mining Equipment Limited – Clayton Equipment, Battery-electric locomotives, *109*, 110
Nelson, Viscount, Vice Admiral Horatio RN, *60*, 164, 165
Newcastle-under-Lyme, Gilbert, Thomas, MP, 163
Newcomen Atmospheric Steam Engines, 14, 167, 177
North British Locomotive Company, *127*
North Staffordshire Chamber of Commerce, 69, 70, 71, 74, 76, 77, 81, 87
    Malkin, Sydney, Vice Chairman, 76
North Staffordshire Field Club, Visit to Broadfields Furnace Site, 174
North Staffordshire Railway
    Acts of Parliament – see under Acts
    Acquisition of Trent & Mersey Canal, 61
    Audley Branch, 121, *131*
    Barnwell, Frederick Arthur Lowry, General Manager, *88*
    Bidder, George Parker, Company's Engineer, 61, 111, 114, 115
    Biddulph Valley Line, *128*
    Birchell, William, Solicitor, 67
    Caldon Low Branch, *128*
    Canal Engineer's Department, *18*, *52*
    Canal Traffic Committee, 23
    Canal Tunnels – Proposed Diversion, 69, 70, 71, 72
        Coal Mining in connection with Tunnels, 71, 181, 182, 183
    Crewe Line, *60*, 121, *131*, *132*, *133*, *135*, *136*, *137*, *158*
    Crosbie Dawson, George James, NSR Engineer, *65*, 69, 70, 72, 77
    Curbishley, Harry, Canal Engineer, *65*, 69, 70, 72, 81, 82
    Electric Canal Tugs, 81 *et seq*
    Fane de Salis, Rodolph, Director, 70, *71*
    Formation, Opening of Original Lines & Construction, 61, *et seq*
        Railway Tunnels, 111 *et seq*
    Forsyth, John Curphey, Engineer, 114, *115*, 119
    Keary, William, NSR Solicitor, 173
    Leek Branch, *128*
    Minerals, Purchase of, to Protect Tunnels, 181, 182, 183, 184, *187*
    Mosley, Tonman, Chairman, *65*, *70*, *73*
    Norris, Richard Stewart, L&NWR Engineer, Northern Division, 117
    Phillipps, William, Douglas, General Manager, 64, *65*, 67, 69, 70, 71, 76
    Pinnox Branch, 148
    Potteries Loop Line, 117, 121, *125*, *141*, 148, 166, 185
    Railway Tunnels, 14, 111 *et seq*
    Rock, Andrew Frederick, Electrical Engineer, 81, *82*
    Rose, Cecil Guy, Engineer, *88*
    Samuda, Jonathan, Secretary, 118
    Sandbach Branch, 121, *126*, *131*
    Stanier, Beville, NSR Director, 70
    Talk & Chesterton Branches, 121, 147, *148*, 156, *157*

O'Grady, Bill, Tunnel Electric Tug Master, *91*

Phillipps, William, Douglas, General Manager NSR, 64, *65*, 67, 69, 70, 71, 76
Potter, James, Resident Engineer for Telford's Tunnel, 27, 29, 30, *34*, *36*, *38*, 42, 44, 45, 46, 48, 49, 51, 54
    Career after Telford's Tunnel complete, 52
    Plan of Strata of Second Shaft of Telford's Tunnel, *43*
Potter & Sons, Canal Carriers, 69
Pottery Coalfield, Section on Mines in Harecastle Hill, 163
Pritchard & Hoof, Contractors for Telford's Tunnel, 30, 31, 42, 44, 46, 48
Price, Sir Frank, Chairman, British Waterways Board, 108
Pye, Cecil Arthur, Station Master Longport, 121

Railway Correspondence & Travel Society: Special Trains, *126*
Railways:
    Birmingham & Derby Junction, 111
    Chester & Holyhead, 119
    Grand Junction, 111, 114
    Liverpool & Manchester, 163
    London & North Western Railway, 69, 114, 117
        Findley, George, Civil Engineer Engaged in Construction of Railway Tunnels, later General Manager, L&NWR, 116
        Huish, Captain Mark, General Manager, 114
        Norris, Richard Stewart, Engineer, Northern Division, 117
        Woodhouse, Henry, Permanent Way Superintendent, 117, 118, 119
    London, Midland & Scottish, *68*, 89, 95, *96*, 121 *et seq*, *185*
    Manchester & Birmingham, 112, 113, 114
    Manchester Sheffield & Lincolnshire, 52
    Manchester South Union, 114
    Nantwich & Market Drayton, 119
    North Eastern Railway, 121
    North Staffordshire, *18*, 23, *52*, *54*, *56*, *58*, 61 *et seq*, 111 *et seq*, 184, 185
    Shrewsbury & Chester, 119
    Shrewsbury & Hereford, 119
    Stafford & Uttoxeter, 119
Railway Tunnel Diversion Scheme, 145 *et seq*
Rangeley & Dixson, Iron Founders, Manufacturers of Canal Mileposts, 110
Ravenscliffe, Mining Rights, 173
Rennie, John the Elder, Civil Engineer
    Alternative schemes for Harecastle Passage, 26, 27, 28, 30, 190
Reservoirs:
    Bath Pool, 17, 27, 28, *62*, 114, *131*, *139*, 147, *148*, *150*, *153*, 156, 166, 183
    Knypersley, 17, 27, 28, 29, 30, *37*, *39*, *42*, 45, 46, 48, 49, 52
    Rudyard, 27
Rivers:
    Churnet, 27
    Derwent, 13, 14
    Fowlea Brook, 147
    Humber, 14
    Irwell, 161, 162
    Mersey, 13, 14, 76, 147, *158*, *162*, *171*
    Tame, 31
    Trent, 13, 14, 15, *38*, 147, 161
    Severn, *15*
    Weaver, 13, 15, 67, 69, 70, 71, 76
        Inman, Ernest F., Clerk to the Weaver Trustees, 69, 70, 71
    Worsley Brook, 161
Roche, Norman, Kidsgrove Council Chief Sanitary Inspector, 178
Roads:
    Attwood Street, Kidsgrove, 188
    Boat Horse, *18*, *23*, *85*, 145, *146*, *154*, *158*, *159*, 173, *179*
    Gilbert's Close, Kidsgrove, 188
    Goldenhill to Acres Nook, 174
    Kinnersley Avenue, Kidsgrove, 188
    Liverpool Road, Kidsgrove, *138*, 166, 184
    Lowlands, Chatterley, *125*, *156*
    Market Street, Kidsgrove, 166
    Potteries D Road – A 500, *148*
    Peacock Hay, *148*, *149*
    Talk Road – A34, 166
    Tunstall-Kidsgrove – A 50, 172

Valentine Road, Kidsgrove, 166
Robins, Mills & Company, Canal Carriers, **31**
Rock, Andrew Frederick, NSR Electrical Engineer, 81, 82
Rock Services (Midlands) Limited, Contractors on Tunnel Repairs, 101
Rose, Cecil Guy, NSR Engineer, **88**
Rolt, LTC (Tom), Author, 26
    Description of Trip through Canal Tunnel, 95, 173
Royal Commission on Canals & Waterways 1906, 63
    Barry, Sir John Wolfe, Consulting Engineer Giving Evidence, 67, 71
    Phillipps, WD, NSR General Manager, Giving Evidence, 64, 65
Royce, Electric Motors for Canal Tunnel Tug, 82

Samuda, Jonathan, NSR Secretary, 118
Sandbach, 15
Saner, Colonel John Arthur, Civil Engineer Appointed to Consider Possible Tunnel Diversion, 69, 70, 71, 72
Settle, Joel, Manager, Birchenwood Colliery, **62**
    Coal Owner, **132**
Settle Speakman & Company Limited, Colliery Owners, **62**
Shaw, Simeon Ackroyd, Report on a Visit to Telford's Tunnel, 51, 173
Shelton Iron, Steel & Coal Company Limited, Etruria, 55, 71, 75, 157, 158
Shirley, Charles, William, Mersey Weaver Company, 69
Stafford, Marquis of – Granville Leveson-Gower, **14**, 17
Stanier, Beville, NSR Director, 70
Steam Engines, Stationary used on tunnel construction, 25, 27, 28, 42, 44, 48, 49, 114, 116, 161, 190
    Dragon Incline, Clough Hall Colliery & Ironworks, 166
    Kidswood Fan, **139**
    Newcomen Atmospheric Engines, 14, 167, 177
    Nelson Pit, **139**, 164, 185
    Tug Haulage, 81
    Valentine Pit, 166
Stewart, Hon. Keith, Canal Shareholder, 15
Stoke-on-Trent:
    Chamber of Commerce, 86
    City Council, 101
    British Railways Motive Power Depot, 157
Stone, Headquarters of the Trent & Mersey Canal Company, 26, 28, 46, 48, 164
Stephenson, George, Engineer, 111, 163
Strickland, William, Report on Telford's Tunnel Construction Works, 44, **45**
Sutherland Family of Trentham, 161

Tarmac Civil Engineering Limited, Harecastle Tunnel Diversion Scheme, 153, 156
Tarmac (Kidsgrove) Limited, 140, 185
Telford, Thomas, 14, **16**, **17**, **18**, 19, 22, 23, **25**, 26, 29 et seq
    Harecastle Tunnel, 29 et seq, 61, 64, **66**, 69, 70, 72, **75**, 77, **78**, **79**, 80, 81, 82, **83**, **84**, 85, 89, **91**, **92**, **93**, **97**, **98**, **99**, **100**, 101, **102**, **103**, **104**, **105**, **106**, **107**, **109**, 110, 145, 164, 168, 172, 175, 176, 177, 178, 179, 180, 181, 184, 185
    Portrait, **43**
Thomas, Gordon Cale, Civil Engineer, Reporting on Canal Tunnels, 69, 70, 71
Trent & Mersey Canal
    Acts of Parliament, 13, 30, 16, **39-41**, 64, **182**, 184
    Beech, Chris, Mining from Harecastle Tunnel, 178, **179**
    Board of Trade, Complaints Regarding Brindley's Tunnel, 64
    Brindley, James, 13 et seq
    Bye-Laws, **16**, **63**, 64
    Cutting first sod, 13
    Duke of Bridgewater, 13 et seq
    Electric Tugs through tunnels, 81 et seq
        Bullivant & Company, Supply of Steel Tug for Electric Haulage in Tunnel, 81
    Festival of Britain 1951 – Trips through Harecastle Tunnel, 177
    Jack, William (Bill), Trip through Harecastle Tunnel, 178
    Goodwin, Jon & Witter Robin, Canoe Trip through Harecastle Tunnel, 108, 180, 191 et seq
    Mile Posts, **110**
    Mileages, 172
    Route of, 13
    Traffic Committee, 172
    Tunnel Diversion Scheme – proposed, 69 et seq, 190

Tunnel Leggers, 19, 23, 46, 64, 82, 85, 108
Telford's Tunnel ventilation scheme, 95, **99**, 101, **105**
Trent & Mersey Canal Society, 108
Trentham, 15
    Lilleshall Company, Shropshire, 161
    Sutherland Family, 161
Trubshaw, James, Civil Engineer, Reporting on Canal Tunnels
    Barnton, 15, **65**, 81
    Morley – Tunnel Case, 76
    Preston Brook, 81
    Saltersford, 15, 81
    Strood, Thames & Medway Canal, 30
    Thames, 49
Tunstall, **52**, 115, 117, 121, **125**, 146, **156**, **159**, 164, 165, 166, 172, 173, 174, 188
Turnhurst Hall, **5**
Twemlow, Francis, Trent & Mersey Canal Shareholder, 27

Vaughan, William, Trent & Mersey Canal Employee, 29, 48, 54

Wade, Reverend Frederick, Tobias, Vicar of St Thomas, Kidsgrove, **60**, **150**
    Sunday Trading, 23
    Tunnel Leggers, 23
Walhouse, Moreton and Family, Harecastle Estate Owner, 166, 167
Walhouse & Bulkley, Underground Coal Mining Harecastle Tunnel, 166, 167
    Contractors Employed by:
        Lowe, Dan, 167
        Stubbs, Messrs, 167
        Winkle & Company, 167
        Winkle & Hancock, 167
        Gibbons, George, Solicitor acting for, 166, 167
Walker Brothers, Wigan, Engineers, **96**
Wedgwood, Sir John Hamilton, Bart, Re-enacted Cutting First Sod of Canal July 1966, 101
Wedgwood, Josiah, **5**, **14**, 17, 26, **55**, **101**, **162**
    Catherine, Empress the Great of Russia, **5**
    Barlaston Factory, **5**
    Bentley, Thomas, Partner, **5**
    Etruria Factory, **5**, **55**
    Etruria Hall, **5**
    Etruria Village, 164
    Grand Trunk Canal, **5**
    Hermitage Museum, St Petersburg, **5**
    Statue unveiling at Stoke-on-Trent Station, **54**
Wedgwood, Colonel Josiah Clement MP for Newcastle-under-Lyme, **70**
Wedgwood Pottery Group, 18
Wedgwood, Susannah, 13
Westport Lake, **108**
Widnes Foundry (1925) Limited; Bridge Reconstruction at Harecastle, 130
Williamson Brothers, Coal Owners, 165, **168**, 169, 173, 174, 180, 181, 182
Williamson, Hugh Henshall, Coal Owner at Chatterley, 44
    Goldendale Ironworks at Chatterley, 58
Williamson, John Henshall, Coal Owner at Chatterley, 61
Williamson, Edward, 165
Williamson, Robert, brother of John Henshall, 61, 164, **169**, **170**, 172
Witter, Robin, Canoe Trip through Brindley's Tunnel, 108, 180, 191 et seq
Wolstanton, Parish of, **58**, 166
    St Margaret's Church, **123**
Wood, Enoch, Pottery Manufacturer, 26
Woodhouse, Henry, L&NWR Permanent Way Superintendent, 117, 118, 119
Woodhouse, John, Mining Engineer Derby, Arbitrator on Mining issues, Harecastle Tunnel, 182
Worsley, Duke of, staying at Clough Hall, 164
Wright, John & Edwin Limited, Wire Ropes for Tug Haulage, 89
Wynne, George, Board of Trade Inspecting Officer, 116

Yorkshire Engine Company Sheffield, Locomotive Engineers, **96**

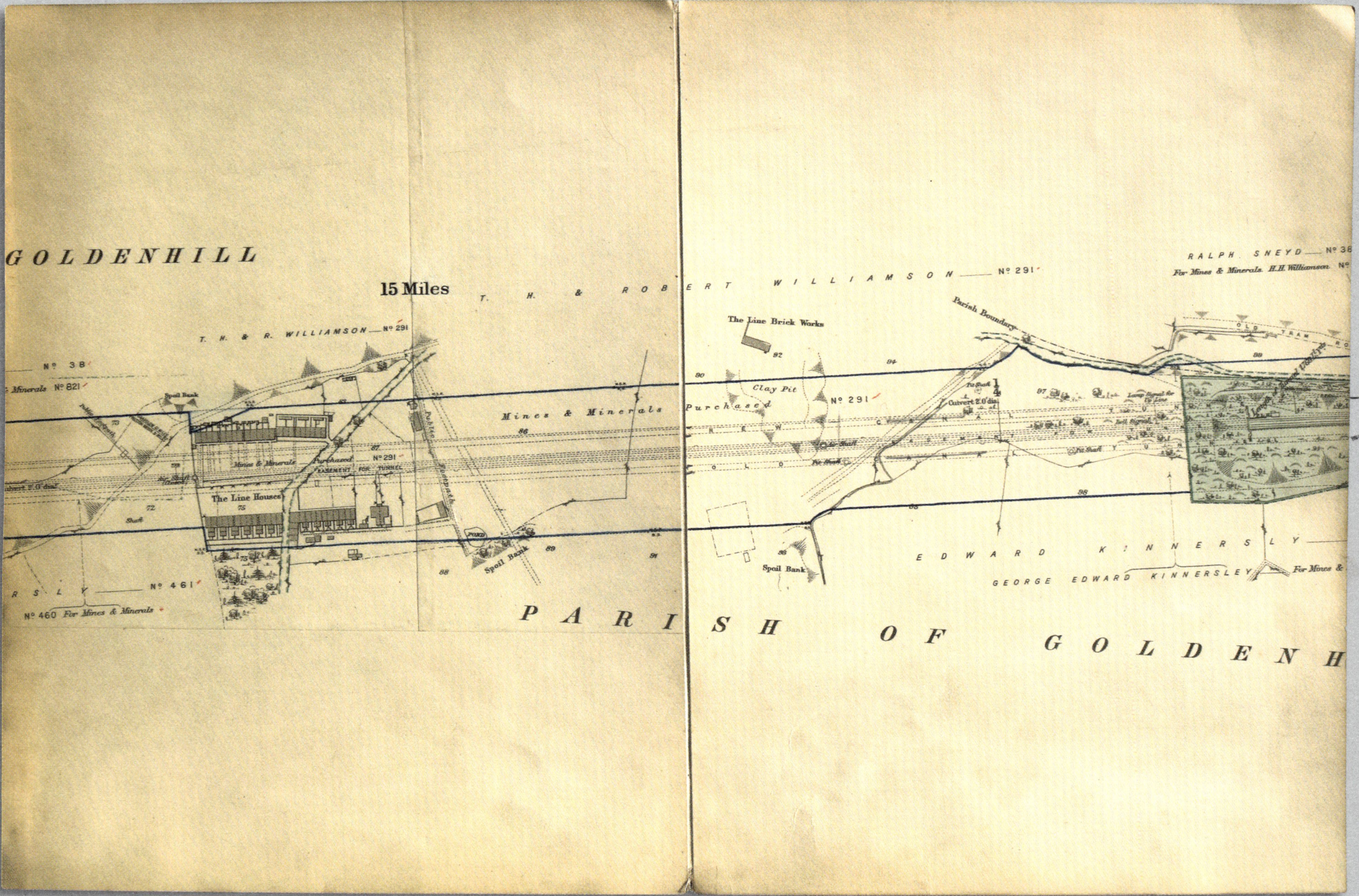

GOLDENHILL
15 Miles
T. H. & ROBERT WILLIAMSON — Nº 291
T. H. & R. WILLIAMSON — Nº 291
RALPH SNEYD — Nº 38
For Mines & Minerals. H.H. Williamson
Nº 38
Minerals Nº 821
Spoil Bank
The Line Brick Works
Parish Boundary
Clay Pit
Nº 291
Mines & Minerals Purchased
Mines & Minerals Purchased Nº 291
EASEMENT FOR TUNNEL
The Line Houses
Culvert 2.0 dia.
OLD TRAM ROAD
Spoil Bank
Spoil Bank
EDWARD KINNERSLY
GEORGE EDWARD KINNERSLEY
For Mines &
Nº 461
Nº 460 For Mines & Minerals
PARISH OF GOLDENH